NEW DIRECTIONS IN THEAT[RE]

General Editor: JULIAN HILTON

NEW DIRECTIONS IN THEATRE

Published

FEMINISM AND THEATRE
Sue-Ellen Case

IMPROVISATION IN DRAMA
Anthony Frost and Ralph Yarrow

NEW DIRECTIONS IN THEATRE
Julian Hilton

PERFORMANCE
Julian Hilton

POSTMODERNISM AND PERFORMANCE
Nick Kaye

THEATRE AS ACTION
Lars Kleberg

A SEMIOTICS OF THE DRAMATIC TEXT
Susan Melrose

TRANSPOSING DRAMA
Egil Törnqvist

Forthcoming

REPRESENTATION AND THE ACTOR
Gerry McCarthy

A Semiotics of the Dramatic Text

SUSAN MELROSE

MACMILLAN

First published 1994 by
THE MACMILLAN PRESS LTD
Houndmills, Basingstoke, Hampshire RG21 2XS
and London
Companies and representatives
throughout the world

A catalogue record for this book is available
from the British Library.

ISBN 0–333–41943–X hardcover
ISBN 0–333–41944–8 paperback

Typeset by Nick Allen/Longworth Editorial Services
Longworth, Oxon.

Printed and bound in Great Britain by
Mackays of Chatham PLC, Chatham, Kent

For Annie Ubersfeld

Contents

General Editor's Preface viii

Acknowledgements ix

PART I

Introduction 3

1 Some Twentieth-century European Traditions Revisited 11

2 Theatre and Language 36

3 New Directions 65

PART II

4 Interventions into the Scenes of Conflict 97

5 Old Masters 108

6 The Performer, My Other? 150

7 The Gendered Scene of Theory 178

PART III

8 Exploding 'Discourse' 201

9 Procedures 245

10 Applications 283

Bibliography 315

Index 322

General Editor's Preface

In the past ten years, Theatre Studies has experienced remarkable international growth, students seeing in this marriage of the practical and the intellectual a creative and rewarding discipline. Some countries are now opening school and degree programmes in Theatre Studies for the first time; others are having to accommodate to the fact that a popular subject attracting large numbers of highly motivated students has to be given greater attention than hitherto. The professional theatre itself is changing, as graduates of degree and diploma programmes make their way through the 'fringe' into established theatre companies, film and television.

Two changes in attitudes have occurred as a result: first, that the relationship between teachers and practitioners has significantly improved, not least because many more people now have experience of both; secondly, that the widespread academic suspicion about theatre as a subject for study has at least been squarely faced, if not fully discredited. Yet there is still much to be done to translate the practical and educational achievements of the past decade into coherent theory, and this series is intended as a contribution to this task. Its contributors are chosen for their combination of professional and didactic skills, and are drawn from a wide range of countries, languages and styles in order to give some impression of the subject in its international perspective.

This series offers no single programme or ideology; yet all its authors have in common the sense of being in a period of transition and debate out of which the theory and practice of theatre cannot but emerge in a new form.

JULIAN HILTON

Acknowledgements

My thanks to Julian Hilton for his support, to John Robinson, and to my students of theatre and drama in Tunisia, Australia and Great Britain – who continually surprise me.

Part I

Introduction

What are the prospects for a 'semiotics of writing for the stage' and how might we justify such a project in the 1990s? After all, it now seems that the fervour that marked early structural semiotic projects has disappeared, taking with it the aspiration and the *belief in itself*, fundamental motor of any intellectual project. More than ten years of growing contestation of the semiotic project itself seems to have vanquished many of its practitioners, who have come to doubt its espoused rationale, and to see with new alarm its 'hidden agendas' apparently aspiring to categorise and control through practices of division, inclusion and exclusion. The new suspicion of semiotics' methodologies and sites of practice, together with the new hesitation (characteristic of wider fields of intellectual practice) to construct models or to pursue globalising (or 'totalising') projects, conspire to render the focus of and the proposals for a 'dramatic semiology' academically and intellectually unfashionable as well as unsound. Today such a project seems – even to some earlier enthusiasts – to have had 'nothing to do with theatre itself'; its ugly duckling, loved only by its semiological progenitors but not by the world of theatre practice itself (Elam, 1989). The practitioner's traditional jibe that people with talent *do*, while the talentless merely talk about doing, was redirected in the 1970s and 1980s from the critic to the semiotician. Unlike the critic, the semiotician – despite Pavis' recent claim to practice "fine art" (Pavis, 1992) – had no cutting rejoinder.

For all that, nothing in this troubled climate suggests that decision-making processes, by any or all participants in dramatic theatre, are not *semiotics at work*. But *which* semiotics is at work, or indeed, *how many*? In the 1990s, alongside a modernist semiotic analysis which remains valid for certain aspects only of theatre practice, we now need to find means to approach those decision-making processes which are characteristic of catalysis, or up-building processes (where one element catalyses another, transforming both) in the diverse phenomena of dramatic theatre. Quoting tradition, to different ends, and gesturing toward other sorts of potential, I shall call what follows a 'new semiotics'. In the

3

terms set out by Schmitt (1990) this 'new semiotics' will be self-conscious, liable to constant update, and relatively open to the past and future of theatre practices. It assumes, *in the event*, that theatre work is always in advance of it, just out of its reach, never to be captured while its life goes on. But this does not mean, for a moment, that theatre and theory do not share a common history.

To the (jaded?) postmodern eye of the late 1980s the semiotic or semiological project seemed to betray a nostalgia for the aspirations and energetic investments which characterised *la pensée '68*: the revolutionary fervour in northern Europe in the late 1960s and early 1970s which challenged established structures of authority. In the case of approaches to theatre, it challenged the widespread critical position of tertiary institutions which took as its focus practices exploring dramatic writing as the posited site and/or origin of theatre meaning, or which reduced the effects of performance to what it might be seen 'to mean' in the terms of established critical *discourse*.

We might ask as a consequence of recent disillusion with this sort of project, whether theatre semiology or semiotics is, more than twenty years after 1968, no more than history. I think not, if only because every action taken in theatre is a decision made, and each decision made entails both a system of equally available, historically specific, options refused, and a spread of implications accruing to both the option chosen *and* to those refused. If these decision-making processes and the knowledges they entail appear to be activated at lightning speed and almost invisibly by theatre professionals, there is still room in a learning situation for the acquisition of a range of analytical theatre procedures I continue to call semiotic. What is certain is that there can be no new exploration of semiotics without a brief appraisal of its rocky journey through theatre practice from the late 1960s to the late 1980s.

For theatre, what followed the carnival which accompanied the 1968 storming of the *Théâtre de l'Odéon* in the centre of Paris (a telling shift in site from the earlier storming of the *Bastille*) were not just new or renewed modes of theatre practice, but a major shift in academic orientation: away from the dramatic text, *to* the stage. But – ironically and perhaps inevitably – only in those terms that were then available. This meant the attempt to *textualise* stage practice through the application of the terms and methods of a semio-*logy*. The textualisation took a double focus:

1. it was to be worked around principles of syntagmatic and paradigmatic combination in performance (lent readily by Saussurean linguistics which had supposed itself to be the exemplary model for all other symbolic practices);

2. it would extend to the reappraisal of the theory and practice of representation, in terms of which it might be possible not just to claim that the stage sign Y 'stands for' something perceived to exist in another dimension of widely agreed social and psychological experience, but to 'scientifically prove' (or disprove) the sorts of judgements of taste and value that the wielders of 'symbolic capital' (in theatre, the drama critic and the academic, and their discourses) have traditionally been keen to proffer.

This concern for proof, in the place of critical 'judgement', was characteristic of the taking of position with regard to knowledge which marked what Derrida (1978) called the *rupture* in critical discourse. The rupture was epistemological (concerned with the possibilities and conditions of knowledge itself), in that it separated out 'traditional hegemonic' from 'newly exploratory' projects and discourses, differently concerned with a common goal: what can be *known*, and what conditions permit us to verify (and speak) a knowledge in and of 'the world' – and its cultural practices – of which the analyst–observer and writer was herself an inextricable part. The perceived rupture was manifested as the difference between two agendas revealed in two fields of discursive practice. The first practice was marked by an implicit humanism – manifested for example in a concern for human motivation and responsibility applied almost equally to those categories of knowledge called 'the author' and 'the character' (for example, Shakespeare and Lear). The second practice thematised (or consistently focused on) its own procedures, either while applying them to text, or indeed *instead of* applying them to text at all.

In his suggestion that

a sign is a reality perceivable by sense perception that has a relationship with another reality which the first reality is meant to evoke. Thus, we are obliged to pose the question as to what the second reality, for which the work of art stands, might be . . .

Mukarovsky (Matejka and Titunik, 1976, p. 5) – theatre critics and teachers might protest – is not telling us anything new at all. What was new, however, or rather newly re-emerging at that time, was that the theorist, schooled by a forceful political interrogation into structures of power, including those over "symbolic capital" (as Bourdieu (1984) sees uses of 'art' to be), sought to replace the project of appreciation of the 'first reality', with analysis of the *bases for* any such conventional 'appreciation'. The traditional appreciation might include specification of hypothetical origins, of the artist's claimed or inferred intent, and of the 'success' or 'failure' of the work to live up to that intent. What Mukarovsky proposed in its place was an exploration of the perceived *first/second reality* relationship (enquiring, that is, into the theory of representation). But analysts then went further, producing a critique of the consensual hypothesis entailed by the *first reality/ second reality* project: it interrogated the bases themselves for any such postulation and authentication of socially-agreed meaning-production.

In the most general of terms, 'the work' (for example, theatre performance) was perceived to be 'text', and the sorts of proofs sought were to be determined through a practice of 'reading' performance, whose intricacies were perceived to derive from the interaction of *codes*, piled thickly the one upon the other along the "paradigmatic axis" of simultaneity, and ordered in time along the "syntagmatic axis" of event and "narrative". The standard against which theatre performance as text was to be measured was thus *language*, which de Saussure problematically (for the English language user) rendered as the couplet *langue* (innate) and *parole* (manifest), plus *signifiant* (signifier) and *signifié*, (signified).

This endeavour flushed forth an old question of theatre esthetics. Analysis of dramatic theatre seemed then to depend, and may still depend, on the ways we choose to answer it. The question has long been this: is theatre an art (or a practice) 'in its own right', and does its status demand genre-specific theoretical discourses and sets of practices, rather than those cribbed from linguistics, literary theory, or, for example, the Metz school of film theory (for example, Metz, 1982); or is it the case that dramatic theatre combines a number of quasi-distinct practices – writerly, discursive, socio-pragmatic, painterly, architectural, ludic (e.g., gestural, mime), vocal, dance, musical, but perhaps also psycho-somatic, amongst others – such that the 'phenomenon of theatre' demands first to be broken down and submitted part by part to a number of diverse analytical procedures; and then to be built up once more, so that we might observe its powers of mutual modification of these apparent 'codes'?

The range of material and approaches included in three clusters of major works – Pavis (1982, 1985, 1987), Ubersfeld (1978 and 1982b), and Elam (1980, 1989) – to which I would add a number of articles by Barthes (1982b, 1986), seems to suggest that there can be no single and stable approach to theatre. But what we need to recognise in the 1990s is that while these writers seem to have shared a common inspiration, and a common 'ground of thought', the 'analytical' (or fragmenting, down-breaking) logic each adopted in the late 1970s and 1980s is not just inadequate to the project to which they laid claim, but was confounded by their own commonsensical and felt response to effective theatre. In common sense terms, it was clear that theatre's specificity was and remains a most peculiar *up-building* process or synergetic combination – that is, of a greater force than that generated by the sum of all constituent parts taken individually. This power through a catalysis in which the real spectators are implicated, is able to mark the *experience* of dramatic theatre neatly off from the experience of all other cultural practices. But how to include this *everyday felt* experience of theatre within the frame of 'analysis' – for this was the aspiration and goal.

In fact, an answer was near at hand: in the mode of expansion of analysis in the 1980s, a felt, commonsensical and anecdotal experience and response, produced 'invisibly' and as though naturally by hegemonically-disseminated dominant value structures determining taste and judgement in the individual as social subject, was indeed a proper field for exploration. But what such exploration entailed was not in line with the earlier aspiration: it required something other than a modernist semiology; it required something besides the belief that language and hence linguistics offered the exemplary model for all other cultural practice; and it required a range of short-term and partial semiotic projects if it was to begin to approach what is **singular** in the experience of theatre.

It seems to me that there are adequate phenomenological bases here for me to assert that, notwithstanding the seminal qualities of the texts I have indicated above, we have hardly yet begun to talk adequately about what is – for some of us – theatre's *felt* specificity. Now, 'feeling' seems in theatre's case to be to some extent at least user-specific and particular-event-specific, and to challenge, as inadequate to that singular event, analysis of cultural practice based on the hypothesis of reiterability.

* * *

In implying that dramatic theatre's specificity lies less in what we might discursively represent as its 'substance', than in the ways in which it enables the production of felt-experience, *in the event*, I am already signalling the distant horizon of the present work. The directions it will take might seem to distance it from the approaches already mentioned. But this is not the case: what we need in the 1990s are the means to expand the project of a semiotics of writing for performance so that it includes precisely what it seemed, at its most rigorous, to need to exclude.

The project for the 1990s cannot proceed without an attempt to approach the epistemes or "grounds of thought" (Macdonell, 1986) – a nicely ungrounded metaphor – which seem to have informed (or given forms to) the French and more widely northern European theatre semiotics of the 1970-80s, as it developed out of the echoes of earlier twentieth-century (for example, Prague School) endeavours, drawn into interactive scenarios with the aspirations of the late 1960s.

But "grounds of thought", although we seem historically to be able to trace their imprint, are, particularly when we lack the distance of time, curiously slippery, unbounded 'entities', which seem to appear primarily through the analyst's motivated quest amongst diverse material manifestations or their traces. It would seem that a 'field of thought' is a short-term mapping of grounds, whose rudiments are constituted by the searcher from across a range of **texts**, rather than from any given one, or from speech. However, "grounds of thought" 'themselves' are already afflicted with

hypostasis (fixed and objectified by an observer, *in her own terms*), from that very moment when we believe that we can perceive them, since to perceive an episteme supposes that I am looking *at* an 'it', rather than *at myself* through the frames I make available. Nonetheless (and strictly for present purposes), goals, procedures, registers and thematic fields on the one hand, and omissions (or absences) on the other, can be perceived to recur across the works which mark the heights of theatre semiotics or semiology in France.

Secondly, I would suggest that it is now clear, after the turnabouts of theory's recent history, that we need no longer proceed in the 1990s through the contestation or rejection of what was valid in the recent past. We have instead to attempt to determine what was missing from earlier projects and procedures; what was not noted or could not then be said in the authorised terms; what was hinted at; and to work then to reincorporate that missing 'something' into the larger project of contemporary knowledge. In these terms, what can now be developed in and for theatre semiotics should be seen as complementary to what was developed in the 1970s and 1980s. However, we need absolutely to note from the outset that complementarity is not simply a matter of bringing together the different on a principle of reciprocity. The joining, here, poses for us the vital problematic of performance semiotics: what transfers between at least two sets of codifications, does the *productive* bringing together of 'the one and the other' entail? In Wilden (1980), digital (sequential, unitary, boundary-marked) and analog (up–down continuum) modes are complementary, the one to the other, *in the world of human experience*. But what we perceive less clearly – because we tend to take it for granted, because it is naturalised – is something that information technology has begun to make clear, in a way that earlier semio-*logies* did not: the point of interest is less the two, than the site of conjunction between the two, where because of that process of conjoining itself, they are mutually transforming. Two observations emerge from this: the one can only exclude the other, take priority over the other, or become the wholesale substitute for the other, within those models of power we begin to see when we study the (dramatic) politics of knowledge. But secondly, that my uses of the semiological tradition will mean that when I select from it, I transform, in so doing, elements of it, by that action. To oppose black to white is a cultural practice (whatever its material basis); but to make them complementary to each other is no less so, even if the process better conceals a specific human intelligence (as decodifier and recodifier), intervening at and indeed *as* their interface.

Chapter 1

Some Twentieth-century European Traditions Revisited

Traditions

The work of Pavis and Ubersfeld (close colleagues in the 1970s and 1980s at the Institute of Theatre Studies of the University of Paris (III)) reveals striking differences between the discursive approaches they separately adopt to dramatic theatre. Pavis' dictionary (*Dictionnaire du théâtre*, 1987) sets out named and alphabetically listed categories of theatre knowledge, which range from *the absurd* via *mise en scène* to *verisimilitude*, and in the most general of terms the text, unfortunately not yet translated into English, would serve as an exemplary teaching and learning tool in tertiary education approaches to a 'French theoretical' appraisal of theatre. But this approach suggests implicitly that the diverse knowledges we draw on in the context of theatre lend themselves usefully to categorisation – whereas Ubersfeld herself will note that theatre works through its *combinatory* capacity, which transforms anything having an extratheatrical 'separate reality'. Ubersfeld's *combinatoire* (combinatory quality of theatre) does not appear as an entry in Pavis (1987).

The title of *Languages of the Stage* (Pavis, 1982) is telling in the naturalisation of its own logocentricity. In referring in the introductory section ("Present Situation of Semiology") to Foucault (1966), de Saussure (1974), Greimas (1979) and Peirce (1931–58), and to the "irreconcilable opposition of two models of the sign", Pavis notes that "[w]hat will be discussed here ... is ... semiology and not semiotics", because theatre, for Pavis, is "*a manifestation of external discourse*" (my emphasis). What I prefer to describe as its *semiotic* workings seem, in this understanding, to be able to be

11

said 'to stand for external discourse': the *non*-linguistic, therefore, is claimed 'to stand', through theatre, *for* the discursive; and to take as its most desirable manifestation a "discourse of the *mise en scène*" or a "metatext" (Pavis, 1985). Taking discourse as its source, and discourse as its goal, via the semiotic workings of the stage, (where "the connection between signs and their referents" or "the reality denoted by the sign" *must be made*), Pavis makes not just of theatre semiology, but of theatre itself, a "*telos* of [discursive] unity and harmony" (Dollimore, 1984). But does this focus do anything other than to authorise (as legitimate source and goal) "the mediation of natural languages", to be "used as instruments of *paraphrase* in the description of semiotic objects" (Pavis, 1987, p. 14: my emphasis)?

The semiology proposed by Pavis would be constituted on the basis of this requirement: "simply to conceive of this [theatre] system as 'syncretic' (a sign system that 'puts into action *many languages of expression*') and make it a meeting point for other sign systems" (p. 15: my emphasis). To this founding perspective of Pavis' work I want to do no more at this point than note this objection: how do we proceed if we take as a starting point for our work in dramatic theatre analysis the supposition that the systems Pavis alludes to as "many languages of expression" are neither "languages" at all, nor indeed commensurable with "natural languages", even if *for some of them* the relationship between what is approached as 'sign' and what it might be thought to 'stand for', is indeed arbitrary (a Saussurean criterion)?

What steps can we now take, through the lens provided by the work of this seminal theoretician, if it seems to some of us that theatre need not and does not take discourse as its source, and discourse as its goal? If theatre works only in metaphoric terms as "many languages", are we doing any more than to remain trapped within this metaphoric construct, by taking *linguistic analysis* as the model for our approach to theatre?

If the Pavis 'dictionary' and his approach in general are reticent when it comes to pleasure, desire, and *felt* significance in spectators' uses of theatre, Annie Ubersfeld's "school for spectators" (*L'Ecole du spectateur*, 1982b) is not. Ubersfeld succeeds not just in drawing systematically on literary and linguistic theory (an extract is translated as "The Pleasure of the Spectator", in *Modern Drama*, vol. XXX, no. 1, 1982a), but succeeds all the more in pleasurably *evoking* theatre for her readers. She achieves this first through photography, and second, through broaching those subjects of human experience in theatre which Pavis (and this is true equally for Elam's semiotics) largely and significantly omits. Despite a background in the study of dramatic writing which Ubersfeld shares with Pavis, and which we might suppose equally informs their approaches to the stage, Ubersfeld's work is actor–spectator-centric where Pavis remains logo-centric; and it is in her approach to the actor as the vital and still (even necessarily, in her terms) *mysterious* focus of theatre's pleasures for spectators, that Ubersfeld's work excels:

> Even if the actor offers us a veritable bouquet of signs, an organised and satisfying discourse clearly related to the global system of stage signs; even if the actor is a perfect enunciator, that actor's role is nonetheless incomplete, and cannot be left at that. Nor is it the case that for the spectator, even the spectator–semiologist, the actor is simply a perfect object of contemplation and analysis. Because the actor is a figure of desire. And even beyond this figure of desire that the actor is or has to be, s/he is – or should be – that gaping emptiness which is the vital condition of the spectator's work and emotion.
>
> (Ubersfeld, 1982b, p. 236: my translation)

Note that "figure", quoted above, is double in meaning: figure of desire, momentary object of the spectator's desire; but also *metaphor* or symbol of desire itself; proferred to stand in for other desires by the conditions of theatricality which form part of the spectator's 'contract' with the practitioner.

Ubersfeld goes on to situate in this gap or emptiness what, for theatre semiology in 1981, remained 'unseizable' (*l'insaisissable*); and in so doing she begins to venture into, but at once draws back from, what is, for rationalist epistemologies, the void:

> This is not just the non-formalisable or hardly formalisable residue formed from the body and the voice of the individual actor, but what we have here is the *residue of a residue*, that gap [between the identity of the character and the identity of the

actor] in which the gaze of the spectator, caught *in the space between*, sets out to cross and to cross again.

Drawing back, Ubersfeld will call on Freudian analysis to re-stage the (pleasing) void through widely acceptable scenarios of knowledge. She attempts, in other words, to make this 'unseizable' residue graspable, through recourse to one model of conventional knowledge. But it is this acknowledgement of the *space between*, which from Halliday (1987) we might call the space of complementarities, which marks Ubersfeld's work out as a veiled guide to the dramatic theatre semiotics we now need to develop: this is a space of energetic investments, but it is not limited to, or knowable in terms of, any of its parameters, which peak in a number of relations between named sites: the actor–character–spectator complex; 'the dramatic author' and 'the *metteur en scène*'. These are complex *conventional* categories of theatre knowledge. Nor can this space of energetic investments be adequately approached through established theories of identification.

We have thus a direction, but something less than a charted path. Ubersfeld's work, despite this step toward ghostly shadows caught as 'un-speakables' within the boundaries of rationalist epistemology, draws back into applications which recall those used by Pavis and Elam, in common with literary theorists in the European tradition of the 1970s and 1980s. At this point we need to begin to explore certain aspects of these applications, looking for the "grounds of thought" which, traceable within their textualisations, seem at least in part to inform and to foreclose them. We need to ask as we do so whether it is now possible to base our own procedures on complementary grounds of thought, and what these might be.

Pavis and Ubersfeld work differently within the same tradition which nurtured de Saussure's own pedagogic practice of theory. In Ubersfeld's (1981) rather terse advice that

[t]here's no point in dwelling here on a theory of the sign, a classic since Saussure: that theory distinguishes between the sign's signifier and its signified, the two bound together like the two faces of a single sheet of paper (p. 23: my translation)

there is no suggestion (such as we find in Pavis and in Elam) that the theory might be of relative, rather than universal 'truth'. At the same time, the concept of a 'theatre sign' seems to have no strict parameters, but to be determined phenomenologically, by the onlooker:

> A true semiotics of performance . . . would show the *meaningful combinatory unit* of performance elements. . . . In other words, nothing prevents us from isolating, as theatre signs, units of widely varying dimensions [. . . such as, at different moments, the actor, but also a specific gesture used by that actor]. So the word sign will be used here with everyday imprecision.
>
> (p. 23: my translation)

But she continues in terms which precisely recall Pavis' discussion of the difference between semiotics and semiology referred to above: "a theatre sign is *that which we can designate by a morpheme or a 'simple' nominal syntagm*" – for example a 'table', in the first instance, or 'a set table', in the second. What we find here, embricated within Ubersfeld's approach, is a modelling of theatre's specificity in accordance with *verbless* units (i.e. not process or energy-oriented) designated by linguistics: she is drawing on the Saussurean hypothesis of the propensity of linguistics to provide the model for the analysis of all other symbolic practices, but focusing curiously on nominalisation.

I should indicate here, in line with the thematisation of procedures I have noted above, that the procedure I have just adopted has wider implications for the investigation into relations between theatre practice and writing with which the present work is concerned. This textualised usage by Pavis and Ubersfeld of a manifest "ground of thought" allows the opening up of an *interdiscursive* field, plus – vitally – a field of *recurring practice*, between the given text practice and other pre-existing and simultaneously existing practices: in other words, it informs a *way of seeing*, and a *way of doing*, as well as a way of apparent knowing, in the world (of theatre). What we are dealing with here is a conception which transcends the logocentric and genre-specific focus of the theory of intertextuality; it opens onto an 'inter-media' association, itself dependent on possible relations between different and heterogeneous **practices**.

Ubersfeld rejects within theatre analysis the quest (which we now see as characteristic of the *digital* mode) for a precisely determined 'minimal sign' or performance unit: she suggests that what we should be talking about is the *semiotic practice* of theatre performance, in which we look less for 'signs', than for those *differences between performance options*, which provide the basis for their articulation and for our recognition. But if this is our brief in theatre analysis, how do we begin to approach that (meaningful) theatre pleasure which depends precisely on the blur of that clarity of difference, separating the one from the other, which conventionally permits what we call articulation? When this blur is produced – 'discrete sign systems' overlap; separate 'realities' merge, and then slightly separate; we perceive 'actorly' work through the complex traceries we call 'character', only to slip again into the illusion – our pleasure grows in the gap between what are elsewhere called 'signs' or sign-systems. Does the spatio-temporally *multivariate* quality of a theatre-meaningful (if not discursively meaningful) pleasure, to which Ubersfeld alludes above before she attempts to universalise and formalise it, preclude a semiotic approach?

Elam (1980) approaches the same question of units under the heading *"Segmenting the text"*, quoting Pagnini's remark that "'one immediately comes up against the *punctum dolens* of every research of a semiological nature, namely that of the segmenting of the continuum into discrete units'" (p. 47). If Elam will conclude that it:

> may be that the attempt to slice up the performance across its various levels, . . . is not only methodologically misguided but also theoretically *premature* (my emphasis)

this is *not* because the writer notes that the human experience of theatre confounds the unitary bias of certain linguistic traditions, suggesting thereby that we need another epistemological support than those afforded by linguistics (or perhaps another linguistics?). Rather it is because, for Elam:

> we must first endeavour to understand better each of the systems at work and to define its *rules and units* and make explicit the complex of dramatic, theatrical and cultural codes which permit *a range of diverse messages* to be brought together to the *united end of producing a performance text*. (p. 49: my emphasis)

Elam's approach remains, in 1980, solidly embedded in the Saussurean epistemology. The spread of that epistemology is considerable, and it engulfs, at its heights, all (French) approaches to human practice and organisation – including those 'scenarios of (secret) knowledge' that typify psychoanalytic modes of explaining human conduct and thereby, by implication, the human itself. What it does not include, as we shall see, are the means to an adequate understanding of those subject-specific hierarchisations and distinctions, *within* the operation of social codes, which fall within, rather than without (as 'deviant to') the various orders which prevail; and which we might suppose it is one function of cultural practices (especially dramatic theatre), to explore.

Each of the theorists noted above will draw on a particular focus-point or peak (*langue/parole*) within the application of the Saussurean epistemology, which is combined with elements from two other sources:

- the conceptualisations and methodologies of Chomskyan linguistics, and

- the narratological analyses typified by Propp

to produce the *actantial analysis* of Greimas (1966; see also Blonsky, 1985, pp. 341–62). Such a coupling of analytical procedures is possible inasmuch as each operates an idealising epistemology favouring *langue* over *parole* (Saussure), competence over performance (Chomsky), and actants and functions (Propp) over folk-tale diversity. This process of borrowings and combinations might be said to characterise the quest for theatre's 'own' analytical discourse and practices – both of which Ubersfeld called, in 1983, a *bricolage*. Each borrowing indicates a certain cunning (which is, in the present context, and in the light of theatre's own practices, a valid mode of operation); but this cunning *was* out of step with its users' declared and 'secret' aspirations of the time.

Elam, Pavis and Ubersfeld differently assess the validity of a generative model to explain not just theatre's perceived unity and diversity, but something like the drives, the 'impulses' or the 'forces' which might seem to energise – and certainly to centre – its stagings. In asking of Molière's play, '*what makes Don Juan run?*',

Ubersfeld (1977) centres in *character*, a question others would ask equally of the author and of many a British *metteur en scène* and actor. The question assumes that the given textuality – here made equivalent to 'surface', and in 'human semiotic' terms made equivalent to 'repeated typical behaviour in the world attributed to a gendered and class subject' – is underpinned by a 'deep' causality, a drive or a complex of drives. In late nineteenth century terms that same, hypothetical 'depth' would have been narrated through the concept of 'motivation', and further attributed to then perceived 'natural' or class conflicts and contradictions. In the late twentieth century the question hints either at a pathological condition or at a class condition, both of which are portrayed, in such symbolic modes as the novel or the drama, as able to produce consistent practices, seen thereafter as the displacement or condensation (metonymic or metaphoric 'stagings') of a founding complex. The perceived founding complex needs then – if we are to play the game – to be inferred on the basis of text elements used as symptoms or indices.

Actantial analysis here becomes a useful 'scientific' metaphor for revisiting conservative knowledges, worked through 'readings' of dramatic theatre: the deep structure/surface paradigm model is amended to focus on a 'creative vision', a 'motivation' or an 'intention' – attributed to either 'author', or 'character', 'actor' or *'metteur en scène'*, as nominated categories of projection – as generative source, while 'performance' comes to be equated with 'surface'.

Greimasian analysis is focused on three pairs of functions to be found, according to the structuralist hypothesis, in the story structure. The couplets are:

> *destinator–destinataire* (for example, the narrator and the ideal receiver);

> *subject–object* (for example, what we 'intuit' as hero and as hero's goal);

> *helper–opposer* (who or which assist or block the hero's desire and actions).

The actant is not necessarily commensurable with either character or actor, but may be something like a force (or, in more recent terms, a **field of force**), dispersed either among a number of focus-points, or 'embedded, as 'internal contradiction' to a named character unit: Antigone, for example, may be both desirer *and* obstacle to her own desire; and in this combinatory aspect we can undoubtedly see some of the age-old bases for the writerly constitution of what will be embodied as a 'complex character'.

Nonetheless, this perception does not eliminate the equally ancient danger of finding ourselves caught up in the hermeneutic circle, whereby what we 'already know' (or 'intuit') can be 'proven scientifically'. In Pavis' reading of Ubersfeld's borrowing,

> she performs a permutation of the [Greimasian] couple subject–object, making the subject into a function manipulated by the couplet of destinator–destinataire, whereas the object becomes the function caught between the helper and the opposer. This detail profoundly modifies the functioning of the model. With Greimas, the point of departure was not a subject consciously fabricated by the destinataire, and attributed then to the destinator. The subject in Greimas could only be defined at the end of the route in terms of the quest for the object. This conception had the advantage of letting the subject–object couplet be gradually defined, so that the subject was not defined in itself but in terms of its concrete actions. Whereas in the Ubersfeld schema there is the risk of over-valuing the nature of the subject, making it a given, easily locatable through the ideo- logical functions of the destinator–destinataire couplet.
>
> (1987, p. 24: my translation)

We can already see why, in terms of the actor–spectator-centric position noted in Ubersfeld, this shift from **text**-structuralism to a theatre-interactive schema was desirable. What it does produce, however, is a **centring** of the performance axis on the subject-function as desire-focus, on what was then called the 'producer–receiver' (practitioner–spectator) relation. It was the actor/s who literally incarnated not just that subject-function, but frequently the object-function as well.

The actants within a 'single' dramatic writing, a single performance, were seen to shift, becoming 'forces' 'moving across' and 'driving' text: from Antigone as desirer against Creon as opposer, to Creon as sole incarnate desirer. 'Justice' as object is cunningly maintained as the spectator's explicit desire, but its sites and definitions are subtly transformed as the dramatic event progresses. The practitioner–spectator axis might turn, as well, on an implicit sado-masochistic desire in both parties, focused – by the writer and spectator – on the actor/Antigone-complex, as the pleasingly punishable site of an Oedipal identification seeking resolution with the Father-function. Ubersfeld mentions symbolic parricide as a possible and unrecognised desire in all parties, but Lacoue-Labarthe (1977; and see also Blau, 1990) observes a more generalised sado-masochism operating through traditional dramas and indeed makes it fundamental to both the tragic mode and to Aristotle's and Freud's uses of that mode. If this is indeed the case, then we appear to have a further – or 'deeper' – 'nexus', in terms of which the actants supposedly 'generating' the *fabula* (Pavis, 1987) are themselves transformations (metaphoric/metonymic) of this conventionally 'transgressive' drive. This is a fruitful game to play, in that it entails a widely ratified staging of conventional scenarios of knowledge, posited as 'causal' in their relationship to performance practice – but is it anything more than that?

The borrowing, and in particular the intersections which are commonly forged in the context of 'theatre analysis' between Greimasian principles and Freudian scenarios, are not particularly surprising: authorial theory, not just in the context of dramatic writing but in that of *mise en scène*, has been combined with the "ideology of 'depth'" (Ulmer, 1989) in order to justify the premise of the necessary existence of a creative 'impulse' or 'vision'. It seems at first to provide a more systematic path to a succinct and reduced (and perhaps reductive) declaration as to 'what the text/*mise en scène* is (really) about'. But there are two brief observations we need to make here:

1. as soon as we return to what we know about *some instances* of theatre's collective practice, and its means of drawing on any number of stage practices not necessarily commensurable with those of writing or of language in use, this notion begins to seem like one more metaphor for a particular sort of singular and single intervention;

2. the focus of the putative *source* of performance – posited to function as does *langue* – rather than on performance as we variously produce and use it, severely limits both 'theatre

analysis' and notions of human desire to strictly curtailed scenarios and formulae. That is, to the generalisable.

What actantial *analysis* applied to writing for the stage seemed initially to offer was the means to locate *forces*, which might then be used as the 'basis' for distributing, focusing and energising the materiality of staging; but this is far from a 'theoretical justification for' attributing to the undifferentiated dramatic writing the status of 'deep' or originary causal principle, capable then of 'generating' a performance held to be marked by its 'genetic' imprint. Apart from anything else, as Derrida points out (1978), the genetic impress in reproduction entails the 'causal' admix of contributions from two participants, rather than the expansion of the putative 'nexus' contained in the one. The troubled theory of socio-cultural reproduction, in recent years, has demonstrated that 'other factors' seem always to be able to erupt into and thereby trouble the very nature of the equation. The borrowing, besides, has simply never permitted us to approach what Ubersfeld notes in performance: performance is constituted not just from homogeneous minimal units (e.g. facework, gestuality, proxemics) for which a common causal principle might be sought, but from the disparate or heterogeneous, to the extent that its constitution is both 'structured', and a matter of *bricolage*, or the (masterless) cobbling together of diverse components.

This mode of composition might seem to recall Saussure's *parole* in its relation to the masterly *langue*, where the former is almost *accidental* to the greater scheme. We are no closer to an understanding of a basic principle relating to the way in which theatre practice – to historically shifting degrees – will draw together components whose successful combination might previously have seemed unthinkable; and will go on doing this, in ways we have to call 'multivariate', confounding any 'rigorous' approach, such as that offered in systems analysis. If our desire is still (as Elam outlined it in 1980) to establish the diverse systems at work and their means of combination, then we must accept that the semiotic project is either wholly historical – that is, looking at past performances; or that what pleases us in theatre is liable to be focused on the *play between* the systems we can establish after the event of performance, and the highly charged systemic category marked 'other', that Lemke (1984) always leaves open.

What emerges again from this inspection is Ubersfeld's cunning: her use of generative theory is modernist, while the term *bricolage* was to become one of the bywords of postmodern theory. The one draws on a universalising, meta-theory of control through pro-liferation of like units according to a given schema; the other on practices of assemblage, motored by energetic force-fields, gathering, borrowing, quoting and decontextualising, refuting any singular control in what is nonetheless (partly because of the unifying force of theatre's architecture and relation) an esthetic 'whole' – but one which can work without necessarily subscribing to already institutionalised principles for harmonious combination.

Pavis, in turn, has drawn on the Brechtian *Gestus* as something like a generative nucleus, pre-forming and in-forming each 'surface' (here, performance) manifestation; but in later work he has preferred to articulate generative theory through the thesis of a pre-existant discourse of the staging (*discours de la mise en scène*) which controls, but does not, for all that, swamp, the heterogeneity of the performance. In tune with this *a posteriori* quest for an *a priori* 'generative principle', and in tune too with the teleological focus, Pavis advocates the quest for 'pertinent signs', where pertinency itself seems to be determined by this propensity for assimilation into a succinct explanatory discourse. Performance, here, if it is to work, will orient the spectator to the reconstitution, after the event, of the *discours de la mise en scène*, a renewed, 'deep' and generative 'what it is about', attributed now to the *metteur en scène*. Every 'accidental' performance 'unit', faithful part of a cohesive whole, is worthy of consideration only inasmuch as it can be said metaphorically to 'contain within it' the seed (or seme) of the generating organism.

Both, then, in the midst of their 'science', perform on theatre's behalf an eclectic cunning and borrowing, and note in theatre practice itself a cunning. But the two differ over the question of pertinency: for Ubersfeld all is pertinent although not all is generated by a master nucleus; for early Pavis, only those signs in which a master control can be determined (or in which a masterly control can see itself?), are of interest. What we find in the early work of both of these story-makers of theatre's working is an implicit theory of creativity as masterly, centred and globalising control; and they take up the 'strong points' of actantial theory to represent the intervention of the *metteur en scène* – or of a vaguer 'ideology' – as *auteur* or string-puller. In Ubersfeld that pleasure in the masterly is undercut by the pleasure of the multivariate, the unstable, the space between. In spite of her recognition of the principle of *bricolage* and – for example – the variables from one night's performance to another which more or less escape the authorial thrust and web, what is 'rigorous' in her approach overtakes her pleasure in the *entre les deux* (the space-between). Both theorists shelve what was then 'ungraspable', as 'fleeting', 'ephemeral', 'impossible to approach', 'beyond' semiological analysis, effectively (Pavis) or wistfully (Ubersfeld) impertinent to the semiological project.

It is time to take these elements back off the shelf, in response to the *feeling* that there was something missing to which theatre practitioners have long drawn attention. How else may we theorise the means by which the various practitioners who work in any performance co-operate and struggle to select from the disparate; sort through and discard; finally 'knowing' (but often without discursive reckoning) what can be of use? This pragmatic 'knowing' is supposed by the generativists to be conditioned by the predetermined and determining 'core' (the 'vision', in the words of many British practitioners), held in the mind of a single powerful figure, and projected out onto, to harmoniously control, 'surface' detail or 'signs'. But such a *romance* of creative domination denies the fundamental experience of **group** work so many theatre companies actually enjoy, whatever the terms in which some of them speak of that work.

Changing contexts

In changing contexts of esthetic process (see for example Pavis, 1985, 1987), we can now see that the 'director' may well let her or himself be led, or surprised; progress tentatively and exploratively in a team (no matter how powerful the project-initiating 'feeling' experienced by a single person), toward the moment-by-moment constitution of a complex and collectively constituted and volatile 'surface', without need for magisterial control and 'depth', but functioning as the means to the propagation of a multitude of paths for exploration. We have moved in our understanding from the notion of a centred, dominant and tyrannical single-subject-specific 'creative thrust', which weaves its web over the harmonious whole and perfectly communicates its intention to 'like minds' who reproduce 'the message' in the image of its maker, to that of a looser and more fluid practice marked by numerous focus points, and permitting any number of 'voyages' by a number of always-singular social subjects – that is, offering the potential of a network of different conceptual and practical schema. Perhaps this is a matter of different generations, different ways of seeing?

The recently articulated but long-felt dissatisfaction with the myth of the adequacy of either actantial theory or an authorial theory displaced onto the person of the *metteur en scène*, has found theoretical legitimacy (Greimas, 1990): the actantial–authorial–generativist theory operates as a power house. In positing a single and singular generative *force* at work in performance, these 'centricists' implicitly overrule what is often the disparate, the fortuitous and the collective nature of theatre practice. Centricists require at the very least a controlling intermediary to actantial intervention into esthetic and practical judgement, and it was the nature of myth-making in the 1970s and early 1980s that this role was most readily to be attributed to the person of the *metteur en scène* as *auteur*. But does the director *write* – and *sign!* – the stage, as the author supposedly does the text? The borrowing of specifically textual terms and models for analysis of live collective practice having a textual input was fashionable, but seemed, ten years later, to be questionable. The questions did not end there.

In both Elam (1980) and Pavis (1982), what we find is less a master discourse than a discourse with two masters (Pavis) or *no master at all* (Elam). Perhaps the latter should have been a relief, but it was not. In a combination which ignored the nuances of Peirce, which would tie his endless chains of meaning-production to Derridean *différance* or deferred meaning-making, Saussurean semiology was combined with Peircian semiotics. The consequence for theatre semiologists in the early 1980s was that "signifiers" (Saussure) were claimed to be identified through their quality as *either* iconic *or* indexical *or* symbolic "signs" (Peirce), standing relatively unproblematically for other orders of experienced reality. But whereas the signifier, for Saussure, evokes the wholly conceptual (and thus never 'material-real') user-transcending signified, for Peirce the sign is "something which replaces something **for someone**" (my emphasis); and, with greater delicacy, it is a REPRESENTAMEN, which stands in . . . a genuine triadic relation to . . . its OBJECT, as to be capable of determining . . . its INTERPRETANT . . . [And the] . . . three members are bound together [in a **triadic** relation] in a way which does not consist in any complexus of dyadic relations. (Peirce, 1955, p. 99)

Wilden (1980) notes that certain uses of Peirce have reduced "[this] complex triadic theory of meaning, with its integral relation to the world and to other minds, to a binary relation between words and things" (p. 268). He goes on:

We recall that . . . the tripartite semiotic theory of the Stoics, for whom the 'sign' included the "signifier, the signified, and the 'conjuncture'" [. . . ,] was reduced to a binary relation between signifier and signified in the seventeenth century. (p. 268)

The blending of pickings from Peirce and Saussure served a need in theatre semioticians working within the European tradition at that time, and not the least because of the delicacy of working with the heterogeneous complexity of a dramatic theatre, and of a dramatic theatre theory then intent on privileging the ambiguous materiality of the stage in place of the relative or apparent uniformity of the written text. Was a chair *on stage* any longer a chair, or was it now 'a signifier', or indeed 'a sign', and what sorts of relationship might be posited with regard:

– to an authorial *metteur en scène*'s conceptual intervention (here the chair must assume the status of concept or concept-component within a symbolic network);

– to a stage manager's material intervention (here the chair is decidely 'a thing' in the material real, and then not just a 'stage thing' in the theatre-real, oriented now however to a collective gaze as much as to an 'authorial' schema and an actorly action, but, more significantly, 'that thing we can manage to find/afford');

– to a dramatic writing of didascalies (*'Upright chair centre stage'*), which poses again the already problematised relationship of writerly symbolic, dramatic authorial intent and power, and the iconicity and indexicality of the performance material-real;

– and to an actorly utilisation which may be simultaneously said to be materially real, verbal, symbolic and a matter of both *Gestus* and actorly daring (i.e. doubly indexical)?

In the 1980 borrowing from Peirce, the answer seemed relatively clear, but it has become less clear with the passing of time. This is not just because of different shades of emphasis placed on readings of Peirce. The growing complexity might have as much to do with the early-twentieth-century brief for semiotics (its then prevailing 'ground of thought'), according to which: (1) communication cannot take place outside of systems of signs; (2) as consequence we are always translating one sign into other signs.

Paraphrasal, again, between the non-linguistic semiotic and the linguistic system? The problem with that brief, as soon as we attribute to *language* the role of referee between systems, should be clear: translation *between natural languages* is not a matter of a neat and neutral transfer from one system's signifier to that of another system. It always activates a complex relation between complex systems (including systems of values, ethos and attitude) which make up 'one culture' and the material real of that culture, on the one hand, and *similar* systems (but not necessarily 'the same') in their relation to the material real, in the target culture. How does the chair-staged function, within this framework for translation between systems? Does it cease to be a 'theatre sign' if I *observe* it – and if I go so far as to 'lose my gaze' momentarily in the richness of its fabric, in its pleasing curve of frame – without 'translating' it into another sign? Without this 'translation', does it cease to be part of 'theatre *communication*?

This now classical Peircian perception is, it seems, *almost* unshakeable . . . if we are prepared to accept strict limits placed on the range of potential of the term 'communication'; and provided we add to it one observation, and then the blurring already introduced through my use of Ubersfeld.

Let's begin with the Ubersfeld perspective: into what 'other signs' do I 'translate' that play '*in the void*' or the *space between*, upon which much of my pleasure in theatre depends? Semiosis *has already occurred* at that instant at which I 'realise' (where this might conventionally be construed as a 'naming to myself' function) that what I am looking at, at a particular instant, is 'the skill of the actor'; that at another, what transfixes me is 'Antigone's dilemma'; that at another, I perceive that 'Antigone's dilemma is equivalent to mine'. Here the *systems* of available options are neat – but what exactly does this constitution of discursive potential (or re-staging of the stage) through practices of separation and categorisation of the blur of experience and feeling, have to do with the pleasures of that perceived theatre real? We might do better explicitly to analyse the ways in which we discursively represent our own subjectivity, as this is or is not accessed by performance, than to claim that this implicit analysis is indeed 'theatre semiology'.

It is clear that we can note a precise number of performance indices which lead us to infer and *name* (to 'translate') what we perceive as 'actorly' in one instant, and 'characterly' in another – after all, Brechtian tradition demands that we separate out these two semiotics. But this notation offers no insight whatsoever into the *play* of dramatic theatre, where that process is conjugated in terms of *a movement from one sign system to another*, rather than the site of its effects (i.e. the spectator's work). It is that movement, and not the 'goal' or pole, which produces the felt-meaning. Secondly, as I demonstrate below, that felt-meaning is not explicable in socio-functional terms, may not indeed be wordable except through use of mainstream 'desire-traps'; but it is user-specific in its onset and in its wanderings and finishings.

Let me return to the 'space between': what we need, in these delicate terms, are the means to note those moments when 'translation into other signs' is impeded, when it splutters, pauses and stumbles; when 'translation' is not possible because systems – if indeed we can continue to speak 'clearly' of these as fact (without addressing the question of the proposed nature and sites and modes of action of 'their' existence) – are not commensurable in manifestation, effect or affect, with each other, nor with the ways different users, within even a momentarily united 'theatre community', activate these.

Once again, does this mean that theatre is non-communicative? Yes – if communication is coded, unitary, digital and always translatable between supposedly like entities. But this does not mean that theatre is not systemic, and it does not mean that in its event, it does not *transmit*. What it does mean is that our semiotics must take note of one fact of theatricality: what in part makes theatre work is its capacity for creating those events which enable us to experience the blur where one system insinuates itself into another, with which it might be logically at odds; the blur where two options – and not one – from a given system, are simultaneously made available, to confound the notion of systemic choice itself, as an explanation of modes of cultural practice. What we need to observe is that a major *communicative* function of theatre lies precisely in this blurring of reasonable communication. But can we not say the same for any number of esthetic practices?

To return to the second point: meaning does not 'occur', felt-experiences do not 'occur' (cf. de Lauretis, 1987, pp. 39–42). These are *produced in and by* (and Lacan would add, *despite) the users* as individualised participants in the activation of socially-determined knowledges and modes of experience, and not anonymously 'within [like] systems'. Of the latter we need simply note at this point that even amongst the socially shared and agreed knowledges of late industrialised societies, different spectators will differently prioritise and discard possible and altogether less possible options. If felt-experience is vital to theatre which works – and it is – and to a theatre which is marketable because it works (and this is part of a market economy's esthetic, and thus part of theatre's semiotic), then we are dealing with the explicit 'personalisation-potential' that dramatic theatre as a social practice seems to make possible. Just how it manages to be simultaneously 'social' *and* highly varyingly 'personal', is precisely what we need to consider.

Segmenting 'experience'

For that early 1980s' strand of theatre semiology the proposed representational relationship with an appropriate and pre-determined 'something out there' (a binary concept), seemed to be best improvised through a fragmenting grid determining one of three basic options derived from the most accessible aspect of Peirce's ternaries:

– *either* the effective transparency of the sign: because of a posited 'likeness' to something 'in the world' (a ticklish concept we might better approach through the theory of complementarities) the 'theatre sign' becomes a glass through which a teleological (as 'origin' or 'goal' of meaning) 'real out there' might be identified and thus apparently 'read';

- *or* its indexicality: 'the sign' is read as a (convenient, meta-phorical) 'arrow' or symptom, said to be pointing (through processes of logical inference) to a logically agreed (and her-meneutically more interesting!) 'something else';

- *or* its arbitrary but supposedly stable, 'collective', associative or symbolic relationship with what it is not like, with its other, which it nonetheless can be read/said to stand for: I can do no more than note in passing, in this introduction, the extent to which the notion of 'a sign' as a minimal meaningful unit in symbolic functioning is a nonsense. But the dominant con-ceptual framework of the period did not permit analysts to give up the quest for the *minimal* unit in favour of the notion of sets of complementarities or vitally **relational** complexes, unmarked in advance by neat boundaries or grids. These are *perceived* complexes which are worked as differing guides to a series of associative leaps by the performance users between parallel planes of similarly densely relational – and relative – cultural experience.

Contestation

Now, the major problem emerging from this borrowing seemed ten years later to relate back firstly to the aspiration to masterly authority and science, and secondly, as a consequence of this, to the 'impurity' of the Saussure–Peirce blending: supposed relation to a 'world out there' is taken from Peirce but it is conceived in Saussurean terms – i.e. as a binary couplet: sign/world, mediated by what was theoretically a rather embarrassingly authorless intervention still implicitly responsible for determining iconicity, indexicality or the symbolic. The term 'referent' is incorporated to replace Peirce's OBJECT (standing for something), but Peirce's user-specific INTERPRETANT is omitted from the scene. The theory (narratological) to this point offered only the new couplet *emitter/destinataire*, to approach the Peircian 'someone(s)'. But, while it appears appropriate to then prevalent one-way theories of communication (from a producer, to a receiver: the spectator is relatively passive), this option remains delicate in dramatic theatre whose emitters are multiple, and whose receivers are diversely but vitally implicated in the event.

Until Benveniste (cf. Kristeva, 1980) offers us the theory of *enunciation,* and Derrida the theory of *différance,* however, we are a long way from the vital and mobile Peircian INTERPRETANT (stands *for someone*), which seems not just to be able to incorporate differences in understanding in all parties to the event of performance use, but to admit into semiosis the complex and shifting subject-functions Ubersfeld's work prioritises.

In the terms of this uneasy game of blendings coupled with both dominant singularities *and* divisiveness and categorisation, theatre productions were said to be 'basically iconic' – e.g. strongly marked by naturalistic detail. To be 'largely indexical' – for example, standing as symptom for a (hypothetical) director's or writer's 'attitude' or 'subtext' (each the product, in fact, of the analyst's or critic's cunning). Or to be 'powerfully symbolic', in that the material and energetic specifics were replaced, by the user, with a generalised statement ('man's hunger for . . . ', 'human striving after . . . ') of supposedly universal verities, which was once again attributed to a creative 'vision' on the part of the 'emitter', despite the fact that it was produced by the 'receiver' critic. That is, the terms of Peircian semiotics or Saussurean semiology were borrowed, but to do little more than function as equivalent to and supposedly 'scientifically' preferable to, the terms of an earlier (yet more explicitly critic-specific) critical practice centred on judgements of 'taste' and of 'style' – (e.g. 'expressionist', 'social realist', or 'symbolist' theatre).

Desire-traps

This new appropriation of old experience, in terms of the newly pervasive model of knowledge that was semiology, serves here as an example of what I want to call a 'desire-trap' (cf. Durand, 1977). A desire-trap involves the wide dissemination of a complex way of knowing (an episteme or epistemic complex) which both imprisons and pleases us in the apparent user-defining 'certainties' it offers: it cuts off (imposes closure upon) our capacity for interrogation and exploration of knowledges. For Ulmer (1989), what I call a desire-trap draws into quasi-everyday, anecdotal terms a theoretical or *expert discourse,* couched initially in a wholly 'scientific' or 'objectifying', third person register. That register is *pleasing to (many of) us* – even, or especially, when we wriggle or revolt against it (de Certeau, 1984).

Quasi-anecdotal (for example, my commonsensical Freudian interpretation of my neighbours' child's misbehaviour); quasi-scientific in the terms of its expanding dissemination through audio-visual media (e.g. technical terms and images of practices relating to economics or government, relayed by news programmes concerned with fair dealing or the unemployed professional), the new 'everyday way of knowing, doing and telling' is drawn on as something like a number of short-term mythical *scenarios*, new means by which users explain their world to each other. As scenarios, they dramatise roles and relationships, sketching out a space for action and both a problematised beginning (uncertainty, mystery, a trouble), possible modes of intervention (e.g. government, private, privatised), and a reassuring 'explanatory' ending. In my own application of it to specific performance in the 1980s, the semiological discourse provided the 'stage' and the 'master discourse' for a new quest into meanings. But the 'end' of that quest revealed no more than a pleasingly ordered and objectifying discursive space and time, within which we 'stage' again, (to applause), what we have already felt.

It seems now that certain of the terms and methodologies of 'semiology' as expert discourse characteristic of late modernism, fulfilled this legitimising function for theatre analysts, and did so for precise political reasons in the post-1968 period. But it seems too that they did so on the basis of a quest for something which could not finally satisfy their desire (if it could seem to satisfy their short-term needs): much early semiotic work on codes of human invention (e.g. the system of options for traffic lights) was effective precisely because it operated within what Pêcheux (1984) calls a "logically-stabilised field", while theatre – like many other cultural practices – presents both an order of logical stabilisation (the theatre technology for example operates within this order), and an other-than-logically-stabilised field. Strangely, both theatre *which works*, and theatre which does not, can be approached equally effectively in terms of their logically-stabilised components. It is 'something else' which determines whether one will close, another sell out for a season. This 'something else' belongs to fields of practice which are not logically-stabilised; they are therefore not wholly of the order of a code; and information technology shows us, by failing to tackle the subject of live dramatic theatre, that they are not even a matter of a 'density of interlocking codes'. (The theory of synergy might suggest that 'something occurs', which cannot be dis-interlocked, in performance conditions, and that if this doesn't occur, then we don't have 'good theatre' . . . but how far are we here from alchemy as theatre's preferred metaphor?) Theatre practice laughs in the face of traditions of science.

Softening 'science'

But times change: perhaps the discourse of science, noting theatre's laugh (among others), might be ready to drop some of its own self-seriousness. As Ulmer goes on to indicate – and this is in line with the renewed need for a 1990s' semiotics of writing for the stage – "[i]n practice scientists often choose to work inventively rather than methodologically", drawing passion, conceit, errors and sheer pigheadedness into their practice, since:

> "seductiveness of content . . . is of the essence because interest must be created at a time when the usual methodological prescriptions have no point of attack".
>
> (Feyerabend in *Against Method*, 1975,
> quoted in Ulmer, 1989, pp. 26–33)

We are in the wings here of the libidinal, passionate stage of theory. But such an observation has had to wait for the emergence of the *postmodern scene*. The concealed passion of that earlier stage was infused with an awe-filled yearning (of the supposedly 'weak' because self-proclaimedly 'instinctive','intuitive', 'creative') after the approval of a supposedly paternalistic, 'objective' master discourse called Science. The trap – because of that yearning – was a pleasurably irresistible (and, it now seems, illusory) prison to inventiveness. It led nowhere: there was no attaining to either equality or reciprocity between theatre semiology and the discourses of 'science'. 'Scientists' (with the notable exception of the CNRS in Paris, responsible for the series *Les Voies de la création théâtrale*) were hardly more interested in what was produced by this yearning and these couplings than were many of theatre's own practitioners.

Rational desires

What we can now note is that the rational desire, in 1968, to expose *structures* of power, operating not just at the level of institutionalised 'visibilities' but within the orders of text-production and use within cultural practice and within modes of writing and *understanding* themselves, made structural semiotics a vital early tool. That tool was used effectively, at first, in a number of different domains: it demonstrated that fields of study (e.g. "orientalism", in Said, 1978) and genres (e.g. 'drama') were constituted by ('either/or') exclusions as much as by inclusions; that writing was less a masterly and singular creativity than a 'collective', intertextual process; that "however distinctive, each work is always a re-ordering of already-existing codes, conventions, and materials" (Allen, 1987); that what could be said to be 'dominant' in societies operated less irrevocably through major political and government institutions, than through the 'institutions' of everyday life itself and the attitudes, ethical judgements and actional modes these inculcate (Bourdieu, 1977; de Certeau, 1984); that 'the individual' is not naturally occurring, but rather a product of history and marketing; that the social subject is constituted within the kinship unit, as social microcosm, ordered according to incest taboo and the community exchange of the female child (Levi-Strauss, 1972).

But the 'foundations' upon which structural semiotics was established were formal, categorising, categorical: observing the marginalisation of a 'minority group' required the identification *by the analyst*, first of a mainstream, and then of a marginalised group as its other, its negativity. But from what position did the observer look? The identification depended on the noting of one or another 'observable trait' – e.g. gender or ethnic or racial or economic feature – by which it would be 'known' and then re-cognised, and upon which the establishment of an A/non-A structure depended; and from which further work would be developed. But the problem implicit in this strategy is now clear: one shared quality does not necessarily create group membership; the analyst herself or himself is implicated in the observation and the naming; and, as Guyattri Spivak pointed out recently (Conference: *Beyond Translation*, University of Warwick, 1988), neither her gender, nor her ethnic origins, nor her politics, nor her activism, *necessarily* meant that she would automatically speak for Indian village women and their plight.

What followed the early successes of structural semiotics as political tool was that certain groups, whether women, ethnic minorities or gays (and, later, heterosexual *men!*), began to raise their voices to declare that the Saussurean principle of *shared* or transcendental signifieds, and consequent agreement as to meaning-production, *did not necessarily apply here and now for me/us.*

Rational difference and 'truth'

The prevailing logic based on an either/or binarism, according to which A's identity was not immanent but able to be discerned through differences from not-A (here female = not male, and is perceived to be male's negative; black is not-white and again the first term is the other's negativity), began to be seen less as a natural system (social in operation), than as an arbitrary symbolic system, derived from our desire itself to note difference as a principle of organisation. This is capable of locking into and ordering in its own image other symbolic systems through which the material real is organised. In this sense applied binary logic was not just political, articulating (mythically charged) oppositions leading to policies for proposed action in the world, but *ideological* where that refers to hegemonically disseminated, conservative positivities (regulating attitude, ethos and practice), excluding and marginalising what was perceived to be different, other, deviant.

The notion of a neatly transcendental signified (equated with a 'truth'), and then, with the shift in theory, the subsequent condemnation of it ('truth' is always elsewhere), might seem ominous for theatre semiotics: Eco, that arch/i-semiologist (1976, 1979), specifies the aim of semiotic practice *as he conceives of it*, to be *to uncover the lie* (e.g. Blonsky, 1985, pp. 3–11). Uncovering the lie supposes the ideal existence of verifiable truths, from which the lie can be clearly distinguished. But we might feel that theatre's province and processes are quite specifically those of the effective 'truth' of (what others might call) the effective 'lie'. If theatre equates 'truth' with the effectivity of illusion ('lies'), in order to provide the conditions through which many – if not all – participants arrive at something like an energetic belief, then theatre has never been subsumed into the realm of the truth regime, and its specificities do not lend themselves to wholly rationalist approaches. Theatre's realm is one in which what counts is what Ubersfeld has long since noted: the efficacy of the blurring of neat distinctions in performance; in which 'making people (momentarily, and partially) believe', and moving them (almost of necessity from one place – of predetermined social certainty – to another or others), replaces the aspiration to whatever might classically be perceived to be singularly truth-*full*. But if Ubersfeld hints at another direction to take, as we have seen, her own semiology blurs the path.

What we need to do now is to 'wander in the cityscape' (de Certeau in Blonsky, 1985), amongst the tall buildings erected by one master (of knowledge) or another, armed only with a strong feeling or two, to see what might lend a hand, and where that movement might take us.

Chapter 2

Theatre and Language

How should we proceed in the light of the scenario of conventional knowledges I have outlined in Chapter 1? If conventional drama consistently demonstrates modes of intervention ('revelatory', or 'successful', or 'tragic') into scenes of conflict, presented to the gaze of potentially 'bound-in' onlookers, then it appears that what we have here before us in the name of 'theatre semiotics' is a classic scene of conflictual epistemology, in which an established masterly way of (rationalist) knowing is challenged by one and then another of its callow offspring. But is Antigone, as writerly figure of impassioned (male conceived and written) *'feminine'* revolt against the substitute Father, *bound* to threaten all that Creon stands (or acts) for, ceding the central place – ob-scenely by death off-stage – to a newly focused, recentred and solitary, 'repentant' and 'wiser', order of the present Fathers? As alternative, can we only conceive of an Antigone triumphant, *who does not need to die/leave the stage,* but who might overturn the order of the Father only to find herself confronted with a country to run, a state apparatus stronger than herself, compromises to be made, and a people keen to see her wedded? Such a scenario would be more compromising than that focused on a principled womanly revenge. But to confront one tradition with the makings of another is to bind oneself in to the endless chain of History: the King is dead, they cry, long live the King/Queen!

It is *modernism* which derives from the desire for, and then advocates, the *clear* opposition of the one to the other: this 'clear distinction' forged between the two, stages *the desire for clarity*, for visual and then speculative precision, dear to the Enlightenment. It is the triumphant rule of modernism which designates as *natural* and as *rational*, clear categories – units, boundary-marked entities, atoms, *individuals*, ideas – on the basis of their neat relation to (a perceived) *what they are not*. This perceptual staging simultaneously and 'naturally' clothes these 'reasonable' distinctions in sets of equally opposed options within what has been a dominant system of values. It is in the 'naturalised' and 'invisible' terms articulated through modernism, that we tend 'naturally' in various domains of human practice to choose right *or* wrong, black *or* white, male *or* female, animal *or* vegetable *or* mineral; here *or* there, in proxemic terms; the actor *or* the character *or* the spectator, in performance terms. It seems still to be the case that it is felt to be natural that if male, anatomically, then 'should-be-masculine'; if male and 'masculine', then 'masterly', 'dominant', oriented to the exterior, to the rational, where these are always understood in relation to 'naturally occuring' negative categories of 'not male', 'not masculine', 'not masterly', oriented to the interior and the body. So that we effortlessly rehearse this articulation, within micro- and macro-social manifestations of 'ways of seeing' (Berger, 1972), judgements of taste, ethos and attitude (Bourdieu, 1984). If female (so this tradition has it), then not-male, man's negativity, to be lived out in 'not-masculine' modes. But theatre confounds this logic. And we might well feel that everyday lived experience (rather than social or political principle and theory) does so every bit as much.

What this means is that traditions of analysis are out of step with the lived everyday and with theatre as one of its 'laboratories'. For Habermas (1983), this disjunction derives from the splitting of knowledge and experience into discrete categories with their own specialists that he traces to the period of the Enlightenment; it develops thereafter in the conditions of societal modernism and the growth of capitalism. Cultural modernism is characterised:

> as the separation of the substantive reason expressed in religion and metaphysics into three autonomous spheres. They are science, morality and art. These came to be differentiated because the unified world-views of religion and metaphysics fell apart. Since the 18th century, the problems inherited from these older world-views could be arranged so as to fall under specific aspects of validity: truth, normative rightness, authenticity and beauty. They could then be handled as questions of knowledge, or of justice and of morality, or of taste. Scientific discourse, theories of morality, jurisprudence, and the production and criticism of art could in turn be institutionalized. . . . There

appear the structures of cognitive-instrumental, of moral-
practical and of aesthetic-expressive rationality, each of these
under the control of specialists who seem more adept at being
logical in these particular ways than other people are. (p. 9)

In the *light* of this hypothesis, should we confront Analysis head
on, armed with our Oedipal tools, to try to take its scene from it,
as, in their day, did the structuralists (after the avant-garde's own
revolts)? But the structuralists tried to banish questions of ethics
and morality from their judgemental scene, unpicking esthetics to
demonstrate that the artefact was structured and hence not an
'originality' mystically charged; and bore, as well, secret agendas
and the mark of power struggles.

Should we instead declare – more modestly and along the lines of
one aspect of Habermas' own project – that what is now needed in
theatre analysis terms (Habermas is pessimistic, in the early 1980s,
about the possibility of a more generalised intervention), is a new
synthesis? This would combine elements of digital and analogical
analysis with explorations of catalysis in esthetics, and with a
consistent enquiry into ethical implications.

To the old master of science, this might smack of compromise. So
that even if a new generation interested in questions of theatre and
of theory quickly answers in the affirmative, this does not mean
that we can easily convince the die-hards in their quest for specialised knowledges: choosing to perceive difference as *complementary*
to the other, and not opposed to it, is 'soft' and 'lacking in (moral)
rigour' to the modernist as absolutist and idealist, whatever the
domain of exploration. In his 'Classical Heritage of Modern
Drama', published in English in 1985, Pavis seems rather ruefully
to consider the same question of *the modern* and the *postmodern*
through a comparative analysis of different modes of staging 'the
same dramatic text'. Once again he is doing so from his position as
categorist, working in the conditions of post-1968 interventions, for
whom the 'classical, modern or postmodern fashion[s]' (p. 17)
relate to specific (i.e. exclusive) stylistic differences in directorial
approaches to dramatic writing:

By transforming *modern drama*, by a sort of postmodern *Diktat*,
into *postmodern theatre*, we have committed an act of risky
imprudence. On the one hand, we no longer know where to

place this ephemeral, amnesiac theatre . . . and on the other, the boundary between modern and postmodern – if we want to go beyond the vague temporal metaphor of the *beyond* (*jenseits, au-del*a) – has no theoretical, generic, geographical, or historical foundation.

Postmodernism may as well be founded on a postcomplex – everything that comes after me is postmodern; *après moi le déluge* . . . [Thus] "[p]ostmodern" *Chekhov* would be the version outlined by Meyerhold (in his critique of Stanislavski) and, to take a concrete example, by Vitez' *mise en scène* for *The Seagull* (1984, Théâtre National de Chaillot). In this case, the work is treated as a text: decentred, without answers, performed no longer as an arrangement of intrigue and agency within the plot, but as a vocal and general enunciation. Even if the spectator certainly hears Chekhov's text, s/he no longer perceives a totality or a center of attraction which would give a clue to the scattered fragments. (pp. 17–18)

For Pavis the postmodern is "much more cynical and disenchanted" (p. 18) than is a principled modernism concentrated on effecting social change. But what we might ask is whether his way of seeing is not terminally bound in to the leftist perspective which peaked in France in the late 1960s, and hence, 'purely' of historical interest, or whether instead it is a vital position for the analysis of dramatic theatre. As collective and social practice perhaps theatre 'should' (axiology at work) be 'political' and 'historical' in Pavis' understanding of the terms. But does the loss of faith in the adequacy of the semiotic project as it outlined its own goals and attempted to justify its own methods in the 1970s and early 1980s, necessarily equate with a global loss of faith? Or are some of us now more cautious of globalising projects and of heady ideals? Does the rejection of a (godly) centre in favour of an observation of the bases for that and other desires, mean that we are 'cynical and disenchanted'? Or are some of us – the present is pluralist – now less restricted in our movements and in the directions in which we choose to look?

The case of Mnouchkine and the *Théâtre du Soleil* provides an example of the development from political radicalism in the late 1960s, through to what might now be called – not just in view of

Pavis' disenchantment quoted above – a postmodern *enchantment* wholly lacking in cynicism in spite of the trappings of property, middle class popularity, and huge government subsidy. In both *Richard II* (Shakespeare, performed in 1982) and *Les Attrides* (Euripides/ Eschyle, 1991) by the *Théâtre du Soleil*, what I found was – in part:

– an *authored* dramatic writing;

– a directorial translation for specific purposes by Mnouchkine;

– a named directorial person and role, combined with a signed contribution by a number of 'co-authors' (e.g. Schaub, Lemètre, in *Les Attrides*);

– a transformable 'proper' (or owned) space;

– a 'classical' stage–audience relationship;

– a cunningly 'filmic' use of the stage–off-stage space, defined through the gaze;

– actors able to work through dance, acrobatics, micro-somatic 'intensities' (which avoid the need for cannibalised actorly 'moral interiorities': Hunter, 1983);

– acutely skilled verbalisation;

– a continuous musical score and performance, on stage, by J. Lemètre, which modulates and punctuates the performance moves and emotional shifts;

– every *appearance* of passionate involvement achieved through belief, no doubt, but every bit as much through sustained muscular 'wastage' (Barba and Savarese, 1985) on the part of all participants (including, in a different mode, the attentive spectators);

– a theatre co-operative which is incarnated in all elements of production and performance.

These were combined with an explicit drawing upon Mnouchkine's own stocks of nostalgia and recall – i.e. with the traces of a singular experience. Now, although I can attempt here to partly codify the systems I perceived to be at work, this does not for an instant mean either that another spectator would similarly codify;

or that, in similarly codifying, another spectator would experience 'the same effects/affects'.

On the evening of 4 May 1991 (*L'Oreste*: *Les Choéphores*) the performers took a minimum of eight 'curtain calls', on each occasion performing quite differently to an audience reluctant, despite/because of actorly exhaustion, to release the performers from the spell. To the 'politicised' in a conventional sense, what the spectators demanded and received might smack of a humanism wholly unable to change the orders of the established social. But if the *Théâtre du Soleil* seems no longer collectively to espouse and enact, as part of its function, a particular party political principle, this does not diminish the small case 'politics' of its working; and what is typical of this theatre's contemporary postmodernism is not limited to the way it combines the heterogeneous, the way it quotes a multiplicity of apparently discordant sources. It is its dispersal – the term 'refusal' would err in another direction – of any *clear*, univocal and strongly directed political action, in the post-World War II through to 1968–1973 sense of the term. This rankles with those in theatre who still warm to the crusading politics of, for example, the 'Brechtian' or the 1968 leftist tradition (see however Wright, 1989 on the postmodernism of Brecht). But this does not indicate a lessening of the political. It indicates, instead, the ways in which myths can change, changing with them certain sorts of polarised roles, certain notions of the enemy and possible modes of intervention.

* * *

Changing directions

In the light of this, let us step sideways: the problem I have outlined is not implicit in the theatre semiotic project; it is, rather, a problem arising from the application of semiology, by certain of its major practitioners, to the wider sphere of social analysis and political critique. Now, theatre indisputably plays a role or a number of roles in that wider social and political sphere, but it also role-plays. It is *at one and the same time* a social action, a political event, *and* the simulation of these.

The Vitez staging cited above is less a "movement of ideological retreat and depoliticization" (Pavis, 1985, p. 18), than the means to a reappraisal of the commonsensical – or historically determined, hegemonically disseminated – belief that the 'archeological' stage can adequately represent History. Pavis apparently believes that History might be retrievable through current representations, provided they are 'grounded' and 'coherent'; or considers that a contemporary history might be substituted for it, as long as the stage refuses fragmentation and amnesia. Cohesion, coherence and 'grounding' emerge again as criteria for *good* theatre performance, and again they imply the globalising control of *mise en scene*. What he seems unprepared to acknowledge, is that the fragmentary, amnesiac, or schizophrenic *onstage* might be esthetically valid practices; that secondly they are irresistibly grounded by their place in a given theatre, in its social context, without this grounding necessarily serving as *control;* and thirdly that fragmentation and amnesia (rather than clarity and coherence) might themselves present a current (hence historically specific) refusal to articulate cohesive explanatory master discourses through theatre stagings. From his perspective, it appears that postmodern stagings in the 1980s did not articulate the overlapping and blurred (hi)stories of late industrialised European societies, because they did not set out determinedly to represent them.

But what we know from earlier Pavis is that theatre is at once a material and socially specific event of energetic productions, and a sign-complex undoubtedly able to be perceived as 'standing for' a number of instances of *what it is not.* That it is also a simulacrum, standing for nothing so much as our desires – in part to play games apparently heavy in implications, games of standing-for, a little of what Baudrillard (1983, 1987) has called sex without secretions . . . This *performance as sex without secretions* somehow emulates the interactive energies of other sexual interactions, but in theatre which works one participant enjoys distance, stillness and an intensified practice of the gaze, while the other can heighten and repeat, almost at will and without worrying consequences or responsibilities, what in the material event we seem to lose in one or many little deaths.

A newly passionate science, coexisting with the technological developments that motor capitalism, and operating as something like its complement (rather than as its antidote), should now offer us the means to overcome the failure of fusion or fission between theatre and established semiological discourses and procedures. What is now needed is an exemplary but momentary *event* of empirical analysis (in place of a 'stable methodology', a 'rigorous model', universally practised upon an 'analytical object'), which might be worked through the application of a number of 'semiotic' heuristic tools. What I am looking for, in the terms with which I began this chapter, is a postmodern theory of dramatic theatre practice which is neither cynical nor disenchanted – but which does not aspire, either, to burst forth from the theatre space to convert the orders of the wider social. Many of the heuristic tools we might specify have always been applied by successful practitioners, but under cover of a body of discourses whose effect has been to shroud the mechanics of stage practice in discursive terms derived from one myth or another: e.g. that of the intuitive creative Artist, or that of the urgency of theatre as political praxis. That both the 'creative artist' and the theatre political activist have tended to dismiss the aspiration and the terms of the semiologist should not perhaps surprise us.

(Re-)locating the orders of discourse in theatre semiotic practice

In line with the changing concept of analytical invention and intervention outlined above by Ulmer we need to try to invite passion (pigheadedness, sheer conceit, errors, and the singularity of explicit anecdote) into our project, giving up the dry sobriety of 'rigour' and the apparent anonymity of a master discourse (articulated through third person deixis, a universalising unmodalised present tense, and a focus on nominalisation in place of process). Within the context of what this project foresees – a semiotic discourse relating to complex cultural practices not wholly governed by language – the act we are now engaged in, through the intermediary of *discourse*, needs to find within its parameters tentative answers to the following troubling question: what might we continue to use, from within the discursive economy, when it is the apparently pervasive efficacy of that economy which has held sway over theatre practice, to transform not so much the practices themselves as the ways in which some of us can know them?

In line with Feyerband, let me note pigheadedly: I am obliged to question the uses of discourse within theatre and its different productions, *through discourse itself*. In order to do this, I need to make explicit the roles and relations that discursive traditions within theatre have prioritised, suggesting different scenes of interest, additional place-takers, alternative processes, a wider range of products. I need to admit, bemusedly, that on specific occasions I have been pleasurably transfixed by performance which, after the event (in that pause which precedes my own discursive production), I have found to be questionable. This seems conventionally to entail a complex parallel processing, which then separates out a masterly performance pleasure in the event, from a discursive product, with as consequence a troubling disjunction of a politics of discourse from a practice of pleasure. If this traditional disjunction of event-pleasure and discursive product is newly visible in the age of Madonna and the films of Beineïx (e.g. *Betty Blue (37° 2 le matin*)) – *should* we admit to liking what would once have seemed and may still seem to be 'ideologically unsound'/'politically in-correct'? – we might now admit that it has always been the case that performance can please intensely in the event, only to be omitted, attacked or accused in secondary recuperations into discourse.

In the 1980s this sort of disjunction (and its implications for what was called 'popular culture') led to attempts at a politics of pleasure (e.g Barthes, 1977, 1982; Carroll, 1987; Kroker and Cook, 1986; Bourdieu, 1985) which however has only recently begun to ponder the question of the experience/discourse disjunction itself. What this means, in apparent contradiction to aspects of the critique of semiology I have attempted, is that we shall need to bring a certain practice of 'socio-political theory' to operate within a new theatre semiotics, just as we need to practise a new politics of discourse within this semiotics. This socio-political practice relates not to 'what theatre represents', but to the political implications of conventionally taken and conventionally excluded options in discursive representations of theatre experiences.

In answer to Pavis', and others', accusation of postmodern depoliticisation, what should now operate is a politics of modes of representation of theatre, not a hermeneutics of a theatre of representation of the fictional political. This may nevertheless entail a new hermeneutics of political fictions, and in this broader analysis we might attempt to note the ways in which the two 'politicals' intersect, and to what effect for theatre and for the wider social. One 'everyday political option' concerns the ways we conventionally use 'superordinate discourse', to allude meto-nymically to those judged to be 'like', through reference to the 'typical' instance. Tyler (in Clifford and Marcus, 1986) suggests in place of the unquestioning use of the superordinate, we seek the means to a postmodern ethnography (and we might want the same for theatre discourse) which should be able to *evoke* "what cannot be known discursively or performed perfectly, though all know it as if discursively and perform it as if perfectly" (p. 123).

Experience/discourse

The gap between the gamut of human experience on the one hand, and uses of language in writing and speech on the other, and the domination not of language over experience but of certain dis-cursive modes over those experiences, where the former are used to comment on fields which are 'other-than-logically-stabilised', did not become an issue for what were (until recently) called the 'human sciences', until the works of Lacan, the neo-Freudian theorist, and the philosopher Derrida, were differently fed into early feminists' rejection of what was seen as a 'patriarchal' tyranny, worked through a 'Word' (of the Father) (e.g. Derrida, 1978, pp. 232–50).

Since the translation and wider dissemination of those discursive materials, critical discourses which accrue to various fields of cultural practice in which language merely plays a role (e.g. in film, popular culture), have set about thematising and questioning the traditions, the adequacy and the shortcomings of widely disseminated discursive norms, in their relations to diverse cultural practices. Many of the terms and conclusions of that critique are now part of the history of cultural analysis, and can best be approached from both historical and relativising perspec-tives. To a very limited extent, linguistics and discourse analysis have succeeded (Halliday, 1987) – despite the resilience of both idealising generative and reductive digital and boundary-marking models – in shifting their epistemological bases from the ideal of 'scientific rigour', the ideals of law and universalisation, to practices marked by indeterminacy, particularity, by chance and the small-scale. They thereby adopt the relative fluidity of models of knowledge informed by quantum theory. But how do we set these out *on the page*, and *clearly* enough, without reactivating the very conventions we now seek to reassess?

Writing and socio-somatic practice

What are the stages in the recent history of cultural analysis which have led to this new understanding of the place and function of writing and language *within* socio-somatic practice, rather than the opposite where the body is seen as ancillary to, equivalent to or inferior to language? Each of these stages, in interventions which have swept across a number of relatively discrete fields of enquiry (e.g. linguistics, literary theory, discourse analysis, anthropology, ethnography), is marked by a renewed interrogation of the established and possible relationships between language and other modes of human action. For our present purpose, focused on the relationship between dramatic writing and other theatre practice, and bearing in mind the different notions of semiosis we have briefly examined in the preceding chapter, we need to retain as tentative and pragmatic guidelines to our critical enquiry, a field marked by certain peaks which continue to show up within theatre practice as we know it: dramatic writing activated by practitioners in the context of a planned staging within a given cultural context; somatic action; semiosis; idealisation and options for realisation; the *metteur en scène*, the actor, character, the spectator, and their possible roles and relations.

* * *

Masterly shifts

In terms of the history of analysis of cultural practices, it is only relatively recently that that 'Saussureanism', which proclaimed the priority of language over all other symbolic systems and its status as the sole system upon which analysis of other practices could be based, underwent its development in the 'Derridean' derivative ('there is nothing outside of text') and in the 'Foucauldian' derivative ('all practices are informed by discourse'). More recently still it has undergone the reappraisal centred both in feminist discourses and in the delicately troubled discourse of a critical ethnography (Clifford and Marcus, 1986), which is concerned with how the outsider (the other) 'understands', talks about, 'documents' and analyses another culture. There are obvious resonances here for our enquiry into the ways in which the spectator–semiotician and the semiotician as critic and analyst, talks about, documents or writes about theatre.

The critique provokes a question close to the theatre practitioner, who hands on tradition through example rather than through theoretical or critical **discourse** (e.g. the teacher of *kathakali* or of *Noh*; the drama conservatory teacher who demonstrates as much as she tells). The implications of the answer spread beyond the reach of theatre's relationship to writing and language, into the realms I have just signalled, and into the theory of signing itself. As Pavis indicated above, for Benveniste and a number of French theorists *language* is the only semiotic system which can interpret other systems different from itself. The questions then are these: does theatre communicate other theatres; does theatre communicate theatricality to others; can theatre comment critically on theatre? The answers come swiftly and clearly, but in a way which troubles the semio*logist* as producer of discourse, as it does the conventionally *academic* teacher and student of theatre whose work is still largely transmitted and assessed through language. Theatre communicates and often critiques other theatre practices each time it is produced – provided we are able to perceive this stream of interdiscursivity and **interpraxia**; to recognise the systems of allusion, quotation and transformation through image and practice, and to acknowledge the positions within it that given practitioners have chosen. All theatre practice, regardless of its practitioners' intention, is caught up, not in a dialogue but in an 'interpraxio-logue', an exchange both with the abstract *theatricality* itself, and with specific concrete instances.

For Macdonell (1986, p. 1) '[d]ialogue is the primary condition of discourse [and, we might want to add, of practice]: all speech and writing is social', even in instances of invention, improvisation, and self-reflexion. In this sense, *mise en scène* is more than a dialogue with other stagings: it seems to function as *heteroglossia* (multi-'tongued') (Lemke 1984) and **heteropraxia** (or multi-modal and internally-differentiated practice).

In order to approach heteropraxia, we need a theory of practice; but first we must determine whether that theory of practice should take as a basic premise the adequacy of language to its development, the adequacy of language to its applications to theatre practice, and, indeed, the adequacy of language as it is conventionally used, to *stand (for us, here and now) for* what occurs in the various practices we should want to include under the heading of dramatic theatre.

Theatre 'talking about' theatre/practice enacting practice

In Balinese tradition the teacher curves her/his body against the body of the student, from behind, the muscles, limbs and digits of the one lifting, directing, flexing and rhythmically moving those of the other. The child learns, through her central nervous system, an un-spoken – and even unshown – complex performance skill. It is a knowledge felt in/as the body. If I ask the performer about a gesture she replies 'Like this, like this', drawing only on the symbolic and deictic properties of language to draw my gaze to some*thing* 'explained', less through showing, than through taking my hand, and turning and flexing it. This is far from an 'exotic' or secret knowledge. By contrast, Stanislavski, caught up within old northern European social codes and grounds of thought, could only approximate through that exteriority which is clothing (in its strange relation to the nervous system); with description, advice and admonition, as substitute for what many of us would perceive, in the south-east Asian model I have just invoked, as an embarrassing somatic 'intrusion' upon the body-space of the student.

But on the other hand, as infants we learnt to negotiate our way around, to tie our shoes and to wipe our noses through guided somatic intervention and example ('Like this, like this!') rather than through discourse. In the examples I give, discourse is a support, and it is inherently 'meaningless' because of its vital deictic and interpersonal relation to a given, (now absent), time, space and human relation. Arguably the generations brought up with television, as well as those fields of education which draw strongly on video, similarly draw extensively on somatic practice – curiously 'transmitted' not just visually and bi-dimensionally, but through a synesthesia we do not yet understand, to the whole body – as a complex knowledge which does not need to be mediated by language. We need advances from AI to understand this sight-through-to-action transfer, from 'grey level' description, to the equivalent of a primal sketch, to a surface 'description' which ruffles the body's nerve network; through to 3-D model in time and space, from which we constitute performance, in the everyday of theatre work.

This seems to suggest that only certain kinds of knowledge *about* theatre are transmitted through language. The use of language outside the professional context, to 'talk about theatre' rather than to demonstrate it, creates no problem if we are satisfied with the adequacy of language to represent theatre experience. If, however, we want to question some of the ways in which uses of language conventionally *stage* only certain aspects of experience, prioritising certain of these over others, wholly omitting yet others in line with what are indisputably dominant modes of seeing and speaking the world, then renewed intervention is necessary. The 1970s were marked by various modes of intervention and by a number of confrontational positions, not the least of which conflated language itself with a tyrannical patriarchy and its modes of oppression. But this led to the exclusion of dramatic writing and of the use of speech in voicing, from dramatic performance (the baby–bathwater syndrome). What emerged from observation of these radical alternatives, these attempts to kill the Father (Word), was the recognition that they in turn bound us in to the same oppositional and exclusivist mentality (oriented to biological difference) that we sought to reject. To reclaim the pleasures of language, feminists and other cultural theorists began to recognise instead that language itself was less the culprit, than that straitjacket which comes from discursive traditions bound up and ratified in certain institutions of learning and everyday practice. This difference in perspective marks the epistemological shift from a modernist to a postmodern (or non-oppositional, combinatory) approach. It is neither a universal nor an uncontested development.

Drama's 'talking about theatre': the case for connotation

But let us come back to the proposition made by Benveniste: it might seem then that a case can be made for the hypothesis that dramatic writing is not so much the 'speech' of 'human' characters, not so much the coded intention of its author, as a "[dramatic] semiotic system . . . interpret[ing] other [theatre] systems different from itself". Ubersfeld has already suggested this in terms taken from Hjelmslev's semiotics (Hjelmslev 1961): if dramatic writing *denotes* elements we then flesh out in terms of the codes of dramatic fiction, it might also be said to *connote* (a further plane of semiosis in which first-order signifier + signified become second-order signifier) not just 'theatre', but a contextually specific theatre mode, as second-order signified. In this case, however, we need to ask to what extent this second signified *transcends* the differences we now see more clearly within the community of 'like' users; and secondly we need to ask what operatives control and extend the dimensions of the connoted complex signified. Where the 'connoted' signified's proportions are not commensurable with the dimensions of the first-order signifier and the user's understanding of the first-order signified, what are the means to a general analysis of connotation?

Thirdly, if we are satisfied with the modification of the schema for denotation so that it includes user and *user-context specificity*, with the implication that second-order semiosis springs from the action of the brought, on certain attributes of the text given – and I see no *a priori* objection to the hypothesis that what is brought to 'dramatic signifiers' by a specific-purpose reader of dramatic writing, for an envisaged staging, will, in its precise types of activation of the textual given, cause that reader to 'see' potential (but idealised) options for different moments of a future staging – then there is still no adequate basis for claiming that this 'connoted' semiosis is a fact of that dramatic writing itself. It seems to be a fact of specific purpose use, but that use – as anyone who has staged a text not using established convention knows – is not necessarily inscribed in dramatic text grammar as complex signifier.

Finally, we need to return to the nature of semiosis itself, and, to some extent at least, to some idea of what occurs in the mind of the reader for the stage when that reader 'activates' dramatic writing. Essentially, we are asking, when using the signifier/signified binarism of Saussure, whether an idealised theatricality seen as something more than a complex image, can be the second-order signified in a reading process, in which the user's first-order semiosis of 'the same' dramatic signifiers, functions as second-order signifier. Difficulty here comes from the way that this consideration plunges us back into the question of the meaningful unit. If, however, we turn to the Peircian semiosis in which signs belonging to one system are 'translated' into signs 'within other systems' – with no indication, in this formula, of the vital Peircian grounding elements (standing *for someone*, which now means *somewhere and somewhen*) – then we enter a virtually bottomless pit: how many sign systems does a dramatic writing 'encode' when signs can simultaneously function iconically, indexically and as symbols in their relation to the stood-for? If theatre functions, as now seem likely, through intensities, which are densely worked sites of intersection variously perceived and differently semiotised by different users within and beyond the parameters of social agreement – working through something rather more 'like' the hieroglyph than 'like a sign' – then we need to ask how many orders and how many sub-systems and minority systems, of how many signs, *can* operate within theatre practice? (Is it "a million", as Shakespeare suggests?) How readily can we claim a direct and causal linking between the dramatic signing and the theatre signing? Who might mediate this teleological relation? For whom, ideally and really?

Connotation in the realm of the unknown user

If what has been called connotation is a user-specific process, rather than either a text-producer-specific or a subject-transcending one, then it would seem that any attempt at modelling and methodology-production must leave wide open and imprecise – open to anecdote, for example – its most significant category. At this point I need to stress the idealised nature of single-user connotational semiosis: since theatre is collective practice we have either to suppose that all members of that collective will share the same second-order semiosis, which all practitioners know is a nonsense; or we have to suppose that *metteur en scène* second-order semiosis will best be able to impose itself as the means to the creative impetus of performance. But Roger Planchon (a particularly complex *metteur en scène* who operates through a traditionally strong 'leftist' politics with regard to his team combined with a minutely exacting control over options preferred by that team) was far from dictating to the stage designer Frigerio the nature of the set Planchon and the TNP (Lyons 1979, Paris 1979–80) would use for Pinter's *No Man's Land*. It is difficult to see how Frigerio's set could be produced **as** Planchon's own second-order semiosis. It seems, rather, that Planchon's staging options developed in his understanding of the dimensions and proportions, the access points and the relation and orientation to the spectators, that Frigerio's anticipated set would offer, after he learnt these, in a process marked by consultation and individual contribution. Here immediate context to actions was singular, as well as social.

If this is the case, then the concept of a connoted semiosis best relates to a singular production (e.g. one person's act of reading). But in theatre's collective work, connotation intervenes *interactively*, as negotiation, after the event of user-specific second-order semiosis. It is not shared in that event, since if it were, connotation would be reduced to the status of norm, convention or stereotype; and what results from this negotiation may even have been unthinkable to another user, until it is produced, and made available to group intervention. Hence it is not *wholly* socially encoded at the moment of its singular production – except to the extent of implicit agreement in the area of late twentieth century European esthetics, and with regard to the nature of the minimal theatrical relation itself (the specular–somatic relation for looking and bodily presence). These however do no more than establish its parameters. Without acknowledging the practitioner's capacity for *flirting with* and for *quoting*, as well as contesting or sustaining the codes of the mainstream, and pleasing while doing so and thereby persuading, we have no means of approaching the spectator's pleasure at theatre's collective and co-operative work.

According to the hypothesis of a shared connoted semiosis, what we should find in dramatic writing is not just 'dialogue' plus 'stage directions', but a coded textualised *interpretation* of theatricality bearing on an entire stage 'world', already allusively coded 'within' the interplay between text givens and like-minded social code users. Socially stable denotational semiosis is seen as this connoted theatre's originary site; and from this site the perceptive code-sharer is supposedly able to decipher (or 'decode') that interpretive theatricality, through a 'close' and sympathetic 'theatre contextualised' reading of dramatic writing, and thereafter 'made flesh' by a 're-encoding' on stage.

If this thesis is valid, theatricality can be encoded within the order of adequate discourse, a 'further meaning-field' connoted by writing and finding its impetus *in* that writing. This is reassuring to traditionalists trained in text use and further text production, where the goal of a process leading to the constitution of a 'plane of connotation' is not a *'presentational' imaging* (Langer, 1942) itself, but a discursive explication of 'pertinent aspects' of imaging. But for those operating outside of that closed field, it does not seem that we can readily justify such a position. In the case of theatre, the conceptual realm brought by the user is not necessarily of the order of a putative 'equivalency' of 'other signs' within the systems of discourse as that notion is conventionally understood, and nor does it function necessarily 'like a language' in our conventional understanding. It is rather a question of non-commensurable multi-dimensional and multi-modal abstractions from and for praxis, in which discourse is activated as one component. Within this complex multi-dimensional figuring *brought* to a pro-theatrical reading of text co-ordinates, we might be able to talk *as well* of the growth in the reader of force-fields and waves. Force-fields are I think self-evident. Waves are activated as a later (and fluid, not unitary or 'codified'), phase of the complex user-activation of the denotational and the connotational semiosis, rather than as a conventional connotational meaning-production.

It may be the case that the force-field production relates to a particular *brought* preconception of a centred *mise en scène* and of a particular (reverent/mystical) theatre relation, which would appropriate and transform what the production makes available, rather than to a universal of theatricality. Rodowicz' account ('Theatre East-West', Japanese Theatre Conference, ICA, London, 1991) of classic *Noh* theatre, for example, suggests that it operates precisely through the short-term constitution of a centralised field of resonant intensity in which the voices of the singers and the rhythm of the orchestra (on two sides of the front stage) intersect with the audible and visible energised body of the *sh'te*, at the heightened plot-performance moments of revelation of identity. If we can generalise, in an attempt to approach the notion of *theatricality*, then it seems that what we are trying to understand are the means to the modulation by the practitioner of an event-specific force-field, already made possible (but by no means guaranteed as a positivity) by the nature of the theatre per-formance relation itself. In the context of Japanese theatre Jan Kott

(Japanese Theatre Conference, ICA, London, 1991) noted that, as with Beckett on stage and Robert Wilson's work, Japanese traditional theatre produced intermittent boredom, but not that boredom which causes us to leave the theatre, or to switch off the television. It is a boredom which keeps us 'bound-in' (Frow 1986) – hence the appropriateness of the term 'force-field'.

From Denotation/Connotation to a typology of complex processes

We are dealing with something rather more complex than the order of connotational semiosis when as readers for staging we activate complex multi-dimensional and multi-modal imaging in advance of a staging. What we might attempt to work with in the analysis of dramatic writing is a return to a Peircian schemata which seems to offer the bases for a fluid typology of 'pre-sentational imaging', according to which we might be able to demonstrate that certain sorts of text relations are simultaneously activated, but differently for different users. Relations are

- *diagrammatically* relevant to theatre conditions and human relations (but unable *in themselves* to define the multi-dimensional specifics of a specific theatre or theatrical mode);

- available, through the activation of conventional models of knowledge, to be **used as** *indices or symptoms* of inferrable interiority and sociality, and through this intersection of (user-prioritised) given and brought elements, to effect material actions (gestuality, facework, moves, shifting proxemic options, voicework, and so on); at a further phase of very rapid user-processing, these are activated again as *metonymic of* (perceiver's) 'real world' relations;

- and available to be used as *symbolic of* other, substantially unlike socio-psychological relations, which are either felt but undeciphered, or conventionally decipherable, by some theatre users in a given context of use.

In each of these types of processing by a user, for others, and *between* writing and the idealisation of staging and theatre conditions and relations, what we should be looking for within the order of the **synoptic** text (see Halliday, 1987: the synoptic text is "in place", mapped, fixed, reduced to its bare materiality) are *relational complexes* of different types and different dimensions, and the bases for a short-term constitution of *complementarities* (and not binary opposites: not male/female, but female ↔ male), which the user then draws into relations of potential equivalency with perceived relational complexes and complementarities operating both in a conception of theatre and in a conception of the wider 'real out there'.

Once again, the perceived 'orders' of theatre and the 'real out there' may become *more or less* available to users, under particular sorts of operative constraints, in a communicative pre-production situation, but here they do not necessarily function 'like a language': we may be able to propose that they can be made to function and become available, in these conditions, 'like discourse', provided we broaden the understanding of that term, snatching it momentarily from the hands of linguists. On the other hand, it may be more satisfactory to suggest that they function, and can only be communicated, '**like a multi-modal demonstration**'.

Let's take another, comparative example, from Zeami's classic *Noh* play, *Lady Han* (included in *Twenty Plays of The Noh Theatre*, 1970, pp. 129–45), and Mishima's modern *Noh* play, *Hanjo* (1973), which borrows explicitly from the first. If we can assume in a first reading adequate language competence and knowledge of *Noh*, then the reader should – provided s/he has adequate access to the fixed stage codes of the theatre of Zeami – be able to project and develop conceptually, *from* that first decoding, another formulation. A conceptual space is crossed, etched in, between writing, fiction and reading, on the one hand, and on the other the knowledge of the specificities of classical *Noh* stagings, which function as enablers to the specific experience. The resultant rigidly codified and circumscribed 'imaginary scene' (Banu 1986) poses relatively few problems for a theory of representation, since the currently maintained traditions of *Noh* themselves enunciate, and are the means to representation. The master and actor of *Noh* readily accept the role of (preserving, reverent, hence by definition conservative) mediator.

But what happens when a modern Japanese reader for the stage works on Mishima's relatively recent 'modern' *Noh* play which takes its title and plot-motif from the Zeami work? Some of the esthetic codes (as well as implicated epistemological shifts) of modern industrialised societies which have accompanied the US presence in Japan since World War II enter the equation, and the enunciator takes, willy-nilly, a position with regard to these. One paradoxical *code* entails the worrying or confronting of traditional codes themselves, and the loss which results from breaking with them. Thus technical perfection or mastery of the given, plus – for example – *hana* (Zeami, 1960), cedes in significance to an esthetics of change and difference, both exciting and hazardous.

The implications go further to encompass other fields of experience which performance and 'theatricality', supposedly connoted, might be said to entail as *practice*, attitude and the bases of judgement, without however their being explicitly *represented* at any point through discourse. Conventional Japanese ways of understanding and dealing with psycho-social 'complaints' through somatic treatment (Ohnuki-Tierney, 1984) are overlaid, for audiences with everyday access to international media, with commonsensical freudianisms. Does *Lady Han* now performed to these audiences 'connote' ancient theories and modes of approach to socio-psychological problems and metaphysical goals? Arguably not, with any force. Yet could we for an instant claim that Mishima's dramatic writing does not *permit* Japanese stagers to work theatrically through, for Japanese spectators, both pre- and post-World War II esthetics in these fields of experience? Can this ambiguity be said to equate, then, with *connotation* seen as the play of semiosis? The question is troubling for the conventional thesis of a connoted theatricality. In the case I have mentioned, the only persistently stable feature of 'theatricality' is the enunciator–discursive–specular–somatic relation of live dramatic performance itself.

The strictly encoded specificities of the *Noh* stage no longer necessarily supply the schematic grids which dominate in the forming of parameters to different readers' imaginary stagings, in a putative 'second stage' of semiosis in work on Mishima. In the same sense, does the proscenium arch, or the *théâtre de chambre*, or the theatre in the round better or more authentically supply these parameters in a way which can be said to 'be inscribed' in the writing? Dramatic writing for staging, whatever the mindset of its author, is open to esthetic change: it is this 'openness', just as much as 'inscribed conventions', which the analyst of performance potential needs to find the means to approach.

The theoretical basis for 'openness'

If 'theatre' is not 'inscribed in' dramatic writing, although theatre relations may be seen *by one user or another, and differently*, to be diagrammatically or symptomatically or symbolically 'made available', by use of that writing, in the precise context of a planned or possible staging, then what we need to call upon is Derrida's theory of *différance* (Derrida 1978) and *déhisence* (Derrida, 1977).

Few theatre semioticians of the 1980s in Europe have had much to say about the contribution of Derrida's work, and for reasons which perhaps seemed justified in terms of the 'text politics' of theatre analysis after 1968. In order to overcome 'literary' readings of dramatic writing it became necessary to demonstrate the inscription of theatre 'in the text', the inscription of theatre's social pertinency, the inscription of ideological positioning heightened by theatre's 'transgressive' potential. It was entirely appropriate, politically, to stress that Sophocles'/Shakespeare's/Mishima's conceptual space was theatrical, first and foremost, to be predicated in other terms only after this investigation; so that 'dramatic text analysis' might be charted in terms of *decodable* spaces of the stage and times of performance, rather than in those of the current state of literary theory.

But Derrida's theory of openness, of semiotic play, and of the bipolar (writer-and-unknown user) production of meaning, which led to the shifts associated with poststructuralism, seems to have troubled this epistemologico-political project. If *nothing* is 'in the text', unless it is put there by the user in terms of her local and immediate context, then 'theatre' as (representable) concrete construct, and performance as a (representable) given event in time and place, can no more be 'there', so much as projected, and then staged in the play of the Imaginary (Lacan, 1977) as it stalls and flirts with the diverse symbolic modes.

The omission of the theory of openness is perturbing: first because this development is precisely what permits us to bring into play different orders of semioisis 'of the one text', differently activated by different users in different contexts, for diverse users and uses *within the one audience.* Secondly, 'theatre' and in particular 'Artaud', supplied Derrida, in the 1960s, with a major metaphor for his critique of structuralism.

We have already seen Pavis' position outlined in 1985 with regard to a postmodernism in theatre which developed no doubt in part from the widespread dissemination of Derridean theory, but the omission remains troubling. Because we can now see that the 1990s user of Sophocles' *Antigone can* bring to that writing conceptual models specific to a 1990s conception of theatre and understanding of current theatre technology, provided certain co-ordinates are available in that writing. Those co-ordinates are, for the theory of *déhisence* which takes as its metaphor the bursting seed pod, akin to the genetic specificity of the plant seed. But this specificity cannot itself control what the seed grows into – hence the need for a bipolar theory: other factors brought from without, such as rainfall, soil quality, fertilization, will determine degree of growth, whether the plant flowers, whether it produces seed. The seed does not connote that growth, nor has it 'inscribed' its specific needs, thereafter to be effectively 'decoded' by the other partner. And if these are not 'in-scribed' into the dramatic writing, but brought, then meaning – including theatre codes and conventions – for a given text, is deferred, postponed, until a context-specific but also singular user activates, will activate, or did in the past activate the writing. (Perhaps it is only the elusive 'theatricality' which remains, activated *as soon as the text is read for the theatre scene.* But this has never been 'in' the text, so much as in the conditions of use, and in the Imaginary of its writer/s and users – i.e. 'in' the *spaces between.*)

The limits of discourse

In the examples I have given what is at work is neither specifically a linguistic process, nor equivalent to a linguistic process; nor is it particularly useful to describe these processes when they are at work in theatre as *discursive,* locating them within the boundaries of a discursive economy (a vast apparatus processing and producing discourse according to established principles and pragmatics of economy and wastage, formulae for the regulation of use, and quantitative and quality control), as the term discourse is used in the English-language mainstream. We cannot confidently speak of 'code', encoding and decoding, unless we are concerned with the codification of what has already occurred, of what *has been produced*, and not with *what might be produced*.

Nor do the practices I have outlined lend themselves readily to that discussion: how do we generalise on and how do we typify a range of experiences (as Actor, as agent performing in the scenario of another, as subject within a fiction written or produced by another, as goal or beneficiary in a material real or a fictional scenario – terms adopted very loosely from Halliday's systemic functional grammar (1978, 1985)) of cultural practice? *What sort of discourse might we now produce, in the light of the various scenarios of knowledge, belief and disenchantment I have sketched out in the preceding pages?*

Talking again 'about theatre'

Barthes (1982a) has already asked in 'The Grain of the Voice' whether we are condemned, in approaching esthetic experience, to hover between predication and the ineffable. Condemned either to speechlessness, or to do no more (and no better) than to qualify the phenomenon (rather than our experience of it) **adjectivally**.

This produces a description which is couched in terms of a named subject (e.g. i. 'Shakespeare's Lear . . . '; ii. 'Warner's *Electra* . . . '), and an adjectival and qualifying *predication* (i. 'is anguished'; ii. 'is gripping and passionate'). The problem is not unfamiliar in either the field of theatre criticism or in the field of theatre analysis. But what alternative options can be found? Whereas the adjective relates to the perception of its perceiver–user rather than to a generalisable 'truth' of experience, its phrasing excludes that use of personal deixis ('To *me* . . . '; '*I find it* . . . ') which would textually identify the given perceiving subject. The sentence structure which predominates in criticism omits the (name/sign of the) perceiver who makes the judgement, including only the judgement of taste lodged in the adjective ('brilliant', 'witty', 'turgid', 'fast-moving'). The sentiment is communicated, but not the source of the sentiment.

For Carroll in *Paraesthetics* (1987), on the contrary, the always problematic relationship of discourse to esthetic phenomena revolves around what might be seen as the **rationalist** tendencies of what we accept as meeting analytical criteria. That is, around what has been perceived, until recently, as the unitary or particle-based nature of language (which seems thus to lend itself to rationalist constructs); and around the fluidity and the movement of an other-than-particulate or unitary, digital, *working*, of esthetic experience, which works in ways which confound neat articulation and established categories of appreciation – so that "[the] *'coup analytique'* is continually countered . . . by the 'coup du sentiment'". This *drama* **of critical experience itself** provokes in the theatre practitioner, with regard to the analytical product and the analyst:

> feelings of injustice and stimulate[s] a sensitivity to what, in a given situation, has not been phrased . . . a search for idioms that testify in some way to the silences of the not yet phrased and the unphrasable, which constitute the stakes of a critical philosophy, politics, and art. (Carroll, 1987, p. 183)

In 'La Peinture est-elle un langage?' ('Is Painting a Language?'), Barthes (1982b) introduces terms which relate to the delicacy of our own theatre semiotic project:

> [i]n truth the question of whether painting is a language is *already* a moral question, which calls forth a mitigated response, a dead response, safeguarding the rights of the individual creator (the artist) and those of human universality (society).
> (139: my translation)

He goes on to suggest that what is needed is "a new way of feeling [and] a new way of thinking", if we are, in analysing cultural practice not wholly governed by language, to cope with the terms inherited from semiology (structure, text, code, system, representation). This suggests that we can break with the prevailing epistemes (or ways of knowing), the prevailing ways of seeing, feeling, judging and saying, which are disseminated in schooling, in esthetic tradition, in the media. A challenging project, and one which Bourdieu's theory of *habitus* would reject; but it is no more challenging than the project for an epistemology of theatre 'sciences' that we have already taken up.

In asking what the relationship 'should be' between visual arts and the language through which we attempt to 'read' and implicitly to 'write' them, Barthes suggests that the painting has no *a priori* structure, but that it is itself (I should prefer now to say 'it functions *for me as*') the system of the textual structures that we differently activate across our act of using it, and that this system of textual structures is infinite: "the image is not the expression of a code, it is the variation of a work of codification: it is not the depository of a system, but generates systems (p. 140)".

But this 'development' from Saussurian linguistics requires a modification of the discourse of analysis itself, such that semiotic analysis is no longer a matter of delivering up a body of 'results' (fruit of a quest sharpened by the certain knowledge of its achievable grail). Rather it is a matter of language constantly *at work*, unfinished, in the attempt to identify itself radically with the processes (in our own case) of performance in which our multi-modal perceptions are included. The spectator semiotician, like other performers, is both caught up in socially constituted and ratified codes, and 'beyond' them, able not just to play with them, but to choose paths within the performance which differ from user to user. These are literal in the case of theatre's multiple sight-lines, and metaphoric in the case of user-differing sites of interest and intensity.

In an unfinished article ('Right in the Eyes', 1986), Barthes begins to indicate the means to this expanding and user-specific semiosis: a kernel or nexus of socially agreed meanings is surrounded by relatively unlimited and uneven ripples or haloes, an aura of user-specific meaning/feeling development. It remains, for all that, linked to the centring kernel, but is simultaneously 'generated' (though not in terms of its array of possible implications for meaning-production) by the user-specific muscular **act** (of the pebble-thrower or semiotician-as-user), as well as by external chance factors. Together with the literal and symbolic parameters of the cultural performance scene (the pool), these both frame and radiate inwards toward the outward-spreading ripples.

The metaphoric modelling is dynamic (or "in flux", Halliday, 1987) interactive and multi-dimensional: the ripples 'caused' by the given body's muscular act with the stone as it meets the water's surface, are not just marked by the outer edges of the pool. They are marked as well not just by water depth and the play of the wind in the area, but by the chance relation of the water and the stone and the impetus with the fish swimming below and the duck, on the pool's edge, which simultaneously lowers itself into the pond.

By reactivating the notion of (the drama of) difference and distinction (Bourdieu, 1985) both within the users' fields of force, and between these and those that press inwards from social others, this fragmentary and unfinished text by Barthes begins to direct us towards the wild side of a given event of semiosis, which Derrida (1977) approaches through the metaphor of the bursting seed pod and wide-flung seeds, and Deleuze (1987) through the *rhizome* or root system (which is genetically encoded at source but wholly unpredictable, possibly asymmetrical, unruly, in its actual growth) used to critique the idealisation and the sterility of Chomsky's 'tree' model. Although Ubersfeld, as we have seen, alludes to the 'unseizable' *between* two semiotic instances embricated within the one (actor to character), we have also seen that she refuses to problematise the tradition of semiosis out of which she writes. The consequence of this omission in the most challenging of French theatre semioticians is that the development of the discourse of theatre semiotics seems hardly to have kept pace with shifts which would have made its own meaningful expansion possible.

The un-speakable

The self-appointedly explicatory function, where semiology's discourse saw itself as able adequately to represent and adequately account for 'meaning-production in performance', can no longer be sustained in the terms initially proposed, no matter how readily that project is maintained in university departments as a pedagogic exercise from which the thematisation of its own procedures is increasingly omitted. The supposed 'analytical' text claimed by its advocates to notate and to *re-present* – and through this representing, to explain to the practitioner what s/he did and to what meaningful effect – seems largely to have disappeared. To some extent at least the analyst is beginning to recognise what other participants in that theatre event have been fairly sure of knowing – if not of asserting in terms acceptable to analysts: that is, that *when it works*, theatre work gives place to the means to something *felt* and virtually **un-speakable**. To something momentary and – for all its force – *weak* (in the sense of impermanancy that de Certeau gives to the term (1984)). To a gasp and a quickening of the pulse. A body chaos of a shortlived but effective kind. Something painful in its pleasing.

What *is* said in the heady moments after performance, after the constraint of a lesser or greater 'polite silence' is lifted from the spectator? '*I was* transfixed'/'I couldn't take my eyes off . . . '/'I went cold all over . . . '. Sometimes '*I was almost in pain*', as with the Jean-Pierre Mignon Australian Nouveau Théâtre (Melbourne) production of Cousse's *Kidstuff*: the actor Julie Forsyth performs alone, and, through an intensely controlled and apparently effortless use of energy, produces for over an hour with scarcely a break the whooping and running and games of a boy child. This is performance in the 1980s sense noted by Ubersfeld, where what is elsewhere the thrall of effective representation, here does not attempt to dispel for a moment recognition of the actor's somatic skill and psychological strength which themselves become part of the performance's 'meaning'. To me this was a *mesmerising* actorly work, of which representation and discursive productivity (standing triply for world and authorial and spectator input) are mere factors in play in an event whose real felt significance lies in performance. In this event, the spectators applaud virtuosity *within* the tissue of the performance: disbelief does not need to be suspended since belief is in the virtuosity of performance itself (which does not preclude, for the modernist in us, the 'answers', but leads us to struggle to produce them).

What becomes clear in the unfinished business described by Barthes is that we are dealing with something which is not in fact wholly 'owned by', nor wholly *presentable* by the *stage team itself*, inasmuch as it requires the energetic participation of one or another, but not equally all, audiences. Something therefore not wholly to be attributed either to dramatic writing, to dramaturgical analysis, nor to *mise en scène* – although all practitioner participants seem to *know it when they see/feel it (in potentia)*, and try thereafter to grasp it, and then to reproduce it. Beyond semiosis? Absolutely not, where this 'unseizability' is not *just* a private or secret matter, but is the stuff of theatre decisions for the collective, and of judgements made in theatre's marketplaces.

If it is not re-presentable discursively, in terms of analytical and explanatory modes available, either by dramaturgical analysis worked through performance reception, or by the analysis of *mise en scène* (where that might be defined as an organising of the stage work or as the means to the intrusion of ideological positions into the staging), without a series of generalisations and dissections and reductions being practised upon it, then we have to extend the range of fields invoked and evoked, the textual modes available, the number of participants involved in the discursive production. Semiotic 'analysis' would become a collective 'up-building' (rather than down-breaking) practice, a multi-media practice; a multi-modal process; a collage or a tapestry drawing on and combining dialogues between participants, anecdotes, archaeological findings, reports, reviews, representations of the found and the discarded, accounts of wrong directions, wrong decisions taken, failures, inadequacies. It would start to look, in this practice, like the variously recorded traces of a full-scale action toward a theatre production; or like what Tyler calls a "polyphony", a "means of perspectival relativity" (in Clifford and Marcus, 1986, p. 127), which might be our only way to approach what I call elsewhere theatre's 'multi-modal heteroglossia and praxia'. This goal is impossible *here*, because this is an authored text, whereas the *evocative* polyphony Tyler foresees combines different voices, including those of all participants, in a variety of textual modes. There exist already one or two examples which have chosen this direction, although the incidence of actorly contributions remains low: for a number of years the CNRS in Paris has attempted such a semiotics in a large number of volumes focused around a number of productions (*Les Voies de la création théâtrale*, Bablet *et al.*, 1970–92). They form beautiful partial archives not just of theatre productions but of modes of discursive, analytical, diagrammatical and photographic intervention by others working in various fields which theatre draws on. They are, unfortunately, and in several senses, untranslatable.

Chapter 3

New Directions

Taste and judgement

The positions adopted by both Barthes and Caroll, cited above, are located in a field of reflection largely passed over in silence (although present in fact) in the early agenda established by structural semiotics. Taste and judgement within cultural practice appeared on the one hand to be subjective, rather than social, and therefore an irrelevancy to projects more interested in specifying the enabling conditions for general practice. Or, on the other hand, it was socially-determined, a clear manifestation of class difference or distinction where 'good taste' is a matter of economically-determined access to a "symbolic capital" (Bourdieu, 1985) whose value was not innate but ratified by conservative tradition. Meanwhile *practitioners* experimented with the 'ritual' and 'mythical' potentialities of theatre, relegating the dramatic text, in some quarters, to the category of that oppressive, imposed 'taste' of the dominant class.

The subjective hypothesis, like the class hypothesis, is a 'drama-tised' scenario for judgements of taste. The first opposes objectivity and subjectivity to form its matrix (the first term is valorised, the second dubious); the second operates through the exploiting class/exploited class binarism, in its development to include other sets of opposed values: 'high'/'low', rare/widely available, elite/popular.

Typically of developments in the early 1980s, in the collection entitled *Formations of Pleasure* (1983), Jameson notes, of the then-recent staging or dialogue of theory in this field of discourse, that it might seem that:

> there has been a whole series of left political or ideological positions on pleasure and hedonism in our recent past, and we

need to confront a few more of those before 'deciding' what we really think ourselves. (What we 'really' think may simply be a residue of one of those older ideologies, in fact.) . . . How do you distinguish . . . between real pleasure and mere diversion – the degradation of free time into that very different commodity called 'leisure', the form of commodity consumption stamped on the most intimate former pleasures from sexuality to reading? . . . [I]f what people today imagine to be pleasure is nothing but a commodity fix, how to deal with that addiction? Who is to break the news to them that . . . their conscious pleasure in consumption – is in reality nothing but false con- sciousness? (pp. 2–3)

The extract is itself cunningly staged by a master at the game of oppositions (see also Jameson, 1971, 1981), around a number of those:

what we 'really' think	versus	*residue in fact of older ideologies*
real pleasure	versus	*mere diversion*
free time	versus	'leisure' commodity
intimate pleasures	versus	*commodity consumption*
imagine to be	versus	*is nothing but*
pleasure	versus	*commodity fix*
conscious pleasure	versus	*false consciousness*

but to what end? The goal is one approved by Brechtian dramatisations:

That there is . . . a politics and a historicity of *jouissance* seems clear, as does its fundamental ambiguity as a socially symbolic experience. . . . [T]he proper political use of pleasure must always be *allegorical* . . . : the thematizing of a particular 'pleasure' as a political issue . . . must always involve a dual focus . . . [T]he right to a specific pleasure, to a specific enjoyment of the potentialities of the material body – if it is not to remain only that, . . . if it is to avoid the complacencies of 'hedonism' – must always in one way or another also be able to stand as a figure for the transformation of social relations as a whole. (pp. 13–14)

The *rights to pleasure,* as distinct from the means to purchase pleasure (if we are to "avoid the complacencies of hedonism" against which Pavis in his critique of postmodern practice has warned us), are to be won through our capacity to transform 'the local' into an allegory for "society as a whole". Let us retain here, in particular, the notion of the "fundamental ambiguity [of] *jouissance* as a socially symbolic experience": this is still significant for the collective practice that theatre is, within the prevailing climate of the 1990s in which one and then another *grounds* have shifted under our feet. In this climate we might newly view the final proposition from Jameson: "the right to pleasure . . . must always *in one way or another* be able to stand as a figure for the transformation of social relations", stressing rather less the utopic "transformation [of] social relations", and rather more the ambiguities of other elements included: *to stand for; a figure of; in one way or another.*

Were it not for recent changes in the composition and politics of 'Europe', this new stress might seem to locate our 1990s enquiry in the boundless zones of simulacra: here 'real pleasure' can so name (and justify itself), provided it can *show* (i.e. produce the signs of) an allegorical standing-for. But show these signs *where*? (i.e. 'in' the staging; or 'in' its interpreting by a spectator? If the former, does this not require, once again, the sort of practice of power ensuring clarity in *mise en scene*, that Pavis advocates?) In such a standing-for, 'the larger good' might be said to be *represented within* 'my intense pleasure' – rendering it more intense. But this promotes a double enquiry: first, isn't this what theatre has always excelled in doing? And second, what is it which can guarantee, in the 1990s, a projection outward from that more intense pleasure in allegory, into the *everyday real*? To Pavis (1985), this question smacks of postmodern cynicism. But did the Brechtian aspiration lead British spectators, at least, anywhere so much as to the warming 'feel good factor'? The aspired-to 'raised conscious-ness' – a retention and a build-up, the other of catharsis – functions as a different use of energy; but it remains, for all that, within the closed field of esthetic pleasure (cf. Weber, 1980 and van Erven, 1988). From sex without secretions, to politics without praxis. Can esthetic **distance**, vital condition for the production in *kathakali* (George, 1986) of *rasa* – a pleasure which is the sweeter precisely for its separation from the everyday conditions of *the real* – produce in the European theatre, for the ('post-Brechtian') spectator of Brecht, exactly the opposite relation to the extratheatrical world?

In theatre performance, as long as some of us work in the space between what are elsewhere perceived to be discrete units (e.g. actor and character; actor and spectator; reality and illusion), activating these as simultaneously-working **complementarities** rather than opposites, then it seems that pleasure in theatre, and the decision-making processes involved in that pleasure, are *bound in* together in a field of play which, for all the richness and diversity of spectator resonances, is nonetheless closed. But does this observation constitute a 'theoretical position'? The alternative, contemporary, 'new European' view is typified by Chtiguel (1990) and Oslzly (1990) – in the context of revolution in Czechoslovakia; by the Presidency of Havel; and by the rather different role that televised 'real life dramas' seem, in recent political change in Romania and the CIS (formerly the USSR), to have been able to play.

Can we say more in *north west European contexts*, than that the theatre in which some of us work is neither transgressive, nor liable to win huge media interest; nor is it *a priori* able to propel actors and spectators to escape the estheticising frames which are a characteristic part of it in material and symbolic terms, and which make its implications – as Jameson has hinted – *almost always* indirect, at best allegorical. *Almost always*, in late industrialised societies: a further but ambiguous exception is provided by the case of the *Théâtre du Soleil* in Paris where the company itself functions as an alternative model of social order, located literally on the margins of the Paris mainstream (cf. Bradby, 1991).

The main implication of these different examples for the reach of 'theatre theory' is that we should newly appraise its local and relative, rather than universal, status. Different examples simultaneously exisiting within what we have called 'Europe' now offer a heterogeneous range of possible implications with regard to theatre's powers of 'effective representation' within highly different political systems, as these function in contemporary 'televised societies'. One obvious candidate for reappraisal after the revolutionary events in Romania is the theory of the 'passivity' of the social subject anesthetised by television (cf. Adorno, 1984) –

a theory reactivated by Michel Touraine (1989) in the context of contemporary French politics.

The consequence of this sort of relativisation is that we can only discuss questions of taste and judgement – as well as subjectivity and agency – to the end of delicately constituting a locally-specific 'general trend', rather than a 'universal' principle. All we seem to be able to note is the vital ambiguity of pleasure as a "socially symbolic experience", while acknowledging the pragmatism of a theatre work which cannot avoid decision-making processes, practised by the few, on behalf of the many. The *metteur en scène* function always arbitrates in terms of a 'personal judgement' which is explicitly a political judgement, articulating a *policy* of *this* performance practice, for the (theatre) *polis*. What this seems to mean is that the personal–political fusion *for a given minority (of mainly middle-class theatre-goers)* is a fact of some theatre; but this fact is not necessarily worked in the terms Jameson sets out, i.e. in terms of the possibility of social transformations, worked through personalised allegories. Its implications may be limited to within that minority and to its sway within the wider field occupied by these second-level members of the 'cultural nobility' (Bourdieu, 1984).

It may now seem adequate to aim to 'affect the audience', where that audience is not a 'social microcosm' so much as a new minority group (defined by the means and the will to 'purchase theatre pleasures'), by a performance emerging out of particular sorts of work practices – such as those of Mnouchkine or Deborah Warner. And in the self-acclaimed pluralism of the 1990s, we have no real basis (despite the development of 'political correctness') for moralising the choices and pleasures of any minority group, as self-appointed ideological police. Further, theatre, as a working model of personalised social organisation might seem to offer us precisely what some of us need: a few moments of *really* (rather than illusionistic, or technology-dependent) highly organised and in part rule-governed relief from extratheatrical *anomie*. But beyond such generalisations, the intriguing question remains: what sorts of pleasures does this group seek, and what sorts of judgements of taste do theatre practitioners seem to operate, *in general*, and on what bases, in late-industrialised societies of our experience, in the 1990s? All theatre decision-makers engage at least implicitly with this question, at every instant of their practice.

It seems certain, now, that taste and judgement are class-determined and wielded over others, *to some extent*; they are not however wielded consistently, in late-industrialised societies, in a single direction, from the cultural "aristocrats" (Bourdieu, 1985), via the symbol-makers, to the cultural 'masses'. 'Those in (cultural) power' might now be seen to profess multiplicity (as the new hegemony). In this case, we need to look at the range of choices included, in any one time and place, in the notion of the multiple, asking what has been overlooked/excluded as 'less important/interesting/viable'. (In 1992, in Great Britain, 'community theatre' and TIE groups are suffering from changed economic policies; while 'new theatre' now seems to excite enough interest to elicit funding from the private sphere. Propertied 'professionalisation' on the one hand, and experimentation within electronic media on the other, seem to mark out anew the wide scene of performance practice.)

'Class', once we note this shift in social conditions, need no longer be perceived as a wholly rigid set of categories condemning social subjects to an eternal status quo. The ruling class/working class division – and their respective cultural practices – are now forced locally to cede to the in-work/out-of-work division, and the former 'class' distinctions, in post-Thatcherite Britain, and in terms of recession in industrialised societies, are no longer readily equated with stable positions in the binary construct. Both within and across classically conceived class barriers, we find a blur and a previously uncharted mobility which troubles conventional conceptual categories.

What happens to semiosis when users within what has been perceived to be 'a single group', sharing a given language or code, have different types of access to, and do not activate the same codes in the same manner, in similar circumstances? More specifically, if taste and judgement are subjective, how do we approach theatre as collective practice requiring group support? But if taste and judgement in theatre are socially determined, how can a theatre project long worked on and passionately produced fail to please some, pleasing others; charm the critics and fail at the box office, or vice versa? Answers provided in the 1980s by theorists of popular culture barely approach the question: theatre is largely neglected by theorists of a popular culture which – with Brecht recuperated into the mainstream, and with the relative failure of the leftist conception of a 'popular theatre' and of the theatre activism of the 1960s and 1970s – continues today to perceive it either as middle class and irrelevant, washed with embarrassing intimations of presence, mysticism, existentialism and excess, or as 'simply too much trouble' in comparison with the apparent freedom and control offered by use of television.

I have noted some contemporary exceptions; other exceptions are historical, and seem to emerge from a particular political/critical position: Dollimore's *Radical Tragedy* (1984), and Stallybrass and White's 'Bakhtinian' exploration of the divergent and discordant 'voices' and practices in carnival, *The Poetics and Politics of Transgression* (1984), propose respectively that a theatre now subsumed into middle-class culture was in its time radical and subversive. 'High' and 'low' performance modes do not just uneasily coexist but cross-fertilise, to create together

> a mobile, conflictual fusion of power, fear and desire in the construction of subjectivity: a psychological dependence upon precisely those Others which are being rigorously opposed and excluded at the social level. (Stallybrass and White, 1984, p. 5)

While it seems clear that the Polish Gardzienice and – quite differently – Tadeusz Kantor's work (e.g. *The Dead Class*) both offer striking and often grotesque actorly practices which confound middle-class televisual and theatrical norms, it is not clear to what exent this oppositional model can be said to contribute to the 'construction of subjectivity' (cf. Klossowicz, 1986; Filipowicz, 1983, 1987): de Certeau's (1984) non-oppositional (complementary) duality may be more representative of current conceptions of the development of a 'late industrialised' subjectivity – however much this subjectivity may be deplored by those who feel nostalgia for what they consider to be "universal values" (see, for example, Dews, 1987).

What we may need today, in place of an analysis of theatre as antidote to social oppressions and exclusions, is a comparative analysis of live theatre performance's uses of event, live exchange and interactive presence, *in relation to film and television* (cf. Pavis, 1992). The latter at least can be approached as a major disseminator and reinforcer, but also an *occasional explorer of conventions* (this is what differentiates the postmodern attitude). By comparison, theatre offers certain sorts of experiences whose specificity means that they complement – and trouble – some of those electronically-mediatised 'everyday life' conventions. Today a televisually-led exploration of conventions does not cause their overthrow (although they may be modified), not the least because the conditions of television use are largely located within the private property of the family unit, rather than in the public space of the fairground. The marketable willingness to multiply choices and to explore conventions, to review history and to assess the presentation of the present through conventional media, seems both to *show* revolt (for example that of French students in the streets/on the screens in 1990), and to defuse revolt *by the very fact of showing it and 'giving it a voice'*. The explorations and 'auto-critique' effected within television's programming – see for example the *Antenne* 2 analysis of CNN 'coverage' of the Gulf War – which never go so far as to propose to viewers that they intervene radically to disrupt televisual broadcasting itself – lack any hint at possible radical intervention by the social subject. 'Consciousness-raising' becomes a spectator-sport, guaranteed a certain 'feel-good' factor, even an elation, which does not, however, seem to lead to the potential for 'social transformation'.

Theatre offers different modes of activity, different modalities of production and representation, in wholly different conditions of use, but today in its dramas and through its own technologies and relations, it is no more likely to do other than to explore certain uses of live human energies in reduced and controlled fictional and public situations, and to critique certain excesses of emotion, rationalism and illusion. (It seems always to have done this.) The raising of consciousness and the advocacy of intervention into like structures within a like-structured order of the 'real out there' seem now to be the stuff of nostalgia. This is either because social subjects share in the means to an exploration of codes and conventions; or because centres of domination are less visible, less attainable (in de Certeau's terms (1984), self-perpetuating and self-mobilising machines); and politics and governing (in Touraine (1989)) less a matter of group representation, than of the marketing of acceptable images.

The differentiated tastes of the 'middle class' (the supposed other of the committed leftist or 'popular' analyst) are approached through cultural theory, but in terms of a derivation from and a manifestation of the desire, sustained by effective marketing of changing products, to 'individualise' the bourgeois subject's self-image. 'Individual choice', from this perspective, is itself seen as a luxury purchased and propagated by the middle class, in part to exclude its perceived other; whereas choice and pleasure, for members of the dominated classes, are determined by and will continue to be determined by what becomes available through the 'choice of the necessary' (Bourdieu, 1985).

The 'I'-eye of the spectator

If something in theatre which works for me pleases me passionately, and if I say so ('It was *wonderful*!), what – if I heed Habermas' injunction to remove esthetic pleasure from the private sphere (Habermas, 1983, p. 14) – affords me the authority to do any other than to write myself in, to the equation? The critical discourse which notes that 'the staging is simply excellent' uses the text-modalities of depersonalisation, but the epithet remains subject-specific, a matter of individual perception, as comparison with the epithets used by other critics makes clear. But is there any progress, on this score, when the semiologist avoids the use of adjective and conceals his own position of perception, by declaring that 'the production takes as its effective axis, worked through an assemblage of complex icons overlaid with indexicality, the opposition reality/illusion'?

When I indicate my particular position and pleasure, I must however – equally in terms noted by Habermas – be able to demonstrate why 'I', here, is a deictic functioning as superordinate (we are all 'I', at different moments) evoking the fact of **subject-intervention** in general, if not the precise moments of that subject-intervention *for me*. But if it pleases me, and not a majority of my fellow spectators, or pleases the majority differently, then how do I approach this gap esthetically and politically? For researchers working with Pêcheux on interdiscursivity (*Mots*, 9, 1984), the new objective is to demonstrate how, in cultural practice which pleases, *singular moments of opacity open up gaps in which a spectator-subject might intervene*, thereby realising an aspect of that subjectivity.

This requires that we seek the means to restage, in terms of cultural practice for the many, the weave and flow of the personal–anecdotal, from a number of speaking and writing subjects, demonstrating the ways in which the given practice makes this multiple and heterogeneous intervention possible. Otherwise the ways in which I judge, and attempt to account for that judgement *in 'the practice itself'*, demonstrate the imposition of a stabilising force which neutralises my own intervention and processings, and attributes effect to the 'product'. The grammatical and deictic options (often third person generalising and past tense closure or present tense universalising) function to pin down, to universalise and to take apart. This sort of stabilisation of the "logically-unstabilised" (Pêcheux, 1984), aims, in de Certeau's terms (1984), at a mastery of space by time perceived as unitary and fixed or fixing.

New directions

The work of two particular theorists seems to me to overlap in ways vital to my perception of a dramatic semiotic project which might encompass decision-making by practitioners for others, and modes of processing by different spectators. They are Michel de Certeau (1984) and Pierre Bourdieu (1977, 1985).

Strategies and tactics

In de Certeau's *Practice of Everyday Life* (1984; see also Blonsky, 1985) we find a number of essays located within the boundless field of critical epistemology. In a chapter published under the title of 'The Jabbering of Social Life' (Blonsky, 1985), de Certeau considers the ways in which 'the (televised) social' has been constituted, and maintains itself. What we need is a study of theatre's particular place (where theatre is not construed as mass media's negativity) within a social order transformed by the proliferation of simulacra whose status as 'true' or 'untrue' in relation to a pre-existing, non-televised 'real out there' is no longer the issue. De Certeau effectively outlines, perhaps in terms which are too general, a technological development which ushers in changes in the ways in which subjects in late-industralised societies can (through televised *visibilities*) know the world. If his hypothesis is valid, then the ways in which theatre itself functions and is used, will equally be modified (cf. Pavis, 1992, but also Ulmer, 1989).

If what we are now accustomed to is the distinction between more effective and less effective simulacra, then theatre's role is no longer to represent effectively a 'real out there', but rather to present a vitally forceful 'real in here', whose status as 'real' derives precisely from its investiture of concentrated and mastered human energies. These are forged by the conditions of live performance itself, and hover constantly – in a way not available through an edited and technologically mediated television – on the borderline between a closely-watched strength and fragility. It is this combination of controlled energies, *caught in the real event of their precarious production*, which makes theatre so dangerously pleasing to some of us. It elicits something like momentary belief, less in any fiction than in human skill and artistry. For de Certeau:

> I take 'belief' to mean not what is believed (a dogma, a programme, etc.), but the investiture of subjects in a proposition, the *act* of uttering it while holding it to be true – in other words, a "modality" of the affirmation rather than its content. . . . Today it no longer suffices to manipulate, transfer and refine belief; its composition must be analysed, *since we want to produce it artificially.* (p. 148)

Might we suppose that each piece of dramatic writing which works for us, each example of staging which binds us in and momentarily captures us, similarly "produces belief" through the art of its artifice? Artifice, in this media-proficient society, is the norm and thus loses any pejorative colouring – except for those nostalgic for 'universal truths' of a utopic past. Effective *and* self-critiquing arts now stand in, through metapraxis, for earlier unquestioned absolutes. This shift – if we accept it requires of the wordsmiths a new set of discourses articulating changed practice. In this set of discourses effective performance becomes the pragmatic goal, in terms of which effective everyday skills are modelled. They replace the earlier model in which the everyday served as touchstone, making the actor and the performance its exception, troubling, double or deviate. But for de Certeau (1984) the pedestrian-as-artist laughs as she wanders through the cityscape – precisely because her arts are not pedestrian at all; and because it is only the -ologist, of whatever professing, who needs to frame her and yearns to 'capture' her through his science, making her both anonymous and typical. (Note the naturalised violence inscribed into the terms of his data-gathering: he selects her, frames her, gets a shot, takes her picture, classifies her, names her, files her, and then moves on.)

What de Certeau offers, in more general terms, are a number of ways of conceptualising cultural practices. Both the institutions (material and conceptual) and their structuring orders, on the one hand, but equally the ceaseless, ungraspable play of individualising human action within those structured orders, can be distinguished as complementary components of all human action. De Certeau structures his reflections around a number of metaphors, and a number of concepts which will be invaluable in our attempt to characterise short-term energetic uses, by effectively *nomadic* theatre practitioners, of writing, energies, spectators and sites of practice; and a number of complementary couplets – e.g. strategy and tactic – which permit us to characterise different, but embricated, modes of action.

His text also offers a means of approach to everyday somatic practices perceived as a mode of **knowledge as action**, on which the performer draws and which the professional twentieth-century performer of naturalism seems to retain as something like a stock of 'psycho-somatic' pre-constructs (at this point they are skeletal *actional frames* oriented around general situational and typical-subject conceptions, always doubled through indexicality, by a relatively unsemanticised 'interiority' and sociality), which will be relationally modified and particularised once they are manifested in juxtaposition with a number of different-source input types: e.g.

– a voicable, named dramatic writing element

– an interactive vocal and somatic complex

– a developing relationship to actorly others

– a developing relationship to the *metteur en scène*

– a complex somatic and discursive knowledge of theatre modes.

The theatre practitioner (including the dramatic writer) I have characterised as *nomadic*, practices, in de Certeau's terms, something like poaching: never owning a text or a writer, rarely owning a space, borrowing the energies of any number of participants, she arrives, works, and moves on. She does not hold the material and conceptual properties (*le propre*) she captures, except momentarily; and she only establishes a property in precarious terms requiring constant renewal. In literature, before postmodern 'quoting' without named sources, this poaching was called plagiarism, but it has always operated without scruples in theatre. Architectural, painterly and photographic, but also everyday 'real' images, constructs, layouts and somatic practices are borrowed and transmitted, largely without the need for acknowledgement of 'source' or 'authorship'. Directors may hire but they also attempt to seduce and to 'capture' the material reality of the actors' bodies and the energies of those bodies, to complex ends. Practitioners 'lease', short-term, not just the theatrical property of the producer-owners, but the somatic (and mental and emotional) energies of spectators. If the owners and institutions are in each instance complicit with this use, it is still the case that there is something like a pleasingly unreasonable and short-termed capture practised by the theatre poacher – who moves on.

The action of poaching is small-scale but triumphant, in comparison to the large-scale seriousness of institutionalised systems, and the poacher makes no real attempt to encroach on the landed authority of the institutions themselves: for poaching to succeed, it needs the system to flourish. To paraphrase Lemke (1984), theatre cannot *make trouble* unless it can get momentarily into the institution. But the institution is not inert: for Halliday (1987) any established system opens to the encroacher, but then 'exports disorder' brought by that invasion, incorporating in its own terms those elements of the newcomer which can be assimilated within a necessarily expanding, dynamic ("in flux") system.

For de Certeau, this small-scale mode of action is 'therapeutic' with regard to deteriorating social traditions; and far from heroic, it involves everyday practices performed not by a minority but by all of us since we are all, with regard to one or another social institution, more or less marginalised. His perspective thus eschews large-scale categorisations constituted in terms of stable binarisms of class, age or gender relations, and their concomitant strategies for the maintenance of the status quo. In de Certeau, power structures and institutions – including the discourses of 'individual identity', the family, commonsensical Freudianisms –

are 'self-mobilising' and self-perpetuating, and they are not 'owned' by any one or other group. But they are more than that: they are pleasurable to us, in that we achieve and maintain identity through them. Here again, de Certeau distances his position from that of those who posit the existence of a manipulative and exploitative dominant group, tyrannising 'the rest of us'. Institutions work to regulate everyday and 'individual' aspects of society, as well as more overtly through schooling, policing, hospitals, shopping centres, town plans, theatres, fields of knowledge.

De Certeau asserts that the users of others' institutionalised products – we might include the script, the play, the theatre building, together with social codes inculcated by the Church, by advertised government policy on drugs or smoking or use of alcohol at football matches – produce a short-termed and 'weak' trajectory. This nonetheless 'sparks' in the short term, through a re-energising of institutionalised products and processes, much as does the actor's play with the stubborn shoe, in *Godot*. To understand this process we need the theory of *synergy*.

What seems to me to be invaluable in this aspect of de Certeau are the implications for a double action on the part of the theatre practitioner. One is a complex work which we can call *strategic*, or institutionalised. This works with and through predominantly socially encoded options – like eating three times a day, in certain societies. The other is a simultaneously activated *tactical* intervention, unknowable in advance in its particularity, which does not oppose itself to the strategic (this would produce 'abnormal behaviour', the avant-garde, or the 'made strange' option noted by Russian Formalists), but which insinuates itself within the parameters of the socially coded and collectively agreed upon, to mark it out as 'someone's work', 'someone's way of doing things', within that collective effort. Complex practices, such as those set in motion by the dramatic actor in rehearsal conditions, seem to function as an **oscillation** between two modes of practice, each of which has a typical relation to time and space. We might represent this *double* input, and the oscillation between them which produces performance action, as shown in Figure 3.1.

The strategic, or institutionalised, is ratified by time (tradition, history, convention), and hence **codified** – it repeats itself across

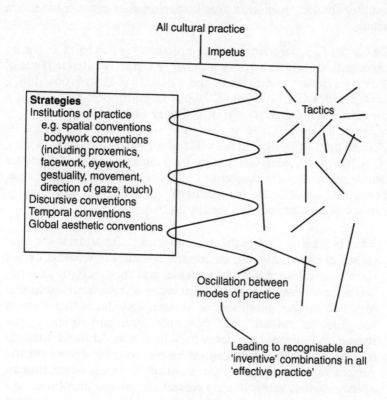

Figure 3.1

individual social actors; it is spatially ratified, in a similar manner: 'making dinner' maps out an **actional frame** (Lemke, 1984) or set of *strategic* actions in a socially-agreed range of *congruent* or *possible* times and spaces. 'Making dinner' *on-stage* maps a further system of institutionalised temporal and spatial co-ordinates (determined now by a relation to the spectator, and a relation to stage esthetic modes), onto the 'everyday' model(s). The tactical, however, a cunning, short-lived and 'unpropertied' mode of intervention, intrudes the individual actor's self-defining modes into the strategic construct. It is always *not yet codified* (but related plainly to the codified). But it will, if successful, be 'picked up' and reproduced between practitioners in the short-term. On the basis of adequate repetition it cedes to history and convention, becoming strategic, institutionalised, so that, in turn, it will elicit in another context, in another practitioner, another instance of tactical action.

De Certeau's separation out of complementary modes of everyday practice finds echoes across a number of formerly discrete fields of 'human science' enquiries in the 1980s. In Austin-Broos (1987), who profiles Clifford Geertz's work in anthropology, we find a concern for the elaboration of a theory of human agency in its relation to the socially typical and normative. The debate is focused on the question of the validity, for anthropological enquiry, of behaviour which seems to be something like a 'private language', and on the danger of excluding the "idiosyncratic, new, deviant or semiotically incongruent" (p. 158) from any enquiry into social functioning. She concludes that:

> what is missing [in Geertz] is an attempt . . . to address the dual issues of rationality and desire: the question of whether or not the historical specificity of societies and their varying cultural codes entail also entirely different logics of behaviour – different logics of motive, intention, repression and choice that we still recognise as 'culture'. . . . Not only ideas and emotions, but reason and purpose too, must be shown to be 'cultural artefacts in man' [*sic*]. The issue cannot be resolved by dissolving the subject of human agency in a study of codes, when human agency itself . . . constitutes a central component of culture.
>
> (p. 159)

In invoking agency Austin-Broos brings her work close to our own concern: the writer, *metteur en scène*, actor and spectator share agency in the theatre production of felt-meanings. For the traditional analyst the problem lies in the attempt to separate out and name individual instances of agency in this production. In a 'new semiotics', we need to attempt to find focus-points of energetic input into the combinatory and complementary practice of a shared agency which must include spectator roles and tactics.

Another vital component for a dramatic semiotics comes from de Certeau's suggestion, derived from analysis of historical shift within occidental approaches to the formulation and inculcation of what we might call 'appropriate' or 'acceptable' knowledges, that somatic actions *are themselves intelligence at work*. To understand the significance of this proposal, we need to acknowledge the extent to which we are conditioned to accept as a commonsense, that actions result from or 'should' result from, thought; that actions otherwise are 'instinctive', 'thought-**less**', or '**ir**-rational' – controlled perhaps by passion or by drives, hence automatically dangerous. The initial binarism activated here, rational vs. irrational, hooks in to a chain of binarisms which include ethical judgements and judgements of taste.

To approach the ways in which the performer – taking as her starting point an intended production in a given theatre space, sets of codes covering many fields of human action, a number of vitally important but volatile relations with others, a piece of writing, and *acts of voicing* – initiates actions which *might seem to come from nowhere* (spoken or visible), we absolutely need a theory of a human somatic action *which is itself a somatic intelligence*, rather than parallel to, the consequence of, or sequel to an intelligence, predetermined by reasoned and willed strategies.

This somatic intervention which is itself an intelligence, "takes as its form not a discourse [to which we might attribute a causal or generative logic] but the decision itself, the act and the means themselves by which an occasion is seized" (p. 21: my translation). It is this intelligence as the act itself that the dramatic performer (like the designer, the painter, the sculptor, the photographer, the musician, the writer and also the scientist) already experiences, not just in the rehearsal process but in performance conditions. The spectator similarly achieves acts of somatic intelligence during performance, which are not commensurable with secondary appropriations made, after the event of theatre, into the acquired and valorised discursive formulae of dramatic critical practice.

But what are the discursive conventions through which intelligence-as-act is approached? The skilled performer, apparently 'on impulse', does not verbally suggest an action, but instead sketches out, with the voice or hand or a turn of the body or a twist of the mouth, a complex somatic option, within an equally complex context combining theatre place, stage space, fictional site, directional frame, and written dramatic complex. This performer brings a somatic symbolic **action**, whose determinants remain shrouded in their complexity, and not a somatic **re**-action to discursive input. But although discourse is not the master here, the pleasurable thrall of *discursive* action is such that that actor is commonly said to 'feel' 'intuitively' that 'response', rather than bodily to know its possible place within a complex webbing of interactive energies, many of which work through and to the gaze. Established discursive convention makes that actor re-active, and not active, responsive and not initiating, 'intuitive' rather than intelligent and – the final condemnatory 'compliment' – *feminine* in his–her wiles and bodily skills and cunning, regardless of gender (cf. Féral on Mnouchkine, 1989).

The supposedly felt (rather than bodily-reasoned) option, if approved (and the means of approval are diverse and often not verbal), is thereafter repeated and tooled and formalised within the larger interactive pattern being established. It does not, however, necessarily solidify to the extent implied in the term 'concretisation' often attributed to acts informed by language, and in this it happily *fails to be lexicalised* as an infinitely reiterable 'gestural option': it does not assume the status of a 'word', in recent occidental tradition, as it would need to do if we were to speak of body **language** (as so readily do logocentricists). And it cannot be said to be either hard-edged or a meaningful unit 'in itself', nor within a system of so-circumscribed options. What is practised here is not a single lexical choice within an established and easily read symbolic order: first, because there is no such thing as a 'single gesture on stage', since each apparent option interacts in time and space with all others present and with what precedes and follows; second, because a known and easily read culturally coded option is inadequate to what others might call theatre's 'poetics', to its 'rhetoric' which, in occidental tradition, requires difference as much as it requires conformity.

Nor does it seem that we can claim to recognise a minimally coded (and thus meaning-filled) somatic option, which might be 'made strange' (as in the convention of Russian Formalism) by a stylistic supplement. Instead it seems that we need to recognise that injection of energy which is peculiar to performance contexts, which converts the everyday to performance. In Barba and Savarese (1985, 1991) this involves the shift from everyday's *minimal wastage* of energy, to performance's *maximal wastage*. This cannot be approached as digital, nor established through conventions of textual analysis.

In recent tradition, the so-called body 'response' which I have noted above is assumed to be 'generated by' – because performed in the context of – verbally accountable and writerly components such as drama. The alternative is to see this option as an element within a complex other-than-digital body-knowledge or knowledges, whose modes of learning, recording and transmission have been neglected by mainstream institutions of a learning more traditionally governed and mediated by a language conventionally perceived to be rational, unitary, digital, and to 'express' clear intentionality on the part of its 'emitter' . . .

The somatic option, in its intelligence-as-work (and not 'at work'), "seems to come from [a] nowhere [of speech]", so infused with the order of language are even the professional occidental practitioners of body intelligence. De Certeau sees here the pleasurable tyranny of the *scriptural economy* – i.e. the hegemonic power of writing and reading in many traditions of education. My own *feeling* is that somatic work should not be included within the writerly or scriptural economy of mainstream learning and transmission – where the metaphor of 'body language' would be legitimised – but rather, that if it is in any way comparable with linguistic function, then we can only say of it that it begins its function as 'something like' the *anecdote*.

The anecdote, rather like gossip, in its deictic and proxemic orientation as informal first person, particularised account addressed to a present interlocuteur and thematising an absent but 'available' otherness, is conventionally excluded from mainstream, 'academic' discursive modes. But the anecdote, for Ulmer (1989), reveals the means by which an *expert knowledge* is appropriated, typified and personalised. Expert knowledge is typified by certain features: third person, universalising present tense, lexical density, nominalisation; structured, for example, through hypothesis leading to concluding synthesis. Personalisation and oral individuation equally exhibit characteristic formal features – although the 'rules of combination' may cede to a tactical play, precisely with the notion of rules: first person, present tense of given event, process rather than nominalisation, deictic density, strong interpersonal and attitudinal effects, paratactic rather than hypotactic cohesion (i.e. use of simple connectors like 'and', 'but', rather than dependency through 'which','who'), strongly interactive somatic options – of eyework, facework, touch, gestuality, direction of gaze, and so on. We may usefully apply this second process to the work of the actor, and – more mysteriously – to the dramatic writer's fragmented but single-source discourse. The actor's 'anecdotes', worked somatically (I include voicework here), are less to be seen as everyday disseminations of expert discourses (although they often involve these), than extra-ordinary performance uses of the practices of an other. They are characteristic of the rehearsal process, to the point of being paradigmatic, and what is interesting in them is the extent to which these complex 'anecdotes' draw the personal into the social. Frequently they relate to a perception of the enacting of a complex *actional frame*, lodged in either a fictional 'possible world' (Eco, 1979), or a theatre 'real world', to whose elaboration they contribute (e.g. '*She makes breakfast*'; 'Play to the audience there!'), but the actional frame is only briefly, indexically or symbolically signalled in the writing or production conditions, while the anecdote, specific to the actor, is even more subtle in its putative 'textual bases'.

Ulmer is particularly interested in the ways in which television intrudes anecdote into expert discourse, in order to *show* through televisual images rich in their appeal to dispersed spectators, what the expert discourse is accustomed only to write or to profess.

Although the expert discourse/anecdote relation might seem to attribute precedence or causality to an expert discourse, apparently followed by a putting into images, such an assumption ignores the ways in which anecdote might use, but transforms and exploits to its own ends, the expert discourse. The anecdote is a quasi-spontaneous mode, which, like the performer in *commedia*, instantly adapts the borrowed, the snatched and the given into an interactive practice, conjugated as much in terms of a perception of the complex interlocuteur's changing needs and desires, and amply demonstrating a somatico-discursive intelligence not requiring 'thought' to precede action. I am assuming that modes and arts of anecdotal embodiment (which ironically I can only render here discursively: 'I went up to the jobs office counter this morning like this and I did this – look! – and then the woman behind me said . . . and they went . . .'), are worked around a showing and looking which draws on/in elements of the discursive economy, rather than the other way around. Now, anecdote and gossip are not unitary, nor available to a digital analysis which works first by marking out boundaries apparently determining 'transactions' – although the transactional may be enacted through partial recourse to these. They need energy, heat, flow, the pressing together of bodies, voice to ear, the darting and play of eyes, the quick and the covert, malice, complicity and cunning. And these terms better evoke fine acting in the 1990s, than does the term 'body language'.

Or is it perhaps the case that the latter term permits us only to approach the strategic, in de Certeau's use of the term, whereas acting (which works) always involves both strategic somatic *and* tactical somatic options. In acting the strategic emerges through repetition between roles, between actors, across performances, between production modes, and is particularly prevalent in certain modes of teaching. Whereas the tactical option, in its 'weak' and shifting cunning, *cannot be reiterated*, not just for fear of finding itself transformed into a strategy, but because the prevailing actorly/performance esthetic asks for work, from any actor, which is 'finely differentiated' between different roles, and for roles which are finely differentiated between different actors.

From this perspective, and in line with de Certeau's way(s) of seeing, it would appear that the strategic and the tactical somatics are complementary in occidental dramatic acting; that neither dominates the other *in reality*, although what we do need to recognise is that the strategic can readily be talked and written about, whereas the tactical resists this and, in so resisting, seems to establish itself 'beyond' conventions of knowledge. It may well be the case that the tactical feeds the strategic, rather than that the force or domination of the strategic *causes* the tactical to spring up as a weak rejoinder. On the other hand the idea that the strategic is part of the institution of acting, and that it acts as a barrier or boundary or norm against which the actor can flex her or his energies and will, is in line with some of the theories of energetic wastage noted in Barba and Savarese (1985, 1991).

Bourdieu's 'habitus'

The term strategy is vital, equally, in Pierre Bourdieu's work in the social sciences, but his orientation to historical materialism and a class-based empirical sociology locates his extensive work largely within the epistemological projects of modernism. On the other hand, in addressing what he calls "the accidental and the irresistible" of everyday human semiotic practice, where "because human subjects do not, strictly speaking, know what they are doing . . . what they do has more meaning than they know" (1977, p. 79), his work does seem to offer us the means to approach the resonant and evocative work of actor and *metteur en scène*, as this potential inscribes itself for the spectator *between* the enabling structure and the tactical intervention.

In *Outline of a Theory of Practice* (1977) and *Distinction: A Social Critique of the Judgement of Taste* (1985), Bourdieu is interested in the question of the relations between social conflict and a cultural practice regulated relatively unproblematically for them, by the wielders of symbolic capital. To this extent his work approaches the question of the input of the socio-economic conditions of lived history into human agency which I have begun to outline briefly above. Now, his response to the question of human agency, and to the question of the formation and practice of attitude, ethos and the judgement of taste, will always be articulated through his analysis of class difference – which might seem at first, within the context of a largely middle-class and apparently apolitical postmodern theatre, to hark back to another age of aspiration and understanding.

The habitus as interiorised regulator of the larger part of taste and the majority of judgements of all kinds, and in consequence of actional options, which Bourdieu calls a 'generative machine' (interview, *Antenne 2*, 1990: my translation), is acquired by social subjects through the material (and class-determined) conditions of their early home and community life. For Bourdieu:

> the different ways of relating to realities and fictions, of believing in fictions and the realities they simulate, . . . are very closely linked to the different possible positions in the social space; and, consequently, bound up with the systems of disposition (habitus) charcteristic of the different classes and class fractions. Taste classifies, and it classifies the classifier.
>
> (Bourdieu 1985, pp. 5–6)

If, however, we locate our politics of everyday life in the small conflictual scenes of individual practice, rather than in the ponderous oppositions of Right/Left institutions of party politics, supposing that major socio-economic difference is always lived out for the subject in the gendered domestic scene, in the family and in the workplace/unemployment office, then the perspective he offers seems to permit us to approach both the dramas and the theatre practices which conventionally interest us.

What is principally of use is the way in which Bourdieu admits the play of a certain indeterminacy in the everyday into his theory of agency within a conflictual society: his social subject is characterised as being both subject to the regularities of social action, *and* able to practise options which are purposeful and apparently 'free' (where that perception of freedom and self-determination is itself conditioned by class, by historically specific social conditions). This produces action through a "spontaneous semiology" (a semiotic, in our terms, in that it includes somatic and discursive action) which is irreducible both to immediately prevailing conditions, and to the conditions in which the habitus was formed.

The scene for the working of theory which Bourdieu sets up is, I think, of particular interest to us when we are trying to determine why it is that one professional production 'works' and another does not:

> [P]ractices cannot be directly deduced either from the objective conditions, defined as the instantaneous sum of the stimuli which may appear to have directly triggered them, or from the conditions which produced the durable principle of their production. (1977, p. 78)

The practices of the actor and *metteur en scène*, their relations to dramatic writing and the relations they establish between each other through practices, are not then wholly explicable through the terms and conventions and aspirations of a social semiotic, where the perceived given is used as symptom of *currently-prevailing* social knowledges and conflicts. They are loaded with 'something else':

> These practices can be accounted for only by relating the objective *structure* defining the social conditions of the production of the habitus which engendered them to the conditions in which this habitus is operating, that is, to the *conjuncture* which, short of a radical transformation, represents a particular state of this structure. (p. 78)

This seems to be the sort of intersection Pavis attempts to codify in his "interculturalist" approach 'Toward a Theory of Culture and *Mise en scène*' (Pavis, 1992). Once again, however, he assumes a certain social consensus – and hence, 'coherence' – within the one (source culture), and another within the other (target culture), failing to come to terms with the postmodern experience of a multiplicity of possible subject positions, actions and attitudes, simultaneously prevailing and available within both, and liable to make the staging, and spectator practices in it, the scene for heterogeneous 'wanderings'.

For Bourdieu:

> [i]n practice, it is the habitus, history turned into nature, i.e. denied as such, which accomplishes practically the relating of these two systems of relations, in and through the production of practice. (p. 78)

It is "history turned into nature" (or personally-lived everyday manifestations of prevailing socio-economic conditions – e.g. mother who comforts child, and not father, who is at work; mother who works and child-minder who caresses/doesn't caress child – interiorised by the subject as 'the way things are') which then acts through (the cognitive and motivating structures producing action in) 'me', in my smallest interactive (voluntary and 'involuntary'/irresistible and accidental) gesture. It similarly acts through the subject in performance, in that gesture I produce and show to that *other* (the *metteur en scène*, the spectator) to whom I have attributed an identity and a potential for judgement. That acting-through activates knowledges, in all participants, which exceed any knowledge obtained from what is immediately available to perception. But in terms of the ideology of depth, what we have to note is that while the habitus may 'generate', it does not wholly encode the given practice, because the latter is as strongly determined by the multiple factors not just of the context of use, but of intervening history.

Bourdieu will attribute to this the term **unconscious**, as does Ulmer, for whom "the analytical account of the unconscious . . . [is] a new version of memory" (1989, p. 25). The implications of this understanding, which breaks from the neo-Freudian tradition, will become clear in Part II. We shall need to modify Bourdieu's notion of "schemes of thought and expression . . . acquired [which] are the basis of *intentionless invention* of regulated improvisation", adding to these schemes our own vital 'schemes of somatic action'. It is only through this addition that we can begin to approach the powerfully resonant work of the actor in pre-performance and performance conditions, and the range and diversity of resonances for different spectators. We may begin to be able to appreciate, through the use of this notion, that moment of decision-making, of the team of practitioners, in which one option is retained, while another is discarded.

For Garnham and Williams (1986) Bourdieu works in terms which – for some of us – seem to relate almost irresistibly to the controlled spheres of human action we find in both dramatic fictions and in theatre performance conditions:

> [A]ll human actors are involved in strategies in situations of which the outcome is uncertain because these strategies are opposed by the strategies of other actors. The problem therefore is to specify the mechanism by which unbeknownst in principle to the actors (for if they knew[,] they would alter their strategy to take account of this knowledge) these strategies of improvization are objectively co-ordinated. (p. 119)

For Bourdieu each social subject's actional potential is generated by an 'exteriority [i.e. social conditions] interiorised' (*Antenne 2*, 1990: my translation), which he calls the *habitus*. This produces something like a 'generative machine' (not necessarily any more 'deep', however, than the human brain, and memory), which in turn regulates a complex array of verbal (and somatic) actions, attitudes and judgements, always in interaction with those of other social agents. For Bourdieu (1990) we are dealing with history and stories literally in-corp-orated or embodied and then manifested in the everyday conditions of doing, liking and judging. In our present context, where the actor 'invents' and 'improvises', we need to multiply this embodiment to the power of **n**, since the skilled actor will have observed, and be able to embody, not just the contradictions of her or his formative lived conditions, but also the observed conditions of his–her social other. I add, then, with explicit *impropriety* (because Bourdieu's subject is always strategic in a gamut of little struggles with different adversaries), de Certeau's *tactics* to the options of the actorly strategist.

The addition of this perspective to that available in de Certeau seems to me to be vital for reasons relating to drama itself, where drama – like class – is an oppositional concept, a binary concept – or, as I prefer, a dense set of shifting relations. It conceives of social subjects or social actors as strategists who inevitably enter into modes of action through oppositional relations with the needs and perceptions and taste, attitude and ethos of other social actors similarly **in**-formed – but informed *at any point* within this shifting density, with differing needs and tastes.

Therein might lie part of the secret of what we conventionally call 'dramatic characterisation': a shifting flux of little oppositional strategies, which are not just necessarily relational – formed *between* characters – but also 'internally' differentiated, within that complex we call character. In dramatic writing these are mediated not just by language-in-use, but by the blanks between textualised language, and by the spaces between two or more character-blocks and within character-blocks. Into these spaces, which tend to be used as sites of emerging difference, and on the basis of whatever models of knowledge accrue to our understanding of the current 'whole human semiotic', we conventionally project strategic or tactical actional and attitudinal shift, which, in tune with the widespread dissemination of certain myths, we attribute to character intention, motivation or psychological specificity.

That we do so needs to be made explicit; that it is a user-**felt** and discursive production legitimised in the classroom needs to be made explicit; that it is a production relativised by our own socio-specific strategies and tactics needs every bit as much to be made explicit. But we are dealing here with one element only of what Pavis (1987) has called for, and that is an epistemology of theatre knowledges, in place of earlier structural semiotics and semiologies. Because what is omitted from this textualised and discursive production is an accounting for what the actor automatically adds to and even prefers to this projection: a proto-somatic sketching of image and actional potential in space and time and in relation to others and to objects, in minimal but telling detail. That is, a time-space 'body-thinking' which is not verbal nor even pre-verbal. At this point, that actorly projection might be a matter of a complex spontaneous semiotics, implicating the actorly habitus to establish outer limits, but drawing already on details of observed habitus of others, mysteriously retained and somatically transformable from options mediated by vision, to somatic action elicited by complex situational factors.

The theatre practitioner, like the changing human agent in a wider sphere, has never been wholly constrained by such strategic or 'strong' options or hegemonically disseminated 'controls'. Both are liable to and revel in what have been perceived (to the dismay of the reductionist) to be 'idiosyncratic', or in de Certeau **tactical** 'ways of making do' and indeed *arts* of making do. These are not opposed to the institution perceived by some others to dominate the social actor. They play within its parameters, and wander without coercion within its controlling *dispositifs* or grids. In de Certeau, once again, the common person laughs, while wandering almost at will, lost in the crowd.

His metaphor for the decision-making of everyday cultural practice – which we might well borrow for the actor – is the pedestrian strolling in the city: although the city itself (like the synoptic text and its patterns of graphemic complexes and blanks and breaks) is an apparently rigid set of routes, crossroads, buildings and sites, regulated to some extent by the system of traffic lights, the pedestrian's choice of path cannot be determined by these – nor even by intention or predetermined goal. The pedestrian's pleasure lies in a certain flowing and responsive, interactive movement, simultaneously caught within the system of the city as institution, and 'free' to inscribe a wandering which lightly mocks, from within, at that rigidity. De Certeau's conception sets apart the rigidity of the structure on the one hand, and the cunning of the subject on the other, whereas Bourdieu embeds the subject within a multi-layered structure, such that the subject's options, in all their complexity, refer back to a series of little struggles, observed, lived, but 'forgotten', with an opposing other.

This coupling of strategy and tactic can be applied not just to dramatic writing and the characters we are taught readily to constitute (and which from the poststructuralist perspective we can see to be wholly contingent upon that teaching and the desire it generates), but to options taken by *metteurs en scène*, by performers and by spectators. So that any theatre event and its *mise en scène* begin to look like a web forged between intensely overlaid transparencies each of which is an organising schema for human action and interaction. These transparencies are made to intersect not just on any one plane but as this 'peaking' forces through, to join them, they intersect on different planes – so that the critic claims that 'this works on many levels'. Theatre's complexity comes not just from the density of this multilayered webbing and swirling, whose outer limits are not clearly mapped because onlooker-specific, but from the fact that entry into and movement within this unwieldy phenomenon is not wholly predetermined. It is relatively open for spectators and for performers, although the movement potential for the latter is relatively more predetermined than for the former inasmuch as 'the actor' is never a discrete unit for the purposes of performance.

The 'freeflow' (but always partly blocked and framed) actions of de Certeau's pedestrian wandering in the city and lost in the crowd are not pre-determined nor generated by maps or guides, or by pre-existing discourses, but seem instead to be a matter of bodily practices which are cunning in the pre-1600 sense of the term: a conning, a conjuring; at best, a somatic artistry. In this quality and following changes in the sixteenth century, such 'artful arts' have been neglected within institutions of idealised knowledges mediated by certain conventionalised uses of language, becoming largely unavailable to mainstream knowledges – but not to everyday practice, performance, seduction, or feeling. The combination of strategy, as de Certeau and Bourdieu rather differently conceive of the term, and de Certeau's tactic, seems to offer the conceptual frame for an approach to theatre actions which are seen to be both strategically inscribed *to a certain degree* within social and cultural institutions, and a tactical conjuring, characteristic of its cunning arts and artfulness.

The actor, but also the director and the spectators, draw repeatedly on both what is given, and – in order to cope with the institutionalised aspects of society, including theatre – on a complex *'art de faire'*: the *art* (and not the accident) of getting by. As art this mode of action has appeal on-stage for members of the collective, for whom it *feels like* an ancient and cunning intelligence-at-work.

The role of writing

If I have seemed to set aside the role of language in this framework, favouring somatic practices, let me indicate at this point that language in its use in theatre performance, inasmuch as it is mediated by the actor's voice, is itself a matter of somatic, muscular practice and artistry; and secondly that the role and function in performance of voicing perceived to be a matter of energetic bodily investment overlaid by socio-cultural features specific to actor and actorly perception of role, are far removed from conventional analysis of dramatic writing, perceived either globally as author-production, or intratextually as character-production. To what extent can we claim that writing of language can activate and mediate between, for example, dramatic writer 'real' habitus and dramatic character inferred habitus, on the one hand, and user (*metteur en scène*, actor and spectator) habitus on the other hand? How does it mediate?

Part II

Chapter 4

Interventions into the Scenes of Conflict

If the theatre performance which draws on dramatic writing were no longer required to be the faithful servant of a putative authorial intention and creativity, but perceived instead (in metaphoric terms derived from Chomskyian linguistics) to be **generated by** a **text** approached as its idealised 'core' (stable and resistant despite the vagaries of performance 'surface'), then it would be appropriate that analysis of the dramatico-theatrical text or performance event should borrow from modes of analysis derived from the fields of linguistics and literary and discourse analysis. After all, *applied* linguistics and discourse analysis have been trying to expand the parameters of notation and speculation within their fields, to include within their spectrum factors called 'non-linguistic' or 'paralinguistic' which might 'flesh out', and modify language use in the scenes of the social.

But – to paraphrase the biblical formula of classical idealisation already invoked by Derrida (1978) on 'Artaud' – is it really the case that the beginning of dramatic theatre is the Word? Is the Word then made flesh, with the consequence that we can eternally *read* within the flesh a linguistic imprint? We need caution here: what is implicated in our spontaneous response is a 'story' of human subjects' access into the complex symbolic, with – prioritised within this narration – the rationale for modes of secondary recuperations through which somatic practice and experience is textualised and effectively colonised by language.

If some of us are still seduced, in working on this story, by *origins*, in theatre's case we might well try to frog-leap logocentricism: if neither the beginning nor what is effective in present performance practice is necessarily the word (so much as, for example, **the voice**), then the element of performance we might most readily choose to focus on as starting-point is 'the body' – or rather *bodies*. The plural is vital: the perspective is relational, a matter of complementarities, rather than singular or minimalist. 'Bodies', besides, as ungendered plural, seems to permit us momentarily to blur the question which has exercised all those who dabble in the neo-Freudianisms of Lacan (e.g. Lacan, 1977), major French theorist of, amongst other fields, the cultural or symbolic: 'the body', in the concrete world of theatre, is always *some*-body. That is, that body is inevitably conceived of, chosen and *described* (and thence *known*) on the basis of biology, as 'male' or 'female', a conceptual grid which seems then to resonate with other elements of the binary framework: man/woman, the masculine/feminine. *Some*-body is already inscribed in complex social perceptions, in the norms of language, and in the ethical and actional modes which accrue to both. This recognition – and the way I have set it out, *effortlessly* – leads necessarily to a question of order: I have effortlessly and almost *naturally* put the sign 'male' first.

What I need to ask as a consequence is a question which makes the leap – from closed esthetic circle to the order of the social – which I have just denied to 'political' theatre. It is a question which seems to emerge *naturally* when the field shifts to 'bodies', but its terms may well change as soon as we recall that our subject here is *performing bodies* (i.e. the somatic symbolic), and not 'bodies in nature'. The confusion, as we shall see, is pertinent. The question is simple: is it the case, *in nature*, that the male is first, the female second? The terms 'male and female' are signs, *standing for* biological difference. This biological difference is material, and not symbolic. But its *significance* only emerges when we enter into the *symbolic orders* through which human societies organise the material and the natural.

It seems that within these symbolic orders – at least, it is historically the case – the *sign* of maleness is *put* first, and becomes the grounding term, within dominant orders or political systems. And that on the basis of this human ordering, the social subject *observed to be appropriate to the category* finds conferred upon **him** a 'commonsense' priority in any number of domains – such as theatre. The male candidate 'naturally' springs to mind, as Kruger (1990, pp. 27–47) claims, when certain roles in theatre work (the producer, theatre manager, author, *metteur en scène*, technician) are considered. In relation to this the 'female' sign is – as Kruger suggests with regard to the mainstream institutions of contemporary British theatre – generally second, so that we find it hard to resist that step which takes us into another, contingent domain: here the often-second sign is reappraised, becoming the (fe-)male; the woman becomes the woe-man, no-man, not-man. She is constrained, *naturally*, to play the 'actress', to perform the natural-material incarnation of what then might be termed male fantasies, in which Woman (a set of values, conjugated oppositionally as negativity in terms of a 'male' perspective) is commonly staged as the (often fascinating, often deadly, often eliminated or negated) site of conflict.

In semiotic terms – because theatre practice occurs by producing and reproducing orders within networks of signs or symbols, human-made, projected *onto* bodies – we must ask once again to what signs (in relation to what substance) this cultural priority has been so forcefully attributed throughout so much of history. Is it to biological difference, anatomy, that priority is granted – i.e. to material difference; or is it the *sight* of difference, and the absence *of that sight* – rather than the presence/absence of the 'organ itself', the 'penis itself' – which determines first and second places within mainstream cultural orders? But if *sight-of-biological-difference* – and not 'biological difference itself' – is the basis for signing traditional mainstream cultural orders, then the question which follows is no question at all.

The question: how do we change a so-called 'male' dominance, when maleness is naturally-occurring, having versus not-having, a matter of biology and unable to be changed without systematic violence **to bodies themselves**? The answer: the question confuses the material and the symbolic. Changing culture (ordered networks of signs) does not engage with biology and anatomy, but with the signs of difference. The signs of difference are not unitary ('male'), nor even neat binary opposites ('male'/'female'), but rather sets of relations between active perceiver and perceived, and their traces, activated in time and space of practice. I have characterised the relational here as sight-of-difference (i.e. requiring two participants and a process): **perceiver-actor + signifying practice + perceived and acted upon**. Change can occur, within this order, *if we can change perceivers' ways of seeing* – it is here that subjectivity and agency intervene – rather than changing the dubiously couched concept, 'what is seen'. But before I develop this theme, we need to concentrate on some of the traditional ways of seeing which the field of 'bodies' entails: into what systems and structures, and for what reasons, and for how long, has the notion of the presence/absence of the phallus – i.e. the orders of gender – ushered us (and them)?

'The body' has already in the late 1970s and early 1980s functioned as preferred political option for those struggling against a Word seen to be in the hands (*sic*) of the patriarchy, where it serves as symbolic tool of phallocratic domination over a Woman characterised as Body. A gender politics of cultural analysis, which sets up the mother-infant complex as a 'pre-symbolic' semiotic (the 'symbolic' here is equated with the linguistic), and which suggests that 'access into the symbolic' can be equated with the infant's access into language (in order to negotiate with the patriarchal social), tends to ignore the acquisition of a **body-symbolic**. This body-symbolic involves the gradual acquisition of specific muscular skills. It produces in part a body practice which is pleasurable 'in itself' (growing control of muscular contractions is pleasurable; in Freud it marks access into culture; in Barthes (1986), playfully, it marks the acquisition of the soul). In part it is a goal-oriented activity, but one which functions less as a *token*, a unit of exchange for services (e.g. nurturer response) – where it 'stands for the desire for something else' – than as a complex move, within a growing affective skill, involving an attempt at binding-in and transfer which will be developed throughout the social subject's life.

One example of this muscular control and its functional and affective effects is provided by what *we call* 'smiling' (i.e. the interactive process, entailing a muscular work *and* its perceiver, rather than 'the smile' as 'thing itself'). It involves a set of muscular contractions, an interactive eyeplay, and a feeling thereby **produced** (in place of our more customary expectation that feeling precedes the somatic event, which we find written in to Stanislavskian tradition). It is worked both *in* the muscular contraction and *from* the interactive play with the other – which transcends, and cannot be reduced to, the complex physicality 'itself'. What we are dealing with here is something like an early *performance skill* in the infant in its relation with the other: the infant is active, hence *acting*, in what functions as a dramatic scene (a relation with the other).

For reasons which relate not just to the Lacanian tradition, to which I return below, it is useful at this point to set up a comparative framework in which we draw together, in order to distinguish between them, four somatic options. These are:

- 'smiling'

- 'the penis'

- 'the cry'

- 'language'.

In a number of recent 'dramas' – or dramatic dialogues – of theory, the latter three are 'staged': they are made to take up the place of protagonist or antagonist, focalised and opposed by virtue of gender or visibility, or as apparently digital (either X or non-X), to a neatly established other. They seem obliged to engage with this other, because of the political positions of their animators, in a battle whose desired outcome is the development of theory itself toward the goal of True (or ideologically sound) Knowledge. But 'smiling' (the process) does not fit into the categories such dramatisations would want to make available. It does not fit (is not a fit dramatic subject) for a number of reasons:

- its condition is processual, rather than object(-ified);

- it is not distinguished by gender difference in its earliest stages (even if the doctor declares the gender of the infant at birth, thereby ushering it symbolically into symbolic orders);

- it is a complex somatic process whose value is not circumscribed by its materiality;

- it is not succeeded by language, does not necessarily accompany language, does not necessarily subvert, corrupt or attack language, although it can surely accomplish all of these inasmuch as it is active within what others might call 'discursive contexts'.

'Smiling', we shall see, has about it something of the laugh of de Certeau's pedestrian, happily lost within the precincts and institutions of theory, able to acknowledge and to act within these institutions (e.g. gender-based smiling practices) but neither wholly controlled by, nor condemned by these.

The body-semiotic

Kristeva (1980), in order to distinguish it from a linguistic symbolic, calls the body's semiotic a *pre*-symbolic, a "*signifying disposition . . . that is definitely heterogeneous to meaning but always in sight of it or in either a negative or surplus relationship to it*" (p. 133: my emphasis). In this appraisal, informed by a feminist politics of the 1960s–70s, we remain within the episteme of the double, and within the scenario of the conflicts of signification. Here the body semiotic is out on parole as language's closely watched inarticulate other:

> a distinctiveness admitting of an uncertain and indeterminate articulation because it does not yet refer (for young children) or no longer refers (in psychotic discourse) to a signified object for a thetic consciousness . . . (p. 133)

Noises, rhythms and intonations in this conception are the mark of the poetic where that is perceived to be the eruption of body into writing. They are always present, but to differing degrees according to genre, and they function as a surplus to the linguistic symbolic:

> Language as social practice necessarily presupposes these two dispositions, though combined in different ways to constitute *types of discourse*, types of signifying practices. Scientific discourse, for example, aspiring to the status of metalanguage, tends to reduce as much as possible the semiotic component.
>
> (p. 134)

The body-semiotic, in this approach, is *dramatised* within – ironically – something like an Oedipal scene of revolt: it is not just a surplus; the semiotic is liable to "attack . . . or corrupt . . . the symbolic function . . . in poetic language". What we find here is the classical *drama* of theorising, which, through the theorising subject's perspective, sets up a conflictual scene of oppositions which spread between and link gender difference and cultural difference.

It is marked by roles and relations and, in the sequence or plot of the presentation, by the conventions of narrative: by desire or goal, obstacle, interventions, climax and resolution. In invoking 'attack' and 'corruption', this 'scientific discourse' (of the human sciences) adopts precisely the positive/negative scenario it seeks to expose; it is bound-in to the same logic. For our purposes, what we need to note is that this drama never fails to revolve around **language**; and that 'bodyness', for Kristeva, never avoids its function *within the dominion of logocentricity*, as a precedent to, or an accompaniment of, or a threat to, a 'corrupter of', language's modes of signification. The 'un-certain' or 'in-determinate' of the semiotic, in Kristeva's terms, both retain negativity as prefix. More than that, they remain language's prisoners, language's other.

This is far from what is needed in an analysis which removes itself from the constraints of a *literary* theory (however much that theory may yearn after bodies). But times change: in the 1990s we are slowly losing the text-political polemics locating a necessarily *maternal* body, which serves as antidote to a 'paternalistic' speech or writing; a mother—infant *chora* whose function has ironically never been more than to precede, and then intrude upon that same **language** seen as order of the patriarchy, *making it strange* and therefore arresting the reader.

The dominant dualist episteme, particularly as this is modelled around language and what is seen to be its other, reappears in the late 1980s in a wider political framework: all those deprived of a voice within the dominant mainstream of the community emit this absence-of-language as effective social intervention, through 'the cry' (de Certeau, 1984; Ruby, 1989). The cry is closely akin to Kristeva's *chora* but it is no longer constrained by *gender* politics. It is no longer constrained by dramatised politics as such, in that the cry is specific to the splintered and dispersed subject, who has no voice precisely because s/he has no group, s/he is unable to find the massed strength to become the mainstream's other. The drama, here, lies in the loss of the polarity which marks the traditional concept of the political. For some this is traditionally the (invisible) place of the actor as social subject, lacking a voice until one is given, lacking a group(-identity) because identity is what is taken on, not what is internalised as self. The Actor, like Woman, in this logic, cannot take (a) place, because s/he lacks (and *should have*: the truth-regime here is displaced into the ideal of *authenticity*), an inherent sign, must borrow one to function effectively in the social. But can we side-step this logic?

Historical shifts

What we find in the historical shift I have been outlining is a reappraisal of a basic dualism, derived from an ancient episteme, still repeatedly legitimised. In the past (see for example Euripide's *Bacchae Women*) the cry of a socially inarticulate (because seemingly not rational) body has been associated with earthy/earthly bodily passions, and devalorised in its relation with the ideal of thought and poetic language. The body's cry is conventionally perceived to be negative precisely in opposition to the perceived ideals of 'clarity' and of potential disembodiment (as thought or as writing) as certain modes of these are advocated in extremes of rationalism and idealism. The 'body's cry', as metaphor for all that is perceived to be rationalist language's other, apparently cannot be broken down into units – phonemes, morphemes and lexical items. It is hence *not articulate*. Nor can it be built up into syntactical blocks (except as something like the goat song, associated – by rationalists – with lust, madness and mating). We might want to see this – Artaud-like – as its strength in the theatre as soon as we release theatre from a blind reverence for a hypercharged 'Word', but only provided we accept to remain within the boundaries of this dualist, categorising episteme. The politics of so remaining, in the 1990s, are dubious.

Body*work* is just this: it operates within a somatic economy – and the brain (and perhaps 'the mind', and 'the psyche'?) is part of this somatic complex and its processes. As such, and despite body-work's slippage and flux which make it escape digital reckoning, it is nonetheless in the everyday a reasoned practice, even if that body-reasoning is so rapid as to appear to be a social or an idiosyncratic automatism: we say, for example, 'it was intuitive/ instinctive/I just *knew*'. It is an artistry, combining a strategic straightforwardness and a tactical *cunning*, which, in the professional actor in particular, is liable to be approached in terms of a 'rhetorics of practice'. It may, for all that, never have been approached by that actor through discourse, nor through the sorts of worded contemplation peculiar to the artist of language, and it may well continue to surprise the professional actor, in what it lets her do and makes her feel, even as she does it.

It seems, if this is the case, that we need when dealing with stage-work – and I should want to include here the work of the designer, and much of the work which passes unsaid between *metteur en scène* and actor, between actor and actor, as well as between actor and writing – to loosen our definitions of what can constitute a 'logic' of practice, recognising that much that enters into play here seems to work through felt-experience, observation and displacement, but that these are overseen by something like a 'theatre logic' and a theatre logistics. This is the case because these constituents are overlaid by and selected amongst and modulated by, the conceptual grids proper to professional theatre, and the decision-making processes these entail. What we need to do, in order to approach this logic and these practices as they are used in theatre, is not to attack language in order to let bodywork in; but rather to shift and soften our understanding of language in use, removing it from its ratified central place, in order to demonstrate that language functions within bodywork, and alongside body-work, as a component within it, but not as its opponent, nor as its Father or master. The new 'logic of practice' will admit felt-experience, and sight, as forces whose functioning is as decisive, in successful theatre practice, as is that of wording. And this admission requires that we reconceptualise the analytical process.

Such a shift means that we need to broaden our outlook, as Wilden (1980) suggests we need to do, to adopt as *complementarities* the "analog" (associative spread) and the digital (binary, linear) as ways of knowing and appraising the worlds of cultural practice. Note, however, that Wilden's own uses of these technical terms taken from Information Technology, slip between their literal value in that IT context, and a metaphoric value within the Saussurean/ Jakobsonian epistemology, where they seem to *stand for* the synchronic axis of simultaneity and the diachronic axis of change in syntax and time. The problem posed by Wilden's produced-equivalence *should* be useful here, since it draws our attention to a long-standing one: if Saussurean linguistics is concerned with separating out two text functions (which in popular usage are then perceived to be discrete), what IT is more concerned with is the interface between the two, where the analogue (directly related to the phenomenon through equivalency, and not digital) is transformed, through re-encoding, into the digital.

Bodies as relational networks of values, in movement, caught within those stage and theatre force-fields which are theatre's optimal condition and production, blur the notion of the *articulate* – which is a long way, however, from calling them 'in-articulate'. They are triumphantly not clear: they are ambiguous (except perhaps in the groundwork of a strongly codified symbolic practice such as the Indian *kathakali* or the classical *Noh*), however much the proponents of what is termed 'body language' seek to use superordinates (*the* arm, *the* hand, *the* mouth, *the* eye) to attribute to the single body's work discrete particles akin to lexical units.

They attempt then to posit syntactical combinations and obedient textuality, failing however to approach what is finally the artistry of bodies-in-action before spectators – an artistry which is ambiguous in its implications, in flux, liable to little fallings away and unevenness, and wholly interactive both within the stage practice and between stage and spectator practices. In this ambiguity, bodies in performance might seem to be, as Ariane Mnouchkine maintains from within recent French tradition, both 'feminine' – despite their biology – and 'oriental' – despite race and ethnicity. This attribution of qualifiers emerges from and in response to one of the most pervasive and strangely persuasive semiotic myths of the twentieth century in the West: Lacan's semiotic theory of gender identity within culture.

In Part III I demonstrate that dramatic theatre intrudes the discursive economy into this specular—somatic order, to the end of blendings, juxtapositions and mutual transformations. Dramatic writing *activated* can be said 'to stand for' (and in) this complex economy, as the diagram of a chair stands, through an equivalency of dimension and relational complementarities, not just for both 'chairness' in general and 'a (constructable) chair', in particular, but furthermore, for 'that chair I might choose to use in my preferred everyday life'. That is, it can be said – in scriptwriting – to stand for 'my everyday-lived experience of' chair, into which attitude and affect can enter. It seems difficult, indeed, to separate out affect and attitude from my perception of the relation between writing and contemporary performance – although this is not the same as claiming that attitude and affect are 'already there' in writing. They 'emerge' from the dynamic ("in flux") activation of the synoptic ("in place") text, within the conditions of a (pre)staging, into the space between. In standing diagrammatically for, it does not command but it elicits; it surely also constrains, iconically. It does more than this: its stagers use its specificities to point to, to elicit feeling from, bodies (actorly and spectatorial) which will (or not) take pleasure from that process. On the basis of that pleasure – whether esthetic or political judgement wills it or not – the validity of dramatic production *in the marketplace* depends. Dramatic semiotics can no longer afford to overlook that factor.

Before we proceed to Part III, however, we need to tread some kind of a path between institutions of semiotics – including Lacan's 'story' of gender and culture – which have recently contemplated possible relations between language-use and cultural practice and into which 'bodyness' begins awkwardly to intrude, in the attempt to see whether this path can lead to new sites and new chartings for the sorts of shifts I have outlined in Part I.

Chapter 5

Old Masters

Social semiotic tradition

In 1984 Fawcett, in *The Semiotics of Culture and Language* (Vol. 2), introduced the assembled writers' project in these terms:

> Semiotics, which I take to be the study of sign systems and their use, is not a subject that has many practitioners who . . . call themselves 'semioticians' (or 'semiologists' to use the term favoured in the mainland European tradition). On the other hand it could well be argued that the world is full of applied semioticians, in that semiotic issues are inherently involved whenever a language is taught and learned . . . whenever a psychologist studies gaze or proxemic behaviour, and whenever a student of art or music or literature is at work. But . . . the student of semiotics is also concerned with the *general* principles of signs and sign systems. [S]emiotics . . . is crucial to an understanding of human nature – both social and psychological. For it is the sign systems that we use for interaction with other living beings that determine our potential for thought and social action. (p. xiii)

Well and good – but we can see something else going on: first, Fawcett's semiotic project remains imprisoned within the framework of the symptom. In this logic, what is 'given' (or observed) is always used as an *indice* of something else – a relation within the clause becomes symptom of ideology. Rising intonation at the end of an utterance not using the interrogative, for example, becomes a symptom of disempowerment. The difficulty with this approach, for theatre practice, becomes clear with the work of Derrida and Lyotard, to which I return. Second, there is something missing – for those of us interested in theatre and *how it works* and how we work it – in the focus on 'thought and social action', as there is in that on 'the *sign systems* that we use for interaction with other living beings'. Is dramatic theatre's working or not dependent on, rather than assisted by, 'use of sign systems' for interaction, or is something else needed if our understanding of dramatic theatre's working is to be developed? After all, as I have indicated above, *passionately 'good'* theatre, and theatre which 'does not work', may equally carefully draw on 'the sign systems . . . that determine our potential for thought and social action'. The criterion used most generally within the fields social semiotics is particularly involved in (e.g. second language learning; trans-actional analysis; ideological analysis), seems to be that of functional adequacy or *effectiveness*. But theatre does not fail, or succeed, on the basis of functional adequacy: unlike the social norm or mean, it needs something more than adequacy to flourish. And 'effectiveness' here cannot as readily be assessed as it appears to be in transactional analysis where the teleological focus (e.g. social function as origin, acquiring goods or services through use of language) seems to assure the delineation and assessment of 'moves' and 'exchanges' practised in a circumscribed and com-ponent-prescribed 'event' of social interaction. What then do we need to 'add', and where might we find the missing ingredients?

Metaphors for absent bodies

In his preface to the French edition of *Travels in Hyperreality* (1986) (*La Guerre du faux*, 1985) – but not, interestingly, to the English edition – Umberto Eco indicates that for Peirce, the lesser-known progenitor of twentieth-century semiotics, "every philosophical or scientific discovery is preceded by 'the play of musement'; a wandering of the mind through the realms of the possible, an amassing of interrogations when faced with specific facts, an attempt to propose several solutions at once" (my translation), and that what is needed in such a quest is a practice animated *by the nose*:

> what Barthes called the "semiological flair of the nostrils", this capacity each of us should have to seize the meaning exactly at that point at which we might be tempted only to see facts, to identify messages at that point where one might only see

gestures, to discern signs where we might be tempted only to see things. (p. iv: my translation)

Once again, and despite his getting the body in the form of *the nose* – responsive, quirky organ of virtually unspeakable knowing – into the semiological act, for Eco the goal is still to replace what 'is sniffed out' ('facts', 'gestures', 'things'), with a 'something else', beloved in its otherness by the semio-*logician* as logocentricist. That is, by a being obsessively concerned with the predominance and value of language (meaning, messages, signs) over other modes of experience of the world.

This bend of the rhetorical knee to the **nose** does nothing to alter the logocentric focus, and something is still missing from a workable semiotic practice for those of us who work in theatre. Nor would it be helpful, in this context, to call the semiological flair 'intuition': this is to turn in circles, moving away from the notion borrowed from Bourdieu which allows for an interiorised exteriority able to affect attitude and ethos and, arguably, what others still call intuition. Even within the bounds of logocentric pursuits, something is not clear: in the tendency toward the obsessive production of discourse and text to 'treat' what is not textual, just *which* meaning/message/sign 'should we' choose?

Incursions

In the midst of this scenario so solidly and often so unquestioningly informed by a language-dominant world-perspective, and into which 'the (hypostasised or objectified) body' is at best intruded metaphorically or in terms of an 'extra-linguistic', 'non-verbal' or 'non-discursive' 'communicative practice' or as a parallel order of 'body language', each always ordered by, equatable or reducible to or translatable into verbalisations, there have however been certain incursions.

One of the theorists of the postmodern, Lyotard, claimed in a short and difficult text not widely discussed among English-language theatre practitioners ('La Dent, la paume', Lyotard, 1973) that occidental theatre remains dominated by a theory of representations, by a double standing-for. What theatre *does*, in the present experience of those involved, is irresistibly reappropriated into the terms of another (past) experience seen as causal or generative, and already available either as 'the dramatic text', or as discursive formulae (or desire-traps). In Lyotard's terms:

> [t]heatre plunges us into the heart of the religio-political, by which I allude to the question of absence; into negativity . . . and thus into the question of power. A theory of theatre *signs* and a practice of theatre *signs* (whether dramaturgy, mise en scène, interpretation or architecture) depend on the acceptance of a nihilism inherent in representation, and indeed they reinforce this nihilism. The sign as Peirce told us is something which replaces something else for someone. So theatre hides, in order to reveal. And our late modernity consists in this dilemma: there is no longer anything to replace, or to represent, there is no legitimate place-taker – or rather all of them are.
>
> (p. 89: my translation)

In the equation of sign and what it is said to stand for conventionally (e.g. B on stage standing for A 'in the real out there'), A is absent, but perceived to be both B's precedent, its order and its hidden truth; and B is reduced to nothing, mere illusion of presence whose being is in A and thus elsewhere, ideal, absence. This, says Lyotard:

> is the scenario of nihilism. Is theatricality condemned to it? By repeating this scenario in its own reading semiology maintains and develops theology, the theology of the death of God, [that absent ideal], of the theory of structuralism, of critical dialectics and so on. (p. 89: my translation)

We need not assume, twenty years later, that this appraisal of occidental theatre is eternally valid – the French stage, for example, is now marked in many instances by an astonishing, controlled physicality which newly centres our attention on the capacity of the actor to withstand and overcome intensified everyday circumstances (such as the frailties of the flesh), where once we expected that the written *fiction* would furnish instances of the exceptional, merely 'portrayed' by the actor. Two examples: *Les Attrides*, Mnouchkine, *Théâtre du Soleil*, 1991; and, in a completely different register, *Les Hommes naissent tous ego* ('All Men are Born Equal Egotists'), J.-C. Cotillard, *Théâtre Montparnasse*, 1991).

But to some extent, and removed from the scene of French theory, performance is still widely seen to '*stand (relatively transparently) for*' 'the author' (approached or constituted discursively as a signature-text, e.g. '*Beckett*'s own misanthropy is exemplified . . . '); for 'the text'; for the *metteur en scène*'s intent. It is also perceived to stand for 'the world-out-there'. And each of these is then related back to present performance as a now-speakable, reappropriated absence, and as a lost – wasted! – ideal.

Performance in this prevailing tradition is a means to discovering what is not performance. And each of these 'discoveries' is rapidly relayed through recourse to what Foucault has called the pre-discursive: these are established discursive formulae which might be seen as (changing and internally contradictory) patterns or indeed *scenarios* of knowledge available in and effectively founding the specific discursive context in which everyday social actors learn and speak, write – and act. As these are already discursively formulated, widely disseminated, but also relatively contradictory within a single 'dispositif' or grid (e.g. the multitude of different ways of 'talking about women's work'), thus permitting the user to contest and debate and differ, we are dealing with a properly *economical* drama of discourse which can conveniently be substituted thereafter for theatre's apparently uneconomical display and event; in which we have apparently as wastefully (because passionately, where passion entails 'over'-production of adrenalin) participated.

Power in the everyday (of theatre)

We might want now to develop Lyotard's position with regard to power – not just as a generative or causal force shrouded in mystery and idealism, which holds us subject, but in terms of the everyday of power as it manifests itself through our discursive options: by an everyday of power I refer to 'common sense', 'obvious' or axiomatic ways of perceiving and talking about 'the world'. Our discursive response to theatre is not just a question of esthetic coding into which user-specific judgement intrudes; it is one which activates the everyday of *axiology* (with its specific discursive options). Axiology reveals itself once we realise that it is widely taught, and *felt*, that 'theatre *should*' represent what it is not;

'should' be the ghost of an absent truth, a hidden agenda, or a covert ideology, always discursively rendered.

There is more at stake here than a discursive or symbolic appropriation, and the games of contemporary theory: there is an appropriation which is widely taken to be right and proper (which makes it a matter first for axiological enquiry and then for ideological investigation). It is an appropriation which is able to overtake felt-experience, to drain it and to regulate and differently (and as pleasurably) re-produce it through transforming it. It permits the respected and prolific British theatre critic, Michael Billington, to comment in the context of a review of Benedetti's work on Stanislavski (Billington, *The Guardian*, 1990), in these terms:

> it proclaims the importance of method . . . and shows how the famous system was rooted in working practice. You could hardly better Stanislavski's note to an actor having difficulty with Claudius's prayer-scene that "the main thing is you are not *living the reason for which Shakespeare wrote the king's words* but the words themselves, you're spelling out their direct meaning'. *Benedetti's book reminds one that Stanislavski had the sanity of true genius.* (p. 22: my emphases)

A complex 'theology' operates here, disseminated through the media's use of Billington's well-established and lightly borne authority. And if I quote Billington quoting Benedetti quoting Stanislavski, it is to reveal the means through which widescale and painless dissemination of notions of 'truth' and value occur: the juxtaposition and dramatising of specific textual clusters, all overseen or staged by Billington here – 'living' (implying actorly interiorisation and its manifestation in actorly work); 'the reason for which Shakespeare wrote the king's words' (authorial intentionality and the attributing of writerly words to a supposedly real human speaking subject who is 'the king'), opposed then to 'the words themselves' (apparently bereft of their intentional essence) and 'their direct meaning' (ditto). These are approved by Billington's valorisation through the use of 'sanity' and 'true genius', and taken together they propagate as 'universal truths' the relationship of a number of absent gods to an historical theatre practice effortlessly relegitimised in this relatively popular medium.

The play of otherness/openness

Such a 'theology', entailing a pleasurable submission to 'higher authorities' of conventional wisdom, is easy to expose but hard to replace. Once again: let's step sideways. What has entered into the game of theory is the notion of openness, playfulness, aided and abetted by the theory of *indeterminacy*, and of the effect of the observer on what is observed. In turn the recognition of the relative openness and indeterminacy of meaning and effect makes the publication of judgements of taste and value delicate. We seem to be back again with 'individual judgement', but with this difference: our quest now is to try to understand the blending of the socially-determined with individual clusterings and hier-archisations of knowledge and effects/affects, on which much successful theatre in Western tradition depends.

Around the time when Lyotard – major theorist of the postmodern (Lyotard, 1984) – was using theatre as metaphoric site for questioning traditional occidental theories of representation, and at a time when 'social semioticians' continued not just to seek out discursive form(ul)ations, 'grammars' and systems for everyday and extra-ordinary cultural practices, but developed critiques of dominant and concealed ideologies and set out briefs for 'making trouble' within different institutions of knowledge and learning (Lemke, 1984), Derrida's own decisive challenge to structuralism became available to English-language readers, in these terms:

The stage is theological for as long as it is dominated by speech, by a will to speech, by the layout of a primary logos which does not belong to the theatrical site and governs it from a distance. The stage is theological for as long as its structure, following the entirety of tradition, comports the following elements: an author–creator who, absent and from afar, is armed with a text and keeps watch over, assembles, regulates the time or the meaning of representation, letting this latter *represent* him as concerns what is called the content of his thoughts, his in-tentions, his ideas. He lets representation represent him through representatives, directors or actors, enslaved interpreters who represent characters who, primarily through what they say, more or less directly represent the thought of the "creator". . . . This general structure in which each agency is linked to all the others by representation, in which the irrepresentability of the living present is dissimulated or dissolved, suppressed or deported within the infinite chain of representations – this structure has never been modified. All revolutions have maintained it intact, and most often have tended to protect or restore it. . . . The Occident . . . has worked only for the erasure of the stage. (Derrida, 1978, pp. 235–6)

In fact Derrida precedes Ulmer and Lyotard in adopting theatre as a metaphor for theory seen as a matter of dramatic scenarios and dialogues, fed by contestations always within dominant epistemes. Secondly he draws on 'Artaud', less as an historical theatre practitioner than as metaphor for his own challenges to the validity of structural semiology. The bells ring gloomily and resonantly for the occidental stage of representations (Derrida, 1968, trans. 1978), and the forewarning that revolution maintains intact what revolutionaries seek to change would seem to condemn us hereafter to more of the same: if oppositionality and conflict are endemic to the human in society, and to the development of human reason and action, there can be no escape. If, however, the oppositional can be shown to be a tool of human invention, adopted and then naturalised because of its usefulness as a means of division, classification, representation and control, then it can be set aside as just that, as one tool amongst others, and the field is thus open to other developments and modes of knowing and acting.

Derrida also foreshadows de Certeau on the subject of the injudiciousness of direct confrontation of the institution and the institutionalised by the marginalised, and it is de Certeau who in the 1980s proposes the 'soft' option of a postmodern tactical making-do, undertaken in the everyday by the users of the products of a range of institutions which offer, as well, the virtue of permitting us to 'know who we are'. There are obvious implications, here, for the twentieth-century tradition of a revolutionary 'Brechtian' theatre practice – from this perspective it becomes no more than one significant development in *theatre* (and pedagogic) practice.

The norm as master

While oppositionality as a tool to understanding has recently been problematised, it does still seem to be the case that we can best see axiology at work within our own cultural practice (where it determines narrations of attitude *and ethos*, deemed 'right and proper', 'natural' or obvious in judgements in and of theatre work), *through* observation of *difference*. Artaud saw Balinese performance through Parisian eyes, and took from it the ingredients for an attack on the familiar (cf. Clancy 1985); we know of Brecht's interest in Chinese performance traditions, and the use he makes at home of these; Derrida takes up Artaud's use of difference, just as Lyotard in turn observes the theatre of presence (rather than representation) of certain classical Asian performance modes (Lyotard, 1980). But what we can now note is that none of these was dealing with radical difference, for the simple reason that by their own acts of spectating, and of speculation (vital components of any 'performance itself'), they intruded their own ways of seeing into 'the other', to transform for them what they thought only 'to see', and to see 'objectively'. Their acts of perception converted the different into so many instances of difference-in-sameness, in which – it now seems – they saw themselves, their own traditions, and their own needs, at the very moment they thought to see the other.

In *quantum* terms, the situation cannot be other, inasmuch as the observer *constitutes* the reality-order-perceived, including herself or himself in it, by that act of perception. A structuring need in a given subject will produce a *perceptual real* in terms of the demands and requirements of that need; and inasmuch as the subject's need is a socially possible one, rather than wholly idiosyncratic, then that perceptual real is no less valid than any other so determined.

What the quest for the *other* – which might better reveal the workings of the given – determined, with regard to certain traditions, was that for classic *Noh* and *bunraku* there was no vital expectation of a social standing-for or representationality; this is not to say that these performance modes are lacking in resonance and in stylised reality effects. Similarly *kathakali* performed at an Indian community feast stands not simply *for itself* – which would betoken a return to a rigid Formalism – but instead it 'stands for' tradition-in-practice, for its artistry, and for the need of a community to reinforce its traditions through cultural practice.

Barthes has already had something to say (Barthes, 1982a) about the classic Japanese puppetry theatre *bunraku*, from his privileged viewpoint as semiotician-in-desire, caught – as was Lyotard, besides, and Artaud before them – in a then-fashionable Old-European yearning (cf. Barthes, 1982b) after the apparent non-representationality of this theatre mode. What he finds pleasurable and useful is always worked through the observational principle of perceived difference-in-sameness: formed in and politically critical of the traditions of northern Europe, and of the dominant mode of naturalism and its psychologising amongst them, what Barthes perceived was a performance mode whose principal delight (for him) was the fragmenting and juxtaposition of elements which, on the stage of naturalism, are marked by their seamless cohesion and the illusion of unity, with all that it betokens of a central power force to control it. The unities of naturalism suddenly become clear: actor-interiority with actor-exteriority (to constitute 'in-depth' that non-thing 'dramatic character'); unity of action with gesture, with options in the systems of voice; unity of supposed intent with manifestation (especially where this unity consists of a carefully constituted contradiction, characteristic of the oppositional or conflictual tradition). Unity of acting modes among actors, of place with fiction, of time and space with fictional 'reality effects', and so on. The political problem this produces was noted by Brecht: the unity depends on *someone's* power and is not natural but illusory, and the spectator's identificatory pleasures with the seamless construct transfix her – as Narcissus was transfixed; and her critical capacity slumbers.

In the use of the one and a half-metre puppets, each animated by up to three puppeteers visible on stage but veiled in black, *bunraku* achieves, for Barthes, the explicit and humanly worked production and adoration of the 'little thing' we each, as infants, seize upon as substitute love-object (Barthes, 1982a, pp. 305–13). But we are not lost in identificatory pleasures, because the seams are visible, the object is perceived to be just that, and its mechanics are underlined, rather than concealed. Barthes does not make clear whether the Japanese spectator therefore constitutionally enjoys a heightened understanding of principles of manipulation, but this is not in fact the point: what counts is the difference-in-sameness with the given, where the sameness is assured not so much by the similarity of performance world-wide, as by the consistent eye of the perceiver: Barthes himself.

The telling difference is particularly clear in the work of the chanter. In *voicing* the dramatic exchanges between, for example, scolding mother and weeping daughter puppets (if I can name them as such, the reality effects are clear and trans-cultural, but the puppet is *thing* standing for human, rather than one human for a fictional other), the single chanter gives body to them in two ways:

1. through internal changes in voice timbre and colour plus rhythm and speed, temporally co-ordinated with the distanced puppet movements which are similarly internally differentiated;

2. through the fact that the eyes of the chanter weep, cease to weep, weep again, as she switches with great speed between the voices, *but not in perfect co-ordination with that shift.*

The eyes weep – but the chanter as self-willed and voluntary actor does not. As self-willed and voluntary actor, she would not weep – her intent would preclude it as it is superfluous to her performance role of voicing. Were she *playing character*, naturalistically, however, that weeping could be used (as we are accustomed to do so) as symptom of actor–character interiority. It is impossible to attribute to the performer, in this instance, a troubled interiority, affective recall, a memory of lived and resuscitated anguish. Something much more interesting is occurring, and what we might begin to ask, along with cognitive psychologists, is whether we can draw on this experience: the performer produces the muscular, voice work of crying; this in turn produces tears; and this in turn might, if the conditions were appropriate, produce an altered psychological state in the performer. The chanter's body *works* something, through a sympathetic muscular contractual relation between voice pitch and throat muscles, in the voicing of a particular character-element; but the visible signs of weeping, produced through this bodywork, are superfluous: it is the puppetwork, and not the chanter, which is the site of *visible* character-signs. The chanter signals this inappropriateness: she must perform a vocal shift, within the diadic mother–daughter voice relation, which is more rapid than are the responses of the muscles and the tear ducts. The tears interfere with that shift, they overlap it, since they are less dynamic and less liable to the working body's muscular control.

Now, we have here a principle of internal difference, and a principle of rapid alternation, vital to the working of the performance of a fiction, but the muscular workings of the body, and their traces, are not digital. What might we say these weeping eyes, in this instance, 'stand for'? They are not a voluntary signifying practice; and they are superfluous to the complex role of chanter who is, nonetheless, a visibility and not 'just a voice-play'. What we might suppose is this: that an acutely ordered work in the body's musculature *produces what we conventionally call the 'signs of emotion'*, even when that emotion is absent from the performer as source, and when it is inappropriate to the performer as visibility. In this case, and perhaps in others, the intense muscular production of the shrill voice, working the tears from the eyes (but with professional control, and not sadness, as source), activates in turn *in the performer* a potential for an experience we generally call emotional. The performer, in this instance of rapid shift between two voices/identities, does not have time to let this emotional potential develop, cannot taste, and exploit it.

But if she could – as can the actor in the traditions which are more familiar to us? Marguerite Duras has similarly experimented, from within these traditions, with the dislocation of voice from body, but the work remains categorised (measured and assessed against unified illusion as norm) as 'experimental' in its effect. My aim here is less confrontational: what *bunraku* seems to me to reveal is a different means to understanding various productions in the actor, within naturalism every bit as much as in our critique of it, whereby certain sorts of muscular work have the potential to **produce** what we semiotise as emotion, and not to *'express'* it (to press it out), as naturalistic tradition would have it. The actor work, if what I suggest is valid, does not then 're-present' emotion (concealed somewhere else, in advance of the work, and always yearned after), but nor is actor-affectivity 'recalled' in the actor, and cannibalised by 'character' or role through the medium of *mise en scène*. Instead it *presents* the potential for it. The schooled performer – and the schooled spectator – thereafter experience it. The chanter works a voice whose specificities we might record, which she has undoubtedly observed 'in the world' and honed using what is singular to her. She *presents* a voice whose power over an immense range of muscular networks – contracting throat muscles, pitch, volume of breath, labial and plosive control, lung power, and so on – causes the contracting, sympathetic muscles of face and eye to produce the somatically irresistible, but **performer-inappropriate** work. In the event, her performance requisites include not just her script and ceramic tea glass, but a folded handkerchief, matching her kimono, with which one hand will wipe these working eyes, swiftly and neatly, even as the voice has shifted from crying child-work to scolding mother-work. (In Old Norse 'work', *virkje*, means 'pushing against a burden'; in *bunraku* it is this pushing against the barriers formed by difference which seems to produce, but not to derive from, the affects experienced by spectators: in my case I am literally enthralled by the effort of the chanter, which in Barthes' terms, borrowed from the discourses of neo-Freudian psychoanalysis, is my own 'little object'.)

In Part III I demonstrate some of the paths we might tread toward a theory of the economy of worked energy in/as performance. But at this point what we need are the means to draw together our contemporary, vast and varied experiences of world theatre, in order that we might develop a contemporary theatre semiotics which avoids the 'theatre anthropologist' fascination with the exotic other (cf. Schechner, 1985; Barba and Savarese, 1985).

Ulmer's 'theorter'

Some time after the entry of the postmodern and poststructuralism onto the stage or scene of theory, Ulmer, as 'applied grammatologist' (the title alone is an explicit reference to Derridean theory and to its possible application in the pedagogic context), points out with regard to *performance* of/and theory, that "everything from politics to poetics [has] become theatrical" (Ulmer, 1985, p. 277). In consequence the quest for an effective mode of analysis of dramatic performance becomes not just more urgent, but wider in its implications. Ulmer asserts that, from the perspective of theory in the 1980s, "theater and theory merge into one activity (which perhaps could be dubbed "theorter")" (Ulmer, 1985, p. 229).

In part this development comes from what the French philosopher Touraine (1989) sees (but bemoans) as the newly emerged (post-televisual) focus on image and performance, rather than on 'universal values' on the one hand, and a politics of *real* representation (established in principle at the time of the French Revolution in 1789) on the other. Touraine's modernist position – unlike Ulmer's postmodernism – is nostalgic for an earlier conception of the social actor and a wider politics of effective representation, in comparison with what he perceives to be current marketing of an individualism lodged in the image, in a government system worked along the lines of successful business management and marketed through the media. As the terms I have emphasised demonstrate, the parallels with the problems for a contemporary semiotics of dramatic theatre performance are evident: in the social real Touraine bemoans the loss of a politics of representation of social subjects, replaced by seductive images without substance; in the theatre certain practitioners and theorists bemoan the disappearance of a theatre of political representation, which might transform spectators into social actors, replaced by one of seductive simulacra (such as a 'Brechtian' staging in a comfortable middle-class theatre).

But Ulmer, as postmodernist, is keen not to condemn and confront, but to embrace the technological devlopment of today's 'media society', not the least to the end of a valorisation of popular culture – the culture of each individual – through an enhanced access for each subject to the technology now widely available in post-industrialised societies (Ulmer, 1989). One of the steps to this end comes through the development of performance skills through the use of the media, in the 'cobbling together' of each subject's 'story' (his-story/my-story) into something like a personalised script for a televisual production.

It is not easy to find parallels in 'text-based' theatre, not the least because such a mode of scripting emerges best from a group 'writing', and such a mode of writing does not readily meet current publishing requirements. The closest parallel we can find in writing for theatre performance might come from women's monologues collected in *Out From Under: Texts from Women Perform-ance Artists* (Champagne, 1990). Vinaver's 'theatre of the everyday' promises but does not convincingly offer this sort of low-key polyphony (Vinaver, in Bradby and Schumacher, 1989), because the strategies of plot, index of writerly conservatism, take over from the desire to replicate the polyphony of everyday life. The contribution of Goffman (e.g. 1956, 1970, 1974) to this sort of approach is clear, but we still need to develop a finer understanding of the subtle dosing of the social and the personal that the professional performer and *metteur en scène* bring to intersect in performance utilising dramatic writing, for a group of spectators.

From 'the sign' to its other

Into this complex framework what we might call on again is Bourdieu's theorisation of the social actor's multiple (and relatively unforeseeable) strategies (or institutionalised, 'normal' interactions), which enact little dramas constituted by the clashes of *habitus*. Let us not forget, at this point, that Bourdieu has recently acknowledged (*"Grands Entretiens: Les Témoins de la nuit: Sociologue, Philosophe, Pierre Bourdieu"*, Prony Production/Antenne 2, 1990) that the social theorist, like anyone else, is traversed by urges, by drives and desires, which will affect the projects and choices, the channelled energies and the interest focus of any project otherwise seen as 'scientific'. What this seems to imply is that the 'dramatised' subject, like the dramatised society, will be involved in modes of action and assessment which will always be more complex in their implications – and thus can be said to have a further reach of representation – than the objectively observed co-ordinates of any perceived 'situation' might seem to suggest. Action, the social actor, performance and the performer, brought into relation with the actorly and spectator other, begin, from this perspective, to assume a complexity of resonance which newly focuses attention away from the 'character' beloved of naturalism, to the play between actor, role and spectator.

Again, de Certeau's theory of unforeseeable tactics which worry at the neat edges of the socially and economically encoded strategies, seems to open a certain space to the singular, but in this conception the social subject is triumphant, empowered by the capacity for little subversions, and laughs. The laughing subject's little powers, here, are altogether too self-aware for a theatre of passionate bindings-in, where there are 'other forces', activated to be sure by the work of single subjects, but negotiated, negated and combined in such a way that the combined energy produced is greater than (individual knowledges and feelings in) any of its constituent parts. And that combined energy then draws in, and along, the theatre professional and the spectator, whose pleasure, in part, derives from the nature of that quasi-collective, quasi-personal experience.

We need a complex theory of marketable performance pleasures and of *multiple uptake founded in pleasure*. In order to draw in that multiple uptake founded in pleasure, our path will mark out an *oscillation* between Bourdieu, de Certeau and a third option: the theory of otherness, as this seems to offer a means to approach these apparent 'other forces'. This theory of the difference which is bound up in our notion of identity ('I' is 'not-you', 'not-he', 'not-she'; 'we' is 'not-them') is both *dramatic* – it is oppositional, within the framework of difference-in-sameness set out above – and it permeates a wide range of discourses of the 1980s. It takes a twentieth-century impetus from discourses and practices of neo-Freudian psychoanalysis of the French school. But the discourses and practices of psychoanalysis are themselves institutionalised modes of knowledge, and we have already seen that the strategic actions which ensue from these models are not adequate in themselves to our need. And secondly there are dangers implicit in this component which derive in part from its development through normativising notions of 'deviancy' or 'inadequacy' or 'abnormalcy'. Thirdly, the theory seems to be couched in terms of gender difference, wherein the norm for theory appears to be male. What is the place of the actor and for theatre practice and for the spectator, in an order marked out between social adequacy/inadequacy, between normalcy/deviancy, between the male defined by opposition to the female, and between exhibitionism or inverse hysteria in the performer, and voyeurism in the onlooker? Can we sidestep some of the institutionalised elements and some of the automatisms of applications of the theory, while retaining what is useful in it?

In de Certeau the 'common person' laughs, because the theoretical discourse, self-appointedly standing for her-him, for 'how/what/who she or he is/does/is done to in the world', does not wholly invade and organise that person's self-world, even as it organises what we take to be its main lines, its larger entities and phenomena. For Ulmer and Touraine, our contemporary 'performance society' makes of all of us performers, and from this point of view the actor does no more than perfect the acquisition of skills, resources of energy, and the means to their use, which function effectively in the particular conditions of *professional* performance. Now, the conditions producing performance and what these conditions activate in the professional actor, and in the spectator, do seem to relate closely to basic 'scenes' of the discourses of psychoanalysis, and to this extent we should be unwise to ignore them.

Uptake founded in pleasure

What I mean by 'uptake founded in pleasure' is this: while my own pleasure at, for example, the Warner/Shaw/Sophocles *Electra* (RSC, Barbican Pit, 1988–9) was not, as I shall relate, consistent in its choice of focus-points with that of my partner, I am assured that my partner's pleasure was as strong as my own. In case this might seem to betoken a wholly individualised pleasure Habermas' social theory warns us against (in Foster, 1983), other members of the audience and audiences would take up aspects related to our differing experiences, without necessarily focusing on moments at which our specific uptake of features was strongest, nor activating the same elements of what might elsewhere be validly called a socially-acquired taste. Without this assumption of strength of collective response, and equally of divergence in the specificities of that pleasure, I am unable to see how a *metteur en scène* can be called successful, how stagings may be said to 'work', but at the same time how different critics are both unanimous in their praise, and keen to select and focus on quite different 'angles' of the performance, and modes of understanding, in order to develop certain sorts of critical discourse.

Discourse as the other of performance?

But the pleasure is complex, and one aspect of it lies in the 'otherness' of a new symbolic production: the 'talking/writing about performance' interaction with it, which follows it. At this point, I am more concerned with other 'productions', and with other economies, whose working signals itself through changes in spectator activity – but at the same time I shall want to try to relate these 'productions' to voicing, to uses of dramatic writing, to 'ways of talking about performance', and to critical discourse. I have already alluded to those 'arrests' or 'captures' which we commonly articulate through expressions like 'I couldn't take my eyes off it' – indicating a fixing or focusing of attention, experienced at different points by different spectators – and which seem paradoxically 'to work' through a working *against* the momentum of plot/performance event. How might we go about relating this complex experience of performance to that eternal 'thing', 'the dramatic text', and to that modernist 'story', the psyche, to which so many contemporary narratives allude? The path to this 'expansion' of meaningful productions in theatre work seems to come through the different contributions to a theory of *imaging* in its relation to the Symbolic (focused on language), emerging in French theory in the last thirty years. Into this vital scene, if we want to work with words, images and pleasures, we are now obliged to draw (some notion of) the Imaginary, in its relations with the Symbolic.

Pêcheux and discourse analysis

Pêcheux (1984) sets out a perspective derived from his appraisal of discourse analysis as it has recently been practised. In investigating 'the epistemological contexts of discourse analysis' he suggests that the latter (and by extrapolation, the analysis of dramatic writing in/for use in theatre performances):

> does not claim to set itself up as a specialist in interpretation, mastering 'the' meaning of texts, but seeks to construct a number of procedures which expose the reading-gaze to *levels which are opaque to the strategic action of a subject* (e.g. the relationship between syntax and lexical options in the order of utterances, with the effect of interdiscursivity induced into this order of utterances, in the form of the unspoken [*le non-dit*] which emerges through it as either another discourse, a discourse of an other, or the discourse of the absolute Other, [the unconscious]). (pp. 15–16: my translation and emphasis)

The question here is no longer limited to what writing can conventionally be said 'to stand for' or to represent 'iconically, indexically or symbolically', or even 'to generate'. Pêcheux's study of these intrusions is complex. He posits three orders of inter-discursive intrusions or admissions (to which will be added other modes of practice) – i.e.:

- another discourse: e.g. contemporary, assimilated feminism, Freudianism, and so on, which the production 'seems to be about' (but without any explicit allusion);

- the discourse of an other: e.g. legal discourse; anthropological discourse;

- the discourse of the Other: i.e. the repressed and un-speakable 'discourse' of my unconscious which conventionally is absolutely barred to my intervention, only available through psychoanalysis which 'narrates' a version of it.

He suggests that we need to attempt to break down, and to look at the interplay between, different orders of discursive and other-than-discursive play. The *mise en scène* and the work of the actor on text and in specific performance conditions might provide us with the impetus, the parameters for and the local cues for our individual and collective production of this play. The means are not fixed, but are conditioned by an exploration seeking those moments at which the given viewing subject perceives material liable – for that specific user – to activate 'traces in a stock of memories'. This is activated through interdiscursivity and other practices which will be both socially conditioned and individually hierarchised and valorised.

For Ulmer (1989), this is the means to the wide dissemination and often the 'fictionalisation' of 'expert discourses': through the media in general, through dramas, novels and anecdote. Here the 'expert discourse' is drawn in as an 'unsaid' of the initial text, plausibly appearing, after the event of one such use – for example, across prime-time news broadcast at a given time – to be 'cued' by commonly recurring syntactic or lexical items. Once broadcast, and then assimilated and reused with local and idiosyncratic modification by given subjects, these appear to function for a subject as 'traces from a stock of memories' which are experienced as 'personal'. The stock of memories is collective: World War II to many Europeans and Americans, of a number of generations, provides one example, 1968 another. It is equally singular, in that the stock of memories is not constant and homogeneous across a range of subjects, nor within a given subject's long-term experience, but liable to be differently valorised and hierarchised, to be stacked up and assessed differently against other such 'bundles', and to come into dramatic opposition with that of other members of a supposed 'single community'. Further, the stock of memories will equally include wholly 'idiosyncratic' options. Although we cannot hypothesise as to the nature of these, what is clear is that any recourse to what we might call the 'wholly personal', if it is to be used as a global metaphor for a staging, must be able to activate effective dramatic resonances for a wide spread of spectators – as was the case with much of the work of Tadeusz Kantor.

In this context established by Pêcheux, otherness – other texts, other discourses – intersects with text elements activated in the reading process, and these are then transformed into, *and felt 'already to be'*, 'traces' of a 'something else'. The latter would seem, however, to be strongly of the order of the user's, rather than of the writer's, felt-world. It seems that through this process the user activates a stream of intertextual and interdiscursive resonances, and that the collective nature of theatre practice is such that a number of users' 'resonance-stocks' will be brought, often through different symbolic modes – discussion/design/bodywork/showing/sound – to intersection, negotiation, contestation and compromise, under the constraint of pre-performance conditions.

The proliferation of different 'readings' (stagings) of a piece of dramatic writing in the 1970s owed much to the practitioner's bringing to the synoptic (or 'inert', "in place" (Halliday, 1987), materially given, pre-read) text, other 'bodies' or scenarios of knowledge (or discourse), to which the text seemed to its reader–director to allude, through (an often-called 'intuitive' appraisal of) specific lexical items, thematic systems, and indices of actional frames. This given-into-user complex then formed the basis for a design construct – and a power-complex, in that it set out to overcode the actorly options – which dominated the visible production. In the climate of burgeoning interest in 'human sciences' where common structures were posited to operate to regulate different orders of human experience, we saw Genet's *The Maids* conjugated in terms of the boxing match, *Galileo* in terms of science fiction, *Hamlet* as Freudian psychoanalytic scene, *The*

Tempest as dreamwork, and a number of 'anthropological' and 'ethnological' stagings of dramatic fictions. The 'iconicity' was in the directorially-posited relationship between one conceptual 'structure' or 'skeleton' derived from 'experience of the world', and another in the use of dramatic writing, and it was summarised along these lines: 'this is positively pugilistic; it *works like* a boxing match'; 'that reads like a session of psychoanalysis'; 'the pace here is like a game of squash' (which is how the Planchon team at the TNP in Lyon are said to have conceived of the play of dialogue in the Kahane translation of Pinter's *No Man's Land* (Seuil, 1979)).

The involuntary subject

What we find in this notion of an otherness 'within', which we cannot neatly attribute to authorial intention, nor necessarily to user intention – the *metteur en scène* may only be exercised by the need to 'look for something usable', where the criteria for a given practitioner's notion of usability may be relatively fluid; or may mediate another 'social structure' as instance of unwilled interdiscursivity – is an element of *involuntary* intrusions, of unwilled connections. We find it, already, in the idea of fascination, where 'I couldn't take my eyes off them': there is a force at work here, with which the subject is complicit but to which she cedes control. If this *unsaid* or discursive otherness of dramatic writing can be attributed in 1970s' practice firstly to the *habitus,* secondly to 'discursive context', and thirdly to 'theatrical context', as these are mediated by a practitioner who often wants to claim 'inspiration' or 'intuition', and only then to the conscious strategy of the theatre practitioner, it can no more be attributed to wholly conscious strategies of the dramatic writer, whom we might now view as mediator to them. In the instance of differing spectator uptake I have briefly alluded to, we need not assume those instances of uptake were determined through conscious interpretive strategies – although it seems obvious that the spectatorial position is one of *willed* desire: I *want to see, want to speculate, want to know.*

But if these strategies are in part involuntary, how do we depict them in discourse, given that the term 'strategy' itself implies a quasi-institutionalised control? The agent, in this case, is either unspecified, or, if specified (for example, through the frame of psychoanalysis), is a mythical, universal but invisible founding scene only decipherable indexically (as tics and coughs are used as symptoms in the patient) from a manifest dramatic conflict. Agency is articulated in this process of deciphering, through a dramatised kinship scene (cf. Levi-Strauss, 1963). On the other hand, on the basis of our 'feeling', it seems difficult to avoid the hypothesis that these strategies emerge from an activity of what is widely called the **un**-conscious (and perhaps the pre-conscious). We have two ways of approaching these notions: through the discourses of psychoanalysis and their various uses; and through Bourdieu's notion of "forgotten history".

Ulmer/Pêcheux: the unsaid

Before we proceed to an examination of some aspects of the discourses and practices resumed under the heading of 'psycho-analytic theory', let us return to the Ulmer and Pêcheux outline. This outline for a complex user and context-specific *production* (both 'expert' and anecdotal) does not lead to 'better' practices of interpretation 'on other levels'. It directs us instead to the elaboration of procedures or work practices, which might elicit, between text givens and user-context specifics, the sorts of practices which can be brought into play in any use of dramatic text in performance. If I add *other practices* to the discursive, it is because as spectator I wish to include such somatic and affective activity as I am involved in when I hold my breath, feel hot all over, cannot take my eyes off some element of performance practice, as well as the heat of my applause (or lack of it). If these moments remain relatively and happily un-speakable, in terms of coherent, explicatory discourse, then it is indeed an other of discourse which (refuses to) act(s). But is more than this at work? The practitioner makes explicit decisions in terms of such spectator activities. What do these decisions entail, and when are they produced?

From 'interdiscursivity' to 'interpraxis'

We need to expand our appraisal of relations mediated by discourse but activated by uses of perceived traces of 'otherness' to include the relations, vital to our project, between dramatic text *and other practices*: everyday practice is conventionally approached as the other (the unwritable, unspeakable) of logocentricism – but equally so of the delicate and magical language–experience relation in theatre. The actor and the *metteur en scène* look, keenly, everywhere, and are able to retain and draw on complex imaging which, through *some kind of transformation,* can produce complex actions and concrete images *never before acted or constituted* by those practitioners, capable of producing in them the *frisson* which a so far unfelt sensation can produce. In this case, it seems that the practitioner's reading practice, prior to staging, will as keenly seek (or engender) 'traces' said to be in the text, traces which *cue other practices*. We need then to expand Pêcheux's terms of reference to include not just interdiscursivity, but 'interpraxis'. I give examples of this in Part III, below.

This 'interpraxis', cued through practitioner-uses of dramatic writing, is not limited to the straightforward processing which occurs through the writerly use of an actional frame – for example, the didascalies '*She makes breakfast'*, which is a highly economical cue to a complex set of processes which actors in different cultures, or depicting other cultures, will quite differently perform, in different types of spatial layouts, and to differing rhythms. The processing has a **'minimal–logical' enactment potential**, highly codified, which forms the strategic basis for an individual 'interpretation' – as indice, for instance, of 'social/theatrical conformity', or of an 'idiosyncratic actor/character complex'. Theatre practitioners do not, however, remain at this order of the 'minimal logical' of their cultural practice (even in the 'theatre of the everyday'). This **complex multi-modal praxis** is another instance of cued 'otherness' of dramatic writing-in-use, and, once again, it is difficult to attribute it to the conscious or willed intervention of any participant – which is far from saying that the practitioner will not at a later phase *lucidly* control, exercise, repeat and thus 'stage' the products of those 'leaps' of involuntary connection. What recurs is the *involuntary* component in that text-to-practice processing, which some of us commonly experience when an image 'pops up in the mind' of something which we *did not know we had seen*. The actor can *in some instances* go further, to sketch out in time and space that complex option s/he does not know s/he has seen.

But what are we to make of those other images which seem to 'pop into mind'? Some of them seem to be akin to those images I do not record, which I rapidly pass over, which trouble me, in certain of my uses of performance. In wide use in recent French theory is a notion which attempts to account for these elements: it is the theory of the absolute Other.

The absolute other

As we have seen, Pêcheux (1984) included "the discourse of the (absolute) Other" in his development of a schema incorporating different orders of intrusion into the reading process. So doing he drew into the range of interpretive procedures (included in mainstream discourse analysis), those which relate to contemporary narrations of a determining force, barred to the voluntary action of the subject, but apparently rich in implications for interpretation and pleasure. But where or what is the absolute Other of the subject, and what causes/permits 'it' to work its works? Does it entail a barred 'language' ('what I absolutely can't say') and if so is such a language implicated in an image-production; does it organise an imaging; is it incidental to an imaging; or is it in fact not a language at all?

It is of absolute importance, in the context of our text-politics of the dramatic-writing/performance relationship, whether it is – as Lacan (1977), in the fullness of his logocentricity ("even Freud was taken in by . . . the idea that thought is communicated without words", in Blonsky, 1985, p. 204) claimed – "structured like a language". The formulation is obscure, but it has vital implications for the theatre stage and for the images we produce on it; for their relation to what is not of that stage; and for the ways in which certain aspects of the stage will start in us something like a dreaming. For Lacan, as for Freud (**but unlike the participants in theatre**), the sole medium available for the intersubjective communication that analysis is, is seen to be language.

But 'language', for Lacan (in Blonsky, 1985), is not after all 'the major communicative tool' some take it to be despite the apparent unitary nature and *clarity* of its signifiers, because "the subject [i.e. the speaker] is marked from the beginning by division". 'Being clear', then, is a widely sustained illusion, and this illusory clarity means that we have to look "beyond the pleasantries about communication" (Blonsky, 1985, p. 204). Instead, language works not by communicating through the neat exchange of tokens or signs between consenting participants, but by **evocation;** and evocation is not precise and unitary *in effect*, but spreads and flows.

The unconscious, if "structured like a language", is not however a 'text', but 'another scene', a 'scene of an Other' (and not this conscious one), into which it however intrudes. Note the connection, here, with Bourdieu's (1977, p. 78) loaded scenes of present action, and their links with 'forgotten history', to which I return below. As scene – or stage – we might suppose it to be characterised by complex moving images and by scenarios, rather than by elements akin to the textual; by evocative forces rather than by the linear combination of minimal and larger units of signification. But, if we want to take this metaphor further, *who* or *what* can we identify as *metteur en scène* of this stage (cf. Lyotard, in Benamou and Caramello, 1977)? For Lacan it is the site where "something's going on, I can tell you"; something which *thinks itself* "rather badly", even as – especially as – we are thinking in the more banal, everyday sense of the term (Lacan, 1977, p. 193). 'Thinking rather badly', here, is curious. What it does imply however is a short-circuiting between 'conscious intent', on the one hand, and on the other what our actions (discursive *and other*) are loaded with, with which they resonate.

Now, what we might suppose from the Lacanian formula, despite his explicit rejection of the notion (Lacan, 1974, p. 194), is that we have before us once again the model of the double, dominated by the process of secondary appropriations: if this is the case, then the evocative scene of the Other is less "structured like a language", than symptomatically revealed – or perhaps *to be constituted* – through language in the context of analysis, where what is said is always that gap which opens up within *what can be said/wants to say itself*, to the analyst. But in theatre we are not constrained by and to speech – although *not speaking* is my condition, and my role in a contract, as spectator.

Not speaking, but looking intensely, my function is not that of the analyst who listens, but rather that of the particular function to/for whom the actor/stage/*metteur en scène* will show something intensely evocative (rather than communicative), on condition that I do not speak; and through which, in these sorts of terms, will equally be evoked elements of that other (materially unseen) scene (the scene of the Other). What is evoked will only be shared if the unconscious is shared in the nature of its stagings. Can we assume likeness here? What are the operatives and determiners of the nature of this Other scene? By way of contrast, what the material stage will overtly show is always conditioned in terms of the practitioners' conception of what the (spectator) other could/would/should/should not see (the scene of the spectator other).

But if we accept the premise of 'greater forces' outlined earlier in Part II, then it does seem, as well, that the evocative force of this material scene is not limited to or by this willed effort. Theatre is peculiar amongst the visual media in that it seems to depend significantly for its evocative effects, on the conjunction of a writing by an other in the names of fictional others, with a *metteur en scène*, but exposed through the work of live actors (and not merely their filmic images), precisely in order that the stage *might* (at best) reveal to us that which the actor as self-willed subject would not show or does not know that s/he shows (because my self-image is always a fiction, a frozen moment of a control impossible to sustain in life). S/he shows her/his incorporation of the others of dramatic staging, for and in terms of the others (spectators) who look and listen. This highly-charged conjucture is, in consequence, not just 'immensely evocative' in its potential *standings-for*, but not wholly controlled by the function of will and intent.

Now, what Lacan suggests with regard to this complex conjuncture of 'relations between divided participants', is that they are all 'mediated by the Other'. That is, they are all subject to forces emanating from the struggles of the actor-unconscious, just as, in other participants, that mediation similarly intervenes. That intense negotiation and compromise, between a number of participants, is shadowed by scenes of struggle, whose terms are *absolutely* Other to the given participant as self-knowing. Nonetheless, this complex hidden scene – and consequently, *mise en scène* as its outward face of struggle (cf. Lyotard, 1977) – is for Lacan constituted from discrete elements, from signifiers (defined by their difference from each other), and consequently **decipherable**. Indeed Lacan's profession, not as writer but as psychoanalyst, depends upon that decipherability: his theory is thus interested. But the alternative possibility – which he draws on Freud to refute – that the unconscious is composed of "protomorphic proliferations of the image, . . . vegetative intumescences, . . .

animic halos irradiating from the palpitations of life" (Lacan, 1977, p. 195), might seem to be more useful to our attempt at understanding the imagings which lead to the constitution and use of performance. Secondly, these "protomorphic proliferations of the image" might seem rather closer to the "forgotten history" as unconscious we find in Bourdieu, provided, and only provided, we begin to acquire our habitus prior to the acquisition of language, and not as a 'pre-linguistic' or 'proto-linguistic' mode of symbolic activity. If this is the case, then our unconscious is the trace of forgotten – and now 'blurred', on partial recall – socio-economic conditions articulated, in the everyday, through gender divisions of nurturing and absence, through acts of affection and domestic violence, through those 'corrections' to the infant which articulate, within the family, the personalised–naturalised socio-economic conditions and relations (*who* caresses and feeds the infant; *who* leaves on a daily basis and is thus less available; *who* bathes/changes/toilet-trains?).

The 'protomorphic' scene, which Lacan attributes to the Jungian school, is rejected by Lacan (1977), because it neglects "the directing function of a signifying articulation, which takes effect from *its internal law* and from a material subjected to the poverty that is essential to it" (p. 195: my emphasis). The unconscious, on the contrary:

> prior to all analysis . . . is *articulated* . . . in its discrete elements. This is most important, for these elements are those that linguistic analysis forces us to isolate as signifiers, and here they are seen at work in their purest form at the most unlikely, yet most likely point . . . (p. 194: my emphasis)

The point of their working is both the most unlikely, and the most likely: most unlikely, because they function in a relation of radical difference (they are un-like) from the subject ("as yet undecipherable hieroglyphics in the solitude of the desert"). Happily for the profession, only the psychoanalyst can bring the subject to the condition of being able to 'read'/speak these (in the terms the psychoanalyst can 'read' already). (Note that this is far from Bourdieu's "forgotten [naturalised] history" (1977, p. 78), since the forgotten can be recalled, whereas the repressed, here, must be produced.) They are simultaneously "most likely", because it is in this relation of radical opposition itself, and itself alone, that their semiosis, or rather, production, can occur.

Challenging the master

Now, the apparently *radical oppositionality* of the Lacanian semiotics of the subject has elicited a largely dramatic response from a number of groups and commentators. For Wilden (1980):

[a]s it is becoming necessary to insist, Imaginary and either/or relationships remain dominant in our society, and in such a way that in general our system's both-and (cooperative) relations are derived from the either/or socioeconomic reality, rather than from the socioecological imperative of 'both system (at one level) and environment (at another)' to which the either/or must ultimately be subordinate if the system is to survive.

(p. xxxiii, n. 8)

Here either/or relationships are marked by and thereafter lead to the performance of *something like a violence*, in the use of the cut or slash itself, and in their practices of inclusion and prioritisation, versus exclusion and devalorisation. For Lacan this violence seems to be inscribed, as the radical break or rupture in the relation between the One/the Other, which alone permits their very definition, since:

it is a truth of experience for analysis that the subject is pre-sented with the question of his existence, . . . as an articulated question: 'What am I there?', concerning his sex and his contingency in being, namely, that, on the one hand, he is a man or a woman, and, on the other, that he might not be, the two conjugating their mystery, and binding it in the symbols of procreation and death. (p. 194)

The subject, in this conception, desires to be clearly either X or non-X, precisely because he [*sic*] fears he might not clearly be the one: it requires the conjunction of the two to produce him. He is *of woman*, and must therefore, to assure himself of his manhood, struggle to contest his own doubts by fighting with the one and mating with the other: "That the question of his existence bathes the subject, supports him, invades him, tears him apart even, is shown in the tensions, the lapses, the phantasies the analyst encounters . . . " (p. 194).

Psychoanalysis aside, this reads either like a critique of certain dramatic works by Pinter, or like a mid-twentieth-century treatise on Greek drama. This is less flippant than it might appear: the scenes are equally dramatic, and similarly marked, and they seem to articulate, in less or more popularised modes, 'expert discourses' of twentieth-century modernism. If this is the case, then what we find in Lacan, in Pinter, and in mid-twentieth-century readings of Greek classics, is less a universal theory of human subjectivity, than a wholly historical, relative theory, informed by historically prevailing epistemes.

From this perspective the either/or 'violence of the Imaginary' is not immanent to the Imaginary and to the subject; it comes instead from the decision-making processes of the wider economy of capitalist societies, here controlled by socio-economic reality (to Wilden a pejorative term), which produce passionate competitiveness between advocates of the one and the other: **either** Left or Right; **either** government-funded women's health services, **or** increased spending on defence; **either** that play exposing racism, or *Les Misérables*; **either** a new library, **or** a new students' records system.

Now, one of the major either/or orders which dominates Lacanian discourse, and the critiques brought to bear upon it, is the drama of gender difference, and the plethora of exclusion/inclusions and value judgements initiation into this order entails. This divided gendered field has seemed, since Freud re-read the Greek myths and constructed his theories from the intersection of his myth-reading and the ways in which he perceived casework, to be the inescapable destiny not just of women and men, but of cultural theory itself – and some 1970s feminist critiques did nothing to diminish this, since the politics of their position reassert the logic even as they attack it.

It seems, for our position in the 1990s, that while this *gendered scene* is no less vital to the ways in which human subjects can conduct their everyday affairs, it might be the case that theatre offers a privileged site in which we can show means to the *effective performance* of modes of play which flow across, which subvert, and which critique clear gender roles – however much, in late-twentieth-century industrialised contexts, we see women actors called upon to embody male writers' representations of Woman. It might seem, secondly, that certain of the perspectives outlined by Lacan (1977), relating explicitly to "a man or a woman" (p. 194), and the notion of the struggles of the One and the Other (but less **between** clearly opposed poles, than **within** the blur of the conjunction of man with woman), might enable us to better understand the troubling scene of dramatic choices and of casting choices. When Mnouchkine consistently throughout the 1980s and into the 1990s, chooses to foreground the intensely worked image of Georges Bigot, which seems to present "something of the order of pain, of a character painful to perceive because he is slightly deranged. So we get the feeling or the vision – and it is this which is superb – of a certain gulf, of loss or perdition" (*Fruits*, 2/3, June 1984, my adaptation), we are obliged and entitled to ask to what extent this woman's work can be typified – as is that of Deborah Warner with Fiona Shaw – by this choice of gendered images of pain which encompass not just the order of the represented but equally the order of the exposed working person of the actor. Since this contemporary theatre practice wins huge audiences and wide acclaim, for both groups of practitioners, it does seem that we have to have recourse to some notion of the Other (here, the Mother-function) as instigator of the sight of real actorly pain for the spectator–other. But this interventionary force which cannot speak its name (for fear of accusations of sado-masochism), emerges *historically* as Actor, and not universally. It emerges quite precisely in the context of a society otherwise dominated by electronic media.

This particular observation of 'women's work' emerges, it must be said, in a climate called 'post-feminist' as well as postmodern. The earlier climate saw a radical confrontation of the gendered theory of Lacan, because of the sorts of myths which emerged from his observations. A version of the 'neo-Freudian myth' needs to be related here, and not just because of its apparent plausibility when we review certain highly popular mainstream productions emerging from Hollywood cinema. It is revealing – but differently; we need to avoid facile borrowings – when we reconsider the canon of dramatic writing, used in English-language traditions.

Once upon a time . . .

The neo-Freudian myth goes something like this: in the beginning, in gender-divided cultures, the child at birth, not by dint of its anatomy ('the thing itself') but by dint of social observations of anatomy ('Congratulations! It's a boy!'), the newborn infant is ushered into gendered cultural practice. We need to be clear here: it is not 'having the thing itself' which ushers the infant in, but the social engagement (looking and naming) with *the signs of difference*. On the basis of **observed signs of difference**, the child is introduced by these and other such mediators, into roles and relations within the larger complex networks of difference. But the story is more complicated than this, since this ushering-in then equips the child with 'appropriate' and naturalised modes of thought and behaviour: the child approached as having *the sign of maleness* sees the child *without the signs* (and this is where woman is negated, is thereafter defined and self-defining as negativity within the patriarchal dominion) not just as other – no-man – but as cut, castrated, as less-than-male; as absence where maleness is the network of systemic options conjugated in terms of presence-of-sign. Conceiving the female in properly dramatic form, the male-child perceives her (and thus looked-at, she perceives herself) as formerly male and now castrated (anato-symbolically, in her actional modes, her relations with man and with the world) and fears that she will cause the same to happen to him. The castration complex causes him thereafter to adopt, to prefer and to produce *fantasies of Woman*, in cultural practices, in which 'she' is staged in dramas which treat this fear, allaying it or overcoming it or demonstrating and then neutralising its threat to the male or to patriarchal norms and values, through the oppositional components of plot. Women as actors in our own theatre lend their work – just as Glenn Close does, for example, in the film *Fatal Attraction* – to these fantasies staged by men, and thus complicate the representationality of the dramas (Electra is a male fantasy of Woman, whereas Fiona Shaw's Electra represents, through Shaw's work, contemporary *women* as well as Warner's enunciation of the male writer's fantasy of Woman); whereas the Ancient Greek and the Elizabethan stages – and *kabuki*, too – used males to perform such fantasies of Woman – Antigone, Electra, Medea, Cordelia, Portia.

What we find in the myth propagated by Lacan's intervention

recalls Bourdieu's *habitus*. But where the latter, in Bourdieu's narration, is determined by class seen to be clearly oppositional – and so determined once and for all – for Lacan it is the observation-of-gender-difference which provides the initiatory scene, in which the onlooker, mediating established gender structures, is entailed as vital (in much the same way as is the spectator in performance).

This seems then to be less final than is the construct in Bourdieu: *if* the onlookers, mediating a shifting gender-scene, could be brought to differently perceive and differently attribute values to newborn infants, then it would begin to seem possible that the major initiation process would not be into a culture marked out along the lines of a gender battle. But this needs a widespread shift in everyday perceptions, enabled by a major shift in the dissemination of alternative epistemes which might, at the very least, coexist with the modernist episteme of identity founded in clear difference. For Lacan's radical semiotic, subjectivity is forged through absolute difference, but he has always been ambivalent, as we shall see, as to the differing values of perception of difference, versus immanence of difference: if biological difference and violence do not dominate the founding scene, but mark an historically specific version peaking under twentieth century modernism – i.e. in the context in which Lacan formulated and published his theories – then it does seem possible that cultural theory and human subjects can to some extent at least escape a social determinism for which biological difference is used as emblem.

But where are female children in the neo-Freudian myth? Besides being 'man's problem', and 'taking no place', the girl-child in the everyday internalises the male's look of fear-and-fascination. She then lives it out through the masquerade which veils her anatomy and becomes her **performance of a 'femininity'** designed to alleviate – and in certain circumstances to speak directly to: the coquette, Madonna, the stereotypical whore used as object – the male's pathological fear and horror: the smile, the downcast eye, the painted lip and lid, the curl and fluff of the hair, the flounce and whisper of 'feminine' skirts; the apologist, the virgin, the mother, the nanny, nursemaid – each (according to the myth) is a classic performance by women (and by certain gays) to the male's fetishisation of 'less problematic' or deproblematised elements of the female anatomy.

When we are working through these sorts of terms, what we begin to see is that consistently in the dramatic tradition Woman is the site of conflicts which test a patriarchal social order, and that as consistently Woman 'must be' removed from the scene for 'resolution', or an access into 'understanding', to 'occur' – removed by death, suicide, marriage, reproduction. This might lead us to declare that if it is now felt that Hedda Gabler 'appeals to women in the 1990s', that 'Ibsen was good with women', it is the suicide, as patriarchal plot-strategy, which seems to play out the male fantasy, and which points up the male anxiety: what does she want? What does she threaten? What to do with it, to minimise the damage? The answer is clear, and rather too consistently performed by male dramatic writers: delete the threat (suicide (*Hedda Gabler, Antigone*)); mercy-killing (*Betty Blue/37° 2 le matin*); insanity; containment, within the new kinship unit, by 'happy (ever after) marriage', reproduction, and so on). In the 1990s 'Hedda', enacted by any woman, could simply laugh and leave, without even slamming the door, thereby taking up Barthes' suggestion for Iphigénie (1963), sidestepping the confrontational.

Or, if the *metteur en scène* wishes to retain a degree of conformity to the text-options, despite contemporary disbelief in the fantasy of a suicide provoked in a probably pregnant woman by an unhappy or missed love affair/marriage/adultery, the decision Warner (Dublin and London, 1991) takes is available: she breaks into the temporal/tension structure at the moment of Hedda's final departure, leaving Tesman and Mrs Elvsted and Brand onstage, in such a way that expectation is suspended and, thus supended, weakens and then flags. The gunshot, and various responses, are thereby defused, the death is trivialised *as plot-strategy*, rather than as 'human choice': the energy gap forced lets in the spectator's questioning, and can thereby be used as indice of possible attitude in *mise en scène* and *metatext* (Pavis, 1985). Naturalism's convention of 'human choice' within social determinism is replaced in gravity by the loss from view of Shaw's finely energetic work. The spectator must spring active into that gap, to attempt to understand its place in Warner's enunciation as a mode of women's action in the 1990s; or else condemn this particular performance-option as wrong-footed direction.

Sidestepping masters of knowledge

If we shake ourselves loose from the desire to *wholly believe*, from
the quest for a universally valid theory and a master discourse able
to explain for us 'theatre itself', 'the spectator', 'the audience' or
'the self', then what we find is pleasing in its smallness: Lacan,
seen from the 1990s, is not 'wrong' – this would be imprudent, and
its force is unnecessary – but historicised. His theoretical discourse
is demonstrated to be less a universal truth, the Other less a
founding scene, than a plausible narration and scenario, couched
in the terms, fed by the dramatised epistemes, appropriate to
certain of the socio-historical conditions and mind-sets available
when it was constituted. As a 'way of (partly) knowing' in the
1990s, it is relativised, rather than confronted, and the pertinency
of some of the observations which emerge from it, as explanations
of certain elements of recent history which still cling on in many
fields of cultural practice, can be retained.

Other approaches to otherness

Wilden's critique was more confrontational: besides suggesting
that we might try to expose Lacan as the master exposing masters
(of knowledge), he goes further, drawing, not surprisingly, on
Marcuse, to suggest that *we already know* what we want to know.
The implication for our approach to performance is this: we should
draw out and replay under performance lights, what we
consistently *do*, casting aside, for the purpose of the experiment,
what we are taught to say about it. 'Knowing', here, like de
Certeau's somatic action as thought, is not lodged in established
discourse, and need not, thus, incline its head to the brilliant,
reflected (false) image of masterly discourse. After all, says Wilden:

> [r]eading Lacan – especially his later work – is so tortuous and
> difficult that one hesitates to recommend him to the reader. . . .
> As one who 'knows', Lacan is above all devoted to the
> destruction of the status of the "subject-who-is-supposed-
> to-know". But we cannot destroy the master by simply taking
> his place; we have to make him IRRELEVANT – and that means to
> reduce his mastery to insignificance by transcending the
> oppositional relationship *in which we find ourselves in a negative
> identification with him. To destroy exploitative mastery, we must do*

more than become the negative complement of the master, his mirror-image; we must know what he knows, which, in essence, is nothing we don't already know. (1980, pp. 29–30: my emphasis)

The terms are strong, and once again they participate in the very logic (and violence) they seek to challenge. But at the same time, perhaps there is something here we can, in the 1990s' modes, use.

What we already (somatically) know

Common sense suffered an assault in the 1970s when it was seen, with some justice, as a major but dispersed locus for hegemonic dissemination of dominant discourses and practices – which did not thus need coercion for their implementation. They could be diffused and painlessly absorbed through the Church, education and the media, and 'uwittingly', reproduced by users of these 'in the name of common sense', in everyday talk and action. But there is no more reason to exclude from some instances of common sense practice, a certain pragmatic validity, than there is to exclude from 'old wives' tales' the possibility that they purvey valid treatments which science is then pleased to be able to 'discover'. We can acknowledge that this is the scene for the everyday enactment of a dominant ideology – of which our ways of seeing, understanding and acting are irresistibly part – attempting to perceive how this grid of knowledges intervenes, and what it makes us but also lets us do, without needing to attempt the impossible goal of overthrowing it.

Otherness in everyday guise

In common sense terms, as I have demonstrated, the reach of the notion of 'otherness', within the ways in which we approach the diverse phenomena of theatre, is considerable, and we can further justify this complexity introduced through use of Pêcheux, by recourse to terms used in the everyday of critical practice: two major metaphors which attempt to deal with the problematic Pêcheux confronts, commonly recur in critical practice, where they function as sleight of hand within the semiotic (and hermeneutic) process. One notes that a given text 'works on several levels'. The other adds that 'reading between the lines', we can work out what the author 'is (really) alluding to'. Dramatic writing, often perceived to be 'under-written' in comparison with other fictional modes, 'holed' (*troué*) according to Ubersfeld (1977), seems particularly susceptible to 'between-line' 'readings'. We need to newly approach this, however, as an inventive practice, always attributed elsewhere in a 'move' which reveals a staging of conventionalised knowledges specific to user-context rather than to the context of text-production. Text-activation is thus an activation of the text's other, an 'unsaid' specific to the user-context. The notion of 'subtext' attempts to attribute what the perceptive, semiotising user activates, to an authorial/authoritative source. *Theatre uses* of dramatic writing, in turn, lodged in a given, double materiality (theatrical and 'material real'), seem to lend themselves to hierarchised strategies of interpretation 'on other levels', as do the 'indexical' and 'symbolic' theatre-semiotic strategies, in that they produce a 'stood-for' which is 'unlike', but apparently 'hinted at by' the performance givens. What we need is a new understanding of the specifics of dramatic writing for staging, where the clause and the transclausal complex are perceived as parameters to a user-experience, *but are not synonymous with that experience itself.* Nor are they a means to attributing a like experience to text producer.

Common sense dangers: mediating 'the whole human semiotic'

By contrast, another practice needs absolutely to be interrogated at the point of its emerging, commonsensically, from 'what we already know'. In this instance, we are dealing with a taught, curriculum-specific, discursive scenario, used in the conversion of a text-materiality into 'something (quite) else'. It is a **minimal-logical otherness** mediated by the reader, entailing, amongst other components, reader-contemporary notions of acting, staging and characterisation. These seem to operate as a series of conceptual schemata or transparencies, overlaid upon each other and 'aligned' with text-specifics, through which, at conventional points, we produce certain categories of knowledge. Attributed through the reading convention of 'character', we find the projection of the user-perception of what Halliday (1978) calls 'the whole human semiotic'. It now includes, for example, the expert Freudian discourse assimilated into everyday interpretive practice. This is projected, with other models of knowledge, onto a writing which is historically or culturally other – e.g. Shakespeare's or Sophocles' or Zeami's texts. The complex textuality from which we derive 'Cordelia' or 'Electra' or 'Hanjo' loses its writerly materiality within a stage script (where it anticipated play by male actors) and becomes instead a 'young woman', 'who', in terms of the contemporary whole human semiotic, 'has' and 'is' what current readers attribute to late-twentieth-century young women . . . including sexual choice and a psyche overseen by Freud. In these sorts of terms, Hunter (1983) analyses the wholly historically-specific construction, popularised through European educational norms of the late nineteenth century, of fictional character in terms of 'moral hygiene', 'moral interiority'.

In Ulmer (1989) we find the suggestion that this process entails the dramatisation and fictionalisation of a number of 'expert discourses', derived from the popularisation of the human sciences, and assimilated into the ways of explaining the everyday through the intermediary of conceptual frames naturalised through schooling and elements of the media. The danger emerges once Freudian discourse is accepted in terms of its own claims: i.e. as a universally valid theory of 'the way we are'. What seems to be at work is a 'social' projection, mediated by the user, which selects and combines text traits as these can be similarly located in 'ways of speaking the world', which constitute (in all their complexity) the discursive universe of the user.

Once again, this depends on a supposition of equivalency between writing 'itself', the putative 'structures' of a 'psyche', and the structures of the social. The one is accepted as able to 'stand for' the other; whereas what we might better teach, and learn, is first the means to an understanding of the historical and local bases for that claim, and second the limitations and constraints imposed on what seem to be combinatory modes of cultural practice, where the combination produces something other than the sum of its parts.

Approaching combinations

If the matching of units and structures of units with others perceived to be 'like', and the relating of these to what seem then to be 'unlike' (said/unsaid; word/body; symbolic/semiotic) offers us a certain schooled pleasure, what also plays a part in eliciting empathic responses, such as liking or disliking, and increased attention and interest, is something which seems to 'stage' image-stock able to transcend and blur or confound 'real-world' categories. Such blurring image relations and their effect, seem to draw in a type of 'feeling' of which the user may be unaware, which may well be omitted from 'schooled' verbal processes, which may contradict verbally-espoused processings, while feeding pleasurably into complex processing within cultural practice. Theatre's 'magic' and its 'alchemy' are inadequate metaphors for this experience, which requires of us a new effort of understanding.

Combining difference: analogue and digital: uneasy correspondences

The procedure necessitated by the theory of the 'un-said' is delicate, since it requires that we draw together two sets of systems, defined on the basis of radical difference (e.g. said/ unsaid, conscious/unconscious), and to which we attribute opposed values (e.g. positivity/negativity, revealed/concealed). The mapping of the 'un-said' **of discourse**, as this is approached by Pêcheux, does not include what is vital to us here: the relationships of writing to bodies in performance, and the relationships within writing in their links with 'anticipated bodies'. Are bodies the dramatic writing's 'un-said'? It would be unfortunate if we were to so define their conjunction in performance; but on the other hand it does seem that, unless we textualise the performing body, then we are indeed dealing with interactions between unlike systems. For Wilden (1980), this sort of interaction requires a digital analytical mode, since "[s]ystemic–cybernetic theory shows that digitalization is always necessary when communication crosses the boundary between different states or different systems – and that it creates the boundary in doing so" (p. 28). From this point of view, performance bodies, meeting writing, are necessarily digitalised, and thereby become available to analysis as a complex of units. For Bateson (1978), this is a theory of negativity – for example, 'X' is defined by its boundary with 'not-X' – and a theory of restraints – for example, that slash is a wall, separating and 'holding back' what would otherwise be perceived as a complex and indivisible whole.

[F]rom the cybernetic point of view, a word in a sentence, or a letter within the word, or the anatomy of some part within an organism, or the role of a species in an ecosystem, or the behaviour of a member within a family – these are all (negatively) explained by an anlysis of restraints.

(Bateson, 1978, p. 376)

The body's 'wholeness', however, and the irrefutable flow of its movement and interactions with theatre's others – even when I 'make a specific gesture', the remainder of my body is actively present, and provides a frame and path to the energetic investment to this small production; it cannot be divided if we are to understand performance – need simultaneously to be approached through a theory standing in a relation of complementarity with (and not opposition to) the digital. Conventionally, this slot is filled by the analogue. However:

[t]here is, in fact, almost no formal theory dealing with analogue communication and, in particular, no equivalent of Information Theory or Logical Type Theory. This gap in formal knowledge is inconvenient when we leave the rarefied world of logic and mathematics and come face to face with the phenomena of natural history [where] sometimes . . . there is continuous gradation from the ostensive through the iconic to the purely digital. (p. 262)

What should perturb us in Bateson's account is his suggestion that it:

would seem that analogic communication is in some sense more primitive than digital and there is a broad evolutionary trend toward the substitution of digital for analogic mechanisms. This trend seems to operate faster in the evolution of internal mechanisms than in the evolution of external behaviour.

(p. 262)

In these dangerous terms, our theatre work, and the nature of the present exploration, are neo-primitive, and can only be retrieved from that 'less-evolved' condition through the sort of quest Pavis typifies: for a metatext or a discourse of the *mise en scène* as manifestations of 'evolved internal mechanisms'. As alternative conceptual frame, we might suppose that the digital and the analogue are always present in a relationship of complementarity, having complementary rather than opposed or differently-valorised values. But we need to remember that the interface between them in theatre work is our own intelligence (often of more than one person: for example, director and technician), which has the complex task of conversion (encoding/decoding/re-encoding) between the two. The digital and analogue, and their possible relations, can, to some extent, be drawn into a relationship of equivalence with de Certeau's complementarities, strategy and tactic. We can then 're-stage', in similar terms, the said/unsaid relation (Pêcheux), reformulating it as the *said and yet-to-say* couplet. This suggests less that the one erupts into the other – as the semiotic does, for Kristeva, into the symbolic – than that the one *used in the context of the other* (e.g. the word used by bodies), is thereby staged in the latter's own specific, simultaneously strategic and tactical, terms. Those bodies bring, irresistibly, the elements of their own Imaginary, but not just in the decipherable terms Lacan signals. Sometimes the Imaginary will intervene as 'nothing more than' (this negativity springs from the sort of value judgements Bateson makes) a particular, *tactical* infusion of heightened energy which is conducted across apparently digital or strategic units.

In dramatic writing, lexical items (table/hand/book/woman) and the naming-function (King Lear/Fool/Cordelia), from the digital perspective, are apparently discrete pips. We can attempt to accept them as such, in the context of reading, drawing them into relations with apparently discrete pips (the thing; the individual) 'in the world'. But dramatic writing once activated engages almost irresistibly with an imaginary scene; and in the hands of professionals, in a pre-performance space, it engages with the intermix of a number of imaginary scenes, newly charged with user-Imaginaries, and secondly with the material-real theatre scene already etched out as a relation with the other. Here we are dealing with the blur between digital or strategic processing and tactical and analogic processings. The latter permits us, as spectators, to appreciate not just a 'possible world' panorama, rather than a cluster of single items, but also a notion of both 'character' and actor as 'someone-in-the-social-world'. Deictics, in dramatic writing (e.g. I/you/he/she; here/there/on/off/in/out; now/then (past)/then(future)), set up parameters to the flow of this analogical work, focusing and restraining the 'spread' of spectator processing (cf. Serpieri *et al.*, 1981, pp. 163–200). But they, like names and lexical items, are only valid as elements of theatre work, **within the relations** they set up within theatre spaces (real and conceptual). 'Table', for example, has no digital function in theatre work, since that apparent 'thing' is meaningless until we locate it within the potential energy-field of a visual or verbal relation with the spectator. Once we do this, we locate the pip within the flow, and its theatre-meaning-potential is thus inscribed in the analogical order, and indivisible from it. Once we accept that 'items', decipherable from a flow through the use of a science such as linguistics, cannot similarly be detached through use of theatre sciences, then we need to elaborate another theory: one of conjuncture, combination, complementarity, synergy, where what are real-world items work precisely because *they lose the clarity of their boundaries.* They function then as peaks or parameters to possible knowledges; but the 'effective theatre content' is always deferred, in expectation of re-contextualisation.

In theatre, unlike in film and television, where the camera intervenes to chart for us the possible movement of the eye, parameters, sites and moments of heightened attentiveness do not preclude my noting, through the periphery of my vision, *something else going on.* This peripheral vision is vital to complex pleasures in Deborah Warner's work for the RSC – (cf. Pontbriand's '"The Eye Finds No Fixed Point . . . "', 1982); but it is fruitless to separate out either the 'parts of the eye', or the 'parts of the scene', as discrete pips.

'Wild' resonances

Beyond the delicate but perhaps unavoidable notion of forces 'staging' what 'comes to mind' in involuntary manner, blending with willed retrievals, it does seem that, in order to understand certain sorts of stage figuring processes and certain sorts of reading processes which do not just 'swell' or expand uptake but which 'resound' with a potential for use, we need to take on the notion of 'forgetting' or of repression. Repression is not interesting in itself, when we are considering theatre processes. It is of interest inasmuch as it seems to produce, and to regulate, certain sorts of productions and transformations of energy.

In suggesting that it is the 'forgotten memory' or the Imaginary that acts – or is activated – here, thereafter intersecting with choices of the reader-user as conscious verbal and somatic strategist and tactician, I am attempting to approach what we commonsensically call 'unexpected resonances', connections and associations which 'come to mind', the blending of image-material which causes us newly to focus attention, to utter 'Ah!' in surprise, delight or recognition, or 'I see!', as the specular turns to speculation and secondary processes. Theatre conventionally positions the spectator somatically in such a way that an Imaginary scene, in each spectator, confronts the material stage (cf. *wayang kulit*, in Java, where the *dalang* and some spectators sit on one side of the screen, other spectators on the other: there are potentially at least two sites for complex projection in this mode). But who or what is it that *stage manages* or directs this highly singular Imaginary scene?

Chapter 6

The Performer, My Other?

In the mid-1980s the term *'imaginaire'*, used to describe the theatre stage, emerges with some force in French commentaries. Suggesting that "[to] represent or not to represent, that is theatre's question!", Georges Banu (1986) explores the recent northern European fascination with Japanese theatre, made concrete in the Mnouchkine/*Théâtre du Soleil* presentation of *Richard II*. In so doing he takes up the thread of inquiry into otherness (and its relation to the one, or the given) which has marked twentieth century theatre theory across the writings of Artaud, Brecht, Barthes and – rather later – Derrida and Lyotard.

But as Banu goes on to indicate, it is not representation itself which is at stake. Rather, it is whether or not theatre can claim, and to what extent it might claim, to represent an extra-theatrical material reality, rather than to *present* the enunciation of a *conception* of that other, the 'real out there'. In invoking the imaginary Banu pushes the question further: to what extent must we now recognise that theatre in general (and some theatres explicitly) presents a complex *imaginary* scene, fed by, and thus representing diagrammatically, indexically/symptomatically or symbolically, hypothetical models of 'forces' deemed to be specific to the scenes of the Imaginary? Brecht, Artaud, and Barthes, we can now recognise, have *imagined* Asian theatre, making of it the scene for the imaginary playing-out of their own desires for the theatre with which they were familiar. That their perspectives are marked by the scenes of their own Imaginary is shown in the ways in which they mythologise difference, producing a drama, a potential for a violence, a complex scenario for change, means to intervention, and something like a potential resolution which might effect change in the other.

For Banu, the project and the processes specific to Mnouchkine/*Théâtre du Soleil* are less confrontational, less didactic. There is no manifesto, advocating confrontation and rupture between the one and the other, but rather (and rather differently from what Barthes admired in *bunraku*) a seamless combination of what is otherwise given as radical difference. In this seamless cobbling together of difference, borne by the global scene but peaking in the work of the actor in *Richard II* (1982), the staging produces (but does not **re**-produce) a personal, nostalgic dream of what *kabuki might be* (and, we might add, of what Shakespeare might be, of what the actor might show, and might offer; of what theatricality might be, in singular (woman's) hands, in the 1980s).

In the seamless combination and harmonisation of historical, esthetic, stylistic and ethnic difference (united only by the desire of the enunciator as symptomatic of wider – but conflictual – socio-cultural desire), the work is explicitly *fiction*. In the terms of psychoanalysis, it is thus marked, irresistibly, by misrecognition. Rather like the subject's image fixed impossibly (in lived terms) in the mirror, but in this instance projected forth onto the practitioner group (the amplification of the one, through the reciprocal contribution of the other), this misrecognition is characterised by a perfection of movement only permitted by an acute muscular control which is simultaneously impossible in everyday terms, and yet achieved, as for example, in terms of Mnouchkine's group's theatricality. It is one particular hallucination of beauty; a painfully maximum wastage of energy, to the functionalist; Romanticism and estheticism, amputated from social representation, in terms of late nineteenth-century social theory; while others will see it to be an instance of the everyday-'political' in its demonstration of the possible *mode de vie* of the theatre collective.

The quest for the imaginary scene

At this point I want to assemble certain personally-mediated impressions of the Warner/Shaw/Sophocles *Electra* (1988–9), indicating, in particular, heightened moments of 'uptake founded in pleasure'. These are, in Pêcheux's terms (1984), moments at which the presentation becomes opaque and indexical to me – rather than transparent – half blocking my practice of neat semiosis. Thus 'dynamised', the presentation functions as the screen on which are activated "traces in [my] stocks of memories". As a second move, I attempt to combine input from specific theoretical fields, which permits me to convert my experience without subjecting it wholesale to closure through the sorts of desire-traps I have noted above. This strategy similarly involves opacity and indexicality, and thus the pointing up of fields of interdiscursivity and interpraxis my processing seems to activate. These are limited by the possibility of knowledge (both cunning and reasoned) which my own 'cobbled' experience makes available, here and now.

Illustrative of the ways in which the expert discourse of philosophy is dispersed and disseminated into other fields of human practice, we might take Deborah Warner's *mise en scène* of *Electra* at the Barbican Pit (RSC 1988–9) as the scene for the manifestation of such a 'post-Derridean' "art of making do", which does not fail to exploit those theatre and social strategies which assure the work's 'productivity' with regard to a wide, non-partisan audience. One of the ways in which it does this is by a lucid use of perspectival difference, which, derived from explicit decision-making in the pre-production process, *enables* the production of my conclusions, without having necessarily 'intended' the precise consequences I experience.

For this production (which is brought into relief, now, against Warner's restaging for the Riverside Studios in 1991–2), the seating arrangement in the Barbican Pit consists of raked rows, beginning on a platform slightly raised above the theatre floor, the fiction's ground before the palace (at the rear of the performance space, marked by two high, closed doors), and rising through less than ten rows. The rows are located on three sides, such that the spectators' entry point is at the base of the central bank (thereby confronting with spectator openness and access the palace closedness and exclusion). The performance floor is divided by a shallow runnel set into the concrete, running from the rear doors to the central spectator rows. It is filled with water and it will be used as **symbolic** of division and reconciliation (actors to each side, hands stretched across the division); for hand- and face-rinsing (**iconicity**: everyday functional and ritual action); it will be coloured, successively, with (Orestes' fictional) real ashes and with the red liquids associated with/standing for the stabbed Clytemnestra (material transformation of substances; **indexicality** and the symbolic).

Upstage right there is an indented circular space, around 1.5 metres in radius, from which prayers to the gods are made and moments of hyperintense somatic work (Shaw) are performed. In its initial state, prior to actor entrance, the space blends the predominently grey, rigid–severe, with the 'experimental'–economical, and the mortuary–monumental. Through the shifting relationships with and within this contradictory blending, the worked passions and movement function as difference-in-sameness, rather than neat opposition.

The production was schematic from one spectator position I chose (above the doors leading into and out of the spectator space), so that the *mise en scène* dominated and 'spoke' the name of the *metteur en scène* as primary agent (or 'actor') in every proposition I produced about it. From a second spectator position however – lower and to the side – no bird's eye view was possible. In this second experience of the production, the flow of blending human bodies with which I was almost level – I looked past and through, rather than down on them – avoided the clear, schematic articulation of what remained, indisputably, 'the same' effective global control. The production was strangely 'everyday human' from the second position, but the means to this transformation are wholly spatial. Proximity and shared level, in this case, meant that what prevailed as 'felt-experience' was the illusion of performer–spectator intersubjectivity. The strategies of *mise en scène* here were 'blurred' through human somatic interaction *on my level*, where previously *mise en scène* was schematic and authorly because overseen, godlike, by me – as that notion is conventionally spatialised in certain architectural traditions. Note that this tradition is consistently interrogated in Mnouchkine's use in the 1980–90s of the flat and wide *kabuki* stage.

The consequence of my shift in perception is that my new summation included as primary agents in the effecting of my responses, not just the 'they . . .' of all actors and constituted character sets, but also my own role as active participant and beneficiary (Halliday, 1985). Here I bracket that set of agents with the name of the implicit *metteur en scène*-enunciator, but I can no longer prioritise it: the working group now overtakes the single signed intervention – or is 'let' to seem to overtake it, precisely by that global enunciator. A change in perspective produces, *within the same performance*, a change in what we might call the politics of the *mise en scène*/actor/spectator relation.

Standings-for/as

The Warner production is not 'erased' by a compulsive 'standing-for' in which its origins and truths might be discerned. It can be approached as lived event, and analysed, quite differently from these different positions, as plausibly in each instance, and undoubtedly in many others. One mode of analysis will see in the production (as in Mnouchkine's *Richard II*), a material scene, fed by those of the dramatic fiction and the Imaginary, which presents a concrete working-through of gender issues. This working-through emerges *from my perspective* with regard to the stage combination of a number of factors: an effective, highly controlled woman's intervention within the teamwork of the group, which dynamises an institution of writing in such a way as to explore both the fiction and gender positions with regard to it. If the ways we theorise the Imaginary are valid, then this working-through is equally evocative of the scenes of the Imaginary of Sophocles– McLeish/Warner/Shaw and all spectators; but in a postmodern, rather than a modernist approach to the psyche, where we see similar components but highly singular combinations at work, elements evoked in different cases will not be identical, producing 'the same' resonances, at 'the same conjunctions', for each spectator.

This multiplicity of specular and imaginary and reading and discursive perspectives and positions explodes the question of 'what **it** meant' and of 'what **she** means by it'. It similarly makes a nonsense of the hierarchical 'working on many levels'. If I want to say '**it** is really and at its deepest level about . . .', and since I must assume that most other spectators saw the production once only, then I have to decide that the present performance (but which? from where?) must represent either what I perceived on one night, *or* what I saw on another, but not both. It presents anew 'the text' – but which 'reading', if indeed the term is valid for the team's explorations in rehearsal? It no doubt represents Warner's workerly and esthetic decisions, but not her intention, about which we no longer can usefully comment.

To some of us, then, diagrammatically and indexically, the

production 'stands for' – or does it rather *stand as*? – Warner's own ways of working with actors; *stands as* the actors' own experience and somatic control and understanding; *as* the spatial specificity of the Pit at the Barbican; *as* representative of certain contemporary British discourses on theatre, feminisms, women directors; *stands for* histories (but also *as* a current variation), of powerful women trapped in the tyranny of others' systems of power; *for* stories (but also *as* a critique of stories) of Woman as hysterical, in pre-Freudian, and assimilated Freudian 'expert discourse' terms. It *stands as* a current British perception of Ancient Greek-ness; *as* the interface between a certain 'historical' evocation, contemporary esthetics-in-practice, and human everyday practice-become performance; *as* an exploration of the uses of energy in small-scale performance conditions, of the contemporary British spectator's pleasure in fictional pain and real actorly physical pain and pain-transcendancy and elation, and so on.

The list, by no means exhausted here, tells us little about 'what I felt' and why I went back again through a certain passion for what it offered, in the space it used, of different angles from which to see the ceaseless and minute interaction of the whole acting team, the face and body of Shaw at one moment, from one angle, the faces of the actor-characters opposite Shaw–Electra, and the faces of those, opposite in the spectating space, watching Shaw's face as it reveals its knowledge that it is watched . . .

The lesson? Presentations and representations are complex and pleasurable matters – and part of the pleasure lies in our semiotic bloodhoundery evoked by Eco, in the pleasure of our converting experience into discourse, in our desire to be able to say 'what it was about'. Part of the pleasure is in that very closure invoked by Derrida – for to say 'clearly' 'what it *was* about' is to assume the authority of historical discourse, of the application of the past tense to felt-experience; is to close off speculation, association and other forms of ('wasteful') brain activity. It is to set in motion the very economical economy of discourse, in which succinct expression is valorised, and produces in its users a certain satisfaction.

But at the same time, the alternative, opening onto multiplicity, signals no terminal assault on representationality itself. The Derridean and Lyotardian texts mount an assault on *mono*theistic theories of creation and of origins having mastery over what we now experience. No theatre practice can do other than present and represent – hence the focus on everyday practices, on their coding and code-blurring, re-presented not just in the work of every performer, but equally in the very fact of our ability to recognise a performer as such, a hand as such, a facial expression as such (and certain performance artists play on just this 'minimal logical' degree of representation).

If we are able to *see* 'it', and indeed to name it 'performance', it is because we are able to re-cognise it (to cognise it again – which depends on an *a priori* experience of knowledge). What we find at work in the Warner–Shaw–Sophocles complex explodes mono-theistic theories of creation, for the simple reason that this complex input makes of the character Electra *staged*, an oscillation *between* the reality of human integrality (mediated by the single mass of Shaw's body), at one pole; and at the other the interplay of Shaw–Electra (and, differently, Shaw–Electra–Clytemnestra, and so on). This interplay sets up sites framing movement between contemporary, contradictory discourses, peaking in certain moments of body interaction, in flux: here, the play's the thing. In order to theorise it, we need firstly a theory of multiplicity in 'the one', which contemporary theory of the subject makes available, and secondly a theory of dramatic theatrical enunciation, into which the flux of scenes of the Imaginary can intrude evocatively.

Fragmentation of 'the one'

This is where we emerge from deconstruction into application: we emerge into a scene neither marked by the One, by His (*sic*) Word, by the Book or the intention, nor by chaos. Instead it is marked by a flux of many contributions **assembled, energised and mediated** by the *mise en scène*, and, both in anticipation and in turn, by the spectating presence and function. In Mnouchkine's staging of the Shakespeare cycle in the *Théâtre du Soleil* from the early 1980s, this emergence is realised in (for example) the open *kabuki* stage for *Richard II*: a stage without paradise or underworld, without wings; a stage refusing height and depth, and therefore automatic resonances. It is realised in a stage practice which refuses the One (on which the recognition of discrete styles/genres depends) by assembling from a wide range of performance skills and 'quoted' painterly (but unframed) tableaux, a collage or patchwork, organised temporally by a version of *kabuki* drumbeat. Within this the Shakespearean writing, translated (Mnouchkine/Shakespeare, 1982) for the purpose (and largely omitting verbs of reflection and introspection in favour of material action), *plays*, adding a further layer of organisation without domination, to those other organising grids or *dispositifs*.

In *Electra* the multiplicity of little presentations, deriving from the interactive experience of writing-in-theatre-use (in rehearsal) and from the perceptions and experiences of the spectators, and able to cause ripples and darting connections, readily differentiates this stage from that of conventional representationality. We are far here from modern readings of the ancient theory of *mimesis*.

Once we substitute for a principle of imitative likeness, a meticulous *diagrammatical* and perspectival iconicity worked in the real and symbolic space of the theatre relation itself, we can begin to see that performance is, in terms I have used earlier, *enunciated*, and hence essentially perspectival and intersubjective. "Enunciation", for Benveniste, needs "an individual act [and place] of use". That individual act of use requires a position from which to speak or show, but it also needs the interlocuteur function; and as long as the latter is multiple, and different, as is the case both within the practitioner group, and within the audience, then *representation* must be seen more as a play between the different, less as a matter of shared codes. Derrida's *déhisence* (1977) and Deleuze's rhizome (1987) – both concerned with the ways the coded-at-source is unexpectedly transformed, once projected forth – provide more useful metaphors here.

Enunciation, thus seen, provides a stage, setting up at least two positions, in both literal and ideological senses of the term. It sets up, as well, in its most neutral mode, a relation of energy, across which intersect both the needs and desires of the spectators, and those of the practitioners. Lacan's refusal of the term communication, and his preference for evocation, seems to be validated here: far from 'emitting a message', or 'receiving one', what we can see *from here* is that that global enunciation amounts to an invocation met by an agreement, to look variously at, and secondly to work on, *what is given, in quite specific ways, to the senses*.

Place-takers

If, as Lyotard indicates, no place-taker is any longer originary and authoritative or legitimate, insomuch as all are valid, the problem we now face is this: how do we show that the success of the *Electra* production, for some of us, comes not in its capacity to represent, and the quality and efficacy and sincerity of its representations (seen as directly and intentionally causal), nor from the 'life-affirming' Nietzschian–Artaudianism of Derrida's approach. It seems to come in its intricate propensity for suggestion and evocation, such that its event provides the scene for something like a spectator-specific 'show', happening at different moments, and differently, within all of the spectators. But 'within', as metaphor for interiority, is problematic: 'within' the spaces opened up between the work of the conscious brain, work in the 'stocks of memories', work in the Imaginary, and work in the central nervous system as it is held and exposed in the particular conditions of (not-speaking/not-moving) tense immobility of theatre spectating.

A personal–political pleasure

The resonances of each spectator's viewing – the ways in which certain colour configurations, from my perspective, evoke others which form part of my active store of knowledges, my store of nostalgia and desire – are both cunningly solicited and unknowable in advance. The decision-making cannot necessarily explain why, from a certain angle, *for me*, Fiona Shaw's lean long body finely and ceaselessly wrought with muscular tension, the slit tunic revealing, in her movement, the point of the hip bone, invite, rather than 'hold', an ambiguous erotic production in me, while for my male companion they do not . . . or is it that he could not say, nor even 'feel', that they did?

I am obliged to assume, since a decision *for the many* was made concerning the choice of Shaw, the costuming of Shaw, the whole then torn pomegranate, within the actorly-constituted context of intense female emotion, that the associative power not of the 'thing itself' but of Shaw–Electra's act of dashing the real fruit onto unpainted concrete where it split open, was universally effective, if not universal in affect and associative specifics. This energetic option seems to 'take its place within a field' of something like 'anger', 'thwarted passion', which contextualises the act, furnishes it with the means to semiotic resonance.

But the act also in part *constitutes* that field. Our use of the act in this constitution does not exhaust it as effective/affect, precisely because it is not a binary unit in a digital structure, but takes a place within a somatically effective, ceaseless energy-work, threaded about in filigree throughout the actorly real. The infinitely fine network of muscular worked control of Shaw's conjuring is stimulated and caught by the performance conditions themselves. These project a massed and relatively fixed, quasi-compulsive spectatorial gaze, onto a woman's body and bodywork. That gaze on a woman is brought to the Sophoclean complex, but it is not foreseen by it: this is Warner's *Electra*, a metapraxis politically charged in late-twentieth-century terms, and no longer the 'male writing' some critics continue to see there.

This complex metapraxis draws into 'meaningful opposition' the processes of pomegranate-**held**, and pomegranate-**dashed to the floor**, with any number of other processes. The textual indice (gerund) is clear: 'What **offer**ings are those?' (McLeish, l. 406). Our use of it in the theatre is complex, but in terms of 'what we see', and then of secondary appropriations, it is worked in semiotic terms between momentarily given participants and processes:

Actor	Process		Circumstance
	(type: Material)		
(f) **Chrysothemis**	carries	pomegranate toward	tomb
(f) **Electra**	seizes	pomegranate	
	dashes	pomegranate to	**floor**

In both instances **Beneficiary** of the process is 'dead father', and whatever 'dead father/king' can be seen to stand for in that/our culture; but the extent of the complex cannot be understood from those elements, since it entails the kinship complex which we retain as 'frame' – or imprint – to all actions. In theatre, this is less a matter of 'the beings themselves' – Orestes (acted, then implicit); Clytemnestra and Aegisthus (verbally explicit) – than the energised or processual relations (for Bourdieu, from the strategic intersections of different actorly, enunciatorly, and fiction-projected, instances of internalised and naturalised history) which give the focus to the acting. We can add to this the active participation (watching/listening/counselling/commenting) of the Chorus, and our own. From this point of view, the body-mass of the actor seems to serve as a parameter to a peak of energy relations and interrelations, rather than a oneness.

Cohesion through Beneficiary, combined with the difference in process, both produces the piquancy, and activates a potential inferential field around the Daughter–Father–Mother–Son–Lover–Onlooker complex, the Onlooker being vital in effect (Derrida, in Blonsky, 1985), if not in theory, in Freud. The effectiveness of this *difference-in-sameness* is increased by a number of traits set in opposition and into *relations of complementarity*; certain of these are further available to be used as indices or pointers to spectator-inference. What is notable here is that we are often dealing with the evocation of a range or force-fields of significance, *activated through user-processings* of a number of given stage 'elements' clustered by that user, rather than with either/or inclusions and exclusions. Both apparently opposed options, plus further associable options, are vital to different spectators' uptake, and it is in their shuffling interplay, like little struggles between and within instances of *habitus*, and between the forces of one scene and another, that we find their significance.

Taking the thrown and broken red pomegranate as focus-point, the force-fields open and ripple and spread around its intersection with actor's energy and enunciating intervention. The ripples and resonances are outwardly constrained in their spread by certain parameters established both by the ingredients of the fiction and by the onward movement of performance-time, but they are similarly constrained by spectator experience and by spectator's *place* and Imaginary's place within the field of that experience.

The un-conscious, again

In performance conditions these are not neat categories (the metaphoric ripples are almost too separate as image); and although decision-making in the practitioners has a stark material face and actional mode, there is no more reason to suppose that each of these potential resonances, and their internal relations, is specifically assessed, addressed, talked through, before being acted upon. That they are 'felt' does not mean that they are a matter of 'instinct' or 'primitive' in the sorts of terms Bateson (1978) sets out. Instead, I am supposing that they may emerge from the way present experiments and conjunctures suddenly resonate with the 'forgotten history' (Bourdieu, 1977) of one or more participants, and thereby be judged to be 'effective'. If Pêcheux's three-part 'interdiscursive' schema has demonstrated the importance of the un-said of the unconscious to discursive meaning-production, in theatre we need to combine two basically different notions of the unconscious, in order to include, as effective in performance decision-making, the transgressive and barred, as well as the fogotten and naturalised: that which socio-historically can no longer be said/thought, which has been forgotten, which cannot yet be said, or which idiosyncratically (in the singular ways we live out history) cannot ever be said – but which, in the particular conditions and combinations of theatre, *might be shown and 'hinted at'*. But the final term poses problems for 'analysis'.

Within French theory Kristeva and Barthes, keen for political reasons to expose subjects' access into repressive social orders, draw on the Lacanian epistemology and its narrations precisely because of its plausible explanation of the effects of culture in and on the subject. In Barthes' 'Right in the Eyes' (1986), he attempts to reinstate drives into a gaze which he perceives to be libidinally charged, through interaction, from infancy. His attempt here is not confrontational; he does not invoke a patriarchal tyranny which might be fought and conquered. Rather he uses the terms of the major French epistemes of the twentieth century to suggest that there is a transgressive pleasure in the workings of the gaze; that, by implication, access into sociality constrains and un-words and disarms this pleasure; and that this can be recognised and acted on, subjected to appraisal and by implication (to Lacan its workings are not ineffable), to something like analysis. But what can 'analysis' come to mean, in this context? The term *signifying* (or *signifiance*, retained in Young (1981)):

doubtless has a specific semantic core, without which the gaze [turned on and produced in – for example – classical painting] could not mean something: literally, gaze cannot be *neutral*, except to signify neutrality; and if it is 'vague', the vagueness is evidently full of duplicity; but this core is surrounded by a halo, a field of infinite expansion in which meaning *overflows*, is diffused without losing its *impress* (the action of impressing itself): and this is in fact what happens when we hear music or look at a picture. The mystery of the gaze, the disturbance which constitutes it, is obviously situated in this 'overflow' zone. Here, then, is an object (or an entity) whose being inheres in its 'excess'. . . .

Science interprets the gaze in three (combinable) ways: in terms of information (the gaze informs), in terms of relation (gazes are exchanged), in terms of possession (by the gaze, I touch, I attain, I seize, I am seized): three functions: optical, linguistic, haptic. But always the gaze *seeks*: something, someone. It is an *anxious* sign: singular dynamics for a sign: its power overflows it. (Barthes, 1986, pp. 237–42)

In theatre – unlike some work for the camera – the actorly-character gaze seduces by its cunning orientation with regard to my own wandering gaze. It (anxiously) acknowledges my own (anxious) gaze upon it (muscles contract, adrenalin builds), and in that orientation to a theatre gaze it largely, playfully, refuses to similarly return, its enunciators interpellate my own looking, in waves and peaks of attention, not just at the one, but at the shifting spaces *between* the actorly-symbolic materiality-in-space.

The gaze and theatre's scenes

I can look intensely, in the theatre, at intensified, gaze-oriented symbolic manifestations of somatic and linguistically constituted human intimacy – constituted for that end – such as (it seems) I might secretly yearn to look at, but 'cannot', outside theatre's scenes; where we seem to agree, without coercion, on certain repressions to looking/showing as sociality itself. It is not only that 'I can look' in theatre; rather, it is that I *must look* for performance to be what it is. This solicited quality of the look, together with other intersubjective processes, tends to draw the practice into the scene of psychoanalysis. But if here we find the objectifying, sexually-charged but non-interactive look of voyeurism, turned on its complementary function of exhibitionism, it is not clear that this offers us an approach to theatre's practices which is as useful as it might have seemed in the context of a 1970s' feminist analysis of

Hollywood cinema (cf. Mulvey, 1977; Bennett, 1990). The theatre relation, as distinct from the relation in the cinema, entails an ethical, controlled, interactive energy-field, which challenges theories of objectification.

The haptic function (Barthes)

In *Electra*, my gaze focuses on Shaw's ceaseless minutely organised muscular work as Electra listens to the tutor's account of Orestes' death, but it is teased away (by movement) to the Chorus' own watching: there is an intense and complex force-field produced and maintained here, and I am drawn by it to *watch their watching*; and because of this movement between them, I then see, on the periphery of that movement of the eye, that, little by little, 'almost imperceptibly' (which makes it, apparently paradoxically, more keenly watched), one girl in the Chorus bends ('weakens') and finally slips, in rhythm with the telling, to the floor. In the Riverside 're-staging' it is an older Chorus member who collapses, and the resonances instantly change.

The relational and haptic functions dominate here: it is little by little, after the performance, that I provide myself with information, obtained not through that active gaze but through a secondary process of appropriations and of reactivations in terms of other scenarios of knowledge. Of the Chorus watching, all maintain tension, all (in the Barbican version) maintain the direction of the gaze on the story-teller but only one orients that tension to a minutely worked collapse so that her 'decline' is conjugated in terms of the telling. I semiotise it firstly in terms of global enunciation, as a strategy for use of the full acting-team; secondly in relation to dramatic writing, by approaching 'repressed feminine passion' as an **actant**, peaking in Electra, but able to be projected equally into other 'female' roles.

What this fragmenting of the spectator gaze produced in me was an intense desire to see the performance again: did she collapse, when did she start, at what point fall? *How much* might I watch her, another time, without 'losing' the differing work by Shaw and Parry, equally intense, equally different, equally fragmented, while the Tutor, telling, faces the 'Palace' space, faces Clytemnestra, his gaze not given to us?

'What I see' is readily recuperated along conventional lines: by inference, from re-utilisation of this complex element of the scene as indexical (Eco, 1977), we take an 'inferential walk', activating diverse frames of *knowledge of the world*. One option for interpretation (Freudian; psycho-somatic convention) re-stages present physical action as 'reminiscence', index of a sustained repression which then 'erupts' into a somatic manifestation. In such a semiotisation, however banal its findings, what we are doing is to attribute psychological identity and an ego to a Chorus member who, in this process, ceases to be a function, attaining the status of character. This complex **somatic** event is now recuperated into three 'texts' we can separate out for the purposes of analysis:

- as the basis for an inference relating to the enunciated *Electra*;

- as an indice of enunciation *pointing to* a *political* directorial decision to decentre the visual, away from a centred 'star' or 'hero' or triangular relation, to another woman receiver of men's tales, a woman elsewhere widely perceived to be 'largely text-functional';

- as an indice of an actor's somatic skill and the complex resonances it can activate.

The fragmented gaze as 'political' work

Warner's team-work, which is articulated in this group practice of different overlapping watchings, seems to be oriented specifically to a *decentring*, so that "'the eye has no [single] fixed point on which to rest'" (Pontbriand, 1982), but can follow a range of different paths to obtain its complex pleasures. As concrete somatic work (it is repeated from production to production), it promotes in some spectators a complex but uncharted eyework. We can attribute to it a clear representational function: a practice in the politics of the theatre group itself which can be said to stand, by implication, for potential political practice among groups outside the theatre.

If we return to Barthes' formula, this gives us something like a second core of signification, in theatre performance terms, where earlier we found one in terms of the fiction. But what is remarkable is that 'core', in this instance, is not performance-component unitary, but collective and dispersed. Secondly, I 'perceive' (or constitute it) through a precise field of knowledges not necessarily accessed by some other spectators. But thirdly, what I now find remarkable is that I almost did not see the Chorus member fall, so intent was my gaze on the Electra–Clytemnestra listening; and I had to return to the theatre, 'to see it properly'. As a consequence, I have to declare that this game of semiotisation, so rich in potential for my own pleasure in the staging, is both a performance **fact**, functions **below the threshold of performance–semiotic necessity**, but also attains a significant order of **singular resonance-probability**.

There still remains the question of the excess, the halo, the overflow, and of its possible relationship to a socially stable core. In addressing these issues, Barthes draws on Lacan, within the same article. Yet what we have seen of Lacan's reading of this epistemological tradition suggests that this socially stable coding is a red-herring, a product of the observer's desire for a solidity; a product mediated by fear of entropy (or disorder) in the Other. It suggests that there is no core so much as one scene doubled in a drama by another, and that the putative core does nothing so much as to attempt to veil – again – the dramas of those scenes.

If we shift sideways from this episteme and its quarrels to quantum physics (cf. George, 1986; Schmitt, 1990, for detail of the developing connection with contemporary theatre theory and practice), what we might find is that such a dramatisation of these scenes is too schematic and altogether too predictable: core there might be seen to be, but it is divisible, and only as 'stable' as the needs of the interested observer are strong. Indeed, in her re-working of *Electra* (1991, Riverside Studios), Warner retains the interplay noted above, but the larger space has invited a more melodramatic, gesture-amplified acting from the named actor–character complexes – making the Chorus both more visible in the theatre space, and less visible in their relationship with the other actors; and secondly the Chorus now are all older, and frequently veiled, in the old Muslim tradition – which resonates for some of us, now, with fundamentalism. In consequence, the range of feminist *political* implications I noted in 1988 is in one direction reduced and in another, extended.

However divisible a core might be, for quantum physics its particles are not analysable in terms of stable dramatisation: their movement is unpredictable, and not consistently patterned, and observation is bound-in to the observed. What this suggests is that our quest for metaphors able to represent experience in theatre needs at the very least to be tentative, wary and relatively uncommitted: theatre practice will shift, just as we attempt to grasp it, and must always run ahead of our understanding and capture. Ubersfeld, besides, has already suggested that theatre practice is *bricolage*; we might then expect the same of 'theatre theory'.

Not one who knows

In the soft light of this unbinding of semiosis, let me invoke one of Lacan's laconic texts on the dramatic subject (of dramatic subjects). Here he notes that:

> Freud proposed the following evidence to sustain the ordering he called the unconscious:
> 1 the subject is not one who knows what he is saying;
> 2 something is said by the word the subject cannot remember;
> 3 the subject behaves oddly and believes that his behaviour is his own.
> It is not easy to find a place for this subject in the brain, especially when the brain shows itself to be most receptive to this subject when it is asleep . . .
>
> (Lacan, in Blonsky, 1985, p. 205)

I might want to intrude here this addition: 'or when it is awake in the theatre, or in the cinema', in order to attempt to account for some of my still un-speakable pleasures, for some of my omissions, for some of my forgettings . . . but isn't the theatre social, and aren't we all, after Brecht, uncomfortably awake? Perhaps this is part of theatre's specificity: awake, I don't dream there, *when it works*, so much as live this almost perfect control of the actor work as hallucination; slipping over it, as a series of transparencies, the stuff of the Imaginary. And this hallucination is not a negativity – although in its shifting and transgressive qualities, it is a pleasurable trouble – because the shift and flow of the theatre components mean that my transfixed state does not take control.

Released from the hallucinatory pleasures, I wake up to *discourse* as a kind of refuge, and I forget some of those pleasurable workings of the Imaginary. Lacan goes on (on Lacan):

> . . . I introduce the following formula: the unconscious is the condition of linguistics. [And] language is the condition of the unconscious. . . . But then what is semantics? It certainly has to do with the languages that people speak and that we as analysts work with; these languages have ambiguity, emotional content, and sense. Are we going to say that semantics is peopled or furnished with men's [*sic*] desires? (pp. 205, 207)

No study or analysis of language without the existence of the unconscious: it is the latter's inaccessibility (it is said to be absolutely barred to us, yet "structured" – for Lacan – "like a language"); hence the absolute ambiguity of its input which bypasses our conscious seeking and drives us to concerted attempts to analyse and disambiguate. No unconscious, however, without language, no un-speakability, no un-said, without the speakable (a nicely exercised binary bind). Language here is a tool used to intervene between the one and the other, in the face of that difference we call mis-understanding. Now, Lacan, in absolutely barring the unconscious from the conscious subject's will, is buying into that spatial metaphor which permits him then to declare that:

> *Behind* . . . discourse, which has its sense, we seek another sense, *the* sense. And we seek it in the symbolic function that is manifested through this sense. But this is another sense of the word symbol now. Here there intervenes a precious fact manifested by cybernetics – something that is not eliminable from the symbolic function of human discourse, and this is the role the Imaginary plays in it.
>
> (p. 207: the first emphasis is mine)

This distinction between the Symbolic, which through the either/or principle of digitalisation (cf. Bateson, 1978) is more or less accessible to conscious manipulation *between* human subjects (although on the basis of the *habitus*, that accessibility varies), and the Imaginary, which Lacan describes as "an inertia" mixed up in discourse, is obviously vital to some of my spectating theatre work. What we need to come to terms with at this point is the return to dualism, but a dualism blurred and blended such that the notion of the extractable *one* is a nonsense: the visible materiality of any discrete body takes as its second term a multiplicity of shifting options, whose 'truth' – recent convention has it – lies in the *desire*-for-truth, and not its resolving. In terms of gendered theory and its critics, this desire-for-truth may be described as desire for the Father: such desire constitutionally cannot be satisfied – provided that we recognise, in terms of that constitution, that it is not the incest-taboo which prevents satisfaction. It is the *symbolic* Father we desire, and not the material, biological father (although we may project the desire onto the material father, or mother, or sibling; but that is quite another series of dramas). Lacan continues:

> The first symbols, natural symbols as they are called, issued from a certain number of prevalent images – the image of the human body, the image of a certain number of evident objects, such as the sun, the moon, and others. This is what gives the weight, the vital force, the emotional vibration to human language. Is this Imaginary homogeneous with the symbolic? No. And it would pervert the meaning of psychoanalysis to reduce it to the valorizing of these Imaginary themes, to the coaptation of the subject to an elective, privileged, prevalent object . . .
>   What cybernetics shows us is the difference between the symbolic order and the Imaginary order . . . *What the Imaginary brings to a subject's discourse is an inertia.* This inertia mixes up the discourse to the extent that when I want the best for someone, I really want the worst; when I love someone, it is really myself that I love; or when I think that I love myself, it is precisely at this moment that I love another. (p. 208: my emphasis)

For Bateson (1978), cybernetic explanation permits us to consider, when something occurs, "what alternative possibilities could conceivably have occurred and . . . why many of the alternatives were not followed" (p. 375), so that we arrive through negativity and inequality of probability, at a theory of viability. "Somewhere", when something which might have happened does not, "there must have been a circuit which could identify error and eliminate it" (p. 376). Lacan's wicked trivialisation, noted in the last few lines quoted above, should not distract us from the theory of interruptive circuits. These intervene in currents, and are powerful enough to invert charges so that the stuff of the Imaginary is converted and distorted as it feeds the Symbolic. The Symbolic, this 'evolved' mode, for Bateson, is thus negatively charged, and heavy with the blocked Imaginary, the 'less evolved' analogue material.

This provides a veritable *drama* of the human actor or agent, since subjectivity as it is acted out always resonates with something more, and with something quite other, than seems to be discernible from the objective qualities of the immediate situation. Note the connection here with Bourdieu's "forgotten" and naturalised "history". If this theory is valid, then it suggests that the working of many other dramas, including the dramas of interpretation, as well as those of acting in the theatre, might depend upon it. 'I', then, is an other, a material body and an artificially controlled body-image reflected back at me (if only through others' eyes). But far from neatly doubling the given materiality, the otherness troubles, erupts into and is mingled in the one. In this way the thesis of an intentional and self-knowing, self-determining *single* subject of language and action, oriented to and moving toward a specific goal, is exploded. Pratt (1986) draws significantly on this critique of the unified subject in her work on speech act theory and ideology, to such an extent that the use of speech act theory in the analysis of writing for the stage (cf. Elam, 1984) is seriously challenged.

What the exploding of the 'single subject' has led us to is a different appreciation of 'character', to a different appreciation of 'author' as category of knowledge, and of the delicacy of 'creating a role'. No longer cohesive, harmonious, a self-knowing/self-deceiving whole, liable to neatly programmed but resolvable contradiction, character is revealed as a writerly practice of division and difference. This is necessarily fed by writerly misrecognition – revealed most significantly, perhaps, in the ways in which character is dramatised as 'problematic', and lodged in a fabula in terms of which *something (in the end, or just before it) will be done to resolve the problem.*

This hypothesis of a dramatic fragmentation and self-contradiction as a current truth of theory in schizophrenic late-industrialised societies, where unity and harmony are perceived to be widely and conservatively imposed fictions of Left and Right alike, leads us to a different appreciation of identification. No longer constrained by a one-to-one relationship forged between 'the spectator' as unit of audience, and 'the character' as dramatic unit, identifications are fractured and mobile 'within' and 'across' the viewing subjects (to encompass the shifting kinship relations we experience within the 'self': my mothering, fathering, infant and sibling and outsider functions); and both within and across the intersection of dramatic characters as these play (as symbolic) across the active and highly charged materiality of actors. Dramatic character (which appeals, which challenges) is a contingency of schooled desire, im-pressed onto a material site (the watched actorly body in its relations with the other) across which we play out the confrontations and reinforcement of the multiple and shifting (discursive and actional) ingredients of our differently constituted subjectivities.

But this 'play across' does not account for the instances of 'fixing' or pleased "inertia", of moments of transfixed attention in my spectating. So that while we can acknowledge to some extent the validity of Wilden's (1980) attack on the "psychologisation of society", whereby every violence is 'explained' and naturalised by reference to the Oedipal scene, it does seem that the theory of a blocked (or forgotten) Imaginary scene offers us one means to attempt to approach some of its pleasures, through certain of the strategies available to us through this field of discourse. We attempt this with full and rueful knowledge that we are producing only and precisely what the current-interrupter, and the consequent hermeneutic loop, makes available.

Lacan, for reasons already noted, remains focused on the plane of language, considering the inertia "brought to a subject's *discourse*" by the Imaginary. But if the role of the performer is to produce, through interaction with others and their own symbolic modes, a performance Symbolic which is neither discursive, nor necessarily "structured like a language", it does not seem to be the case that this precludes the practitioners from deciding precisely on those performance options which 'resonate' with 'something more' than can be attributed to the given moment of enacted dramatic fiction. I am assuming, in consequence, that something like a 'tension', if not an inertia, is "brought to a subject's [practice]", in the combinatory conditions of theatricality, and that it is this 'something' which determines what is appropriate to performance.

As spectator, besides, my role in theatre depends on my willing short-term restraint from discourse; and the activation of my senses is such, in this classic 'bombardment' of difference, that the discursive potential we retain, and prepare, when silent, cedes its place to other sorts of activities. So this modification seems to be appropriate: 'what the Imaginary brings to a subject's **practice** is an inertia', which breaks into, to 'stall', the movement and telos of linear progressions. We need to add, since we are complicit with the stage's modes of working: an inertia which breaks into the movements of looking of different spectators, at different moments and to socially diverse, often pleasurable ends.

The Imaginary and the Symbolic

The Symbolic, like the wheel of human invention quoted by Lacan, seems to be driven relatively willingly and consciously, turned to our ends. It is movement and direction by a voluntary subject. The Imaginary leaks the potential for inertia into this willed model of directed movement, blocking, inverting, undermining and dramatising the conscious wielding of the Symbolic (of which the discursive stream is one instance). And this inertia ("it was simply *stunning*"; "I couldn't take my eyes off it"; "I was fascinated, enthralled") both forges a drama with the directed movement of (linguistic) symbolic modes, and is founded in a complex drama of conflicting interiorised, repressed or quasi-repressed urges and drives, of a dreaming mindstuff of image-material. In Rose's (1986) reading of Lacan, his:

> account of subjectivity was always developed with reference to the idea of a fiction . . . [T]he concept of the 'mirror stage' . . . took the child's mirror image as the model and the basis for its future identifications. This image is a fiction because it conceals, or freezes, the infant's lack of motor co-ordination and the fragmentation of its drives. But it is salutary for the child, since it gives it the first sense of a coherent identity in which to recognise itself. (p. 53)

But this sight/site of identity is 'already a fantasy' since firstly the child is simultaneously, *in and to appearance*, in two places at once – both looking, and *apparently* looking back – a relation we can indicate by a play of deictics or shifters and of case. 'I' is both 'here' (looking), and 'over there' ('that's **me**', in the mirror; on the stage); while in the theatre 'I' is both 'this here/me' and 'that there/it/she/fictional or actorly I'. The two are not arbitrarily linked, but linked by desire and need, by looking and its energies. Secondly, what the child sees is *image*, fixed and caught, and thus a fiction, an idealisation, in that the child already knows itself to be, as socialisation develops, 'uncontrolled', immature in its muscular control. Is this 'imperfect control' the spectator knows in herself, the source of some of the pleasures of the actor's highly charged and controlled work on the stage of Mnouchkine and Warner?

The moment of recognition, Rose continues, "only has meaning in relation to the presence and the look of the mother who guarantees its reality for the child". We need, if we are to escape the chains of gender politics, to replace 'mother' by 'nurturer', i.e. by the symbolic-Mother *function*; and to add – if we wish to retain this institutionalised, mythologised scenario – the non-look of the absent Father-function, with whose law speech must engage to acknowledge and temper the pains of absence or loss. This addition is necessary if we are to draw fully upon the three-ness of the Lacanian model. In this dramatic scenario the nurturer stays (and is thus conceived of as s/he who is there), and, now separate from it, who looks at the child; the socialising Father-function is one which eternally departs, into the world, thus taking its gaze from the child, thereby visually denying it. Sociality is marked therefore by loss, and what is lost must be named, so that these verbal symbols can stand in for it, and for its incarnation, for that child. Similarly its *name-sign* stands in turn for the child, for the departing social or Father-function. In Mnouchkine's theatre that name seems to signal the combination of the nurturing-function and interventionist-function, and the fact of the naming seems to testify to the need for the look (*mise en scène*) which guarantees reality (Rose, 1968) to some of us.

Rose continues:

> Lacan is careful to stress . . . that his point is not restricted to the field of the visible alone: 'the idea of the mirror should be understood as an object which reflects – not just the visible, but also what is heard, touched and willed by the child'. Lacan then takes the mirror image as the model of the ego function itself . . .

The 'I' with which we speak stands for our identity as subjects in language, but it is the least stable entity in language, since its meaning is purely a function of the moment of utterance. The 'I' can shift, and change places . . . (p. 54)

Lacan plays insistently between the material-substantial (the mirror; anatomy; the mother), and the symbolic (the reflecting relation, e.g. with the eyes/voice of the other; the interventionary tool or action; the nurturer). It is this play which seems to make his theory so powerful: there is no struggle to know *'real' determiners*, between nature *or* nurture, if nature itself is always already perspectival.

Unstable entities

The middle-class audience at *Les Choréophores* (Mnouchkine/ Eschyle, *Théâtre du Soleil*, Cartoucherie, Paris, 1991–2) applauds with a sustained energy I perceive as hungry; perhaps sadistically too, through a wholly acceptable – because not physcially but symbolically applied – sadism. We applaud with what humanists amongst us might semiotise as gratitude for this use of sustained and apparently joyful energy, controlled beyond the dictates of everyday commonsense uses. In northern European technologised secular society, in which main energy production and use is mechanical and not human, it is hard not to experience this actorly effort (i.e. to semiotise it spontaneously through the *habitus*) as *generosity*, the gift.

What happens here, for me, recalls the "sex without secretions" noted by Baudrillard. What we might note about it, as is the case with other *simulacra*, is its curious quasi-detachment, in the conditions of theatricality, from a role organised by social norms and stereotypes of gendered responses, and supposedly lodged in the material body. At this safe distance from, but bound in to the site of projected desires, I can play at the full gamut of responses. The stage–spectator relationship, neatly defined in this theatre space and less threatened than charmed (like the infant–image relation across space?), provides the scene for the potential eroticisation of *any* element of stage and performance, *almost* without regard for socially-defined 'appropriate' gender roles. Akin, in this, to the explicit esthetic framing in certain Asian traditions which underlines theatricality itself (cf. Miller, 1984), this distance, far from intensifying my awareness of 'biological identity' (as in the so-called 'male gaze' in Mulvey, 1977), operates on it a short-term liberation.

Work which can be semiotised in this way, and which has the potential to play within the fragile and equally symbolic scene of my Imaginary, does not require that we reconstitute as guide a 'metaphysics of presence' – invoked by so many theatre practitioners in their quest for a 'truth', 'honesty' or 'authenticity', to counter the fact of the illusion they create; but it certainly requires an endlessly 'updated' ethics of energy use in performance, since of such productions, as active participant, I want . . . *something more* than the materiality of what I see around me, and something more than my conventional roles and relations within it. That 'something more', 'something else', is by definition a matter of fine and skilled judgement of the limits of taste. Such an ethics of productions is always active. It intervenes in Beineix's judgements at the beginning of *Betty Blue*, where we see almost too much, but *still not what we want to see*, just as it always entered into the scenes of nakedness which characterised the heady days of the early 1970s.

In Rose's reading of Lacan we seem to progress toward the imaginary scene of contemporary theatre, and to something of the scenes of the Imaginary, because:

> [l]anguage can only operate by designating an object in its absence . . . [and] symbolisation turns on the object *as* absence . . . [T]he child hallucinates the object it desires
>
> (1986, p. 54)

and then locates or invents a materiality which serves, for that child, as symbol, standing for the presence of the Mother, and standing in for her in her absence (e.g. a blanket to suck). When we realise that even in the presence of the parent which succeeds that invention, the blanket will continue to serve as symbol of absence and presence, we begin to perceive the extent to which the child's subjectivity is forged as a symbolic *ternary* drama, in which the material 'thing itself' (e.g. the blanket) is the vehicle for a double symbolic function relating to the child's way of seeing itself in relation to the Mother. It symbolises the (now almost pleasurable) pain of loss and the (anxious) pleasure of substitution, and in this it resonates with my anxiety and anticipation as I enter the theatre.

Where theatre differs from this formula is in the fact that theatre 'equally operates by designating objects **by their presence**, and symbolisation already occurs, turning on that object *as* presented to the gaze, as well as on absence. The spectator *sees* – but cannot touch – the objects she desires, and the seeing is doubled by the hallucination which precedes it':

> For Lacan, the subject can only operate within language by constantly repeating that moment of fundamental and ir- reducible division . . . Lacan termed the *order of language the symbolic*, that of *the ego and its identifications* the Imaginary (the stress, therefore, is quite deliberately on symbol and image, the idea of *something which 'stands in'*). The real was then his term for the moment of impossibility onto which [the symbolic and the Imaginary] are grafted . . . (Rose, p. 54: my emphasis)

Theatre becomes then, at its best moments, and for some of us, the now momentarily possible, hallucinated 'impossible real'. It works a synergy in which the grafting-on of my automatically-substituted Symbolic and Imaginary, merely adds to and personalises its momentary force. In the light of this, we need to modify Rose here, too: "the **actor and spectator**, like other subjects, can only operate in symbolic modes by constantly repeating that moment of funda- mental and irreducible division". The theatre relation of separation *for* performance to occur, re-enacts, irresistibly in material as well as symbolic terms, the scene of this division; and it then projects the dramatic construct, which re-enacts it again, through the order of the fiction. More acutely anchored in the Lacanian myth of the mirror-phase, the actor's Symbolic and the spectator's Symbolic are specular–somatic. Both are worked, albeit differently (but in shifting complementary modes), through an active relation to (what gendered grids crudely call) the Mother-function, and in a quest for approval through the Father-function. We return to these gendered terms below.

Something more, something else

I have suggested that this otherness is to some extent determined by the changing conditions of sociality itself. In Freudian terms these seem to be worked, at the earliest stages of their acquisition, through a body semiotics inscribed between culturally specific approved/disapproved muscular control and muscular laxity. If this is the case, then the 'something else' I seek is liable to be transgressive of interiorised code or convention, but not necessarily of specific codes: displacement or condensation permit a breadth of (still culturally-specific) standing-for to function here. Barthes notes, quoting Lacan, that the psychoanalytic economy tells us that:

> In our relation to things as constituted by the path of vision and ordered in the figures of representation, something shifts, passes, is transmitted from stage to stage, in order to be – invariably, to some degree – elided: this is what is called the gaze. . . . In a general way, the relation of the gaze to what one wants to see is a relation of deception. The subject presents himself [sic] as other than he is, and what he is allowed to see is not what he wants to see. Thereby the eye can function as an object, i.e., on the level of privation.
>
> (Lacan, *Séminaire XI*, translated and cited in Barthes, 1986)

Seductive traps

Much can be hypothesised in terms of an actorly disposition to explore for us, wholly within the performance relation, aspects of constraint and taboo the rest of us will less readily explore in public. In these sorts of terms, the apparently random 'bricolage', which seemed to challenge generative theories, can be understood as a quest, in one and another practitioner, after that object or image or actional complex, which – through the investment of heightened energy – will seem momentarily to represent, and to thereby assert again, and then only partially to close over, the singular experience in each of us of the wound of loss.

In performance terms, this *finding* ('this is my thing') energises the object/image/actional complex, weaving into and through it an energy field literally incorporating the specific performer. In this process of energisation and force-field constitution in time and space, elements of the performance can be said – potentially – to *re-present* the scene of the spectator's own loss. It represents, as well, the location of the 'little thing' which stands in for the lost one, and the emotion-range entailed in that loss/finding. (The *fort/da* principle I refer to here is described in many other sources – cf. Derrida in Blonsky, 1985, pp. 236–58.) The 'little object' here might be any 'worked' somatic practice of the actor, as much as it is an object or an image, or a puppet, in Barthes' view of *bunraku* (Barthes, 1982).

Chapter 7

The Gendered Scene of Theory

Wilden (1980, p. 503) notes of Lacan's discourse that "[f]or women . . . the 'oedipal relation' stands as the Imaginary representation of a life-long disaster". Similarly, in Threadgold *et al.*'s *way of seeing* Lacan:

> [f]inally, [this] is a theory which is inescapably phallocentric, since the mechanism, in Lacan, which enables entry into the symbolic is dependent on the resolution of the castration complex. The differences and distinctions which make the subject's access to language and representation possible are founded *on a marking of* sexual difference, conceived on the primacy of one sex over the other. It is hard to see how, in these terms, if "the Law of the Father" is "the Law of the Culture" in general, patriarchy is not woman's inescapable and irrevocable destiny. This would make the concept of ideological struggle impossible, since it would involve struggle against the very conditions in which language itself is constituted. The subject is always, by definition, "inside" patriarchal language/ideology.
>
> (Threadgold *et al.*, 1986, p. 21)

We need to tread warily here: what is the relation between 'the male', 'the patriarchy' and 'the masculine'? Is the patriarchy the order of the fathers, or of the Father – i.e. of the symbolic Father – which real women can represent as well as can men? If we look back to the 'neo-Freudian myth', as I have narrated it, what we have once again to note is that gendered cultural difference seems to be symbolic, not lodged 'in' (but im-pressed onto, and then lived through) the body's (perceived) biological specificity, by the semiotising gaze of the other. It is constituted and reproduced, on the basis of observation by the other of the sign-value of the

178

infant's body, throughout other networks of oppositional values and practices (boys' sports; girls' change rooms; boyish behaviour; sciences versus domestic sciences).

If admission into social hierarchies is dependent upon observed difference, then it should be the case that a shift in modes of perception will bring about a shift in modes of admission and in the bases for valorisation. Indeed it seems to be the case that we have recently remarked, in certain societies and in certain limited domains within these, a change in awareness and a change in practices and in attitudes (cf. Kruger, 1990). If we can soften and unsettle *perceived* and implemented differences within the observer's relation to her culture, then it would seem that we can gradually unsettle the relations themselves, both within what we term 'gender difference' – to include 'masculinity' and 'femininity' as other than biologically determined or acquired and performed on an either/or basis – and between the relations of gender and other relations within the symbolic networks of culture.

To do so is, however, to blur the drama, and possibly, in some cases, to take away the pleasures of oppositionality itself: Tadeusz Kantor (cf. Banu, 1990) clearly indicated the need for a wall (political oppression) for his theatre artistry to flourish; narratology conceives of the obstacle as vital to the structure of the fable; dramatic conflict is not just an Ancient notion but a consistently utilised structural principle in news broadcasting. On the other hand, to extract the drama from bodies (materiality) and to relocate it in the blur between shifting roles, relations, performances and masquerades – i.e. within and between the networks, hierarchies and modulators of signifying practices – has always been theatre's game, and a particular source of its pleasures.

In the present context, this unsettling of established norms of difference does not blur the drama of the Lacanian scene, so much as that of certain scenarios, used by others to different but always political ends, which take up elements of Lacan's discourse. One of the failures for certain groups of feminists has come from the confusion of gender with biology – i.e. of the symbolic and cultural, with the material and biological, of performance with biology.

Now, if tyranny is *male* and the tyrannised *female* – i.e. defined by biology, rather than specific to the institutionalisation of certain roles and of action – then the situation of tyranny cannot be changed without a change in biology itself. The only means of attack, in this scenario, perpetuate the same exclusivist logic they seek to overthrow:

1. *separatism*, to exclude the male from sexual and cultural practice, producing, in our area of practice, 'wimmin's theatre', 'women-only dramas';

2. *radical inversion*, replacing 'male-dominant/female-dominated' roles with 'female-dominant/male-dominated';

3. *castration*, real or symbolic, in the attempt to take from the male what this logic sees as its specificity.

What is nonetheless clear is that certain developments in the master discourses of the human sciences, seem to have fuelled women's anger (even as they fed the developing 'poststructuralism' of other (male) theoreticians): formulae borrowed from the structural anthropology of Claude Levi-Strauss (1963) suggested that *women* – and not Woman – are consistently tokens (i.e. become symbols) of exchange between groups of men to the end of avoiding incest (or are excluded from or marginalised within communities). So that the everyday life of a biologically-identified subject seemed to be wholly determined not by any self-defining factors, but by the cultural value attributed to biology by men, within a community. Communities were mapped out, in all modes of organisation (architecture and other spatial divisions; division of labour; mating, reproductive and parenting roles, and so on) apparently on the basis of biological difference; so that no individual intervention, nor political change – because biology and the incest-taboo would persist – could change what was determined once and for all before birth. This is biological determinism, elevated to the level of a totalising theory of society and culture.

The Lacanian refusal to be clear, in comparison precisely with the clarity and systematic order of structuralism, is occasionally of use: in positing as determiner not biology ('the thing itself'), but the always interested *perception and signing of identity*, the Lacanian scene does not deny the possibility of change within the order of perception, as that 'spontaneously' articulates (and feels and assesses and judges through) the acquired social. It is that possibility of change which we must seize upon, and work with, so that when we think of an interesting writer, a good technician, a useful producer, a promising director, we do not automatically think that the most visible male examples best manipulate these modes of theatre intervention.

Generalisations and the singular

In this sort of scenario for cultural acquisition, in which we see the im-press, and then the ex-press of what comes from the cultural relativity of perception, but which is thereafter perceived to be 'natural' and commonsensical ('Men are naturally more aggressive, so it makes sense that . . . '), Lacanian theory sets up what is almost, but not quite, an elaborate catch 22: once established, the perceptual matrix (masculine/not-masculine ↔ 'male'/'not-male') functions as the key to a network of other co-ordinates, so that 'psyche' and kinship complex and society seem to unravel from and in tune with this scenario.

But there are always what seem to be meaningful exceptions to the rules provided by generalisations within the human sciences. The *habitus*, which would seem to take up everyday differentiations in actions within a gendered scene, interiorising these exterior conditions, may indeed activate an initial order of judgement, ethos, attitude and typical actional modes, according to these perceived oppositions (father's roles and mother's roles, as these are reinforced or countered by gender roles in schooling and media representations). But in the 1990s it does not seem that this 'structuring' perspective is able wholly to account for the sorts of singular contributions different subjects – including different spectators – make to the events of theatre. If this is the case, then these sorts of theories offer us only an order of strategic knowledge, action and expectation. The singular, which excites us, remains of the 'order' of the tactical, about which we can, clearly, say very little at all.

The scenes of the Imaginary

We can no longer usefully attempt to specify the images and scenarios of the Imaginary each of us activates, in different ways, in the uses of theatre. This is not simply because the Imaginary is marked, in part at least, by taboo and the dangers of transgression. There are indeed certain stereotypical scenes which persist (the desire to couple with/to kill the father/mother), marked by (a now historical) stability in gender division of roles, values and actional modes, sustained by the authority of certain discourses and traditions (drama amongst them). But despite this we must acknowledge that, if the Imaginary is marked by misrecognition and the production of fictions, it follows that there will be a gap between the images produced, and the everyday material real these might otherwise seem 'to stand for'. It seems to follow, too, that theorising itself – as this is marked not just by reasoning, not just by a certain acute observation of the material real, but equally as it is im-pressed with the scenes and images of the theorist's own Imaginary – will similarly be marked by misrecognition.

An attempt, for example, to ascribe only to the real child perceived to 'be male', a founding fear of castration and a rivalry with other males, leading to combative actional modes aiming to contain, constrain and exchange women, and which ascribes to the girl child a founding knowledge that she is 'man's problem', does seem to err in projecting mythical oppositions and scenarios, in the name of theory, onto the material world in which we are active – thereby ensuring that certain consequences will follow. This is easy enough to do, along the lines already noted.

Such a projection ('he hates his father'; 'this is the mothering urge in her') might *seem to describe* certain 'realities' as we sometimes perceive them – although most of us are happy to admit that we 'know of certain exceptions' (often including ourselves). But the implications of our accepting this as a theory of human subjectivity, valid for every human context in which gender difference is marked out at the order of signs and thereafter lived by human subjects organised by male-first/female-second divisions, are heavy. If, however, we accept that this might offer us a means of understanding certain mainstream cultural practices, but not other practices, at certain times (including the present), then we are opening a space to a relativity and a pluralism which are characteristic of recent developments in other fields.

From the perspective of this expanded viewing, it does seem that the historical phenomenon on the stage of classic naturalism – like today's highly competent televised naturalism – depended on the powerful function of a sociality which was defined significantly through a network of constraint and taboo. This took sexuality as its prime site, and was worked in the drama through a matrix of oppositional gender relations which borrowed the gender identity of the actors as its screen. It is not clear, however, that today's use of the scripts of classic naturalism needs to work through the same matrices. Stagings we now call *postmodern* are capable of both blurring that historical specificity, and of constituting a critique of it, by relativising it.

Approaching the blur

Wilden's concept of the couplet analogue and digital, perceived through the modernist episteme to be opposites, seems – once they are reconceived as complementarities – to offer a means of approach to processes through which the im-press in the Imaginary feeds into the Symbolic. The modernist tradition has distinguished two separate strategies for transformation of the transgressive material so obtained – condensation and displace-ment – and there seems to be no obstacle to our approaching somatic practices of the stage through this couplet. In this reconceptualisation these are no longer discrete alternatives. They are always implicated the one within the other – no condensation without displacement, and vice versa. For Wilden, the *analogue* conceives the given as equivalent to a flux of associative images of otherness (e.g. the breast for the mother, the mother-breast for the Mother, for nurturing, for the feminine and so on, including in this range *whatever I cannot name here*), where these function for the perceiver as equivalencies.

In the given example a focused aspect of the performance-energised body is seen as able to compress or condense within its signifying potential a field of associative values some of which are transgressive to the perceiver. But when we are operating through the digital framework, the given is perceived to stand as unitary symptom for another unit or phenomenon which is not, or which cannot, be given: my incestuous desire, which I cannot avow (even to myself), or assuage, but 'should' punish myself for, is displaced into compulsive eating, or self-mutilation, or obsessive practices. In Lyotard (1980, p. 90) the pain of the toothache is displaced: I dig my nails into my palm, producing and controlling a substitute pain, to draw my own attention from the inadmissable source.

Hedda, Cordelia and Antigone function, to the gendered scene of theory of the 1970s and 1980s, in the symbolic mode (writing) historically chosen by male enunciators, not as *women* (which the writing is not), but as Woman, i.e. as fantasies, which either condense or displace neuroses lodged, in these examples, in the male. As contextually 'inappropriate' tokens for exchange – they contest the laws/will of the fathers – in them, their writers conflate the cunning mask and masquerade of mother–daughter values, with 'strapped-on' assertiveness and father/Father/law-threatening interventions as actional modes, refusing socially conservative mythologically 'proper' functions. As 'monsters' (exposed, visible distortions: the monster is the ob-scene (off-stage), cannot be figured or brought to the stage/gaze) of the Oedipal scene, they 'need to be' eliminated from that scene, to facilitate its return to 'reasonable' (gender divided, patriarchal, nuclear family) order.

As *metteurs en scène* we do not 'simply cast', so much as inscribe a path through a multiplicity of imaginary scenarios (some of which are secret from us), so that it peaks in a certain type, a certain body mass and colour, a certain energy-potential, as these can be seen to interact with other such choices. The mythologising is so strong, but so insidious, that many of us enact it as automatic, as 'common sense'. Exposing the myth demonstrates that it need not be so.

In the final scene of Sophocles' *Electra*, this representation of Woman as incapable of material action is materially re-placed, on stage, by the representation of the male, the brother, 'able appropriately' to engage in the 'men's business' of killing. In the Deborah Warner production for the RSC (1988 and 1991), in place of 'triumph' or 'victory', Shaw, her energy given over to the brother for the kill, picks and plucks at tiny fallen objects on the floor, which she 'tidies' as earlier she picked and plucked at the skin on her legs. It is hard not to predicate the character as 'empty', 'neurotic'. Such – this contemporary woman's *mise en scène* can be seen to suggest – was the effective lot of (man's representation of) Woman to the Ancient Greeks, even if/especially if the actual Ancient Greek performance eschewed such 'ungodly' explicitness.

Reductions

The gendered scene of theory can be called reductive – because it is worked around a tight matrix – but it is seductive, if only because it is still strongly rooted in what is conservative in prevailing social orders. Mnouchkine, for example, explicitly 'feminist' in her work, will frequently choose the male actor for stagings because she feels that contemporary northern European society so effectively teaches the woman to veil her 'self' that it is the male actor who can best 'unveil' what is effective in contemporary performance (Kiernander, 1990).

Can we now replace 'male mainstream' and 'patriarchal culture' with ungendered terms? What we might find is that some women – and some men – now prefer to work within the mainstream (Mnouchkine and the *Théâtre du Soleil* are now an institution of French theatre, and an institution of French cultural life); while some either contest and confront, or simply sidestep the mainstream and its institutions (e.g. text, property and subsidy). Wilden was formal about the **Imaginary** representation of lifelong disaster for women: the Imaginary deals in misrecognition, in fictional images, and some of the *terms* of Lacan's theory equally practise this. It might seem, then, in terms of de Certeau's strategy into which the tactic insinuates itself, that the Oedipal myth and the neo-Freudian mode of explication present an institution and a set of strategies of knowledge. Simultaneously, from within this institution – it has to have gaps and interstices if it is to mark off its property and its propriety (*le propre*) as 'its own' – there is currently (although there has not always been in all places; nor is there now), in some places, public space for the tactical which we all, according to de Certeau, always practise regardless of the ways in which the strategists try to contain and classify. "*We are all marginalised*", writes de Certeau, by the Orders (i.e. the institutions of power and property) which prevail: the actor as much as some women; in some cases, some men as much as some women.

One tactical insinuation I might want to make at this point, mindful of the formula of 'theatre which works' with which I began, is this: 'the phallus' – so named through the wicked, gendered gaze of the false master of knowledges – 'stands for', symbolises, **effective use of energy**. Is not the professional actor at work, then, regardless of gender, in Lacanian terms theatre's 'phallus'? We might now prefer to call this theatre's energy-focus or energy-peak, driven by the actor's own and the multiple and contradictory urges of writer and *metteur en scène*, and spectator. In this case, is there any reason whatsoever for retaining a term, to *stand for* this phenomenon, which we commonly relate, otherwise, to male anatomy?

Unravellings

If the phallus stands for using energy effectively, then 'castration' is a wholly metaphoric (and misrecognised) severing, standing through condensation and displacement for the inhibition of one or another means of intervention into the social: in the rapidly changing socio-economic conditions which have succeeded those in which Lacan worked and theorised (and played out socially-approved *games* of devilish authority marked by anxiety), we might now want to replace the radical cut with the different means of hampering effective energies, adopted within contemporary society. In the case of *Electra* at the Pit, Shaw's somatic work, intensely energised, performs two *strategically* (but not tactically) contradictory functions in this regard. First, the energy is turned in on itself, in terms of Shaw's body, rather than outward to either another body or to material objects. There are two exceptions which work inversely to reinforce the blockage: one, the pomegranates she dashes at the concrete floor (symbolic blood-spilling, indexical futility); the other is the 'brother' she embraces intimately and with passion (more a lover than a sister or mother), thereby invoking incest taboos and 'fruitless' or dangerous passion. Inward-turned, ineffective in the space and events of the performed fiction, Electra is exiled to the space we see, listened to only by the chorus of women and under protest by others. At its heights the performance elicits the everyday term 'hysteria' to mark the actional-inhibition/severing of the character. But secondly, in terms of the practitioners' enunciating role, both in general (a woman directed by a woman) and in terms of *what we see* (Shaw and a fine network of interactive women's roles), Shaw *gives a wholly convincing performance* of both passionate and effective control of herself and her spectators. Shaw *is*, in theatrical terms, the effective uses of energy. My own uses as spectator of this effective energy, aided by the Sophoclean writing, are not straightforward. They are marked, at certain moments of intensity, by a fascination, an inertia, which thrills quite precisely at the way the pain of the (woman) performer is entailed by this particularly strong and mixed-gender display of strengths.

In this sense *my* inert pleasure 'might be said to' – 'might be staged as': the desire-traps in use here make these scare marks vital – come from the way the performance 'sets the scene for' (but does not control) the shifting 'battle' between my conscious and Imaginary scenes, waged between approval and glee at a female perceived as attempting or taking appropriately effective modes of intervention in and on the world (Warner, Shaw *et al.* plus 'Electra' as character-focus), and my simultaneous urge to watch that effective role challenged, thwarted, punished or apparently self-punishing (Lacoue-Labarthe, 1977). However effectively I overtly espouse women's effective intervention (thereby enacting it myself), for the *institutions* of psychoanalysis and for Bourdieu's theory of forgotten history, I have an internalised but repressed/forgotten urge which does not simply undermine some of my own strengths, but which applauds punishment or humiliation in symbolic representations of this actional mode. I do not limit this punishment to my (dramatic) self but I expand its implications – such is the force of the kinship myth – to my own working mother (if such is the case), since I carry the complex image of that historical contradiction within my own subjectivity.

I thus 'want' to see certain qualities, as these momentarily peak (and reciprocally 'interfere' to produce an axis of probability) in Shaw–Electra–my mother–myself, punished/fail/exhausted; even as I want, simultaneously, to see her/them/myself triumphant and free. Because of this the work 'vibrates' for me, I am momentarily transfixed. It vibrates the more strongly in that it offers the structures for and the gaps and interstices to both my strategic and my tactical interventions.

* * *

Identifications

It seems then that we need to intervene in a discursive 'body' which plainly has some relation to 'what was going on for me in *Electra*', but which presents, to certain political perspectives of the

1970s–1980s, and to certain of my own ways of seeing in theatre in the 1990s, a number of difficulties we might want to sidestep.

Identification, long implicated (in discourse, since Aristotle) in "binding in" (Frow, 1986) and in the 'uptake founded in pleasure' I noted in Chapter 2, is not a simple, straightforward, one-to-one process. If Narcissus is transfixed by his image in the pool, and rooted by it to the spot, there to be transformed into the flower, the Greek myth is careful to provide a scenario, complete with other participants, desires and processes, which establish Narcissus as only one pole in a complex, where the relationship between this and other poles is determined not by exclusive difference, but by relationships between partial elements – hence, by complementarity. The *play* of dramatic writing comes from the spatialisation, and the shifting distinctions, between a number of contradictory elements conventional psychoanalytic discourse now locates 'in the one' – i.e. in what we might call the psychological scene of any single subject.

In this appreciation of human complexity, derived in part from Freud's reading of dramatic scenarios (de Certeau, 1986), and in the developments which have emerged through the neo-Freudian work of Lacan and his critics, what we find, when we are concerned with the connections between dramatic writing and stage practice, is that the human subject is not 'just' divided and internally contradictory (a veritable drama), but that to those divisions are attributed a powerfully loaded symbolic identity (e.g. Mother, Father, Child), which is itself implicated in this narration of access by the subject into sociality, language and culture.

In this scenario the subject cannot escape a theory of culture finding equivalencies for certain of its functions, in the infant's development as isolate subject within a *nuclear family* kinship scene. It is the historical and local nature of the nuclear family that permits us to unpick the theory's *terminology*, and to replace it, retaining as valid only the *functions* and the networks outlined therein. This should set us free from the dangerous trap of one-to-one equivalencies based on a tenuous symbolic relation (if Mother therefore female; if phallic therefore male; if Hedda therefore 'a woman').

"I" is an Other

In the more recently troubled climate for theory in general and for political theory in particular, it seems appropriate here to reconceive the Mother–Child–Father complex as a relationship of *complex complementarities*, indissolubly implicated in each human subject, and within all cultural practice. Here its different 'faces' inform different aspects of brain-in-body work, in context, and the contradictions and interdictions which constrain this informing lead to the formulation "'I' is an Other, or The Pleasure of the Voyage", to be found in a number of contexts, including Ubersfeld on pleasure (1982a).

Voyaging: Processual Theory

I suggested above that 'effectively using energy' might be meta-phorically figured by the term 'the phallus', but the metaphor is not particularly apt because of the relation of term to material body objectified. What a *processual* theory is concerned with is the acquisition and perfecting of *actional modes*. These are not innate, since muscle is acquired, and does not seem to be limited by genetics nor definitively on the basis of gender. In shifting to a processual theory not determined by the sight of anatomy, we remove from the axis of equivalency the anatomical features of 'real-world maleness' as cue to a given mode of access into the symbolic; we cast off, in that instant, the real-world-into-semiotic basis for typifying both the 'Father'-function, and institutions within the social, as 'phallocratic'.

We are in a position to erase not just the male-centred terminology accruing to aspects of psychological function and of social function, but also certain terms of the political challenge: for Father-function substitute *'institutionalising/socialising-function'* (for this is largely what is so named); substitute *'nurturing/vegetative function'* (for this is largely what is so-named) for Mother-function; for Infant we can substitute *'reactive/learning-function'*. In no instance is any function wholly determined by immanence, but by shifting needs and relations of complementarity. Lacan's own equivocal writings justify this movement: he stipulates that "the *idea* of the mirror should be *understood as* an object which reflects – not just the visible, but also what is heard, touched and willed by the child" (Lacan, 1936, cited in Rose 1986, p. 53, my emphasis).

What we can now constitute is a scenario, in which *within* any of these three peaks of a functional kind, there is the possibility of action which will either be called 'typical' – i.e. which is *strategic*; or which will be called 'idiosyncratic' – or *tactical* – which insinuates itself within and between normativising institutions and their strategies; or – which is currently more likely – the blurring slippage of a combination of the two.

Given the institutionalisation and the acquisition of strategies at any juncture in this spectrum, and the possibility of widespread tactical improvisation, we can now suppose (as was not politically appropriate in the 1970s) that both the somatic and the linguistic can similarly intervene and are used at any *place*, by any participant, to a number of possible ratified, mainstream, or transitory, idiosyncratic ends – and this includes a socialising somatic function in the hands of a male nurturer.

The Symbolic and the Imaginary

Let's come back to the Other, via the rocky and multi-tongued path marked with a white stone by the name 'Lacan'. The quest, here, is for the current limits to understanding the possible relations between imaging, somatic practice and language-use, in dramatic theatre. As Wilden (1980) notes:

> It is not for nothing, then, that Lacan's Other so closely resembles the impossible God of Sartre's *Being and Nothingness*, nor that the *manque* [or lack] of which he is the locus turns out to be a sort of displacement of the bourgeois anguish of the existentialists . . . Since Lacan specifically refuses semiotics . . . , the phrase "the unconscious is structured like a language" either means that the primary process depends upon processes peculiar to language alone – that is to say, language represents a model – or it means that there is some sort of analogy or similarity between language and the primary process. (p. 445)

Wilden's distinction between language as *model* to primary processes, and language as *analogous* to primary processes (and vice versa), takes up two aspects from amongst the most widely known elements of Peircian semiotics (i.e., iconicity, indexicality, and the symbolic (cf. Elam, 1980)). The relationship of model to manifestation is **diagrammatical**, and regulates relationships between points and planes. It is on the basis of this diagrammaticity, that the one can then be *used* as **indexical** of the other: plan can be inferred from manifestation, and vice versa. The 'likeness' here is between the "internal organisation" in the one and the patterns of the other. On the other hand, if language and the primary processes are linked by analogy, then the link between the two is arbitrary and conventional; the one can stand as **symbolic** of, but unlike, the other, and if we break this down, what is perceived to be a unit of one is the analogous one, standing for the whole of the other.

According to this hypothesis, we can agree to substitute language for the unconscious. But such agreement is always political, culturally-determined, strategic, rather than irrefutably valid. It is not located 'in' the entities, but in use of them, in their users, and in those users' desire to make connections. In the terms set out above, this means that we can, in theatre, prefer a tactical approach, along these lines: the primary processes are non-digital either–and semiotic matter, and are structured like a staging. Their functioning is ordered by the specular–somatic economy. This perspective makes us less a suitable candidate for a 'talking cure', with its peculiar relationship to the analyst, and more of a candidate for the Japanese traditional Morita (somatic) therapy, noted by Ohnuki-Tierney (1984): a sustained modification in somatic practice will produce a modification in the workings and stagings of the primary processes.

Primary and secondary processes; repression

Wilden takes up the distinction between primary and secondary processes in order to approach a user's language-production and image-production. The primary process, he explains, is an "analog" (or up down, vertical associative axis) continuum of differences – manifested in writing in something like the "thematic system" which describes the different elements I associate around a notion like 'religion' (e.g. 'she crossed herself'; 'the bread and wine'; 'the *imam* entered the mosque'; 'beyond belief'; 'somewhere beyond'; 'a good Christian woman'). These permit the establishment of what French text analysis has called a '*fil conducteur*': a conducting wire, through which a cycle of energy passes. For that theory, however, the *fil conducteur* is 'already there' in its thematic specificity; for us, although it is enabled by text parameters, it is *brought and activated by the (complex) user*.

Wilden (1980) continues:

> But the reactions of the primary process give rise to a secondary process which discovers certain paths of discharge [of invested energy, activated in a reader, e.g. by use of certain terms] other than those available to the primary process to be necessary. The primary process and its free energy thus corresponds to the pleasure principle, regulated by inertia, or by the reduction of tension to zero, whereas the secondary process, whose energy is bound . . . , corresponds to the reality principle, regulated by constancy, or by the maintenance of enough tension (unpleasure) to deal with the exigencies of life . . . For Freud, the primary process is FULL . . ., the secondary process is full of holes . . .
>
> (p. 269).

First, we find activated a complex free-play of complex images, which can be infinitely substituted for each other. At the 'next stage' of reading for performance, or of processing within performance-use, a problem-solving strategy breaks into this primary free-play to regulate, control and thus *produce* it, *to some end*. In tune with the modifications we have noted above, it should not be assumed that the different 'levels' on the pathways of the primary process mark out single or simple images, nor that at a given point they are static or fixed. But inasmuch as I have suggested that they are 'staged', then it is clear that they are limited in their 'spread' by a framing, and that on the basis of that frame we can seek correspondences with a perspectival, 'framed' 'real out there'.

Somatic practice as secondary process

We need not assume, given the field in which we work, that the secondary process (conventionally – when it is assumed axiomatically to involve language – full of discontinuities permitting the marking out of a willed, but holed strategy), necessarily entails use either of language, or of something structured like language (e.g. 'body language'). Structured, instead, like a staging, it is marked out by strategic modes of action and their peaks, and by tactical modes which insinuate themselves into the interstices left by the strategic (which is always marked off by one or another boundaries). The strategic modes overlap, and the tactical, equally controlled (and less controlled) by the practitioner, fuses with them in performance.

What we need as a consequence is something like particle and wave theory, to replace digital/linear and analogue theory – if it is indeed the case that language-in-use (rather than in a dictionary), in complex situations and contexts, still can be said to depend on the either/or of digitalisation. The wave is a regulated continuum, marked by peaks and troughs, ebbing and flowing.

Lyotard has already suggested that the secondary process might be *somatic*, rather than linguistic (Benamou and Caramello, 1977):

> According to Freud, this mise en scène [or narrative staging in the retrieval and recounting of dreams in analysis] works by means of a set of four operators: condensation, displacement, the taking into consideration for plastic representation, and second ary revision. It may be that these are universal operators for mise en scène. But it is certain that contrary to the hypotheses of Jakobson and Lacan they are not linguistic operators . . . Even if for certain ones (condensation and displacement) *we can find equivalents in language*, we would not find them on the . . . level of enunciation, but on the very complex level of rhetorical or stylistic *formulation* . . . (p. 90: my emphases)

Here language is not the fundamental model, to which all other practices are to be compared, but instead language is inscribed in other 'very complex' formulations, since, for Lyotard, "the most simple utterance carries with it a primitive rhetoric. Its being uttered, its arrangement have already made it *a diminutive stage*" (my emphasis). Language in use seems, in this conception, to operate within, and be transformed by, the complex conditions of staging. But so too are other modes of practice, *within which lanuage is staged*, to the extent that my production of them, in the conditions of theatricality, can surprise me (I can surprise my self).

Difference and pleasure

This 'surprise' comes in three ways, two of which are 'institutionalised' within literary theory (see for instance Jakobson, 1973) and elsewhere: what I 'cannot' show can be transformed through two strategies, already discussed:

- a metaphoric realisation: through *condensation*, which draws together two or more items on the up-down continuum, on the basis of a perceived relation, so that the one slides in front of, to shield, the repressed other(s); or compresses the repressed material, representing it through a core or 'nodal point'. Here the manifest material seems 'fuller', richer in implications, more 'loaded', than its material amplitude warrants. We should say that its *signifiance* (Barthes, 1986), which we derive by reference to culturally-determined systems (up–down), is not commensurable with the plane of its expression;

- a contiguous realisation: *displacement*, where an apparently incidental indice shifts sideways, dislodges or 'translates' the centre of interest of the repressed material, and replaces it within the message (cf. Lyotard, 1980, p. 90).

Once again, there is a lack of isomorphicity between sign-complex and its *signifiance*, which we derive by a sideways movement to sign-context; but the impression is that we are given a clue to a problem or enigma of the enunciator(s), whose nature as well needs to be unravelled.

A third way, corresponding with de Certeau's tactics, is both 'within' institutions, and 'illicitly there', 'up to no good' – but not visibly enough to provoke ejection. Here the Other in me is not wholly barred since in certain contexts I lightly disrupt taboos, but in such a way that my interlocuteur/spectator, slightly shocked, also grins. My intervention does not change anything in the short term, although it may in the long term – since systems are dynamic, "in flux" (Halliday, 1987) and open; but what is important about it is the way it makes me feel as a user of cultural practice.

The unconscious as mise en scène

In his 'The Unconscious as Mise en scène' (Benamou and Caramello, 1977) Lyotard takes up certain aspects of neo-Freudian theory in order to restage them according to the (other than oppositional) principles of the postmodern. This text relates to the way in which I have approached *Electra* through certain aspects of psychoanalytic discourse: that approach might seem to involve a 'writing in depth' to be located 'behind' the material relationality of performance, where it establishes a dark cave familiar to readers of Corneille's *Illusion Comique*. In conventional semiological terms, I should write of the opposition between stage and cave: interior–concealed–enigmatic (psycho-hermeneutic) and exterior–overt–clear (performance-work), internally dividing these spaces in terms of gendered oppositions traced between body-type, discourse-type and actional modes as these relate both to the order of the fiction and to the order of the actorly real; and, in post-Kristeva (1980) terms, I should insert into this the gender specificity of analyst as perceiving and writing subject.

But one of Lacan's lessons comes to trouble the neat spatial model whose concealed 'cave' smacks of a secret truth – the more true because hidden: the exercise I perform above is a staging of my experience of and in a specific production, in terms of the scenario of a desire-trap. This is both irresistible, an imposter bearing the illusion of truth, and it is constitutionally unable to satisfy (because worked through misrecognition), even as it snaps shut in (only apparent) satiety. It is an irresistible stereotype, wholly relative to history and not an absolute knowledge, because that experience 'fits into' and is legitimised by a widely disseminated and pleasurable closed staging of knowledge. Thus it is not, for Lacan, a 'truth', since it remains a 'possible knowledge' for contemporary criticism. As a possible knowledge it is literally, to Lacan, laughable, in that it neatly omits – and conceals from itself – a further 'can't-be-said/known'.

We should applaud the cunning of its formulation, and enjoy it because of the tactics we can improvise as the means momentarily to unlock the constraints of closure. We need to accept that in the case of Shaw's somatic working within the fine network of interaction between all performers (Shaw's imploded energies and those of other women performers are constantly and differentially marked) it is impossible – and unnecessary – in the late twentieth century, to avoid the strategic narrative leap from performance to popular everyday stories (Ulmer, 1989), of troubled interiorities forged within the social stage of shifting gender dramas. But when we leap, and are momentarily and partially caught, what we absolutely need to acknowledge (as de Certeau suggests) is the extent to which those institutionalised ways of knowing are in fact agreeable to us: we derive from them an aspect of our social identity even as we attack and deconstruct them (from within the university as seat of power legitimising our endeavour . . .)

* * *

From un- to other-conscious

The drama of the psyche I have outlined above is a social drama, as the work of both Bourdieu and Rose demonstrates. This 'socialisation', and relativisation of interiorities means that 'the unconscious' is no longer an explicatory mechanism 'in depth'. It works on the same plane as other knowledges, but expands outwards – like the ripples, in Barthes; and like those ripples it is simultaneously active and acted-upon by the impress of the social we each of us simultaneously, but differently, activates. So we need to erase the negation of *un*-conscious, releasing what the term might stand for from the bind of the binarism. What seems to emerge is that the play of the Imaginary, arguably bringing that 'inertia' to my processing of Shaw's work (in particular) in *Electra*, involved an activation 'in me', in response to performance specifics, *of other dramas*. While still concretely engaged with what was before me, I played out any number of roles – including that of privileged spectator, of beneficiary, killer and victim – in my interior scene of dramas retained from childhood experience and the experience of adulthood.

What is striking in the work Warner and Shaw produce – like that of the Mnouchkine team in Paris – is the extent to which the dramas I could play out were instigated by an intensity of body-work, within which the dramatic writing resonated first as *voice*, second as means to 'organise' fields of force. When I combine the somatic–discursive practice with those other dramas it can activate in the spectator, it begins to become clear that what we are dealing with in dramatic theatre which works is less "structured [twice over] like a language", than working like a **somatography**

(Lyotard, 1977). Such a somatography is far from 'already given' (as though the ripples and the impress were already and universally formulated in their tricks and turns). It emerges in the intersection between production and spectator-experience of performance, not just in that it involves a multifaceted body graphy (with no 'depth' necessary) worked on the active stage, but because it elicits in the singular practice of each spectator a **voyage of the eye** resistant to authorial control.

Toward an open somatography

By somatography I mean a 'charting' and a tracing, practised by the spectator's eye – which is not constrained, as it is in cinema and television, to see only what the camera selects and what the director edits and sutures together. It also entails a strategic, institutionalised mapping of borders and commonly-agreed centres of interest which we can objectify; but overall it is not limited to an exercise in submission to another's master plan, organising attention and selective inattention through performance choices. Instead it is that 'wandering in the city' that de Certeau writes of, conditioned undoubtedly by the blocking and dissecting *quadrillage* (graphing) of road and building, by the *dispositifs* (grids) of traffic control and pedestrian control, but relatively unforeseeable, for all that, in advance of spectator uses.

In the case of these diverse tactical and strategic *eye-wanderings*, which escape in their idiosyncratic practice any wholly significant *a priori* structuring by writer or practitioner, what seems to be most powerful within the user-somatography, somehow escapes the event of catharsis. There is no catharsis possible (which is no doubt why Aristotle relegated performance to a minor place, preferring the discipline of the writing), unless it is lodged today in the energy and the action of final applause. This displacement comes because the practitioners do not (need to) know where the wanderer will stop, what intense pleasures s/he will take, at what moment. Not single, linear, causal, and oriented by a telos of order to a little death and a 'resolution' of complex and contradictory desires, the multiple possible wanderings of the eye, in Warner's production, focus on and worry at little instances which trouble it, to which the production offers no solution – but no despair, given the lucid passion of Shaw's work in the theatricality of performance for the other.

The somatography is open, for Lyotard, since the wanderings of my eye flicker between a number of scenes, as well as across the material scene before me. The 'interior(ised)' scene is user-specific, unspeakable, since:

> we must not say that the unconscious stages the message of desire. We must at least say that desire is not a legible text [because investments are contemporaneous with each other, wholly contradictory the one to the other, while located around the same regions of the body and hence contrary to the rules of intelligibility and chronology], and that it need not be given a disguise by a mise en scène in order to be represented, since it eludes interpretation on its own, due to its dischronisms, its polytopisms, and its paralogisms.
>
> (Benamou and Caramello, 1977, pp. 87–98)

The Warner–Shaw–Electra staging is not doubled **at source** by what I sniff out and attribute to its *auteurs*, but serves as the screen on which are projected and intersect an unknowable number of scenes of the unconscious. Its materiality frames these, and they are framed again by the theatre relation itself. Through its own precisely controlled interactions, it uses a fiction and theatricality to provide parallel (but not equivalent) instances. Its *effectivity* is multiplied in and after its event by its propensity for multiplication of the ways in which we can each utilise it. The result is that:

> [t]he idea of mise en scène tends both to expand inordinately and to overextend itself to the point of vanishing. And it is in this way that it becomes congruent with the theatrical, critical, artistic, and perhaps political inquiries which make up what Ihab Hassan calls "post-modernism" and which Freud's explicit and implicit esthetics resolutely ignores. (Lyotard, 1977, p. 95)

Part III

Part III

Chapter 8

Exploding 'Discourse'

At this point the difficulties should be clear: how to set about elaborating *in discourse*, a number of currently valid procedures for a *local* and historically specific approach to writing for use in one or another dramatic theatre practices, where the emphasis is placed not on a conventional globalising hermeneutics (without needing to exclude this pleasurable game of meaning-production), but rather on writing-in-use as somatico-actional potential, and as potential for what I want to call the theatre psycho-soma. Such an appraisal of procedures needs to be able to acknowledge the actual processes (rather than, necessarily, the ways these are conventionally discussed), specific to the diverse range of contemporary practitioners of dramatic theatre, and to establish a new understanding of the ways in which these different processes *combine*, in the fact of theatre, to the end of producing a performance potential and a performance practice characterised not by semiotic unity and harmony, but rather by the curious quality of a *clustering* of semiotic potential, within what has in the past been misrecognised as 'the theatre sign'. There is a clear agenda here: to explore the co-operative–experiential path to theatre processes evoking 'felt-meanings' and knowledges, through contextualised work by groups of singular social subjects.

By 'somatic' I am loosely referring to the sorts of everyday practices (and also 'extra-daily' practices: Barba and Savarese, 1985, trans. 1991) considered by de Certeau and Bourdieu to be strategic. Such practices, in dramatic theatre, take up writing, but use voicing (and the reach and activities of its 'resonances') amongst other modes of somatic practice. But in the actor (and sometimes in the spectator) they require no vital discursive input at either a causal or an organisational level, which might "essentialize the accidental and sensible into the substantial and intelligible" (Ulmer, 1985, p. 31). Instead, it seems at this point that it may be specular–somatic work (peaking often in the sight of the body voicing) which *plays out* for all participants, but differently, the accidental and the sensible in a ceaseless negotiation. This aims both to evoke, and to excite in the spectator, the production of a deferred, user-specific, 'substantial but not necessarily intelligible' effect and affect (cf. the requirement for 'coherence', in Pavis, 1992). Now, if theatre performance is indeed to work this evocation and this excitement, it begins to seem to be the case that we – and the practitioner – quite precisely *cannot* adumbrate in advance of these singular effects/affects, the ways in which they might please.

By alluding to the 'psycho-soma' – and despite the automatically pejorative value of this term in the English-speaking tradition, where a trouble of the psyche is repressed, but erupts then in the body, manifesting what Freud called 'reminiscences' (the tic, the cough), something like real, but 'fraudulent' somatic symptoms (or performances?) – I perform what Ulmer (1985), quoting Derrida's 'White Mythology', calls 'catachresis'. This is:

> the imposition of a sign on a sense not yet having a proper sign in the language. . . . there is no substitution here, no transfer of proper signs, but an irruptive extension of a sign proper to one idea to a sense without a signifier. (p. 57)

Here the sense 'not yet having a proper sign' relates to the actor–spectator experience of theatricality as I have begun to outline it above (Part II, Chapter 3). It is from this perspective, where we fracture an established value – much as Artaud wanted for the term 'cruelty' (Schumacher, 1989) – in order to make speakable what has been felt in theatre's uses of actors, that we can begin to work with an apparently offhand remark which is not uncommon in current approaches to theatre practice of dramatic writing: in noting that a particular staging would not explore authorial intention or interventions or the means to 'readings' conventionally bearing the signature-mark of the *metteur en scène*, one actor suggested that meaning could only develop, for them, in that specific socio-historical conjuncture of forces, from the *'feel of the words in the mouth'*.

I shall want to go further, in terms of the psycho-soma (cf. McDougall, 1982). The work of voicing, of certain sorts of dramatic writing, *in the context of performance* (i.e. for and before the intense but silent demand, channelled through tense body-stillness and the collective gaze of the spectators), produces a complex work in the entire body, such as we noted in *bunraku* (and in other contexts that work which is superfluous to *bunraku* can be used). It is this complex somatic work *in the precise situation of theatre*, which seems to be able to activate what we call the emotions and the psyche, 'bringing forth', and making visible, what we semiotise as affects. Such emotional 'colouring' may be no more than that: 'something' in the voice, a 'shine' in the eyes; not unitary or articulate 'signs' or 'meaning-production' for the fiction or *mise en scène*. But performance success may well depend upon it. The audience as vital massed and ambivalent but always *energetic* force is scarcely mentioned as a major determining factor in Schechner's investigation of Ekman's work, where, instead, he notes that "evidence is accumulating that the difference between "ordinary behaviour" and "acting" is one of reflexivity: professional actors are aware that they are acting" (Schechner, 1988, p. 263). In the appraisal by Benamou and Caramello (1977) of performance-rich postmodern society (noted above), what they suggest, on the contrary, is that such evidence is rapidly dissolving: once we lose the certainties of the truth regime, many of us become happily aware that we are always acting. Professional performance, then, depends upon something else.

What removes the work of the psycho-soma from what is traditionally termed 'psycho-somatic' illness, is precisely this question of **relationship to the other**: where traditionally the psycho-somatic depends on a repression and a displacement, and on the production then of a symptom (little 'reminiscences' traced on the body), the psycho-soma as I approach it works precisely because of a complex **permission to show within enabling constructs** (like a system of parole), set up between actor and *metteur en scène* (function). It works within the specular–somatic economy of performance, in which one of its functions is quite precisely to access a *real*, perceivable, **performance** emotion (into which the fiction can lock, or play). This is dependent more upon the conditions of saying and showing something energetically intense *in performance*, than on anything like 'the words themselves' – although the clauses, here, seem to serve as a series of minute and relational enabling structures to that specular–somatic staging. This seems to be what we see in Fiona Shaw's work for Deborah Warner, where the 're-living emotions' of Stanis-lavski derivation cedes to a somatically-*lived* emotion of highly energised performance, which, because of the enabling frames and controls of performance itself, can slot into the currently-prevailing conditions of lived history (Holland, 'Hearts of Darkness Brought Home to Derry', *The Observer*, 1992, p. 52). Playing *for* that audience heightens the emotional production, transforms the way in which it is felt and semiotised. This lived-performance-emotion is what we see again in the work of Georges Bigot in *Richard II* (Mnouchkine/*Théâtre du Soleil*, The Cartoucherie, Paris, 1982), where the incessant *kabuki*-style beat and the choreographed move-ment, coupled with the demands of the theatre relation, produce a somatic 'excess' which is by definition 'moving', 'emotional'.

We are not dealing here with "emotion prototypes" (Schechner, 1988, p. 264) needing to be 'targeted' through an *a priori* decision-making based on text/'subtext' analysis (which would, indeed, seem to produce "mechanical acting" (p. 264)). Instead this emotional (and interactive) field of force or resonance is a flow, subject then to being profiled or 'outlined' (as one process of a complex somatography), by the facework and bodywork produced in (interactive) voicing of certain sorts of writerly constructs. In Shaw's work at The Riverside, her entire muscular range is choreo-graphed *in tune with* the voicing (and breaks) by all participants in the performance process.

The concept of the 'feel in the mouth', and what emerges from it, is thus far from fanciful, an obfuscatory or romanticising metaphor. It can be approached in a number of ways consonant with the new directions I have outlined in the preceding sections, and to which I shall return. Such 'mouth-feeling' entails and also activates a number of somatic processes, amongst which I include those of the different types and centres of brain activity, in their capacity for retention, recall and (re-)production, where the mechanics involved remain difficult to specify, however much we can recognise their function in the fact of theatre work, and make decisions which depend upon it. The problem here is neat: theatre practice in the 1990s is itself a *theory of theatre practice*, and thus entails a theory of complex human practice. But how far can we carry this, as non-specialists, without being guilty of the 'naive scientism' against which Halliday, amongst others, warns us (Halliday, 1987)?

The feel of words in the mouth seems to activate something more than 'speech acts' (or actioning) and 'actional frames' – permitting the production of "reconstructed [complex] behaviours" toward a staging of the fiction marked out in terms of 'objectives' and 'superobjective'; or thematic systems as hermeneutic traces – toward a global interpretation. It will activate, when particular sorts of text options are used by a skilled actor, what Pêcheux saw as the complex order of the 'unspoken' and of imaging. This unspoken (and the 'unacted': resonant images of singular impossible or 'forgotten' practices) includes – and we need to be clear about this – the organising, structuring and spatialising functions specific to the intelligence of the professional actor at work.

But the work of the psycho-soma is characterised, as well, by the potential binding-in of the complex functions and processes of what we more conventionally call the psyche, to a body-wide network of complex muscular contractions, activated through the central nervous system – e.g. the throat muscles, the lungs, the arms, hands and fingers, the eyelids, eyebrows and eyeballs, neck muscles, stomach muscles, posture, a range of sphincters, and so on. Now, recalling the work of the chanter in *bunraku*, we need to note that this activation does not seem to depend on an *a priori* 'feeling', subject to 'affective recall', so much as on the intermingling through voicing of a work in the conscious mind, with a work in the Imaginary, and a work in the complex musculature of the whole body – for a showing. It works interactively, and intersubjectively, with other bodies (actorly, imagined and spectatorly). At this point, it seems that we might conceive of the psycho-soma as marking out, and regulating, a movement or oscillation, always *between* the fields and functions I am able, through conventions of language, to represent. It is not equivalent, therefore, to any one, nor to a combination, of these. It is located somewhere between the nameable.

This multiple 'passage' of 'words in the mouth' will be manifested in the professional actor's practice, from the start of rehearsals, where we might want to ask less 'what does Beckett mean here', or even 'what does this mean', than 'what am I drawn to do, where, how, and to whom; *who might I seem to become*, with these words in my mouth, *in this place*?'. (It is appropriate, in our own terms, to add the further tentative question: 'And why?')

This marks the onset of what Ubersfeld calls "the pleasure of the voyage" *for the actor* (Ubersfeld 1982a) – and hence, in potential, for one or another spectator. From this actorly 'beginning', the *metteur en scène* can shape and orient the actor-work to a broader orchestration characterising the *mise en scène* – of which we should note two aspects: on the one hand, that broader orchestration develops through that contribution, in tune with the negotiation of the actors' somatic production, instead of preceding it. '*Good theatre work*' will demonstrate the *metteur en scène's* potential for discovering in and eliciting from actors what has not yet been seen, been used, what has not yet become an element in that actor's repertory of skills. But on the other hand – as we shall see from the casting practice of Warner in *Electra* (at the Barbican) – the play of the *metteur en scène's* own Imaginary, intersecting with the actional, attitudinal and ethical–judgemental functions of her complex *habitus*, has already interceded in her own global, pre-rehearsal reading, to inform her choice of inter-actorly potential: interactive potential in body-mass, facial types, skin and hair-colouring, age, energy-potential, muscular state and tension-sites, have already been assessed in their potential interrelations, prior to actual rehearsal work.

Side-stepping, again

If we shift the term 'psycho-soma' sideways, away from its local, culpabilising resonances, then we begin to understand what Shaw was doing in *Electra*; how this work bound mind in to body, without any requirement that her own *equivalent* interiority, her personal 'affective recall', be necessarily engaged **as source** – but with the full expectation that certain sorts of bodily contractions would emerge through her voicing of certain sorts of constructs, in the complex pre-performance situation (i.e. in her complex specular–somatic relation with the other); that those muscular contractions themselves might be said then to 'generate performance meaning-potential'. This is not a willed 'recall', but a calling-forth through her central nervous system, which was activated, and which then *acted* under the simultaneous control of her highly developed rational and passionate mind, again in its relations with the performance other.

What is called forth is an energetic potential *not already semanti-cised*, except in the most general of terms, but made available for differing semiotising, by different spectators at different moments. We can see this 'semantic neutrality' in the case of what we call 'tension', alluding to a general bodily state. This is available to be differently semiotised within a number of scenarios. In terms of its interactive force and its situational framing, that tension might be semiotised as positivity in 'seduction' and 'performance', as a negativity in 'pain', or in 'impatience', or in 'stress'.

Voicing and the psycho-soma

From the perspective of a somatic theory and of the psycho-soma, different modalities of language-use will take their proper place as one field conflating highly economical and often poetic modes of symbolic practice. In the actor it is *voicing* in complex theatrical contexts (for the gaze of the other) which makes these available to brain functions as well as to the materiality of a dramatic theatre they can be said to inform and, inasmuch as voicing is part of a whole interactive somatics, to constitute. The actor-work through voicing, here, differs from the pre-rehearsal and the rehearsal work of the *metteur en scène*, and the two should not be conflated.

In dramatic theatre these different modalities are perceived to be grounded in processual 'possible human relations' (i.e. determined by actions between participants), intensified and singularised by the conditions of performance, and framed (in a way that is not yet understood) by conceptual modelings and imagings – including 'kinship scenes' – both 'derived from', and indeed to be perceived *as* one microcosmic manifestation of socio-cultural context. At this level, we are always, irretrievably, dealing with an order of social iconicity (human relations on stage and in the theatre relation, diagrammatically represent *perceived* extra-theatrical relations), but iconicity here is vitally overlaid by an order of indexicality (the particular modality explored and chosen is used as symptom of, and we let it *point (us) to*, the *metteur en scène*'s enunciation of that representation).

Writing invites a complex voicing, and as such it takes the voice-in-body of one and then another actor as social subject (whatever the period of dramatic composition) as its immediate and effective context. 'Context' is manifested as an animate sign-complex 'charged with signs' in the sense that it takes as its typical or emblematic site the network of signs established and negotiated *between* what is produced through given actors' complex habitus (a specular–somatic symbolic fed by the Imaginary or by Bourdieu's unconscious), in its possible interactions with the input of other practitioner-team members. It is manifested, as voice is activated, in the interactions of body-mass, body-type, typical/singular actional modes of the actors and their manifest attitude to these, and as the spaces between these complexes, and in the relations set up with objects and spatial barriers.

Voicing articulates complex relations, through the clause and inter-clausal relations set up within the texture of the fiction, which intersect with the double instance of actorly and character enunciation, and are informed, further, by the global enunciation typifying *mise en scène*. We can use these relations, once performance voicing occurs (and in our imagined pre-voicing, in reading), firstly as diagrammatical frameworks for stage actions, and secondly as complex *symptomatic* networks, from which we conventionally derive, by inferential processing, concepts of 'singular human interventions' to be attributed to any of the 'peaks' or historically prioritised contingencies of theatre performance work: for example, character, author, *metteur en scène*.

It is this complexity of inferential productions, and their often contradictory constituents, which make our semiotics so delicate a matter (cf. Aston and Savona, 1991 for a renewed investigation into modes of conventional 'literary theory'-based analysis). What should be clear here is that neither *writing* 'itself', nor discourse, in any simple and clear sense, can any longer be considered to be the matrix or generator of performance – which requires the unchartable contribution of those 'singularities' (and not generalities) over which human scientists shrug their shoulders, ruefully; but that writing and discourse can be considered to operate amongst others of its *possible organisers or enablers*, taking their place in performance which is 'generated', instead, by a very complex set of perceived and 'felt' correspondences. Such correspondences are relative to user-perceptions. They are perceived and felt to operate between: relations observed (by someone) in writing; changing conceptions of socio-cultural conditions; the avowed and unavowed desires and needs of a group of practitioners; their conceptions of the social and the audience as symptomatic of this. Dramatic writing is then either poached within, or *lent to* and adapted, renewed, and relativised by, those circumstances.

Somatic work and the psycho-soma

Where do we find the bases for such a somatic theory and a theory of the psycho-soma? As I have demonstrated above, few mainstream theorists in the fields which might seem best to relate to the questions vital to a new dramatic semiotics – i.e. discourse analysis, social semiotics and semiology, and the discourses and methods of psychoanalysis – have done more than glance at the possibility that aspects of cultural practice which language and linguistics cannot contain, but can seem to 'allude to', 'evoke', 'encapsulate' or 'heighten', might function in ways altogether different from those charted by the different schools of twentieth century mainstream linguistics. And although specific elements in Bourdieu and de Certeau (discussed in Part I), and in Lyotard, Barthes and Derrida (in Part II), have provided guidelines to a new practice, it is not clear that any of the latter group, in the sources quoted, have sufficiently broken through the thrall of logo-centricism to be able to conceive of theatre practice as anything other than an *other* of language, axiomatically approached as language's negativity, its bedevilment, its Fool.

For Ulmer, citing more recent Derrida – and for de Certeau – any effective intervention requires the formulation, for theory, of new philosophemes through catachresis; and the limitations placed on earlier attacks on tradition came from their advocates' inability to break with the philosophemes (or discursive units of philosophy, in which we probably see textualised the more elusive episteme) of Platonism and the tyranny of the *eidos*. Ulmer cites Heidegger for whom "*Thea* (cf. Theatre) is the outward look, the aspect, in which something shows itself. Plato names this aspect . . . *eidios*. To have seen this aspect, *eidenai*, is to know." He continues:

And the second root [of theory], *horao*, means "to look at something attentively, to look it over, to view it closely." When translated in Latin and German, *theoria* became *contemplatio*, which emphasizes, besides passivity, the sense of "to partition something off into a separate sector and enclose it therein."

(p. 32)

'The body', 'looked at' (because it is apparently highly visible) by logocentricists through the seemingly ordered grid of language, was thereby partitioned off, separated and enclosed. Theory, Ulmer continues, in its etymological development, comes to mean, "the beholding that watches over truth". The 'truth' of 'the body', in performance, was only *clear*, if the body could be approached as, and called 'text'. What feminists might still assert, however, is that there are other modes of knowing, which function prior to sight, and which have as strong a claim to 'truth' as does what follows: the woman with child knows that child in her body, before she or the world sees it. I am not returning here to biological determinism, in order to construct a gendered theory upon it. Rather, we need to recall this message: there are valid ways of knowing which engage with a somatic intelligence not dependent upon aspect and categorisation. The actor has always felt this. It is time we said so.

In introducing the psycho-soma, I am trying to locate not an *other* of discourse (of *eidios* and of *horao*), but an 'elsewhere', which is always active in uses of and analyses of discourse (even while it explodes these from their apparent location within language), but which has not yet been effectively spoken or written, even though theatre practitioners 'know it when they feel it', and ceaselessly draw upon it if performance is to work. This is an elsewhere of both sight and 'truth', where sight assumes the role of official metaphor for speculation, for contemplation and for knowing, and where 'truth' is equated with an immaterial, passionless enlightenment, with what is brought clearly to sight.

The psycho-soma relates to a wide field of knowledges activated in performance amongst which are prioritised knowledges acquired through uses of emotion; knowledges worked through the body but not clearly available to sight and categorisation; knowledges acquired not through distanced inspection but through workings within the networks of nerve-endings and musculature, as these activate complex and varied resonances in the memory and in the Imaginary. These may do no more than become visible in the shine in the actor's eye, in the muscular definition suddenly etched in her shoulders and drawing the eye, and which we applaud. It is most specifically concerned, in dramatic theatre, with the ways in which voicing involves a taking into and a giving out from the actor's body, in relationship to other bodies including our own, of the particular sorts of little stagings the clause complex makes available; of the curious work of the 'I' which occurs when we take into our bodies, through voicing, the words of an other, in order to show something/to seduce yet an other, through a complex bodywork and in the name of others.

As fleeting, subjects-specific felt-knowledges, these can only be approached through theoretical discourse if we adopt the Derridean position, according to which we try to isolate:

> the specific features of those senses that have not been conceptualized ... and to pose them as an alternative, as models of thinking and writing, to the distancing, idealizing notions based on sight and hearing. The theorization or thematization of the non-objective senses provides the new concept.
>
> (Ulmer, 1985, p. 34).

We need to recognise – if we are to work with the ways in which theatre (which works) achieves the strange fusion of the personalised–social – that if 'distancing, idealising' functions, bound up in traditional semiology, are inadequate to our understanding of the close–intimate–internalising qualities which lead to, and are then incorporated within successful dramatic staging, then we are obliged to try to locate the *sites* for a new conceptualisation.

If we are to understand the play of writing in the actor's work, we have to be able to *think* the 'feel of the words in the mouth', in situations, in a given context (each rendered as different sorts of force fields, acting on and modifying/modified by the rest, and able to resonate momentarily with the 'forgotten history' of one or another of us), while retaining as the unquantifiable and vital component in this conceptualisation, the individual input of the 'risk-taking' actor.

What emerges from this quest is a realisation both pleasurable and intensely frustrating (and more pleasing in that frustration): what the best of dramatic theatre art achieves is what Carroll (1987) citing Lyotard calls the vital *unfulfilling* quality of art:

> According to Lyotard, the mistake of all psychoanalytical approaches to art and literature . . . *is to treat the work as a symptom*, to treat literature, for example, as an "exteriorization in words of a profound phantasmatics". To do this is to imply that desire is fulfilled in the work, that there takes place in art and literature a "reconciliation between primary and secondary processes, between the ego and the id". . . . Lyotard insists that Freud's most important contributions . . . [lie] in the way his theory at its most radical moments indicates that *the work "does not fulfill desire but unfulfills it"*. (pp. 41–2: my emphases)

The social semiotic, as much as the psychoanalytic approach, treats the work as a symptom, leading to a legitimate knowledge; and as we have seen, Bourdieu similarly approaches everyday cultural practice as a new exteriorisation, symptomatic of an interiorised exteriority. Can we sidestep this tradition of 'reading off' the one from its other, by suggesting that what excites and what challenges in theatre uses of dramatic writing, for different practitioners as for spectators, is less *what it fulfils* in legitimate (or already-established) terms, than what it stimulates. That this process is the more satisfying, the more it resonates or ripples forth with further possibilities? This is where the risk-taking occurs: what might happen if I see/feel/show something more than I have as yet experienced – and then more again?

The psycho-soma at its most intimate (but still public) working, in those pre-performance conditions in which the *metteur en scène*'s role is currently vital, operates through something like the taste of words (some of which I have not dared say aloud) in the mouth; of the bite (and the nip: cf. Wilden, 1980, p. 249) of those words or the muscular contractions entailed in the voicing; which elicit, initially, both something like actorly-specific habitus, and something more, belonging within the realm of the excluded, forbidden, omitted or discarded 'residue' we retain from the more accepted conditions of everyday life. It is this half-accustomed, half-dangerous 'bite' and this half-known, half-exotic 'taste', which activate a work in the

Imaginary to which the 'risk-taking' actor is responsive, without for a moment 'giving way' (even to the forceful semiotic thrust of the *metteur en scène*) – since the pre-performance context is itself peculiarly 'social', and functions through a curiously intensified, and goal-specific sociality.

Now, the *metteur en scène*, in early rehearsal work, may tend toward a global reading, which will be 'held', to oversee local decison-making; which will be attentive to the wider spatial implications of the actor's work; and which is careful of the interrelational aspects of the momentary dramatic and theatre relations. This in effect establishes her/his intervention as an energy-focus 'of the whole', however disparate may be its parts. But it seems to me that the actor, working in expectation of locating a means of access (through context-specific voicing of writing) into the realm of a conceptual (or symbolic) 'everyday' of (other) human action, has a quite different relation to writing (as *voice, in body, in sight* potential) from that of the *metteur en scène*, and equally from that already established in a silent, private reading of the text, where quite different mental and physical procedures operate. That the latter can affect the former, when voicing occurs, is evident; but what is clearer still, in early re-hearsal conditions, is that there is a sometimes startling process of discovery, for the actor, as soon as s/he voices certain elements in these precise conditions; and the actor's global somatic intelligence works apace with this somatic (voicing-in-context) realisation, in ways which were literally un-thinkable in that earlier silent, private, 'literary' reading activity.

The little actions awakened by the complex 'taste and bite' are thus both socially derived in their content and conjunctions – both from accessible 'can-show/say' material of imaging and from the less accessible 'can't-show/say *yet*' conditioned by social censure internalised; they are 'other', in that they are activated by responses to a scripting by an other, in terms of a conceptual otherness; and they are necessarily 'personal', first because they are derived through the presence and body-mind work of a singular actor, and second because theatre operates through a work within the personalised–political. Such actions are thereafter part of the *specular*–somatic economy – produced by bodies for, and through the force of, the onlookers, through willed transformations and unwilled (but retained) inclusions, which are juggled and shifted and combined through the active intervention of the collective energies of a group of practitioners.

What is ironic in the present context – and this marks a point at which the work of the actor splits off from the work of the spectator (and from the analyst–spectator) – is that in theatre we have a field of cultural practice which seems to operate largely, and literally, for the senses of sight and hearing – the 'objective senses', for Ulmer – but which does so through other senses in the actor. So that if the actor (and *mise en scène*) work largely through (by making visible) and for sight, through exteriorisation to a seeing implicated so powerfully for Lacan in the mirror stage, s/he does so through an *in-corporation*, through voicing in contexts, of word-complexes. If showing/sight is privileged thereafter, for that actor – who presents a heightened and professional instance of *splitting off* into a complex *actional potential* always infiltrated by, and energised by, a doing shadowed by a highly critical looking-at–doing – what must be noted are the complex processes through which writing infiltrates and shapes the voice, awakening its idiosyncratic and ludic traits, and activating the complex somatic processes which constitute the actorly contribution to the larger image-making meaning-potential of the stage.

Dissolved 'equivalence'

Dramatic writing works within this specular–somatic force-field, *but it should not be subsumed into it as one of its parts*, where sight dominates it, since the actor's language in performance functions as choices taken within a complex (polysystemic) system; so that the chosen options retain the properties of poetic language while becoming a constituent of dramatic action (see Matejka and Titunik, 1976). Secondly the complexities of 'bite and the taste', in all that is brought by a given actor, seem to initiate an idio-syncratic, as well as socially-coded work in the specular–somatic production process, without our being able to suggest that the given elements of dramatic writing are either commensurable with that work, or necessarily able to stand diagrammatically for it in its particulars.

The lure of seeing (see Blau, 1990), used as the conceptual pathway (an Idea, worked through synesthesia or bodily transfers) to other body-experiences, remains strong within theoretical discourse informed by the dominant episteme. For Barthes (1986), sight itself has a 'reach' which includes a much wider range of somatic experience:

> As signifying site, the gaze provokes a synesthesia, an in-division of (physiological) meanings which share their impressions, so that we can attribute to one, poetically, what happens to another . . . hence, all the senses can "gaze" and, conversely, the gaze can smell, listen, grope, etc. Goethe: "The hands want to see, the eyes want to caress." (p. 239)

This may well account for some of the pleasures in theatre *for the spectator*, for some of the skilled actor's work in transferring what has been seen into a complex bodywork, and for some of the pleasures for the actor, of the symbolic spectator as well as the real. Nonetheless, at this point, we need absolutely to separate two complex processes: first, the practitioner-use of dramatic **writing**, where what is perceived to be unitary (phonemes, morphemes, words, phrases, clauses, utterances, character, and so on) is part of what determines the taste and the muscular feel of voicing, its minimal–logical relation to the spaces and objects and relations of sociality; second, the spectator's use of the dramatic, which effectively no longer appears to that perceiver as such in its unitary particulars, since these are transformed in performance into other sorts of human acts (e.g. 'individual speech' rather than single-source writing). As spectator I cannot fully know, through the objectifying senses, what the actor knows through feeling and doing, nor what has gone into that feeling and doing in the space between writing and performance – so that the conventional 'page to stage' formula which hints at understanding on the part of the analyst needs to be questioned. What follows from that assertion is this: as spectator I lack the means to analyse a number of real causal factors (such as individual metabolism, individual daring, and the combination of these between actors cunningly cast), which in a given instance have transformed writing into performance.

Quite different processes are involved in these different uses, although all arguably work through the psycho-soma, and need to be explored as such. But unless we carry out an analysis *as (and not 'of') actors in pre-performance conditions* – which I cannot do here –

then we have as well to recognise that a reader's analysis of 'text', where s/he plays out all roles, at best, in the scene of her imagining, is wholly unlike that irritating, provocative and productive experience of a group-reading under the keen nose of that other, the *metteur en scène*. (The terms 'irritating', 'provocative' and hence 'productive' will take on a particular value in the somatic theory which follows.) My imagining, in the solitary reading process, is not inhabited by the image of the real other (the performer), and as a consequence the activation of my Imaginary, which occurs with the *loss of control/observation of heightened control* experienced when the professional performer intrudes into the field of my vision, does not play a part.

Looking beyond sight

What happens when we try to break from the thrall of the specular metaphor, for the purposes of an analysis based on the feel and taste and the bite of writing in and between bodies? What we need is a theory of energy, in which that feel in the mouth and the bite involved in/as the articulation of words or clauses – working through the interaction of singular-body metabolism, pre-performance conditions, and the nature of the writing – seems to take up an energetic activation (specific to performance itself), to elicit an energetic build-up, a set of blocks to energetic release, and so on. As Lacan learnt from cybernetics, we can learn from developments in information technology, as CDi and CDTV – compact disc interactive video modes – are about to emerge, in the early 1990s, into our fields of vision and experience. Ulmer (1989) is particularly interested in the implications for a theory of energetic perception derived from such a "shift in communications technology", which seems to alter the way in which the sensorium is organised:

Derrida . . . examines the science of electronics, which reveals that a major difference between Newtonian and Einsteinian physics is that the former is a theory of *action at a distance*, while the latter is a theory of *action by contact*, based on the experiments of Faraday and Maxwell in electromagnetism. "The old 'action at a distance' theory postulated that the electrostatic field was merely a geometrical structure without physical significance, while this new experiment ["that the mutual action between two electrically charged bodies depends upon the character of the intervening medium"] showed that the field had physical significance. Every charge acts first upon its immediate surroundings." (p. 35)

In Ubersfeld's estimation of the 'unseizability' of what draws in the spectator and binds her in a to-and-fro movement *between* actor and character, she is bringing the Newtonian gaze to rest on (almost without perceiving 'it') that 'intervening medium'. This is something like an intersection of electro-magnetic fields, something like the clash and blendings of body-heat ('Those two hit it off'; or, 'There's no chemistry between them'), and of the place of writing in this scene. And because of this shift, it is at this point that the *spectator's* semiotics of performance, worked through the objectifying gaze, distances itself from the *action by contact* which is that of the actorly semiotics, where semiotics refers less to decision-making among *meaningful* systemic options, than to decision-making between *felt* and feeling-engendering options as the bite of the words, at that particular conjuncture of the personal and the social, excites them. Ulmer takes up this question:

> Let us say, then, that Derrida's goal is to shift the ratio in the sensorium away from the domination of *eidos* to a new balance . . . requiring a new term to replace "idea" as the name for thought. Derrida himself suggests that the other of *eidos* is *force*, (which, as movement, duration, quality, energetics in general, lends itself to electronic formulations), but he rejects any temptation to reduce the problem to a simple dialectical opposition. (p. 37)

It is not easy to "shift the ration in the sensorium . . . to a new balance", not the least because, as Gregory (1987) notes:

> [t]he brain can increase one sort of input and play down another. Selection starts at the receptors, continues where the nerve fibres enter the brain and spinal cord, and can operate at any synapse within the central nervous system. In order to concentrate on listening, we may find it helpful to close our eyes; to concentrate on a pain, we may want people to stop talking. *One can learn to neglect an input* habitually. *Ballet-dancers learn to suppress the input*

> *from the organs of balance in the inner ear, in order to avoid vertigo when pirouetting.* (p. 525: my emphasis)

In order to concentrate, through acquiescence to *literature's* dictates, on 'the meaning of the words/writer', and in order to concentrate, through the veils of film theory, on the specular function in theatre (cf. Bennett who imports feminist film theory wholesale into analysis of 'theatre audiences' (1990)), *we have learnt to neglect habitually the bite and taste of the words in the mouth in theatre, and what this shows.* We have learnt compulsorily *to see* what we in fact experience elsewhere, and in this unbalancing of the sensorium – in which we sit around a table preparing a text, trying to 'see what it means' – we have overlooked the actor *as active.* In the attempt to redress this neglect, we need to tread in delicate areas:

> All inputs to the central nervous system, gustatory, auditory, visual, and from the skin, the organs of balance, the bladder, the alimentary canal, the muscles and joints, go to the cerebellum, the *reticular formation,* and the thalamus. Those that can eventually become conscious *and cause a sensation* go to certain neurones of the thalamus and thence to the cortex. In the thalamus each input has its own territory, though there is also some mixing, with different sorts of input going to the same region. (p. 525: my emphases)

The last sentence recalls Barthes, cited above, on synesthesia, but at that point, and through that way of seeing, we found no escape from the maze of dominant epistemes. What we need now is a means of access into the energetic activation, through the bite of the words in the mouth, of a 'something in the actor', enacted, in turn, as a multi-layered complex experience and experience-potential. We are dealing with what Derrida calls "force", but this is a term which reverberates with negative connotations in many contexts, where it is conflated not just with coercion practised by the 'forces' of order, with terror practised by the forces of the dark, but with what have been called 'unbridled' passions and drives, liable, in Nietzsche for example, to appropriate, injure and overpower 'the strange and weaker', practising 'suppression, severity, imposition of one's own forms, incorporation and . . . exploitation' (Nietzsche, *Beyond Good and Evil,* cited in Dews, 1987).

This is not what we are dealing with in terms of theatricality although such uses of force may be figured and enacted through the dramatic fiction. There have been instances, for example in the 1960s and 1970s in Europe and the USA, in which theatre groups have, in the name of one or another principle, almost coerced, certainly 'imposed their own forms' on spectators – but rarely more than symbolically, i.e. to an extent which broke with the ethics-in-action of the theatre relation itself.

In more general terms, what we are looking for are the means to a theory of uses of energy in performance, out of which all other developments – such as the production of 'ideas' – develop, and develop such that the idea is greater than the elements of performance which lend themselves to a socio-functional analysis. This basic input from the sciences of the brain seems to signal an area for exploration.

Force, as Derrida indicates, is not the absolute other of *eidos*; in broad terms, in performance which regulates and channels exceptionally developed energies, it is the main and perhaps the only means to the idea, because finally it is only effective performance which, in those few instants in which it edges toward the *sublime* (combining elements of pleasure with elements of displeasure) excites what Lyotard calls 'sublime enthusiasm'. In Carroll's appraisal (1987), "[w]hat makes this enthusiasm a sublime feeling is the extreme tension, or the tension of extremes, it contains within it" (p. 180). Carroll cites Lyotard's appraisal here (borrowed from Kant) of the French Revolution approached as dramatic spectacle as much as political event, and notes that:

> enthusiasm [in these spectators on history] is not a feeling directly linked in any causal way to the drama being observed from afar. It is linked to no definite object, but emerges out of and manifests the gap between . . . baseness . . . and the nobility of the Idea of freedom . . . evoked in circumstances that in themselves seem as far removed from that Idea as possible. Sublime enthusiasm is . . . constituted by horror and joy at one and the same time. (p. 181)

I have already indicated the 'mixed feelings' of my pleasure at the Warner–Shaw *Electra*, where it was the painfully 'almost-excessive' somatic work of Shaw which took me through and beyond character and fable to something (if I semiotise this through the codes of humanism in the world of the 1990s), like a perverse 'actorly generosity'. The complex mix of heady pleasure and horror at this 'excess' is already familiar from recent work of Mnouchkine/ *Théâtre du Soleil*. It was this company which restaged the French Revolution in the heady and enthusiastic climate of 1968 – but at that time a rather more conventional notion of its 'politics' seemed to prevail. In the 1990s, this theatre group tends to amputate that work in indexicality, which in dominant naturalistic tradition leads the spectator to constitute a fictional world of identificatory pleasures (psychological and social, worked in terms of the constituted character); but it leaves no 'disenchantment' in its place. It is the intensely worked somatic energies and skills which seem instead to enthrall the spectators, and which those same spectators seem – in the rapture of sustained applause – to perceive as a pleasurably painful excess (in which sado-masochistic desires undoubtedly play); as something like a *gift*:

Enthusiasm is a modality of sublime feeling. The imagination tries to furnish a direct, sensual presentation of an Idea of reason . . . , but it does not succeed and thus experiences its impotence. But it discovers at the same time its destination, which is to realize its agreement with Ideas of reason through an appropriate presentation. It results from this blocked relation that instead of experiencing a feeling for the object, *one experiences when confronted with this object a feeling "for the Idea of humanity in us as subjects."*
(Lyotard, in Carroll, 1987, p. 181: my emphasis)

'Effective' use of forceful energies leads to what a maximum of us will agree, at quite different moments and for different reasons, to experience as 'an appropriate presentation'. In this context, 'ideas' come much less from the writing, than from those effectively felt *uses* of the writing; and whether some of us like this or not, those effective uses are not enshrined 'in the writing itself', since even amongst professional groups the effectiveness of performance is not a consensual affair. But what can we find in effective writing which can – if our modes of approach are apposite – enhance practitioners' uses of energy?

It seems to me that writing we call effective *in the 1990s* must offer the potential for a voicing which, for one reason or another, *vibrates* in the body/bodies of the voicers, with resonances which swell into the separate spaces of collective spectating, taking individual directions, thereby, *as part of the event*. This means that we need a specialised theory of 'vibration', permitting us to begin to understand what it means to claim that the bite of a clause articulated is a complex *muscular* act, which works, as do all muscular actions, not just at its manifest site, not just through 'the central nervous system', but through the reticular formation. This seems to be a brain centre involved not just in processing, but also in the retention of a mysterious trace or 'recall' of muscular contractions already experienced.

But we need something more than this, because theatre work is collective, and the *metteur en scène*/actor–actor/other practitioner relation is a curious one. I have earlier borrowed Barthes' metaphor of the pebble and the ripples: in the case of theatre work – such as work on a Sophocles text – we need to contemplate in pre-performance conditions a minimum of three 'pebbles thrown', three possible 'workings' in *possible experiences*, in different symbolic modes, entailing not just pre-verbalisations but imaging and the potential for voice and other somatic practice; these are in effect three sets of individually hierarchised and modulated resonances.

Bundles of potential

A bundle of performance semiotic potential, held together by the differing energetic input of group members faced with the demands for immediate concrete work and of a given performance schedule, and ceaselessly negotiated not just between these different inputs but in terms of the conditions of theatricality themselves as these 'press in', does not 'articulate a dominant position' or interpretation, able to overrule contestatory and ambivalent input, to produce the sort of coherent oneness still sought by Pavis (1992). Instead the bundle is established (even within fairly conventional 'dominant' *metteur en scène* practice) as a small-scale performance parameter 'containing' a cluster of different contributions which produce, even 'in the moment' of what looks like 'a single action', a tension and a certain semiotic heterogeneity. Here the global enunciation (*mise en scène*) 'in-forms' (but finally cannot wholly dominate: oppression causes tactical activity) a moment of work by the actor(s) in their always active relationship with fictional forces, objects, spatial factors and the spectator. Every 'instant' – whether traditionally called 'a sign' or 'a signifying practice' – is thus not single (although it 'peaks' in attention-focus), but multiple, and it is time for theory to recognise this heterogeneity 'within the one'.

Each 'bundle' is 'pressed in upon' and thus constrained by the conditions of theatricality (for a showing, for the other, in terms of X performance conditions); but it is simultaneously liable to be marked by a lively but uneven activity within the bundle, between different participants' contributions: heterogeneous particles (half-formed ideas, feelings, input from the shifting and partly shrouded scenes of different Imaginaries and different symbolic modes) of semiotic potential. This seems to produce some of the interest in theatre practice: decision-making toward a staging does not eliminate small-scale difference even within this 'single performance moment', and indeed this difference-within-oneness can both produce a piquancy, and multiply the potential for use by different spectators.

In terms of the proto-symbolic, the actor might bring to initial group work a potential for voicing and other somatic action; the designer a complex image or set of complex images; the *metteur en scène* a proto-discursive hermeneutic, an initial seizing of wider connections with a number of models of knowledge or master discourses and practices (and a position with regard to these), but also a feeling, an energetic enthusiasm, as well as a tradition of working, an im-print in visual as well as hermeneutic terms. These different symbolics cannot any longer be usefully approached as either semantically or semiotically 'the same', although in pragmatic terms they need to be able to peak, to be used effectively together to produce concrete actions in specific spaces and times for an imagined other. What is of interest, in terms of the tradition for discourses and metatexts of the *mise en scène*, is that neither 'discourse' nor 'metatext' (cf. Dolan, 1989), traced to a precise conjuncture of late-twentieth-century northern European and American performance and critical practices, can any longer be seen as wholly determining or exhausting the semiotic potential of all highly diverse particles 'bound' within the bundles representing decisions made in group work; but far from these other particles therefore being seen as 'extra-semiotic', it seems to be the case that they must be termed 'other-semiotic', *performance*-semiotic, 'other-world' symbolics and potential.

Representations

What I am proposing here is doubly difficult to render diagrammatically, since we cannot depict, on the page, the radiating 'haloes', nor the degree of energetic thrust from the performer/practitioner/participant. In two-dimensional terms, and hence metaphorically rather than diagrammatically, the interaction might be represented as shown in figure 9.1.

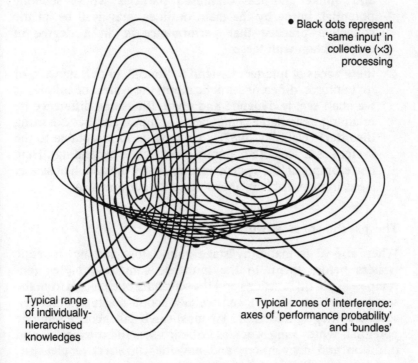

● Black dots represent 'same input' in collective (×3) processing

Typical range of individually-hierarchised knowledges

Typical zones of interference: axes of 'performance probability' and 'bundles'

Figure 9.1 Three-participant group semiotisation of "same input".

There are a number of factors we might want to note here:

1. energy of input differs (for example, between *metteur en scène* conviction, actor uncertainty and designer esthetic) and thus 'ripples' are differently driven, causing quite different force to and upon ripples approaching from other directions;

2. ripples around a 'pebble' represent, in each instance, **individually-hierarchised** and experienced socially-determined knowledges *and proto-practices*: the latter are vital because different practitioners bring somatic knowledges and image-material, as much as 'ideas';

3. ripples intersecting develop **zones of interference** (between often un-like inputs); these zones take the form of bundles of performance probability, marked by both forceful and persuasive 'outlines', and 'containing' – and this is vital – like and unlike and less organised particles whose semiotic potential, borne by the main outlines, may well be, in the collective practice that performance is, in a degree of contradiction with these;

4. these zones of interference tend to 'cancel', to pulsate with, or to 'reinforce' different semiotic input: the system of culture, as we shall see, is dynamic and open. It absorbs difference by retaining assimilable components of input, and by 'exporting disorder' (Halliday, 1987) – i.e. what is unacceptable to the system as it seeks to maintain itself (while expanding). Here one example of 'the system' is supplied by the notion of *mise en scène*, in its possible relationships with performance.

The psycho-soma at work

When appeal is made, by stage enunciators and by dramatic writers before them, to the immense somatic complex (encompassing brain functions and the screening of elements from the scenes of the Imaginary), can we talk about 'meaning-potential' somehow lodged 'in drama'? We must surely talk about a semiotic potential, which ranges across esthetico-somatic convention and tradition and conventions and novelties of affective pleasure, without, for all that, being able to suppose that through any conventional analysis of dramatic writing, we necessarily get much closer to an understanding of what an actor/*metteur en scène* complex *does*. Mnouchkine herself seems – rather like Barthes (1986) – to suggest that the actor/*metteur en scène* complex mediates potential knowledges through action, without being wholly responsible for the uses of those knowledges:

> I tend to feel that the goal of text analysis is to attempt to explain everything. Whereas the role of the actor and of the *metteur en scène*, distancing itself from recent tendencies, is not at all to explicate the text. Their role is to illuminate, of course, and not to make things more obscure. But the spectator has to be left something to discover. There are waves, resonances: the actor strikes a gong or drops a pebble into the water, but without trying to predetermine the ripples that result from it, to fix them so that everyone can count up the precise number of rings rippling forth. What is vital instead is that the actor drops the pebble just so, where it needs to be dropped, so that all the emotional, philosophical, metaphysical and political resonances can be produced . . . A text analysis takes place according to a different rhythm, it can enumerate its components. An actor can't do this: at every moment the actor must produce an essential balance. The audience probably receives – according to the level and the needs of each – what each member is destined to receive. (Mnouchkine, 1984: my translation)

A difference of apparatus, participation and rhythm opens between the work of text analyst and that of the practitioner; a schism opens in Pavis' neat couplet of "production and reception"; a series of gaps opens within the ranks of the spectators. What Mnouchkine invokes, as well, in her use of the term "destiny", is something like Bourdieu's *habitus* – but the understanding here is fluid in that Mnouchkine does not stipulate a class-origin as the basis for judgement of taste and meaning-production. What she adds to our understanding of resonance is that it is both internal to the actor, and must also seek its balance with the 'felt-knowledges' and their productions in the *metteur en scène*(-function), responsible for the orchestration of fields of force throughout the performance space and event. We need thus to integrate a model of negotiated interiority–exteriority of resonance, into the conceptual space opened up by the notion of the singular 'taste and bite' of words in the given actor's site and practice within theatre's specular–somatic economy. We have the potential for this once we remember that the psycho-soma is a condition of theatricality itself, where 'theatricality' marks out a field in which an actorly production is solely enabled by its relation to the other's somatic activity, intensified gaze, desires and needs.

The reticular 'trace', which can be recalled, and thus 'felt again' (if appropriately accessed) is both *detached from* external material reality, and *worked within* the materiality of the body, but always *for that other*. It is not limited, but 'spreads' or resonates not just through the affective–limbic system (whose status and function are disputed), but in nerve-system and muscular 'movements' which seem to bear some relationship to, and elicit, iconic and indexical processing. This may be because in the one a 'muscular-contraction trace' seems to equate with, or provoke, a diagrammatically 'equivalent' body-pleasure we might call emotion (from the physicality of 'feeling' to its emotional equivalence, worked through the same site); and in the other the 'muscular-contraction trace' seems to trigger or point to or function as symptom of another type of feeling. But even amongst 'same-culture' groups, it is not clear that the processing through iconicity and indexicality will follow the same paths to the same sites.

Semiotics and pleasure

At the sight of a favourite chair, in a room or on a stage, or when I see its image, or through a speaking ('That's my favourite chair'), my body either really, or in anticipation (in a symbolic process worked in the brain), reclines, and tension points soften, and the body relaxes. Then a sigh of pleasure runs through that same somatic system, carried by the breath, and it brings with it other shadings of quiet emotion – which may have no specific content, no drama accruing. What seems to happen is that the personal-individual intersects with socially habitual, hierachised muscular contractions, accessing brain functions associated with what some experimenters call the affective limbic system (controlling emotional association), to produce a composite 'felt-knowledge' which expands beyond, while implicating, social codes and conventions.

Stage practitioners make use of these sorts of processes, often cunningly in that they 'sense' them (a somatic intelligence), through an acutely developed power of observation, recall and understanding of the visual–tactile abstract–material associative and transpositional capacities we all constantly utilise in everyday life and our imaginings which make up part of it. What they manifest, professionally, and what we need to try to develop in students of theatre, is this acute knowledge of the psycho-soma and the ways in which it works and can be worked in theatre.

Body therapies and the psyche

This does not involve esoteric arts, but rather the reinstating (and in our case the prioritising) of body-knowledges into the realm of approved knowledges. Psychologists working in what they call "cognitive therapy" are currently exploring the possibility, always assumed in Japanese traditional physiological approaches to problems 'of the psyche' (Ohnuki-Tierney, 1984, pp. 81–4), that somatic exercises and *tactile* recall can intervene in the modification of psychological states. The tactile always involves muscular contraction as well as nerve-sensation, and the muscular contraction hypothetically activates the limbic system of emotional recall: in recent developments in cognitive therapy, the recall of the feel of the foot crunching on sand when one walked on a beach *and was happy*, may permit the depressed to break out of a cycle of 'negative thoughts' into which they are locked. The actor who performs the laugh seems thereby to be able to produce that laughter's feeling, but as a consequence of action, rather than as action's pre-existing thought or feeling.

This *walking plus crunchy feeling plus happiness* is a complex activation of the psycho-soma, with the notable input to therapy coming from what here is given as the second element in the formula: the somatic action, involving leg muscles, muscles in the feet and toes, a relative lack of tension in the upper torso and facial musculature, and – it would seem – a brain attentive to sound + feel + smell, plus a non-focused long-shot type of eye-activity.

Such an activation of the psyche through the muscular-tactile is wholly familiar to the twentieth-century occidental actor: it makes up part of her repertoire; and we need to recognise that the actor's work in the psycho-soma always simultaneously retains that control which permits the tension to be amplified, thrust forth, drawn back, to maintain and enhance performance energy and interest.

The ideogramme and the psycho-soma

What Esslin (in Redmond, 1987) calls the complex 'ideogramme' of actorly work, which functions to make available a shifting hierarchy of semiotic potential, is overseen by that work of the pyscho-soma which is specific to the conditions of theatricality. But while we can begin to chart some of the zones of resonance, as does Barba in his work on the performer of *kathakali* (1983, p. 21), it is now clear that the changed attitude to code and convention prevailing in the theatres of north-western Europe does not permit us to outline and categorise with the same clarity:

> *Mudras* – which are gestures (whose significance is given in advance) composed by hands and fingers – are visual ideo-grammes able to be substituted for oral language. Every mode of Oriental dance uses *mudras* which can be categorised into four distinct groups:
> a. gestures inspired by the symbolism of religious ritual
> b. mimetic, imitative or descriptive gestures, reproducing a character, a situation, or an attribute
> c. gestures borrowed from everyday life, but highly stylised
> d. invented gestures having a suggestive or subjective value (suggesting, for example, the intensity of love of a husband for his spouse).
>
> (1983, p. 21: my translation)

These gestural options, he suggests – and we need to add, the resonances activated in given spectators by their use in performance – are strictly co-ordinated with body movement and facework. But the value of the *mudras* can be wholly inverted if they are produced in an active rather than a static position, or in different combinations. While this recalls the classic definition of structure according to which the constituent parts of a system are organised in such a way that that organisation itself – and not 'the sign' – produces the meaning(-potential) of the whole, it sets off alarm bells as we begin to slip back toward the insidious pleasures offered by the systematising, codifying approaches of the 1970s. The so-called 'minimal gestural unit' is not a performance value, but no more so is any objectified 'structure' divorced from the perceptual strategies and tactics of one or another spectator. The peformance value is *combinatory*, and it includes within 'it' the voyage of the singular gaze (as well as the social gaze) of the single spectator within the group.

But in the attempt to assess the range and type of resonance-potential, we might well adopt something like the Barba schema, with appropriate modifications, suggesting that 'the same' sign- complex, in – for example – method acting, in performance conditions, can simultaneously, for certain spectators, be seen to 'represent':

1. Western acting traditions – which range from the twentieth-century view of the Ancient Greek and the Elizabethan, and encompass the Stanislavski naturalism, contemporary naturalism, the input not just from Artaud and Grotowski but also from Genet's 'sign charged with signs' (Innes, 1981) – and an actorly and a staging position with regard to those;

2. the material exteriority (processed iconically or mimetically), and the hypothetical interiority (processed indexically), attributed to 'character in fictional context';

3. a gendered enunciation (actor and/or character complex), activating empathy or antipathy;

4. a stylised borrowing from everyday life of the performance context;

5. the singular 'idiosyncratic' contribution and the inventiveness of the given professional actor, as this negotiates with the other (actor, *metteur en scène*, and spectator).

The list is far from complete. What it is vital to recognise is that it is the somatic intelligence of the actor which must work to mediate, regulate and (with the *metteur en scène* function) negotiate activity in this site of resonant interaction, as it is made available to spectator uses. The psyche (as in the term psycho-soma) is thus not single in its functions – but no more is it split between 'rational' and 'irrational' or 'passionate' and moralising forces, and nor are its different components locked in a life/death struggle.

Vibration and the psycho-soma

Now, once we approach vibration through the psycho-soma, what we find is that an appreciation of the physics of the phenomenon –

which could arguably be applied to 'the body' as medium and to the theatre relation as concrete site (akin to an echo chamber) – is inadequate to our needs. This is so because the vibrations I am talking about here play in a constant movement between voice as muscular apparatus, and mind and brain which combine the reticular formation with both the limbic system and other brain functions and centres (e.g. primary and secondary sensory areas of the cortex, plus association areas: see Gregory, 1987, p. 525). They progress rapidly into the wider reaches of body through *motor areas*, but equally they are both chronic (they persist) as well as diachronic (they change or develop). In this sense, action is not first 'thought', 'in response to words', but rather animation of muscular options in the widest sense occurs through the 'reactivation' of elements in the reticular formation, when this embodying occurs with the 'bite and taste in the mouth'.

What we might note of the latter is that they are simultaneously experiencing and receiving input from the wider environment, which means that this *vibratory potential* through voicing is also responsive to interrelation with the same sorts of processes in other bodies, in situation, and within the wider theatre relation and social context.

Vibrations are obviously unlike the neat linear movement from signifier to signified, from index to what it is claimed it points to: they play out a to-and-fro, uneven, and – although they resonate further in coming into contact with other surfaces – an often goal-less movement, marked in peaks by performance (actor–spectator interactive) intensities, where they may 'shudder' with the inertia noted above; and consequently they are equally marked by fallings back, ebb and flow, brief dissolution. They might remind us, in this, of Barthes' ripples.

This means that we are dealing with a *psycho-socio-cultural* vibration, with a properly *semiotic* vibration, worked through the materiality of theatre's uses of writing-as-voice (as breath, sound, resonance, in and between bodies, in time and space), tuned and punctuated in terms of a certain systemic potential and a process of decision-making. But unlike conventionally appraised semiosis, this vibration both produces no neat capture of readily retrievable 'meanings', and can no longer be convincingly relegated to the realm of the 'ungraspable'. My casting choice of one woman actor instead of another, where both are conventionally attractive, may depend on the observation that one can twist her limbs 'sinuously', where the other, of equally refined musculature, is tensely energetic – so that whereas 'the same words', in 'the same context', might 'mean the same', just as the two actors' presence on stage might 'mean the same' in terms of conventional approaches to sociality and gender, the internal body and energy relations of the *mise en scène* are wholly changed by this difference in body tension. Theatre depends on vibrational potential, and decisions (often unspoken, un-speakable) are made, for example, in casting; options are examined, selected amongst, retained or rejected, which relate to and attempt to organise *to some extent* 'the social' and 'the esthetic' dimensions of that production; but what we now need to recognise are the 'felt' and recently un-speakable bases for some of them, acknowledging that a woman director will select a particular woman actor not because she has learnt the 'male gaze' (Mulvey, 1977), but because she too, because of the guaranteed distance of the theatre relation, has the capacity to eroticise the bodies and energetic work of others in stagings.

Basic elements of vibration theory

The adoption of conventional poeticising approaches to language and vibration is not adequate to our purposes: we are dealing with the wholly nebulous 'reach' and play of a vibration not 'contained' by the use of certain sorts of sounds (or phonemes amd phonemic clusters, in the scriptural order), nor explained through the attempt to match a sound to affects – although it should be clear that sustained repetition of phonemes – e.g.:

CHRYSOTHEMIS
> Are you so eager to give up your life? 393

ELECTRA
> My life? A fine life, a life to wonder at! 394

> (McLeish, 1979, p. 16)

(rather than 'the phoneme itself'), across character-units, to which is added stress marked through punctuation, *potentially* organises not just use of breath, intonation and – in ELECTRA's case, rhythm – but *may* evoke, in a given performer, echoes of an already-experienced (but not necessarily personally experienced) body cry. But to recognise these factors is not enough: we are no closer to a specific semiotic fact of vibration, which seems to confound semiotics. The problem is this: there can be a significant 'taste and bite in the mouth', an intense energetic investment *in the acting body*, without this body manifesting, in minimal-logical or commonsensical terms, any discrete somatic 'action' (gesture, movement), oriented to beings or objects or spaces in the world. For all that, this 'lack of discrete signs' can coincide precisely with a body-phenomenon which can be semiotised. Here, 'something happens in the body' under the gaze, and no semiotics of action, proxemics, relation to the other, direction of gaze, gestuality, relation to the object, facework and so on, can explain for us the difference, in performance for the spectator, between the body which 'shimmers', with this intense and contained investment of energy, and the body which does not. Shimmering or vibration or dilation is not an articulation, it has no visible unitary parts, it may not even register on any tools of measurement we can employ, *but we see and sense it*, and we can use it as symptom (if we so choose) in an oscillation between meaning-production for the fiction, and the meaning of (this) performance (for me, here). Performance by a given actor 'which works', may depend entirely on the way s/he can summon this up, modulate and regulate it.

In seeking a 'physics of actions in theatre' – amongst which we include the action of energy-containment, and of complex brain-work – we need to draw on the contribution of basic physics, remembering as we do so that dominant and conservative epistemes inform what can be known here as much as they inform discourses in the so-called human sciences. In invoking dramatic writing and the work of the psycho-soma, through the bite and taste of voicing (as this comes to intersect with the force-fields other participants in theatre production will seek to establish), I am not just looking for a theory of energy, vibration and electromagnetic fields, but of the *resonances* that certain highly schooled somatic uses can differently produce in us. If we take the professional violinist as a model, what we find by comparison is that the actor (in the relations of theatricality) simultaneously plays, *and is the instrument played*.

Beyond technical perfection

We already 'know' perfectly well, because we can feel it, and it pleases us, that the 'great violinist' is more than technically perfect, and that in 'the poor violinist' a lack of muscular honing and control can produce vibration without resonance. And we know, further, that the concert violinist, in concert conditions, 'feeds off' the reciprocal energy production of the performance relationship with the spectators, because the receiver of electromagnetic radiation can also resonate in tune with that radiation produced through the particular conditions of performance. (We need to develop our knowledge not just of what the performing body is producing, and how, but also of the spectating body and the effects of its eager self-containment in a state of particular muscular and affective tension; and the effect of the massing of these bodies, and the complex mixture they bring together of desire, need, hunger, nervousness and ethical considerations (cf. Pradier, 1990).)

The resonance can be re-converted into a different form of energy, and in the best of productions (e.g. the Mnouchkine/*Théâtre du Soleil: Les Choréophores*) that converted energy in the spectator is willingly constrained – and probably necessarily. Desire is maintained, and elicits energetic production in the performer – until the curtain call at the end of the performance (which might seem, today, to substitute itself for the traditional moment of dramatic catharsis). Then it bursts ritually forth, given back to the performers who, in the *Théâtre du Soleil*, perform again and again with renewed energy-in-exhaustion: with a lift of the chin, a holding of a muscularly complex position before swinging into movement to the demands of the music. As spectator I experienced this as 'generosity', rather than 'simple professionalism'. Perhaps I can combine the two, and overturn claims about postmodern disenchantment and cynicism: the professional performer in contemporary theatre is required to give something unavailable to us through electronic media, and sometimes gives it; and for a number of complex psycho-physiological reasons (familiar in other aerobic practices), finds that production painfully elating, liable to produce in the brain (in body) natural morphines.

The relations of theatricality are vital to the production process: in a closed system the total quantity of energy remains unchanged, but in the dynamic open systems of theatre, strongly informed by the different planes constituting 'environment', the total quantity of energy is unstable (just as cultural practice, for Pêcheux, is a logically-unstabilised area for investigation). In performance which works, it would seem that the physical space of theatre acts as a potential echo chamber – not just for sounds, but for heat, hormonal productions and excretions, and so on (Pradier, 1990) – in which invisible substances are bounced off surfaces to other surfaces, eliciting other somatic 'productions', and resonate. We already 'know' about this: we talk about the 'chemistry' of certain actor–actor and actor–spectator relationships. But the term conceals more than it reveals.

Kinetic theory

What we know in general terms about kinetic theory, or the theory of movement, is that when a substance is heated, the atoms and molecules which make up that substance move and vibrate more violently, emitting radiation. In the bodies at work in the theatre economy – and we include the spectators here – these 'substances' are multiple, immensely difficult to pin down, apparently unavailable to a classic analysis based on visibilities and boundaries, but absolutely vital to that economy.

In the most general terms, let us suppose that an increase in energy – by any sustained means (including voicing of certain dramatic writerly options, in performance conditions, as we shall see) – produces an increase in vibration, in any number of sites and substances, with variable effect and affect depending on a number of further factors. Energy, for example, can be internal or external: if internal, it tends to manifest as vibration in the particles from which the body is formed; whereas external energy can be in the form either of force (exercised on someone or something: Shaw on ORESTES; Shaw on the pomegranate), or in the form of electromagnetic radiation. It would seem that in the case of Shaw and the psycho-soma more generally (where this comes to be semiotised as a (somatically produced) 'character trait')), we have an internalised energy, working through the bite and taste of certain clauses in particular as these activate the Imaginary, which interacts with the exteriority of the stage situation, and with the need-to-show/experience/feel that theatricality entails.

In the given instance (Shaw/ELECTRA), for the most part that interiorised, vibrating energy cannot be exteriorised as force, partly because of Shaw's distinctive mode of somatic action (see too her HEDDA in the Warner–Ibsen *Hedda Gabler*, Dublin and London, 1991), and partly because of the paucity, in the allotted clauses (Sophocles, *Electra*, trans. McLeish), of **Material Processes** (Halliday, 1978, 1985, 1987) through which we act, through language, in and on the world. As a consequence, and because of the fine 'excess' of her energetic input, the interiorised energy resonates in her body, and is projected forth as electromagnetic radiation which I semiotise – by seeing it as symbolic of known instances of 'real frustration/impotence in the world' (of my experience), apparently pointed to (indexicality/enunciation) by the sustained action of Shaw as element of the production team. I willingly attribute this, despite my explicit knowledge of the actorly role which works the opposite, to the character I constitute within the order of the fiction.

Any 'science' of this vibration and electromagnetic radiation, as these function within the internally shifting specificities of any performance event, must now admit to *indeterminacy* as its major principle: however precisely we can attempt to verbalise 'what is going on here', we are by definition unable to name the constituent parts of any given event, since these vary not just with spectator difference, but arguably internally, and with the shifting input from 'outside', as socio-cultural changes intrude into theatre conditions through the social subject as medium. Together these elements of uncertainty – which may well go some way, once we know more about electrons, neurons and electromagnetic fields, toward explaining after the event, why a performance might have worked on one occasion and not on another – seem to provide some basis for an acting training which privileges all kinds of muscular development and control.

Systemic–functional linguistics

For a second approach which permits us to draw writing in to our field of experience, and in order to test the hypothesis that the clause is a little stage which dramatises manifested participants, dramatising, as well, the speaker of the clause in his–her relation with the other, what we can use here is the input from

Systemic–functional linguistics (I return to this in detail below). At this point we might note that:

1.　repetition is part of the Textual Function, regulating syntactic combinations – here that intrusion of sameness into difference tends to 'hold back', in a situation of tension, the 'onward movement' of the clause;

2.　in terms of the system of Transitivity, line 393 is marked by a Relational Process ('Are you': static) followed by a metaphoric use of a Material Process ('to give up': action in-the-world); whereas line 394 adopts in the position of Rheme (last informational elements in a discourse unit, with the consequent status of 'new' information), a Mental Process ('to wonder at') which is once again static;

3.　line 393 uses the intersubjective marker of the interrogative (putting a question *to someone*) – and we move towards predicating the character accordingly as 'interactive', 'oriented to the interlocuteur' – whereas line 394 is marked by de-personalised uptake: repetition of 'life'; transformation from 'your' to 'My'; function of quasi-response; but marked strongly, in the Rheme position, by a subjectless Process ('to wonder at').

I return at length below to these concepts and terms. The voicing of these lines, by two actors, already 'vibrates' with these minutely marked interrelational meaning-potentials, which we equally – apparently 'intuitively' (because so rapidly: habitus is interiorised, and thereafter lived) – process in a general practice of context-specific reading, as minute symptoms in a vaster tissue of clausal-relations. These relations peak in what we call 'character', in terms obedient to the exigencies of genre: i.e. in a number of clusters of 'contingencies in the flow' of global dramatic discourse (Halliday, 1987). 'Character'-type – i.e. marked by *possible* traits, *possible* qualities, derived through the projection of elements of a wholly relative, user-specific 'whole human semiotic' onto named clausal and interclausal relations – is dynamic, *contingent* upon needs brought in the text-and-user interaction; whereas character-name functions as an exigency of dramatic genre.

That this exigency of dramatic writing can be approached as wholly contingent upon theatrical stylistic decisions, is revealed in those productions which enact 'character' as voice-over, as cut-out, as multiplication of actors, rather than as 'wholly and singly human'. What appears to be an exigency (an 'established convention') of a genre – e.g. dramatic writing – will cede to the contingencies of use – e.g. dramatic writing used as literature; used as script for televising; used as script for staging; used as script for naturalistic staging, or for avant-gardist staging; used to reinforce or to challenge conventions.

'Common-sense' predications: the "whole human semiotic"

In minimal–logical and commonsensical terms, however, we then think to 'know' (by predicating, or adding qualifiers to named subjects) each of these clusters individually, as 'character-in-a-world'. I can readily predicate (through my own perceptual 'staging', and prior to any such systematisation as the one I have just performed) CHRYSOTHEMIS as 'strongly interpersonal', ELECTRA as 'generalising and abstracting', relating 'personal issues' to 'general principles'. What I am thereby doing is bringing my interiorised perceptual 'staging techniques', through application of a 'whole human semiotic' I both mediate (socio-historically) and live out, to bear on the ways in which in general we transform writing into ways of 'acting in the world, for someone'.

And it is on the basis of this intrusion and this 'staging', that my minimal–logical and commonsensical 'feeling' is that, in gestural terms equally, CHRYSOTHEMIS is oriented interpersonally to ELECTRA – in the fictional imaging might touch her arm, direct her gaze to her – but that ELECTRA is oriented to herself, or outwards to a generalised space. What we lack however is any adequate basis for assuming, because of this, that any actor or group of practitioners will enact such 'zero-level', concordant options *in performance*: performance (*for someone*) will generally entail a globalising or cobbled-together 'overlaid' stylistic/esthetic convention, which will be brought to intersect with the minimal–logical, either to sustain and reinforce (while slightly transforming) certain aspects, or to set itself against them, or to flirt with them, quoting them to different ends. What this means is that another minimal–logical grid comes to bear: that of culturally-specific theatricality.

So that the minimal–logical and the commonsensical might be overtaken and then in-formed by an avant-gardist, a postmodern or a *Gestus*-determined organisational schema. In this case we might want to assert, with Halliday, that divergence from norms re-activates those norms through their very disruption of them, since we know full well that the most conventional theatre practice is always meta-theatrical, however conservative its implicit statement regarding theatricality. But invoking the norm, the convention, through exception to it, does not have the same implications for late-industrialised theatre as it seems to have for linguistics, where shifting from the convention is often perceived to impair socio-functionality.

While this rapid processing occurs, and amidst that *tension* I have noted in (1) above, we find reverberating the 'semiotic reach' of the phrase 'My life!' in the mouth and thus through the psycho-soma of a given actor: a neat bite, invested with energy and tension, vitally informed by the subjectivity of any actor as *person-in-the-world*, this translator's option, as comparison shows, is effective in that it privileges brevity, exclamation, the personal and the felt:

CHRYSOTHEMIS:
  With no regret for life as you know it now?
ELECTRA:
  Life as I know it? How marvellously fair!
                              (Watling, Penguin, 1952)

CHRYSOTHEMIS:
  But hast thou no care for thy present life?
ELECTRA:
  Aye, my life is marvellously fair.
                              (Jebb, Bobbs-Merrill, 1950)

CHRYSOTHEMIS:
  Have you no care of this, your present life?
ELECTRA:
  Mine is indeed a fine life, to be envied.
                              (Grene, University of Chicago Press, 1957)

None of the three offers an equivalent to the tight, process-less, exclamatory and personalised initial clause (in ELECTRA) which sharpens the bite of Shaw's mind-in-body, and draws the felt-subjectivity of each spectator, although each roughly maintains the processual and the interrelational indices of socio-functionality we have noted in the McLiesh option. We must conclude, from this, that the 'bite and feel' are more effective in performance terms, than are the socio-functional components.

Dramatic discourse staged, as speech-in-force-fields

Although there is obviously a basic on–off operative principle in our everyday uses of mechanised energies, somatic energies in theatre performance are not mechanised (whence the pleasure of co-ordinated movements); and secondly, force is not unitary, but has reach and spread, currents and duration; and it is a basic potential (although not always a fact) of the conditions of the theatre relation. In the complex 'ELECTRA: My life!', the tension activated by the options I have noted above, and the energetic peaking, are not cut off by the stressed conclusion to the clause, for the simple reason that we are dealing with a wave of energy, marked by peaks and troughs, initiated much earlier in the text (plausibly with ELECTRA's cries at line 90, McLeish, 1979) and newly focused here, rather than with units. That energy *must* be carried into the scriptural space between the clauses, and then across that 'gap', for the simple reason that the semiotic complex is not broken where the clause break occurs, that breathing goes on, that the spectating presence remains hungry and wants feeding; and that finally the conditions of speech are less inclined to mark out in unitary fashion those boundary-markers (capitals and punctuation) we formalise within the scriptural economy.

In everyday terms, the situation in which actors work with the *metteur en scène* is always 'highly charged', often 'electric' – which is to say that what has been thought of as metaphor, taken from electromagnetics, has always been used to communicate the nature of performance and production conditions. The problem which confronts the actors today – and probably the *metteur en scène* similarly – is less one of locating meaning in writing leading to an interpretation, than of locating in individualised actorly uses of written language, the means to a heightening and a tempering of that 'highly charged atmosphere' as it feeds the individual and the interactive. The intention is that it can be effectively utilised in performance, both played through over a given period of perfor-

mance time, *and* repeatedly thrust forth *and partially withheld.*
Dramatic writing which is powerful in evoking the scenes and
blockages and forgotten traces of the actor Imaginary as well as the
strategic, calls forth, sets into situations which block, and then
draws back energies. We call this plot.

Wilden (1980) notes that energy, according to Freud, is basically
misunderstood, tension being perceived as a negativity, and the
release from tension as the desired goal. He signals:

> the necessary TENSION in open systems . . . . We are reminded of
> Freud's . . . definition of the pleasure/unpleasure principle in
> terms of release from tension. We see at once that . . . for the
> higher-order system, SOCIOCULTURAL humanity, release from
> tension (i.e., Freud's pleasure) is a utopian myth. . . . [The
> fundamental error of the Freudian model is that] tension is
> DEVIANT or an environmental intrusion; whereas in fact tension
> is one of the products of organisation itself. (p. 143)

This clearly recalls the 'unfulfilling' quality of esthetic pleasure
noted above. The actor, without tension – activated, explored and
retained – is professionally neutered. Could Freud, in his quest for
the release from tension, ever *understand* the actor, or is Freudian
theory liable only to cause us to perceive the actor, in that
professional sustained tension, as *highly problematic*? What
direction might we instead adopt if we find that this element of
Freudian theory is invalid, because wrongly based?

Sustaining tension

In the southern African country of Malawi, village women sing
and dance in a circle, incorporating into that dance everyday
actions – sowing seeds, reaping crops, digging the soil – which
become performance actions by dint of the fact that the rhythm of
voice and dance involves two forward movements, plus one back.
The energy is thrust forward, into the everyday action performed
to the music of drums and voice, and transformed spatially into
the pre-performance complex. But *performance* itself depends on
the way energies are used within this complex relation: here
energy does not achieve the flow-through which characterises the
functional everyday act. Flow-through would be everyday-

economical rather than watchable, since it leaves the body slack and uninteresting to the onlookers, lacking in muscular profile and delineation. Instead each double forward beat is partly held in and drawn back, before the next forward movement begins from the residue of that preceding energetic thrust.

Everyday practice and performance practice

It seems then that a greater energy than the everyday action itself requires is thrust into its performance, but this energy is not permitted to flow through into the functional achieving of that action. Instead it flows through to 'heighten' the performed action (by a complex muscular definition which draws the onlooker's eye) and then is held back, so that the action both frames itself, and its energetic residue feeds into the next. Any actor in training can achieve this 'watchability' by the performance of a simple everyday action, with an input of energy to the muscles involved which is superfluous to the functional needs of the action. This is, for Barba and Savarese (1985), the principle of 'maximum wastage'. In the opposition between everyday somatic technique and the 'extra-daily' Ugo Volli notes, in a text we should have to call ethnographic in orientation, that:

> everyday techniques of the body are . . . not necessarily used constantly by the entire population: leaping and bearing loads, eating and love-making, giving birth and walking, sleeping and climbing . . . These techniques are considered to be "natural", "simple" and "normal" in every culture (certainly in the variant which is specific to it, in terms of which other ways of "getting by" are seen as "improper", "clumsy", "stiff", "affected", "bizarre", and even "ridiculous"). *The law which organises them, at least for the user, is that of minimal effort and naturalness: the sought-after effect* flows out of the technique seen as its cause and condition. Any member of a culture, within the necessary conditions associated with gender and age, masters everyday techniques learnt within the most elementary social group . . . most often in an informal way, without temporal limits imposed and without any means of external verification. . . . The extra-daily techniques . . . require some sort of formal apprenticeship, taking a quite specific and pre-determined duration: they influence the status of the users, conferring a

social, imaginary or real power. In general we can note *a deviation* from the "normal" uses of the body, an alteration of rhythms, of *positions, of uses of energy, of pain and effort.*

(p. 117: my adaptation and emphasis)

Volli is obviously approaching something like *habitus* here, as soon as he includes not just actions but attitudes and judgements with regard to the 'natural'/'unnatural' performance of actions, but he does so first without explicitly noting a classist or oppositional frame to its acquisition or its quality, and second, with no mention of that 'forgotten and naturalised history' which will seem to 'underpin', to 'resonate through' and to 'load' conjunctures in any materially given situation of extra-daily practice. In this sense, his work is lodged too forcefully in a material, energetic, present moment.

He notes that *performance* techniques alter rhythm, position and energy-use, while maintaining fairly closely the technical specificity of the everyday action. We might ask, at this point, whether dramatic writing for the stage might not conform, to a certain extent, to other (everyday) instances of human discourse, but altering rhythm, positions and uses of energy in line with the specific needs of dramatic performance? Our uses of dramatic writing in performance or pre-performance conditions might not conform to uses of discourse in singularised practice within social situations (and therefore be said diagrammatically and indexically to be able to 'represent' these as minimal–logical enabling structures); but factors relating to theatricality do exercise certain shifts, do prioritise certain factors not stressed in everyday conditions, do energise certain sorts of functions and relations. We need to remember, in the light of the pleasure given spectators by the singularisation by a specific performer, and secondly in the light of the differences (as well as the regularities) between the ways in which we all live the everyday within our community, the difference between enabling structure and enabled practice: we must note a complex web of **enabling structures**, as these are activated (in a number of different ways) by uses of dramatic writing in context, but not the precise colour nor content or singular sorts of work 'within' these structures. Nor can this work be effectively 'explained' or 'accounted for', after the event of it, by reference back to those structures.

Caution is needed inasmuch as most *functional* theories of discourse, and theories which tend to demonstrate how 'the social' organises discourse to the end of its own conservation, are conjugated in terms of goal and/or efficacy, while dramatic discourse in theatre used as dialogue cannot be said either to derive from, nor to aim at, wholly everyday social functions (theatre-use itself is extra-daily), however much it might draw on (but always converting by framing) these in the constitution of its fictions.

Most approaches to everyday use, within the mainstream, tend to work through some kind of typification or generalisation, whereas it seems plain that there are both conventions or strategies proper to dramatic performance writing which distance it from practices of the everyday, and tactics in that writing and in uses of the writing, which *play* within both everyday and theatre conventions. The actor(s) and other members of the group will work both strategically and tactically with regard to that writing and the prevailing conventions of theatricality. It seems then that what is vital to an acquisition of everyday communicative competence in first and second language learning, or functional competence in the performance of social transactions – both fields of major application of discourse analysis – is once again largely inadequate to our approach to other modes of effective cultural practice, even though it does seem to be the case that the performer generally attempts to undergo some mode of partial secondary acculturation in performance conditions. But for all that, the performer does not primarily seek a functional 'survival course' in an established second culture (fictional/theatrical), so much as the means to constitution of a somatic poetics, an *'arts of the everyday of an other'*.

A metaphoric and possibly singular 'capture'; a metaphoric and singular 'intensity', both relegated to the order of the 'less congruent', the 'marginal', the 'other-than discursive', the 'instinctive', or the 'personal' or 'idiosyncratic' in theories of socio-functional competency: these need to be prioritised once again in our dramatic semiotics of theatre which works. The conclusion seems to be that while Volli's observations are derived from and best relate to highly codified performance practice which curtails what some of us might differently see as appropriate actorly individuation (*Noh, kathakali*, etc.), permitting a practice of generalisation in the discourse of analysis, the sorts of practices we are interested in here are – in their capacity for pleasing us – much less available to rigid codification. They seem to spring up as something like a rhizome (Deleuze 1987) or a tactical 'making do', which 'relate to' enabling structures, without which they cannot exist, but which cannot be foreseen or controlled by those structures.

Chapter 9

Procedures

One important element emerging from the work of the Pêcheux group (1984) is the quest for a range of *procedures*, which might permit us to demonstrate that different elements of a given text, in use, will become *opaque* to (permitting partial reflection in), activate memories in and thus potentially 'vibrate' for, different social subjects. 'Opacity' is as vital to the actor's quest for a relationship of felt-experience to, and insertion into, the drama (through, if our hypotheses are valid, a perceived blurring *within* the regimes of 'character', and of 'thematic system') as it is to the spectator's processing and pleasure. But it might be less vital, in 1990s' *mises en scène*, to the director's work, in the sense that in *mise en scène* we might now equate directorially-experienced and effected opacity with a single-source over-determination leading to the imprint of the directorial signature.

In work on writing for staging the quest is complex. We are looking for procedures leading to general recognition of the sorts of textual sites which *in quite different ways* (i.e. specific to the modes of intervention of director, actor, designer, spectator(s)), privilege the active intervention of a subject; for the means to recognise the ways in which the intersection of writing and user occurs, such that *traces are activated within a stock of singular memories*. We need to recognise, whether our intervention here is conservative or critical, that within mainstream north-western European contexts, 'character-relations' serve as contingent **site** of such an intersection; but that this complex of complementarities does not 'in itself' permit us to generalise on the causal effects to a singular activation for a given subject. This is what we have seen, I think, in the ways in which my own uses of Warner/Shaw's *Electra*, in performance conditions, differ from those of other spectators: we cannot usefully generalise on habitus and its echoes, even within a 'single middle-class audience' drawn from a given 'late industrialised' British city.

The Pêcheux approach suggests that something still liable to be called 'analytical procedures' might however be brought to operate in cultural practice, without the loss of what is both singular *and social* in cultural experience. But for the 'analyst', here, the vital consequence of the loss of the authority traditionally accruing to the establishment of 'general' or 'universal' principles is that we are both 'dispossessed' and 'responsible': the results of the application of procedures must be relativised, and attributed neither to 'text itself' nor to users in general (and this is a delicate freedom, a delicate burden). Let me set out here a number of initial and more developed procedures I have found to be useful.

1 The book and the script

Approaching dramatic writing as *script* and not as 'book' or 'text': we need to intervene in the 'products' of the print and publishing economy, and in what de Certeau calls the 'scriptural economy', in order to break out of the tight order of the 'literary' – which is still overshadowed, by dint of the book's place as material and economic entity within the system of marketing, by the aura of thing-in-itselfness. Reprinting the play as script, explicitly *toward a staging*, in a form which leaves adequate space for users' notation, seems 'magically' to transform our relationship to it as thing. That 'magic' should be enough to demonstrate that the scriptural economy is not a theoretical abstraction, but a field of relationships and values organising the everyday real, within which we seem to make spontaneous choices and free acts. The power of the book is tied in to the ancient history, the more recent history, and the future of literacy – the latter newly to be appraised in its relation to a televisual society.

2 Embodying 'discourse'

We need to approach dramatic writing as *discourse* where that means having diversely contextualised *pro-somatic potential*: it is processual, despite its material, synoptic ("in place", cf. de Certeau, 1984) state, lodged in and activating a complex situation of use, and in one or more complex contexts of use. Because the term 'discourse', like 'text', currently functions less as a unit of meaning, than as a site in which different users play out a number of different meanings, it is necessary at this point to sketch in some parameters: I am using *discourse*, in this specific context to mean *writing-in-use* in pre-performance, *and then* (this marks a change, as I have indicated) in performance conditions. So that the term here entails a complex set of *dispositifs* which overlap, and which are variously activated and made to intersect at different points of use:

(a) *a complex enunciator* (whose complexity cannot be prescribed in advance), which activates writing *in a number of ways* which I set out below. This enunciator is not equivalent to a 'speaker' (it is closer in one instance to the *bunraku* chanter in its separation of interiority from somatic work) since each performance use of language derives from many acts around an element of writing, by any number of performance practitioners;

(b) *a complex interlocuter* in advance of 'the spectator', and who performs a number of specular-somatic functions both in real spatio-temporal relation to, and with regard to, the complex enunciator, the enunciation, and what is enunciated;

(c) *a written component* which I have called the '**synoptic text**' in its given pre-activated materiality (note however that the designation 'dramatic', prior to our use, already activates expectations and procedures for conventional usage): here it appears as a range of printerly codes and, characteristically, a wide range of clause types;

(d) *collective and individually hierarchised knowledges* (not necessarily discursive; we need politically to prioritise somatic knowledges) of what I shall call current, historical and future/potential performance conditions;

(e) *a collective and individually hierarchised knowledge* (as in d) *of current, historical and potential/future performance modes and spectatorial activities* – amongst which I would include the expectation that dramatic performance will explore (rather than disrupt) the 'models of knowledge' brought in (f) below, through typification, individuation, dramatisation and processual enactment;

(f) *a range of 'models of knowledge'* – e.g. Freudian but also Jungian or Kleinian analysis; chaos theory; Buddhism – which are differently drawn into any discursive situation by different participants, but which are involved to a lesser or greater extent as articulation of widely disseminated, dominant and less dominant epistemes.

These are activated, within pre-performance conditions of the use of writing, in a number of ways which emerge from the conditions produced by the enactment of points (a)–(d) above. Here we can distinguish between three discursive and practical modes through which these models of knowledge can be introduced:

- the 'expert discourse' and its practices;

- the commonsensical discourse and its practices;

- the anecdotal discourse and its practices.

But we need to note as well the possibility that such knowledges can be introduced through the specular–somatic economy of bodily showing and looking, once the dramatic writing is activated in, or to establish, a given material and human situation, in the context of theatre performance.

These are vital complementary components of discursive and somatic pre-activation and activation of dramatic writing for staging. And inasmuch as they are vital and complementary, and act upon each other to modify each other internally, it is fruitless to attempt to nominate one or another element as a suitable case for semiotic analysis. Secondly, no attempt by one or another single analyst can claim equivalence to the work on dramatic writing undertaken by any production company working professionally in the 1990s: in combining the collective and the singular, company production work on writing – however much that work is inspired or cajoled or commanded by one or another participant – presents the marks of a small-scale social interaction which informs, but is not neutralised by, all decision-making. Furthermore the complementarity and the interactive modification of all components and knowledges (we are dealing here with what is called **synergy**) together issue a formidable challenge to any analyst accustomed to producing models to clarify and stabilise aspects of that theatre work on dramatic writing.

3 Habitus and the strategic

We can approach dramatic writing, in use, in pre-performance context, from the perspective of *habitus*, combining in this approach not just the notion of institutionalised strategies, but also that of the tactic, supposing that while the social subject has interiorised and will act on the basis of factors derived from a lived experience of one position amongst the range determined by external economic conditions, that social subject has equally mastered modes of coping with, making do in spite of, and finding complex pleasures amongst what might otherwise seem to be imposed (might even find pleasures, too, in those impositions).

Nothing stops us assuming, along the lines of Bourdieu's theory of habitus, that this 'feel in the mouth', in a complex situation and context, with specific actors, would entail a range of *socially coded strategies, activating attitudes, judgements and actional modes*, which would be marked intricately by interiorised social conditions, as these were mediated by the habitus of the given actors, and overseen and intersected with by a similar capacity for judgements of taste and ethos in the *metteur en scène*. The latter, however, paces and punctuates these differently, with a differently cunning eye to, and lucid control in terms of, the global conditions of theatricality. Nothing stops us assuming, furthermore, that these same actors in their use of certain verbal constructs, will with great rapidity **somatically enact** socially encoded **actional frames** (more complex than speech acts or 'actioning': cf. Austin (1962) and Pratt (1986)) by which I mean that the 'feel in the mouth' will, in activating 'feelings' and muscular contractions in the rest of the body and in the interactive and intersubjective spaces, permit the actors to sketch out little actional complexes (like 'trying to take off one's shoe while someone is watching' and 'watching someone trying to take off a shoe while someone else is watching'). Because of the habitus these do not need to be fully signalled in didascalies or dialogue, in that, in their social encoding or institutionalisation, they can be economically signalled by a small complex of cues or indices (e.g. Participant, Process and Circumstance, in Halliday, 1978).

Further, we can suppose that this 'sketching out' would entail not just 'recognisable acts' provided through social encoding, but also acts informed by stylistic choices – a somatic rhetoric – which would be oriented around, and would thus enact, something of the performer's (and the group's) *place* and *position* (the one being founded by larger social and cultural orders; the other being willed by one or another complex force in the individual actor).

At this point, this is something less that a globally-determined *Gestus* (Pavis, 1982), although what seems clear is that this rhetorical choice will be recognisable within the group, group-encoded, even if it cannot be said to be socially encoded to the extent of a transcendental transparency. But secondly, this may be the site for the given actor's own tactical intervention with regard to a perceived orientation of the group. Thus, in tune with de Certeau's intervention, we are free to suppose two further possibilities:

- that certain clusters of words in the mouth would 'feel like' institutionalised strategies attributed to character by the actors, while others would 'feel like' tactical interventions ('acting out of character') equally to be attributed by actor to character;

- that in the light of this – *and of other factors* – certain of the actorly 'felt' activations would produce strategic approaches (ratified e.g. by Beckettian or Ibsenien tradition or by Paris theatre tradition of the 1980s), while others might suggest a wholly tactical intervention, which does not confront but plays with(in) those traditions.

This intricacy of intrusions into the institutionalised and the encoded indicates why we need the notion of the tactical, in de Certeau, and of 'traces in a stock of memories', in Pêcheux. How else do we cope with the performance fact which emerges once we have arrived at some specification of '*context*', at some specification of the '*situation/s*' it englobes and informs, and of the '*actional frames*' and '*speech acts*' englobed and informed by situation, only to find that what the skilled actor does, in that regulated framework, is not quite what could have been foreseen (even by her–him); not quite distinct enough to be called 'marginal' or 'deviate' (or avant-gardist, or revolutionary, or a 'particular political stance'); and – which seems more testing still – which is 'absolutely illuminating!', in those complex circumstances? In de Certeau's terms the actor has made a tactical intervention, while acknowledging, at the same time, certain strategic components which are vital in assuring that the complex option is 'recognisable', minimally 'meaningful', or *possible* (although unthinkable)'.

In terms of Pêcheux's suggestion, we can hypothesise that something in the given conditions (of which the feel in the mouth is one) has produced an opacity, has opened a position for a subject's activation of a singular stock of retained images, muscular contractions, feelings – and 'ideas', although I am less certain at this point that it is the idea which dominates, even though the actor may 'think through' (i.e. verbalise) the action in the process of forming it.

Now, if nothing prevents us tracing the socially encoded elements within uses of dramatic writing, drawing on a socio-functional conception of 'language in the world', we need to do so with this explicit proviso: we do not, and it seems *cannot*, 'solve' the question of writing's place in theatre pleasure by so doing. I have already indicated that for Wilden, Freud's mistake was to seek as optimal a *release* from a tension I have also claimed was vital to the very definition of 'the actor'. In Carroll, cited above, we find the same question approached in terms of all users of art: the tension, vital in that use, able to activate quests for enlightenment and understanding, also ensures that those quests is finally unfulfilled, that tension is maintained. This is how and why pleasure goes on, and it is the answer to my attempt, in Chapter 6, to play out my unspeakable pleasures in terms of established scenarios.

It is the analyst's desire-to-know (to hold, to contain, within discourse) which motors the application of diverse socio-functional models to a dramatic writing which, required to be symptom of the social and then of the ideological, as much as of the psyche, happily resists – and can only please by resisting – that desire to know, *thereby sustaining it.* Knowledge, satiety, satisfaction, are similar to the release from tension: they are the death of esthetic pleasure, not its accounting. What is ironic is that it is precisely the enigma, the intrigue, the slipperiness of the writing and of its uses in theatre, which excite our interest in the first place. There is satisfaction, but rather less excitement, in use of a recipe, in the following of its instructions and controls (of a quantifiable, digital kind) through to the production of a perfectly conforming example. What we need to ask of the application of socio-functional models, in the light of this recognition, is that they help us to expose the points at which the writing-in-use escapes them.

4 Dramatic writing as proto-somatic symbolic

The use of dramatic writing, in a constitutable fictional situation, in a pre-performance and performance situation, and in a given, contradictory, socio-cultural context, needs to be newly approached as a *proto-somatic symbolic, for* individualised uses within a (social) group, rather than as a writing into which a body 'intrudes', which a body somehow 'illustrates'. In the *individual* reading (this 'private scene' and staging), note the precise points at which the reader feels 'bound-in', feels a sharpened interest or curiosity, a desire-to-know of one kind or another (relating to the fictional components, or relating to what might be said to organise the fiction, or relating to what the user 'does with' elements activated in the reading). Note then the points at which a keenly observed imaging starts, and those points at which you feel drawn to *'see'/show something experienced,* to others, without that experience being transformed into discourse. I am including acts of speaking amongst showing, here, because speaking in/as performance is rather more a somatic act involving muscular work in mouth, throat, face, eyes, body tensions, gestuality, than it can be called a linguistic act (unless of course we restore the *tongue* to ling-uistic, acknowledging that that tongue in action engages the entire nervous system, as much as it engages the brain). In my own case, in reading Shakespeare's *King Lear* in view of a showing, an action, I am intrigued (Latin: *intricare*), I am bound-in, perplexed enough for a complex imaging to begin – and for a work toward a showing to start, at this line, and not before:

COR. [*Aside*] What shall Cordelia speak? Love, and be   61
    silent.

                                (Shakespeare, Methuen 1982, p. 7)

In Sophocles' *Antigone* (Penguin, 1974) it is the lines:

ANTIGONE: . . .
    It is against **you and me** he has made this order.
    Yes, against **me**. (my emphases)

which, fairly conventionally, bind me in. In Sophocles' *Electra* (Cambridge University Press, 1979) I am initially bound-in by (or experience *opacity* through) the lines:

ORESTES:
  Or else my sister, unhappy Electra.   81
  Shall we stay here a moment, and listen?
SERVANT: **No** . . .

What do these have in common for me as 'divided' or dramatised subject, symptom of a schizophrenic society? Analysis requires a certain rule-bound procedure, from which a certain degree of generalisation can be made: each of the examples cited permits a spatialisation, and an opposition of components within the one, *within* the character-complex, and between the speaking character-complex and its fictional other and reading other: into these gaps, and into other such interstices, my complex subjectivity and individually-hierarchised knowledges are projected. Each focuses, albeit through quite different modalities of enunciation, on one or more (historicised) representations of Woman, in my case for a female reader, and in so doing they involuntarily open up for me a schism between two notions of gendered actions, and two or more meaning-dependent cultural contexts of use. The spatialised components, and my implication in this setup, produce something like an arrow-tip, pointing, through me, to a 'spaces between' which I want to explore, but shall not 'resolve', by a work in the somatic–symbolic order. This work *figures*, but does not explain, the nature of the symptoms, the nature of the systems invoked for/in me.

The difference within the one, made opaque and activated by this reader, and outlining the places into which I, as subject, can intervene, elicits the figuring, but cannot thereby be said to point to, or to be equated to, an explication 'put there' by the writer, nor, furthermore, to any I might bring: the *force* of this figuring is, for Lyotard, situated *between* the space of the system, and the space of the subject. Since it is not quite of the system, it cannot readily be named without imposing restrictive closure; since it is not quite of the order of a subject, no subject can effectively take on the role of adequate explication; since the subject either 'forgets', or 'loses' repressed stuff, which nonetheless resonates, that subject cannot readily account for the figuring.

This recalls Ubersfeld's formula: is what she calls 'character' *of the order of the system(s)*, while the actor is of *the order of the subject(s)*? Perhaps this oversimplifies matters: 'character' derives from systems available in language and within the spread of interdiscursivity and interpraxis; but onto the choices made from those systems, and combined, the user *projects* elements of her subjectivity, derived in turn from the user's perception of the 'whole human semiotic'. Character, too, then, contingent upon current and conventional production-requirements, is located between system and singular social subject. The actor, in turn, is both 'whole human', and systematised/ing, in a professional *production* of specific, systemic options – 'walk *like this, here, or there*'; 'widen the eyes *like that – no, like this*'; 'toss the head *like this and not like that*'.

The parameters of the space between

We are beginning to etch in certain parameters to the *space between*, if only because we are multiplying the sites in which we can locate it. Its unseizability recedes, as soon as we note quantum theory's capacity for explaining that a number of alternative realities, thought to be exclusive, either/or options, can simultaneously exist. What we are looking for is a movement within the overlap of two or more 'orders', where these 'orders', still, do no more than to organise (but not specify nor internally control) 'what goes on'. In de Certeau's terms, we are looking for the fissures, the interstices into which movement can spring or creep, where formerly we were taught only to see the institutions and their strategies.

The question remains: a movement of *what*? There is one answer we can provide to the enigma posed at the beginning of this work, but it is no answer at all; a sort of fool's gold – or should we say, in an attempt to overcome the ancient quest for truth implicated in that formula, a *real performance*? What is it that Ubersfeld 'is looking at', but cannot see/seize between the two? The answer is ludicrous in its simplicity: it is the play of the spectator's subjectivity–sociality, which operates **between** the two organising grids and the two complex frameworks of knowledges. What Ubersfeld did not see, because of her wish to objectify from a distance *what she looked at*, was the play of her own subjectivity in the sorts of gaps I have marked above.

5 The 'systemic-functional' approach

The next procedure is complex, and it provides us with so comprehensive a frame that we can draw together, through it, a number of diverse elements already mentioned above. It is derived in general from Halliday's (1978, 1985) Systemic Functional linguistics, and in particular from the article (1987) in which he draws quantum theory explicitly into his field of discourse.

In 'Directions from Structuralism', Hasan (1987) notes of Systemic–Functionalism that in it language is seen as a "resource for meaning" rather than a "constraining reproductive mechanism" (p. 118); that "system is a resource for process"; that departure "from system is as much a 'regard' to system as [is] conformity" (this can obviously be related to de Certeau's tactic worked *within* and with regard to, rather than in opposition to, institutions and their strategies).

She notes, further, that for Halliday "consciousness – and so ideology – is an artefact of processes of meaning"; and that while experience "from the point of view of the sensing subject may be 'raw sensation', . . . experience of the world both outside us and within us, if it is to be shared must be constructed through semiosis" (p. 119). This is clearly a point at which Halliday's conceptual frame distances itself from what Carroll and Lyotard perceive to be the 'unfulfilling' quality of esthetic experience which, despite its being shared, does not need to be wholly constructed through a 'solvable', socially-symptomatic, semiotic practice. She continues – and I take the liberty here to intrude into her text – in these terms:

> As a mode of semiosis, human language [or, for us, all human symbolic practice] 'performs' an *ideational* function: it permits the construction of sharable experience. . . . Sharing implies some social relation: the *social relations* too are *created/altered/maintained* through language. This is the *interpersonal* function of language realised as a specific aspect of the organisation of the lexico-grammar. All sharing is situated – it is situated in the contexts of that community and is recognisable as some kind of

social process within the terms of reference set by the community's culture. Discourse, talk, writing – managing its continuities and discontinuities is the *textual* function of language. . . . If, arriving in the middle of an ongoing dialogue, we are, more often than not, able to say what is going on, how the interactants see each other, what social activity is at issue, this is not because there exists a mysterious telepathic bond between members of a community: it is because language constructs our world for us. (p. 119)

The logocentricity which persists here is depressing, and in terms of cultural analysis in general, it is short-sighted: it does not cope with our capacity to "understand what is going on" in a situation in which dialogue does not feature, nor with our inadequate understanding of situations in which language is used (in Bourdieu's terms, these are frequently loaded with "forgotten history"); and it does not cope with our capacity to suppose that something quite different might be going on, beside an entirely congruent practice of socio-discursive interaction, which is neither dependent on that verbal activity, readable off it, parallel to it, nor neatly available to be discursively accounted for. In such instances language does not "construct our world **for us**". It is one highly economical organisational mode, but it is neither essential, nor necessarily dominant, nor symptomatically explanatory.

But let's persist, because this linguistic metadiscourse focuses not just on institutionalised functions and their strategies, but on the dynamism of open semiotic systems: Halliday (1987, pp. 135–54) notes of language that:

(a) it "is not constrained by the need to refer", but can be opaque, and can play;

(b) it "creates the natural order", and therefore "another language", or a variation in language (add: **or in other practices**) will create another order;

(c) "Every language **[or system of practices]** is constantly renewing itself, changing in resonance with changes in its environment";

(d) "all social–semiotic systems are of a particular kind known as 'dynamic open systems'". These are **metastable**, in that they persist only through constant change, which takes place through interaction with the environment;

(e) "in the course of such interaction, **the system exports disorder**", thereby renewing itself and gaining information [**or new practices**].

Halliday presents us here with an appreciation we can apply to the conclusion to 4 above: by trying to solve the enigma, to remember 'forgotten history', I have "exported [the] disorder" of my inert and then turbulent relation to moments of Shaw's *Electra*, from the system of possible knowledges, thereby increasing entropy (or disorder) in the surrounding environment. But I have retained the order(able), and preserved systems through developing them.

Such an act is consequently conservative – it preserves the order of knowledges by activating one or more of its models. But it is also tactical, since it tries to make tangible, through that activation, what cannot be seen but can be felt *by someone, somewhere, at some time*. It is tactical, once again, in that in so doing it makes no clearer to analysis itself the nature of the *space between*, in which subjectivity plays.

Wilden notes that this "exporting [of] disorder" is a means by which a dynamic open system or ecosystem (such as culture) changes:

[S]ince the environment is essential to an open system . . . an 'intrusion' from the environment does not necessarily lead to dissolution, loss of organization, or simply to another level of equilibrium as it does for the typical closed system. It may lead rather to a restructuring or to an elaboration of structure, at a higher level. The reason is that environmental interchange is not a RANDOM or UNSTRUCTURED event, or does not long remain so (remain as 'noise'), because of the mapping, or coding, or information-processing capabilities of the open system: its adaptiveness. (p. 143)

If we call *'mise en scène'* and *'acting modes'* a *dynamic open system* (Halliday); an *ecosystem* (Wilden); an *institution and its strategies* (de Certeau); or an *historical stabilisation within an other-than-logically-stabilised order* (Pêcheux), then what we find, from the point of view of semiotics and its movement towards codification, is that we can only approach 'system' in historical terms, codifying established options or strategies. We cannot codify, in advance, cultural change; but we can, to some extent, produce a metasemiotics of the process of selection and retention (similar to the 'hourglass' process noted in Pavis, 1992). But we can only approach present and future theatre options, which are brought constantly by different actors in changing situations in response to environmental and personal factors, through the dynamic open category of any system, marked 'other'.

For Halliday (1987, p. 144) "[t]he process of reflecting on natural language", (add: **or on the first somatic options** brought to a **work by the actor**), "can be modelled in terms of . . . four levels of consciousness". These are:

"meaning" (semantic level):	level 0:	"motifs"
	level 1:	"words"
"wording" (lexicogrammatical level)	level 2:	"phenotypes"
	level 3:	"cryptotypes"

"Motifs" are "what the text [**or practice**] seems to be about [**or doing**]" at first reading or experience of it. "Phenotypes" are words, groups of words, types of phrases (cf. Carroll, 1987, p. 164) – to which we should want to add all **classed** modes of somatic options, relations and clusters or actional frames: here I can only **name** them; but the actors enact them in their complexity – oriented to the other, as well as iconic – often without naming them or needing to use language or to 'think' them: *feeding the baby; thinking; going out to dinner; running; making passionate love.*

"Cryptotypes" are the "hidden grammar" – or in our own terms **the complex logic and common sense of practices** – which organise these phenotypes for and through more than one social subject; here we find the transitivity patterns from which many of our apparently spontaneous or intuitive 'assessments' – or rather, productions – of dramatic character, and of 'possible world' active relations, derive. I return to the system of Transitivity below.

Language – and symbolic practice in general – is said then to represent reality non-referentially,

through the unconscious cryptotypic patterns in the grammar

[or logic of practices] which create their own order of reality independently of whatever it is they may be being used to describe [or show, or enact]. [. . . T]he features of the 'crypto-grammar' . . . function way below the usual level of consciousness[. . .]. The language of daily life, which shapes our unconscious understanding of ourselves and our environment, is a language of complementarities, a *rheomode* – a dynamic open system . . . [Its] reality-generating power may be incompatible with explicit logical reasoning.

(pp. 142–3: my emphasis)

Let's get rid of Halliday's spatial metaphor: the features of the cryptogrammar, or cryptologic, function *way beyond* the usual *order* of consciousness – which makes them an other-consciousness, an other-ordering, but neither unconscious nor disordered. In Bourdieu's habitus, as we have seen, these finely and diversely prefigure (or in-form, but not predictably), and then potentially 'load' with resonance (for an onlooker), everyday actions and judgements. Once we intervene in the Bourdieu and Halliday metaphoric realisations, what we find is that the rheomode and the habitus have something usefully in common: the practices of everyday life, through which we enact our somatic knowledges of ourselves, are established in relationships of complementarities, rheomodes or dynamic open systems, and their reality-generating powers – intriguingly – may be incompatible with explicit logical reasoning.

Extra-daily practice and dramatic writing

Halliday, like Bourdieu, implies the existence of something like a malleable and open-ended but effective 'regulating mechanism' which seems to be able at the very least to oversee the production of both stategies and tactical actions (and attitudes, and judgements) in everyday life. But if we are to make use of this metaphoric construct in the present context, we need to consider again the relationship between everyday practice and dramatic theatre practice – sometimes called 'extra-daily' (Barba and Savarese, 1985, 1991).

Dramatic writing in its entirety, governed as it is by scriptural, generic and publishing codes and conventions, is (despite attempts to demonstrate the contrary: cf. Burton, 1980) removed from 'natural language' used in everyday life, not the least because its different 'orders' of enunciation are multiple and multi-functional; and it is subject to the constraints and controls of more than one genre of symbolic activity. So that while it draws on and *stages* in its clauses and genre-strategies specificities of the everyday – its use of deixis, of the tenses of a here-and-now framed by a past and a future, of instances of turn-taking, uptake, initiation of speech and so on – toward the constitution of an 'everyday natural order' of a fictional 'possible world' kind, such elements of a singular writerly control are **directed toward performance for the other**.

What we need to do, in the light of this complication, is to modify the formula, looking at the way the language of dramatic writing can be said to **"shape our conscious understanding of the actor–character complex in its fictional and theatrical environment"**, where it functions as a "system of systems of complementarities, a complex rheomode – a complex dynamic open system" whose power to generate **'symbolic theatre realities'**, although possibly incompatible with logical reasoning, is entirely compatible with a logic and a common sense and a theatre sense of practices and of felt-experiences.

This orientation to the *performance other* means that schisms which now seem to rend the acting subject in the everyday, and to dramatise that subject, are intensified, multiplied, and, however, overseen by a series of singular controls which are both purposeful and involuntary. These controls energise 'everyday' options, and orient them in space and time, so that **they do not change in kind so much as in presentation and in combination**. We need, then, the means to understand both their relation to socially-determined and assessed modes of practice, and the means of their conversion.

Logocentricity, once again

The problem of logocentricity, this time posed by Halliday's approach, continues to try to limit our parameters and our understanding of causes and actions: his outlook works out from language, to the worlds it 'creates', and not vice versa. By contrast we have seen that the actor knows and 'can create' possible worlds somatically – as do we all – as much as verbally, and in ways which do not seem to be 'structured like', nor necessarily to 'function as' language. Can, and generally does, work inward from the somatic process to the available writing perceived as a potential for voicework, since 'not yet textualised' somatic skills, and not writerly skills, are the tools of trade, are what s/he professes, as a professional.

But the approach does offer us something here, if only because we see at work both a systematising aspiration (permitting us to approach strategic practice) and the refusal of closure (which permits us to deal with tactics and with cultural change). We need however to break into its clauses, **substituting the actor and** *metteur en scène's* **terms for those of the linguist**. What we can foresee, in terms of institutionalised or strategic actional modes, is the constant intervention, in performance situations, of overlaid transparencies or grids, each of which functions as a **level 3 actional cryptotype** in theatre's numerous 'cryptologics'. One will relate to the spatial and proxemic knowledge the actor in a particular culture operates through (regulating, amongst a number of performers, relations in performance space, and relations between performers and spectators); another to gestuality and actional frames; another to voicing options whose relational modalities we hear at work as soon as professional actors read an unfamilar text aloud.

These actional modes are not 'instinctive', nor 'spontaneous' although they are instantly at work; they are schooled, somatically, interactively, and oriented to an onlooker. They entail a somatic other-consciousness, capable of activating 'forgotten (hi)stories' – or, rather, practices; and this other-consciousness seems to work in part through that synesthesia to which Barthes (1986) draws our attention. It is an other-consciousness because the body often knows what the conscious mind does not know it knows – or will not say. One of the most useful aspects of Halliday's functional grammar for our present purposes comes from his focus on process: **the cryptogrammar 'construct[s] reality by not descri-bing' but by enacting it**.

* * *

5.i Process orientation

CONTINGENCIES IN THE FLOW

In this conception, 'things' of the dramatic writing, generally approached as 'character' and 'objects of the stage', can be redefined as **'contingencies in the flow'** of performance, as peaks within processes, determined by the demands of specific performance force-fields. In this way we can understand the apparent 'stylistic' variation between the ways in which one group or another, one culture or another, can dispense with or prioritise character and prop in performance modes. 'The flow' is a matter of driven, interactive, intersubjective energies which traverse both the present spaces of the theatre and stage relations, and tie those in to traditions of the past while forseeing a future of cultural practice. Character (rather than role), an exigency of conventions of dramatic *literature,* can equally be seen as a contingency in the flow of certain performance modes and the expectations and needs these articulate; whereas actors themselves are **exigencies of most performance modes**, and energise and mediate the flow.

The play of objects on the contemporary stage can be seen as a matter of indexicality used as pointer to one or more force-fields of performance – which is what we saw in the Warner–Shaw use of the pomegranate. 'Institutions', from the same perspective, take on the sense of widely ratified networks of strategic actional modes – contingent upon culture and user-decisions and mediations – which organise and act in other ways to determine 'individual actions' and choices. As contingencies, relative to changing circumstances and users, rather than as exigencies, institutions are able to assume a certain dynamism and adaptability, however much they may wear the mask of exigency. The 'institution of theatre', 'major acting styles', the 'dramatic canon' and 'dramatic conventions' are much better understood as historically contingent clusters of phenomena, lived out personally as desired and natural, rather than as necessary and monolithic. What we tend to call 'new theatre' recognises this historically-relative contingency.

In the Shaw–Electra I am supposing that 'imploded energy', as major somatic character trait, is derived by Shaw from a recurring 'feel of the [clauses] in the mouth/body', in space and time, for the other (typified by Warner), where the precise contribution from dramatic writing to this somatic trait comes from the repetition of specific choices in the transitivity system, made by the writer. But the observations I have noted here must be activated in terms of the contingency of models of knowledge currently available to us, and those significant to my own experience (e.g. feminism's fascination with and interrogation of neo-Freudian theory). They can only be *effectively* activated through an **overlay of transparencies**:

- the synoptic text (the simple given materiality of paged graphies);

- overlaid by enunciatory factors (Warner/Shaw/RSC/Pit/ Sophocles);

- overlaid by available models of knowledge which are mediated by any of these.

Through these, the **points of convergence**, marking sites on the **axes of probability** I have noted above, can be 'stitched' (as quilting marks out a network of webbing between layers). These points of convergence are wholly contingent upon the specificity of the enunciatory layer – in the case of *Electra*, this is 1990s' feminist – which mediates both culture and individual hierarchies of knowledge within culture. The individual hierarchies of knowledge specific to a cluster of enunciators must in turn be modulated by the terms of Shaw's own 'felt-experience'. 'Traits', here, are contingent somatic–processual enactments of writing-in-performance focused in the convention of character.

5.ii *The transitivity system*

A further vital aspect – and with it a procedural focus – comes from Halliday's Transitivity System:

Transitivity specifies the different types of process that are recognised in the language, and the structures by which they are expressed. The basic semantic framework for the representation of processes is very simple. A process consists potentially of three components: (i) the process itself;(ii) participants in the process;(iii) circumstances associated with the process. These provide the frame of reference for interpreting our experience of what goes on.   (1985, p. 101)

'What goes on', in our dramatic theatrical terms, is never *simple*, and single, but let us begin here. The Transitivity System includes a number of options, each of which permits a user to perform different social *functions* in the world, and to codify this complex formation. This system shows us the clause as a complex, *staging* Participant, Process and Circumstance, and representing *patterns of experience*. It should be clear that 'effective dramatic writing', marked by those consistencies which permit us to assemble character as 'identity' and sociality as 'one'; and by those differences on the basis of which we both 'recognise different characters' (and thereby develop a conception of the social), and note difference 'within' character (calling this 'development', 'growth' or 'well-roundedness'), is internally orchestrated in part through differences selected 'intuitively' or deliberately by the writer and the other users from within the transitivity system. These combine with **Rheme/Theme options, Paratactic and Hypotactic cohesion** choice, and **'attic'** versus **'doric'** options (to which I return below). Together they establish for us the means to constitute a preliminary **'common-sense' order**, prevailing in a conceptual 'possible real'. They peak in character-types, justified and argued for by our invoking of real-world categories through which we semiotise textual complementarities.

The Transitivity System offers us this reckoning of elements staged in each clause of dramatic writing. Where the clauses are attributed to networks of names (characters), this appraisal offers us a means of appreciating the textual bases for our constitution of character as clusters of speakable actions-in-the-world. Options are:

- **Material processes,** or processes of doing or acting upon;

- **Mental processes,** or processes of sensing, thinking, feeling;

- **Relational processes,** or processes of being or having,

   together with three secondary process types:

   - **Behavioural** processes (e.g. breathing, dreaming, smiling, coughing);

- **Verbal** processes (saying, speaking, meaning, telling);
- **Existential** processes (e.g. 'there **was** a picture on the wall'; '**there's** someone at the door'; '**there's** something I need to tell you').

In table 9.1 I reproduce Halliday's Table 5(7) (1985, p. 131: my modifications) in which he summarises process types, their general categories of meaning, and the participant functions they conjoin. It should be noted at this point that as soon as Halliday moves from the first to the second column, he is engaged in an **ethnographic practice**, in that his writing in social meanings for linguistic options is informed by an *a priori* 'reading', and hence stabilisation, of the English-language-using social order. It is not entirely clear that these categories and their interpretants are equally valid for other cultures through language-uses which might appear to be comparable.

Table 9.1 Process types, their meanings, and key participants

Process type	Category meaning	Participants
MATERIAL: action event	'doing' 'doing' 'happening'	Actor, Goal [ACTANT]
BEHAVIOURAL:	'behaving'	Behaver
MENTAL: perception affection cognition	'sensing' 'seeing' 'feeling' 'thinking'	Senser, Phenomenon
VERBAL:	'saying'	Sayer, Target
RELATIONAL: attribution identification	'being' 'attributing' 'identifying'	Token, Value Carrier, Attribute Identifier, Identified
EXISTENTIAL:	'existing'	Existent

Source: Modified from Halliday (1985, Table 5(7), p. 131)

CHARACTERISATION AND SYSTEMIC ANALYSIS

This system seems to offer a strong base for analysis of character-constitution and character-complexes, from a pre-psychologising point of view: i.e. from that of participants-type, relation, and process-type. We learn, through the application of widely disseminated 'expert discourses', to project 'moral interiorities' (Hunter, 1983) into it. These incorporate the stuff of ethical judgements and judgements of taste. In part this projection is based on our 'intuitive' recognition of the difference between – for example – material-process-dominant and mental-process-dominant named clause clusters (or characters), a difference which is 're-cognised' by us precisely because we note and predicate those around us, in the everyday, on just such a basis, however normative and crude that mechanism might now seem to us. I am supposing, in line with our present focus on the somatic–symbolic, and on the production and uses of energy, that we similarly predicate others on the basis of material-process-dominant versus mental- or verbal-process-dominant energy uses and actions in the world, which we find to be 'typical' of a person or character. For example, 'She always touches people a lot'; 'He never gives anything away, the strong silent type'; 'She smiles a lot at people, almost automatically'.

But in noting here again that I am concerned with the ways in which we 'commonsensically', and apparently 'intuitively' 'constitute character' in the everyday and in theatre uses of dramatic writing, let me stress once more the difference between the everyday-intuitive, on the one hand, and the uses we make of that everyday-intuitive in dramatic theatre. (The singular noun 'character', so easily used here, stages a misapprehension: no 'character' is constituted except differentially, with regard to other clusters of contingencies in the dramatic writing.) In the latter context the processes are overseen, and overcoded, by any one or a number of those conventions bound up in what we understand as theatricality (e.g. maximum wastage of energy; orientation to the spectators' presence and active gaze). As a consequence a semiotic processing which produces actions-(including judgements)-in-the-worlds of the perceived everyday, becomes in theatre (where it is framed by other spatio-temporal codes), a **metasemiotics**, leading to and incorporating within it a **metapraxis**. In theatre terms, 'intuitive acting' is a matter of internalisation of additional somatic and psychological codes, to those internalised through the habitus. What the 'intuitive' professional actor indicates through her use of the term is probably that her operative modes are not formulated discursively; but this does not mean for an instant that they are not formulated and schooled somatically and theatrically. Theatrical coding overcodes the 'everyday-spontaneous' practice, in such a way that it overlays the latter, pointing up some of its elements, exposing others, lending them then to critical in(tro)spection.

5.iii *Practice and metapraxis: complementarities*

A metapraxis, in simple terms, can frame, mimic, investigate and 'critique' practice, *in the very instant of performing it* – and we might suppose that a 'truly effective theatre' always does just that. But this involves a complexity of standing-for, which obliges us to work with the enunciation–enunciated model, despite the difficulties this entails with its apparent implication of intent. This might seem to approach, via another route, that 'doubleness' by which Ubersfeld (1982b) was fascinated. It seems to me that from the point of view of the *metapraxis*, what we might propose with regard to the *psycho-soma* of the actor, is that the felt-experience of that actor, who mediates a vast number of codes and conventions including those of fiction and character, entails and prioritises the interrogative and critical aspect of the metapraxis, but that this is wrongly approached – through the myth of the 'naturalness' of acting – as 'introspective' or 'studied'. Halliday (1987) incorporates this concept of a metasemiotics/metapraxis in his later work, as we shall see.

5.iv *Writing/subjectivity/character*

This seems to lead us *through writing* to our conventional conflation of subjectivity and text in dramatic character. Traditionally, Halliday approaches the question of subjectivity through the category of the subject: "determined from outside the Transitivity Systems; the latter then assign to the subject a particular feature representing a participant role or role-combination from the set 'actor, initiator, goal, attributant'" (1967, p. 46). He continues:

The notion of subject conflates three distinct roles which, although they are typically combined into one element, are nevertheless independent of one another . . . These three 'kinds of subject' relate to the functions of language . . . The logical subject is the actor; this is a transitivity role . . . The other two have a different source, though they are no less meaningful. The grammatical subject derives from the interpersonal component in language function; specifically, it has to do with the roles taken on by the performer and receiver in a communication situation. The psychological subject belongs to the textual component; it is concerned with the organization of the clause as a message, within a larger piece of discourse'.

(1970, pp. 159–60)

Many of us 'automatically' **predicate** 'character' by attributing complements to a text-name (e.g. King Lear, Electra) and a Relational Process (e.g. 'is'/'has'):

(a) Relational Processes:

    (i) 'King Lear **is** . . .': relational attributive

    (ii) 'Electra **has** . . .' : relational possessive

(b) Complements:

    (i) 'King Lear is **anguished**': attribute

    (ii) 'Electra has **no real power**': possession

where in fact we derive these from the application of a contradictory 'whole human semiotic', which is socio-historically determined and mediated by us. This application, rendered in relational processes about 'being' or 'having', which thereby replace the text processes themselves, will be adjudged 'more perceptive' or 'less astute', on the basis of both the number and the complexity of connections we can make with available models of knowledge. But there are plainly strong textual 'enabling structures' intersecting to facilitate this act of user-bringing and user-inference, and it is in the means to recognise these that the Hallidayan Transitivity System is so useful.

I should add again here that this 'social semiotic' of dramatic text is both 'minimal–logical', and 'commonsensical'; and because all practitioners bring theatre knowledges to bear on this, and transform it (not the least through the conditions which expose it to the spectators' gaze), the *use made* of this application cannot be foreseen – and we should not bemoan this, if esthetic practice has to 'unfulfil' as a condition of its efficacy.

I have said that the clause is itself, as Lyotard asserts, like a little stage. This is because the Process (or verb used) is actional, a happening-in-the-world, and because that Process is activated and framed by Participants effectively 'dramatised' because set in opposition by, the spatialisation the clause performs:

I	thought	you	did not.
Participant 1:	Process	Participant 2:	(ellipsed Mental
Senser	(mental)	Senser	process: know)

(Antigone, in Sophocles/Watling 1974, p. 127)

Here the Phenomenon ('you did not') is anaphoric with (refers back to) 'ISMENE: . . . I know no more'. That is, with a (negated) Mental Process of knowing or feeling. '[Y]ou' here, participant in an embedded clause, is 'staged' as weaker than 'I', because that embedded clause is dependent upon both the Senser 'I' and the Process 'I' initiates; dependent that is on Antigone as thinker or Senser.

But who *stages* this 'weakness' grammatically? There are two possible answers here:

(a) Sophocles, provided that Ancient Greek observes the same sorts of grammatical options as English, and provided the way in which they are 'constitute worlds' is similar. There is no *a priori* basis for this assumption, unless we assume equally that subjectivity in the world transcends socio historical context, producing the 'universally human' of some traditions of literary criticism. Because we cannot sustain this assumption, what we note is that Halliday's 'social semiotic' is necessarily ethnographic. On the other hand, the translator 'into English' is doubly an ethnographer (of Ancient Greek conditions, and of recent Britishness); thus:

(b) the translator (E. F. Watling) on Sophocles' behalf, and on the basis of that double ethnographic intervention: mediating between two representations of culture.

What is common to both answers is this: the *writer* performs this clausal staging, and not 'Antigone' (a contingency in the flow). The actor takes up this writerly enunciation, takes a position with regard to it (producing elements of metapraxis), and further mediates the *metteur en scène* intervention. So that the 'standing for' we engage with is multiple, and by no means 'internally' homogeneous.

Knowing or not knowing (attributed to ISMENE), and equally the statement of reflection, considering, thought (attributed to ANTIGONE) are used by the reader as components in a process of 'understanding', which goes far beyond the limits imposed by text-givens: that process activates knowledges-of-the-world, which we 'stage', inserting and opposing or dramatising the two named characters as *different participant types brought into juxtaposition*. It is on the basis of the amassing, by the user, of similar differentiations, and the ability then to 'restage' them in terms of differentials and complementarities perceived in the world, that we 'intuitively', 'perceptively', predicate those two characters as such and such a type of person-in-the-world.

But the actors may not need that predication, that verbalisation. They may in fact somatically 'sense' the same differentiation when the one looks for the taste and the bite of a Mental Process 'held back' by an embedded anaphoric clause, when the other finds herself 'held back' by the five lines studded about with the forcefields of negativity and equivocation:

> I have heard **nothing** about any of those we love,
> **Neither** *good* **nor** *evil* – **not**, I mean, since the death
> Of our two brothers, both fallen in a day.
> The Argive army, I hear, was withdrawn last night.
> I **know no more** to make me *sad or glad*.
> (Sophocles/Watling *op. cit.*, p. 127)

Neither of the two Material processes used here – 'withdraw' and 'make' – is attributed to the character as Agent acting in/on the world. The character shifts between Mental Processes ('hear', 'know') and Verbal Process ('mean'), both concerned with sensing and speaking (oriented to mind and mouth) rather than with actions in or of other parts of the body, and in a minimal–logical and a commonsensical reading or enacting of actional potential, the character is wholly static – which does not for an instant mean that the actor–character complex lacks energy and tension: it cannot mean this, in the energised conditions of performance, where the amassed gaze of the wilfully self-imprisoned spectators bears so powerfully upon the actor's presence and actions.

So although 'rooted to the spot' by a minimal–logical semiosis of transitivity options and textual and interpersonal options, the actor none the less voices, and in that voicing must vibrate within that energised stasis, drawing the gaze to the minimal muscular definition which comes from such an imploded energetic investment. Must do this – or else risk the loss of the spectator attention ('It went flat'; 'I nodded off').

6 Tactical incursions into established procedures

We are approaching an understanding of dramatic performance within theatricality, through differentiation from performance in the everyday – and this brings us back to de Certeau's contribution to a poetics of the everyday. He approaches 'everyday practices' initially through a critique of Foucault's scenario for social control, worked through the minute spread of 'disseminated technologies' perceived to control even our most apparently 'spontaneous' and 'individual', 'natural' activities:

Everyday practices . . . are difficult to define – we might provisionally call them *procedures* . . . The problem of the relationship of such procedures with discourse is clear at once. Procedures lack the repetitive fixity of rites, customs or reflexes – modes of knowing no longer or not yet articulated through discourse. Their mobility means that they are constantly oriented to a diverse range of objectives . . . but without their depending on verbal elucidation. But can we say they are autonomous? Discursive tactics . . . can be the formal grid for other-than-discursive tactics.

(de Certeau 1980a, p. 97: my translation)

In terms of the metapraxis I have just outlined, and with the 'bite of the words in the mouth' to the forefront, what we need to determine is whether we can propose that for the actor, in many cases, *somatic tactics* initiate the process which will 'harden' strategically to become the *formal grid for performance practice*, including discursive practice. This seems to be what is happening when Mnouchkine shows the actors an option, rather than speaking it; when the actor says 'Look at this!' (or does not even need to say it); and when the *metteur en scène* suggests 'A bit more like this'. It is a common function and a common procedure in a theatre of co-operation. From this perspective the actor seems to be de Certeau's tactician, a poet of the everyday – but we know, every bit as much, that the actor can only work those tactics through mastery of the strategies through which she takes on the name of actor. It is her capacity for favouring the tactical, through the use of the strategic, which marks professionalism in less rigidly codified theatre traditions:

> Little known producers, poets of their business, inventors of paths within the jungles of functionalist rationality, consumers [or actors] produce something ressembling 'wandering paths' . . . They trace "indeterminate trajectories" which are apparently lacking in sense because they are not cohesive with constructed, written and prefabricated space within which they move around. These are phrases which are inconceivable within a place ordered by the techniques organising systems. Although they utilise as their material the vocabularies [and systems of practices] of received languages (TV, newspapers, the supermarket or urban dispositions) and although they remain framed within prescribed *syntaxes* [or actional frames . . .] these 'wanderings' remain heterogeneous within the systems they have infiltrated and in which they sketch the ruses of *different* interests and desires. They get around, come and go . . . like the sea which insinuates itself between the rocks and labyrinths of established order. (pp. 82–3)

Let us come back to Halliday for more discursive clues to an 'everyday practice', in terms of which we might better understand performance's uses and modifications of it. For Halliday (1987), humans "construe":

> two macrocosmic orders of which we are ourselves a part: the

social order, and the **natural** order', and we do so through
'**natural** languages' and theoretical metalanguages [or '**unverb-
alised practices and metapractices.**' Thus] language [**and other
symbolic systems** are] as much a part of evolution as we are
ourselves; we did not manufacture [them]. It is an evolved
system, not a designed system: not something separate from
humanity, but an essential part of the condition of being human.
(p. 135)

In this 'evolutionary' process, in the:

last hundred generations or so . . . our [natural] languages have
spawned various metalanguages [to accompany the new
semiotic modes of measurement and experimentation] – the
languages of mathematics and science. These are extensions of
natural languages . . . kept tied to [them] by an interpretive
interface . . . (p. 136)

Thus: 'our spontaneous **practices governed by the habitus** have
spawned various **metapractices** [to accompany the new semiotic
modes of interrogation and experimentation] – **the practices of
performance and performance sciences.** These are extensions of
[**spontaneous practices**] kept tied to them by an interpretive
interface' *which is what we are trying to practise here.*

6.i 'Attic' and 'Doric' modes

Halliday notes as typical of the ways in which language (and other
symbolic practices) develop the distinction after 550 BC between
'attic' and 'doric', characterised by "the explosion of process
nouns in scientific Greek", which marks off 'natural order' (or
'spontaneous') practice from metapractice. That is, a shift to what
he calls a "conscious effort in understanding", which we have
similarly noted to be both **typical of mainstream uses of performance, and not necessarily worked through language**:

For our active construction of reality we [have] to be able to
adopt either a dynamic, "in flux" perspective or a synoptic,
"in place" perspective – or a mixture of the two, with a
complementarity between them. . . . Represented in this new

"attic" style, the world is a world of things, rather than one of happening; of product, rather than of process; of being rather than becoming. . . . [W]here previously there had been one mode of interpretation, the dynamic, now there were two, the synoptic and the dynamic – or rather, two poles with varying degrees of semantic space possible between them. There are now two ways of looking at one and the same set of phenomena.

(pp. 146–7)

He continues:

The . . . everyday, commonsense discourse, is characterised by a high degree of grammatical intricacy – a choreographic type of complexity . . . : it highlights processes, and the interdependence of one process on another. [It is hence akin to the Dionysian principle of blend and flow, of merging rather than separation]. The attic style, that of emergent languages of science, displays a high degree of lexical density; its complexity is crystalline, and it highlights structures, and the interrelationship of their parts – including . . . *conceptual* structures . . . (p. 147)

In Halliday's research what emerges is the difference between choreographic, 'everyday commonsense discourse' (or practice), and the 'emergent languages of science' and their practices, regulated, for example, by actional frames in performance mode. What is of interest for our project is the extent to which we, as 'everyday users' of writing in performance, will apparently intuit, and will differentiate 'human types', and predicate and more widely constitute character, as actional complexes to which we attribute qualities – often noting, for example, 'feminine traits'/ 'logical persuasion'/'very human qualities' – on the basis of a **stylistic wave which ripples between peaks and troughs** marked by dominance of one or another of these separate but complementary 'styles'.

6.ii Semiotising cohesion: hypotaxis and parataxis

Secondly, we can add the phenomena of **hypotaxis** (i.e cohesion through dependency of clauses [*or actions*]) and **parataxis** (cohesion between clauses [*or actions*] of equivalent rank joined by simple conjunctions, e.g. 'and', 'but') to these choices. The first seems to lead to a predication in terms of the mental–verbal, rather than the material–gestual, and in terms of hierarchy. Used in combination with the lexical density and crystalline structure of the attic – we find this consistently in French theoretical writers – it is utilised as differential indice of the 'whole human semiotic', and we tend to predicate the speaker or writer as 'intellectualising', 'complex', 'cerebral' (or even 'obscurantist'), active through discourse rather than materially. Much English-language theory – see for example discourse analysis in this tradition – prefers to attempt a 'simplification' of the difficult through a choice of cohesion through parataxis. What I have just performed here is an ethnographic act of an everyday kind we consistently use in theatre, 'sketching in' national or ethnic 'types' on the basis of language specificities – and this tendency marks one of the most serious obstacles to effective translation for the stage, precisely because it demonstrates that 'understanding', cued by but distinct from synoptic text, is culture-specific: to translate the cue does not ensure cultural exchange. Secondly, the sketching-in is minimal–logical, and not yet of performance interest other than as enabling structure or parameter.

If the 'choreographic' 'commonsense' of the doric 'dances' (cf. Barba, 1990) it is not the least because of its stress on **process**, rather than on lexical density and nominalisation of processes: this seems to lead to our predication of the 'peak' (or character-focus) as process-oriented in an actional world, marked by interdependency of options (e.g. 'First do this, and then this, which works like this, then try the other one, which comes in later'), rather than by the hierarchy and stasis with its consequential imploding of somatic action of the attic (e.g. 'My advice to you is that your preferred choice, characterised by its requirement of a considerable endeavour you show, by the way, no particular taste for, necessitates a consideration marked by all due seriousness').

Obviously if we modify Halliday here – supposing that **somatic practice and relations in the world may be language-constituting** – to add the distinction between a **'doric' and an 'attic' somatic practice in performance**, what we find is the difference between two typical uses of energy in space and time: the equivalent to the nominalisation and lexical density of the attic is typified by the constrained actions of the detailed classical naturalist stage, and by the heightened use of actional strategies, the institutions of a given performance stylistics, and a maximum of actional frames. The 'doric' would seem to favour tactical interventions, and the loosening of the hold of predictably-detailed, socially-agreed actional frames or stylistic devices, coupled with a similar loosening of temporal divisions like scene breaks. It seems probable that we could more finely develop this distinction.

6.iii Applications to the meta-somatic

If such a distinction can be observed in our everyday uses of 'spontaneous speech' and of writerly speech, of 'spontanous action' and of 'schooled' actions – and we all dispose commonly of both registers, while the performer must be able to produce the 'schooled spontaneous' as well – the metapraxis contained within the praxis *of performance* introduces that blurring of the 'attic' and the 'doric', where that blurring is itself, as we have seen, a characteristic of theatricality. In performance we are looking for that soft wavering between a schooled praxis which we can 'attribute to character' (it is in fact a basis for our constituting character), an apparently spontaneous practice we can similarly so attribute, and at the same time a further, organisational transparency which 'hones', 'orients', and energises these practices in such a way that they demand and command spectatorial attention, and – in the late twentieth century – direct that spectatorial attention no longer just to character but to the actor–enunciator complex. As I indicate above, the recent Halliday makes provision for what might now appear, to our own way of seeing, as a complex overlay of transparencies, whose shifting focus-points, for the spectator, come from fluctuating energetic investments:

> in the course of semiotic activity [of constructing our little universes of doing and happening] without really becoming aware of it we have also been construing the two macrosemiotic orders *of which we ourselves are a part*. (p. 134: my emphasis)

In other words, we are consistently 'writing/inserting ourselves into the picture' we think we are 'only observing', and thereby transforming it; and in **praxiological terms**, we are constantly both acting in the scene we believe we are 'only living', and living out the complex scene in which we might otherwise seem only to be performing: that 'scene' is not limited by the reach of the fiction; it extends into the theatrical relation, and the wider relation of theatre with the social. And each of these 'ripples' is entailed by the performance of and within the fiction.

6.iv Scene/frame/control

What shifts within these frames does indeed seem to be something determined by and located in our capacity for what we might have to accept to call 'self-observation' – however much this metaphor continues to bind us in to the order of looking. But what is it that we 'really' see – given the degree of misrecognition Lacan intrudes into our self-gaze? When I look, I control muscles, I both energise and freeze, attempting to wreak 'in the mirror' a body enhancement (but still I never see what I want to see), which I then release, on looking away. It would seem that the performer does not look away, but maintains this self-gaze and control as a condition of her craft. To approach this, perhaps we can take a cue from that other *out-of-the-everyday* everyday practice of *seduction*.

Seduction seems, when it is at work in situations in which 'something else is going on' (activities we can approach through the grid of the actional frame, or through the conceptual categories of institutionalised practice or strategies), to be both tactical – because it is highly interactive, highly responsive to the vagaries of situation and environment – *and* shared, albeit within a limited force-field or force-fields (which we cannot actually quantify in advance). What seems to enter into seduction is a particular, 'maximum wasteful' investment of energy beyond everyday requirements, a build-up of that energy which is at the same time 'anxious', patchy, inconsistent; plus the added factor of a typically *not yet adequate* follow-through of that energetic thrust into commensurable actional modes.

Can we talk *analytically* of seduction? This is a somatic skill, an intelligence-at-work in a highly volatile interactive situation; a cunning intelligence, and one which does not seem to be driven by pre-established discursive input, although it is finely marked by choices and developments. It is characterised by a maximal investment of partially-retained 'non-functional' energy (not functional in everyday terms), and it is liable to produce certain sorts of changes which seem close to those in the 'dilated' or vibrating bodywork of the performer. If we cannot approach the problem in down-breaking terms, perhaps we can do so in the up-building terms of *catalysis*, from the hypothesis of a theatricality akin, in part, to the energetic investments, mutual catalysis and transformation in the processes of seduction. The problem facing us, in more general terms, is acknowledged by Halliday in these terms:

> The problem of turning the cryptogrammar of a natural language [or everyday somatic practice] into a metalanguage for reasoning with [or a metapraxis for teaching performance, or seduction] is that it has to become automatised – that is, the grammar has to be made to describe instead of constructing reality by not describing, which is what it does best. (p. 144)

But this observation points up precisely our advantage within the somatic economy, over those who remain trapped within the scriptural. The relatively automatised (because repeated) somatic work of pre-performance production (and of seductions) *still constructs realities* by enacting them interactively (breaking precise predetermination: this is *déhiscence* at work) in situations, in context and to any number of explicit and implicit ends. Whereas within the precincts of the scriptural economy, for Halliday:

> writing puts language in chains; it freezes it, so that it becomes a *thing* to be reflected on . . . Writing deprives language of the power to intuit, to make indefinitely many connections in different directions at once, to explore (by tolerating them) contradictions, to represent experience as fluid and indeterminate. (p. 148)

A little strong? As soon as we take dramatic writing into the scenes of theatre practice, do we not *partially* liberate it from these chains (the system of parole, again), while retaining the organising frames of enunciation precisely in order to activate the equally pleasurable notion of complex enunciation? What writing becomes, Halliday adds – and the metaphor is useful – is "destructive of one fundamental human potential: *to think on your toes*" (my emphasis). Now, I have claimed more than this: the performer thinks **with** her toes. What our somatic economy of theatre permits – when writing is activated in it through voicing, and in which it vibrates – is the escape of a particular mode of writing from those chains, the slippage from its synoptic ("in place") 'imprisonment' on the rigidity of the paging, into its possible states of dynamic ("in flux") becoming. But this 'becoming' is not shrouded and mysterious, as long as we re-establish somatic practice as a legitimate 'body' of knowledge. 'Becoming', then, is available, because of our acquired literacy skills and our newly acknowledged **'logics of practice'** (which are theatre training itself), to "structuring, categorising, [and] disciplining" (p. 149) interventions, **which produce a meta-praxis in conjunction with a practice.**

6.v Re-embodying 'discourse'

Halliday continues:

> we invent a filing system for language *reducing it to writing* . . .
> For the first time language comes to be made of constituents –
> sentences – instead of the dependency patterns – clause
> complexes – of the spoken mode. And with constituency comes
> a different form of the interpretation of experience.

What this means, for Halliday, is that:

> [w]riting brings language to consciousness; and in the same
> process it changes its semiotic mode from the dynamic to the
> synoptic: from flow to stasis, from choreographic to crystalline,
> from syntactic intricacy to lexical density . . . Written language is
> corpuscular and gains power by its density, whereas spoken
> language is wave-like and gains power by its intricacy. (p. 148)

> . . . Thus writing changed the social semiotic on two levels.
> Superficially, it created documentation . . . more fundamentally,
> it offered a new perspective on experience: the synoptic one,
> with its definitions, taxonomies and constructions. The world of
> written language is a nominalized world, with a high lexical
> density and packed grammatical metaphors. It is these features
> that enable discourse to become technical . . . (p. 149)

Through the features of the somatic economy of theatricality, writing is simultaneously lived, and framed by practitioner enunciation; and current metapraxis, in its orderly – because repeated – tactical and strategic conduct, makes us newly experience experience, which is not *re*constructed, in the sense Schechner (1985) gives to the term, but both constituted anew, with each changing audience, and simultaneously 'chained', or framed by a theatrical enunciation. It operates pleasurably for us, in the late twentieth century, in an oscillation *between* lived praxis and metapraxis.

Halliday suggests that:

> we can all learn to talk in written language, and a few people can manage the harder task of writing in spoken [where] by speech I mean the natural, unself-monitored discourse of natural dialogue: low in grammatical metaphor, low in lexical density, high in grammatical intricacy, high in rheomodal dynamic . . . these are the features that keep it open, in the far-from-equilibrium state in which it enacts, and so construes, the semiotic parameters of our social, biological and physical levels of being. The frontiers of knowledge, in a post-quantum nouvelle alliance, need a grammar of this kind to map them into the realm of "that which can be meant" [**or shown**]. *But this mapping does not depend on reference, with the grammar being used in an automatized way to describe.* If quantum ideas [of force, field and flow] seem inexpressible, this may be because we have tried too hard to express them. They are almost certainly there already . . . (pp. 150–1: my emphasis)

We can all learn to perform the logic of practices which orders and co-ordinates multiple instances of habitus, and a few people can manage the harder task of writing performance potential, of writing for a performance voicing, which will combine grammatical metaphor, high and low lexical density, high and low grammatical intricacy and rheomodal dynamic, in order to provide the materials for the constitution of a global conception internally and multiply differentiated, from which we produce character and plot.

Halliday cites Lemke (1984) with regard to "social semiotic systems":

> such a system can include itself in what it is describing [or **enacting**] – because it is a theory of praxis, of practices which

operate irreversibly, ordered in time. Thus a grammar can also be, at the same time, a theory of grammar [**just as a practice entails a logic of practice**]. [W]e have learnt from quantum physics [and phenomenology] that the observer is an essential component in the total picture [or in the global experience].

(p. 151)

The spectator, then – as we found in our reworking of the notion of theatricality – is only shiftingly and perspectivally the actor's other, and vice versa. It is the shared desire to show/see/experience, and the shared experience-of-the-world (of the specular–somatic economy and its pleasures), which makes possible a binding-in and a circuit of energies which does not transcend so much as itself establish the theatre relation (as distinct from the theatre's architectural specificities).

This perception of energy is similar to that stressed by Volli: 'public techniques', are marked by a necessary *amplification of presence* – or energetic intensity and dilation – *in order to 'break with automatisms' of the body*. This produces a 'second physical culture', de-automatised, modelled on both the everyday and on the relation of theatricality itself, which is both cunning, conning, a conjuring or somatic art, and lucid, in that this art is, in the widest possible sense of the term 'enunciation', *goal-oriented* (just as is so oriented that seduction I brought in above). Volli cites Barba to indicate that this is not a shift between 'being' and 'representing something', but between 'being' and *performing*. *Performing* means *working* energies:

> what is substituted for the energetic economy of an everyday characterised by techniques of posture and movement chosen by each of us whenever possible because it is the most convenient and least fatiguing option permitted by a culture in terms of the specific goal, is an order of wastage in which energy is dissipated in order to capture the attention.
>
> (p. 118: my translation)

As we have seen, this is not entirely accurate because energy is not so much dissipated to capture attention, as partly 'thrust forward', and partly drawn back and withheld, to maintain itself and draw attention to the still-energised body. The soft-body, produced by a full flow-through of energy to a given goal, is of no performance interest in theatre at all. Through maintaining energy within the body the performer achieves maximum visibility and will experience, at length in the conditions of performance, something like elation, which then feeds in to the somatic practice, which 'shines' with it: this is the essential metapraxis of the live performer within the 'late-industrialised' context of electronic mass media; and as metasemiotic it functions in part as an alternative (live-interactive) and highly controlled use of human energies, in a relationship of complementarity with those familiar mechanically-produced energies of our minimal-wastage everyday.

Chapter 10

Applications

Beyond the constitution of the character-complex on which any *conventional* dramatic production depends (a postmodern critique might show precisely the contingent nature of this dependency), what we are looking for are the means to recognise and locate the writerly components which, in intersecting with the diverse 'models of knowledge' outlined above, provide the 'dispositifs' or grids or 'enabling structures', on the basis of which we can constitute the outlines of a stage 'possible world' (Eco, 1979, pp. 3–43). In the interrelationship between writerly and 'other' elements, we can localise *in terms of a given production*, in its socio-cultural context, what seems to have been the role of a dramatic input into a theatre relationship of felt-knowledges, capable of ordering both the given space and time of the fiction, and the interrelational space of theatre and the time of its event. Halliday is useful here, once again, because of his insistence on the 'reality-creating' nature of symbolic practice, in place of earlier and still-perpetuating notions in which symbolic practice is supposed to 'reflect', 'express', or neatly to 'represent' a pre-existing and independent 'reality'. Where realities are conceptual and perspectival, implicating in them their perceivers, and hence dynamic, rather than fixed, representations both enact, and 'stand for', complex *conceptual reals*. As a consequence the stage construct, processes and work are a 'residue of a residue' (more condensed?) of a perceived 'real', where the latter now seems already to be multiform, and internally divided.

The dimensions and the 'nature' of the symbolic constitution of that conceptual 'world' can best be derived and developed outward from the intersection of actorly *uses of* the clausal 'stages' and the interclausal complexes, with the enabling structure formed from elements prioritised in a 'theatre hermeneutics' (cf. Palmer in Benamou and Caramello, 1977) of contextualised dramatic writing

283

(cf. the 'metatext of the *mise en scène*', in Pavis, 1985). This actor-centric focus is far from the stereotypical 'power structure' of the 1970s, dominated by a tyrannical author and/or the *mise en scène*, and equally far from the 1980s' attempt to codify spectator 'reception'. It supposes, first, that the actor is the prime mediator of power in current theatre practice, and second that the spectatorial binding-in, and the pleasures this makes possible, works explicitly through that actor, and no longer through the abstract category of character, in the ancient Aristotelian model.

The conceptual order and the perspectival orientation are always worked through relationships of complementarity (spectator-actor/actor–character), rather than through any apparently 'single phenomenon' – whether this be a named 'character', author, director or 'subtext'. We need in consequence to work outward from the clause through 'hard' conceptual categories ('institutions' of cultural tradition, and their strategic modes) such as theatre genre, acting style, mode of *mise en scène*, moving then to some of the myriad 'organisational' or 'strategic' phenomena or practices which find themselves incorporated in our understanding of theatre as a crossroads for all modes and practices of knowledge. For example, deixis/proxemics, actional frame, thematic system, speech act, gestuality, facework and so on; bringing in, at a later point, the blurring and slippage between categories and modes of knowledge-in-practice which comes from the notion of the tactical. What I propose in this chapter is to attempt to trace in the McLeish/Sophocles *Electra*, re-read now after my experience of the Warner–Shaw staging (Barbican 1988–9, Riverside 1991), those elements which it seems to me, *in the event(s) of my spectatings*, were taken up and prioritised by the production team. I demonstrate to what extent hypotheses as to the possible bases for this intervention, in that staging, are useful and plausible, and I make brief comparative reference to the Mnouchkine *Choéphores*. This provides a useful counterpoint in that it uses 'the same myth', 'the same characters', produced by a different writer, translated into French rather than English, and staged by a different group of practitioners. The *metteur en scène* in this case explicitly espouses feminism in the 1990s (Kiernander, 1990), and the Paris theatre is now legendary, attracting huge government subsidy; whereas the Warner *Electra* was produced in the 'experimental' conditions of The Pit and the Riverside in London.

We can approach the synoptic writing now through three major focus-points:

- **location and specification of actional frames** relating to strategic or institutionalised 'practices of everyday and extra-daily life';

- **location and specification of thematic systems,** which threading through text and production, provide one of the bases for what we call 'character complexity', and 'subtext';

- **exploration of clauses and interclausal relations,** worked in terms of the generic overlay which provides named characters, and anticipates the establishment of interrelationality.

1 The 'information focus' of 'first' text elements

The initial bases for our constitution of ORESTES as character come from the interclausal relation SERVANT ↔ ORESTES, and I am extracting *interpersonal* indices which derive, in the first 86 lines, from **mood,** from **deixis,** and from the **interrogative + take-up** complex. Although on the basis of habitual centring strategies the reader will probably be more interested in constituting ORESTES as character, this is scant comfort to the actor working as SERVANT, who has no less a need to locate the synoptic, interrelational bases for a somatic work leading to constitution of character as complex psycho-somatic action. What should emerge, however, from the detail of *complementarities* given below, is that ORESTES is in turn modulated in terms of SERVANT, and vice versa, so that what we find here are the beginnings of a subtle orchestration:

SERVANT ↔ ORESTES:

Processes, Participants and Mood Options

We are	Listen (Imperative)
Look,	guide my aim (Imp.)
we are	we must obey
We must	you must
it is time	Bring back (Imp.)
we must	Tell them (Imp.)
	to work, old man
	You know your orders

> see they are obeyed (Imp.)
> we must
> * *(hears Electra: thematic system c. kinship*
>   Shall we stay? (Interrog.)
> No: we must
> Hurry

SERVANT is marked by a stronger use of the interpersonal 'we', which, with the modal 'must' and the elided imperative of 'it is time', I tend to semiotise as unity and encouragement, and this semiosis works through the complementary imperative mood (singularises the giver of commands), which dominates this section of ORESTES.

ORESTES names S. as 'old man', personalising (it is intimate in our current understandings, albeit possibly pejorative), but disindividuating (unnamed) and functionalising, whereas SERVANT addresses O. and P. as 'dearest of friends'. There are two points which strongly modulate any rigidity of relation, however:

(i) SERVANT is suddenly strongly marked by the 'I–you' deictic relation after the attitudinalised 'When they butchered your father, I . . . you . . . I . . . you . . . I . . . you'. 'Butchered' is a marked option in the system whose neutral option is 'kill', and the marked option functions in semiotisation as indice of attitude. And both actors will seem to 'instinctively' (i.e. commonsensically, strategically, minimal-logically) modulate their somatic relation (spatial relation; gestural relation; direction of gaze; voice timbre and stress) accordingly.

(ii) at ORESTES: 'Or else my sister . . . Shall we stay a moment', i.e. at the concrete intervention of the **thematic system** of *kinship* (ELECTRA's voice), ORESTES suddenly becomes the questioner; addresses himself to SERVANT, which provides negative take-up; rejects the suggestion, adding an imperative: 'Hurry'. I semiotise this switch from command to interrogative as 'weakness' or 'dependency' in O., and as a shifting-to-complementary strength, in S.

This suggests, again, the bases for a somatic shift so well-learnt (**habitus + acting codes**) that it will appear (wrongly) to be 'instinctive': O. onstage directs attention elsewhere, to an other of the given situation, breaking the established energy-field of the

'I–you' interrelation of the fiction (*but having exactly the opposite effect in the energy-field of the theatre relation*, which it heightens through difference). The S. command (*new*, hence we perceive a marked imperative mood) intervenes to redirect attention to the given situation of plan and deed. It is difficult to avoid noting, here, the **indice** of a current model of knowledge I myself bring to the activation: the kinship bond (sister), overlaid by gender opposition (**thematic systems**: kinship + gender) – in which woman wails, man acts (Ancient Greek consensual **habitus**, determining 'appropriate' actional modes); and that ORESTES wavers between the two, choosing the 'male role', at this point, over kinship.

The feel of the words in the mouth, for both actors, will derive largely but apparently 'instinctively', from this modulated interplay, marked by clusters, and by change (= **textual function**), which collectively will 'feel like', and be enacted as, the beginnings of 'emotional/relational complexity' (see 3 below).

2 Transitivity options – extract from source text[*]

SERVANT
> Orestes, son of Agamemnon, son
> Of the warlord who led the Greeks at Troy,
> We are in Argus – the ancient land
> You pined for, and longed to see again.
> Look, over there: the sacred plain
> Of Io, child of the river-god;
> Down there, the Lycean Agora, named
> For Lycean Apollo; there, on our left,
> The famous temple of Hera. This place,
> Where we are standing now, is Mycenae –
> Golden Mycenae, rich in death,
> Palace of the dynasty of Pelos.
> When they butchered your father, I took you
> Away from here, on the orders of Electra
> Your sister. I saved you, I brought you up
> To manhood, to avenge your father's death.

[*] Sophocles, *Electra, Antigone, Philoctetes*, trans. K. McLeish (Cambridge University Press, 1979).

Orestes, and Pylades dearest of friends,
We must make our plans at once.
The dark blanket of stars is put away,
And birds are carolling the rising sun.
Before anyone stirs, it is time to talk.
Our long waiting is over: now we must act.

ORESTES

My faithful friend, everything you do,
Every word you say, proclaims your loyalty.
Just as a thoroughbred shows its mettle

. . . .

This is my plan. Listen carefully,
And if I miss the target, guide my aim.
I went to consult Apollo's oracle,
To ask the god how I was to avenge
My father and punish his murderers.
This was the answer:
'Go yourself, helped by no army.
Use tricks to snatch the punishment.
They killed; they must die.'

Transitivity Options, lines 1–37

		Processes		*Process types*
S:	warlord who	led		**material**
	We	are		relational
	You	pined for		mental
		longed to see		mental, mental
		Look		behavioural
		named		verbal
	we	are standing		relational
		is		relational
	they	butchered	your father	**material**
	I	took	you	**material**
	I	saved	you	**material**
	I	brought	you up	**material**
		to avenge	father's death	**material**
	We	must make our plans	modal +	**material**
	blanket of stars	is put away	passive	**material**
	birds	are carolling		behavioural

	Processes		Process types
anyone	stirs		**material**
it	is time to talk		relational, verbal
waiting	is over		relational
now we	must act	modal +	**material**
O: you	do		**material**
you	say		verbal
	proclaims		verbal
	shows		causative mental
	pricking up		**material**
	snorting at		behavioural
you	are first		relational
This	is	my plan	relational
	Listen	carefully	behavioural
if I	miss		**material**
	guide my aim		**material**
I	went to consult		**material**
	to ask		verbal
how I	was to avenge		**material**
	punish		**material**
This	was		relational
	Go		**material**
	Use tricks to		**material**
	snatch		**material**
They	killed		**material**
they	must die	modal +	**material**

What can we discern here? S. is Material Process only in 'relating the past'. In all other attributed materials, we find a modalising component, which 'softens' its action-on-the-world potential. It is this processual opposition between active-past and static-present which 'flavours' this position in the prevailing climate. O., on the contrary, is strongly marked by Material Processes, which seems to imply energetic action-in-the-world. But these are in turn modalised by circumstances: Material Processes here are proposed by the oracles, or asked of S., by O. Rather less frequently do they relate to O.'s own actions. A second point comes from the distinction between enunciation and what is enunciated. In the theatre context the actors together constitute a situation, in this case something like a conversational exchange (which performs various genre functions with regard to knowledges to be made available to spectators). This establishes a double situation of enunciation:

> Actor–enunciator:
>> *character–enunciator/enunciated*:
>>> **(enunciation)**:

The actor enunciates to produce the enunciating character, while producing, through voicing 'what s/he says' and does with words (Austin, 1962), as well as the fictional situation of enunciation. The Actorly enunciation takes as its context the given theatre context in and as part of its larger cultural context, which it mediates. Now, what we find in the given instant is that the Actorly enunciation, in the terms set out in the two preceding chapters, is an **enactment of theatricality** itself, in the sense of involving the activation and resonances of psycho-soma, and through production and mediation of the 'maximal wastage' energy input I have noted above.

But both S. and O., in the fictional situation inferred, are largely static, provoking a certain difficulty for current stagings. The situation entails arriving at a place; the showing of the place and its naming; the describing of the relation of place to O. in actual and mythological terms; the discussion of future actions. What, given this fixed situation, can draw and maintain the attention of the spectator by activating this maximal input of energy? This input, besides, cannot be constant, but must be modulated. In my experience student actors, looking for the bases for (naturalism's) *actioning*, complain that the characters 'do nothing but talk' – by which they mean that in the lack of Material processes there are few means to an externalisation of energy as force, oriented to an other or to an object.

Energy use, here, is modulated in tune with the clustering of Process types, such that the clustering, in particular, of Material Processes in S., will invite the thrusting forth, mainly through voice and small gesture, of an energy which will 'swell' the more because of the surrounding other-process types; and this precisely because of the relative fixity of the somatic and proxemic situation. And that this will be experienced and semiotised, by the spectator, as attitude – excitement, indignation, impassioned recall, as the case may be.

3 Textual function

The third focus is the **textual function**, which permits us to note cohesion through initiated **thematic systems**; cohesion through **hypotaxis** or **parataxis**; and through **repetition and change**. These together demonstrate the clustering principle noted above, and its potential (minimal–logical) effects/affects throughout the sequence. We tend overall to semiotise these in 'literary criticism/ whole human semiotic' terms, similar to those used in the introduction to the McLeish translation:

> thought [balances] thought, argument [balances] argument . . . . One of the most striking things about *Electra* is the way [Sophocles] uses such balanced, controlled means to express violent and complex emotions. The formal style adds tension to the drama, and allows him to highlight his characters' feelings and motives . . . (p. 4)

While we remain caught within the order of the *motif,* as Halliday uses the term, i.e. concerned with 'what happens' and 'to whom', we can play the game played here, but it supposes a wilful blindness to writing as *work,* as strategy and tactic, which draws on certain sorts of phenotypes and the cryptotypes in the expectation of producing certain sorts of effects/affects, not in the reader so much as on a real or imagined stage. 'Characters', of course, do not have feelings or motives since they are named clause complexes juxtaposed with each other within a textualisation enunciated by a single writer (or mediated by translators in that name). But once we separate out the overlay of transparencies to differentiate the synoptic order from the dynamisation we produce in terms of culture and our different accesses to and uses of it, then I think we can see how certain sorts of writing components, juxtaposed with others, provide the stage on which 'feelings and motives' become a matter of our own, highly relativised projection, and hierarchisation, of complementarities.

In the table which follows I attempt to show initial **thematic complementarities** (something like a band of 'opacity', in the terms set out by Pêcheux, 1984), which I derive from 'projecting' the synoptic text into the frames of double activation entailed in *staging a fiction in the conditions of theatricality.* I have noted above that our reflected image is always marked by misrecognition, rather than by 'true likeness', which seems to suggest that these opacities will evoke, rather than reflect or neatly communicate. The thematic complementarities constantly intersect and blur through my own reading of the writing, in the context of a possible staging. Analysis is concerned with their extraction, and separation, and what the exercise does is to reveal certain sites and strong points of their working; but catalysis is concerned with what builds up from their intersection and then with user-resonances. What this means is that any performance moment will potentially be marked by a thematic 'thickness', which nonetheless varies between these sorts of points.

What is the nature of these systems in this instance? We are constantly concerned here with the different relations and values of the verbal and the somatic. In the light of these concerns, I begin to produce **thematic complementarities** in these terms, supposing then that any staging of the fiction I might currently propose would be marked throughout, and through diverse modes of figuring, by them:

Suggested thematic systems

(a) *Truth/performance/falsehood*

O: faithful friend
Use tricks
snatch the punishment
spy on

a clear report

No one . . . will recognise you
who will suspect

Tell . . . this story

trusted ally
confirm with a solemn oath
your story
we must obey
trick/
Our enemies with the glad news

(b) *Words and/or deeds*

S: named for
the orders of Electra
make our plans
it is time to talk/
now we must act

O: everything you do/
Every word you say
proclaims your loyalty
good advice,
encouragement
This is my plan.
Listen carefully
To ask the gods
This was the answer
oracle was clear;
a clear report
Tell them this story
You bring news

A bad omen
call the living dead
pretending death I live
stories of wise men
pretended death/came to life
born from pretended death
play our part

you must confirm/
solemn oath
Make that your story
telling it
Deeds, not words
stories of wise men of old

(c) *Kinship: Mother–Father–Infant–Functions*

S: son of Agamemnon, son/Of the warlord
Io, child of the river-god
they butchered your father
Electra/Your sister
I brought you up to manhood

to avenge your father's death

O: My father

my father's grave
I avenge my father
Agamemnon my father
my sister, unhappy Electra

Who might O. 'be' (= act as)? What we add here to the shifting complementarities already observed are the thematic systems initiated: O. will be (acted as) he who advocates pretence and legitimises it in the name of the gods; who advocates action but who can be distracted, and held, by the voice of a woman; who commands the other but can be commanded. (And what does Pylades 'do', in this sequence? Given *nothing*, by the writing, except presence, the actor is bound in to a thankless position. This requires a strategic intervention – what does theatre do, in such situations – and a tactical one, on the part of the actor: 'what *should* I do – and *what am I inspired to do?*.) And SERVANT? S. is acted as he who is concerned with history and family, and with place and its meanings; who has been effective Actor in a past drama of an other, and who continues to intervene while generally maintaining interrelational norms we semiotise as 'respect'.

Symptomatically of the experience of centring traditions bound up with quantity of actional interventions, I cannot recall, two years after the event, the appearance nor the actional modes of S. (Morand in Warner) – although I recall *what he does* in functional terms. In the case of Hutchinson–Pylades I cannot even claim this much. My scant recall of S.–Morand is compounded by the entry-point into the performance space – through the central doors beneath the middle rows of the spectators – and by his functional orientation to the others (especially CLYTEMNESTRA), which turns his telling into the means of showing their reactions. Speaking is not dominant here, in performance terms; instead the listening/ reacting is dominant, and in this stress the role becomes almost purely functional. This is much less the case in the Riverside staging with Philip Locke, to which I return below.

Interpraxis

ELECTRA–Shaw watches SERVANT and CLYTEMNESTRA, and I watch differently the three of them, focusing on the former and the latter, but equally on a fourth point, to which I return below. What is surprising two years after the event is that now I can hardly 'see' (i.e. retain a complex image of) SERVANT–Morand. My recall of him as 'functional' probably derives, first, from the theatrical fact that in this instance both CLYTEMNESTRA and ELECTRA perform the role of spectator–auditor to another's performance – which is in fact my own role; second because SERVANT is outside the kinship unit itself and its assured place as scene of our complex emotional dramas; and third because SERVANT here enacts the truth–performance–falsehood thematic system of male-character intervention activated in the play's initial stages. This produces a complex alienation in a spectator bound in to the emotional–visceral kinship scene that Shaw + Parry sets up. But it is invidious for the male actor. On the other hand, perhaps it is appropriate, in terms of Sophocles as complex, named genre strategy, that I continue to perceive SERVANT in these terms – expository; message-bringer; unnamed; foil to the others – and not as 'character', despite the modulation and orchestration I have noted in the transitivity and deictic and mood analysis. This seems to indicate that Morand's acting mode relates to a set of choices of the metatext of *mise en scène*, and that in the intervening three years before Warner's re-staging, that decision has been rethought. Locke holds the gaze, actionally (movement and gesture are amplified) and because of a certain physical plasticity.

Now, SERVANT as processed synoptic options and voicing options, set forth in terms of transitivity modulation, *does not need* to be performed in the mode chosen for Morand. A sharper observation of the potential for voice modulation, through a blocking of voice derived through an unformalised perception of elements revealed to us in this sort of analysis, is fully explored by Locke, and singularises the actor–character complex for me (made it more transparent, as site for subject-projection into the human semiotic-in-the-world, rather than opaque, blocking and reflecting my own act of subjective perception back on my quest for enunciatory potential). The more forceful energisation – more and faster body movement across the space, where the others crouched, still; more gesticular work and voice shading; finer detail in facework and play of the gaze – invests the role with the muscular 'profiling' which draws the spectator's eye. Through this greater specular–somatic energy-focus, we curiously 'attend' better to the functions of narrating/advising/commanding. But there are implications for the notion of metatext.

To strengthen SERVANT, in the web of interrelationality which is the character-network, has implications for both ORESTES and ELECTRA: the notion of trans-actorly orchestration is vital at this point. Casting is not haphazard but animated by an acute understanding of this interrelationality: a strong ELECTRA, in line with late 1980s' notions of Woman, might seem to be in accord with Ancient Greek ideals for the daughters of the kings; but is she to be as strong as, less strong than, or stronger than ORESTES? If stronger, or as strong, the classic logic of the drama is compromised: if ANTIGONE can bury her brother, why must ELECTRA await ORESTES' return before a killing of mother and murderer can occur? If both as strong as, or stronger than ORESTES and at the same time *unable-to-act* on the world – because the writing largely refuses ELECTRA Material Processes, and makes them negative or passive when they are attributed – it is vital that the *mise en scène* **show** this handicap in the actor's work and relationships. Hence Shaw's ceaselessly imploded maximal-wastage energies, and the casting of Ibbotson (smaller than Shaw), plus the wholesale retention of his muscular, somatic potential. Note too, in this respect, that the drama ends on a note of inconclusive *word-play* (**thematic system:** words–deeds; **transitivity options:** Verbal Processes rather than Material Processes), so that even when centred, ORESTES–Ibbotson seems weaker than an ELECTRA–Shaw become spectator on the deeds of men.

In the 1988 Warner production the facial, gesticular and vocal range of O.–Ibbotson is intensely restrained, so that although the initial synoptic bases for dynamisation in terms of 'character

complexity' noted above are clear, what is interesting is the extent
to which the Ibbotson–O. complex *does not interiorise energy*, but
orients it outwards, toward the oracles, the place, the enemy other,
and to 'the deeds' (all marked by process change and repetition in
this initial ideational set). Each is an abstract and not a material
orientation, so that O. does not enage visibly with the materiality
of the staging. Of these focuses, in this production, only the
enemy-other (Mother, adulterer) will be figured, visible, materially
present – but only once slain, the material acts of vengeance
against that other remaining ob-scene, offstage. The outward-
projected force springs into the air animating the body, and hovers
there, almost thwarted by a Goal or Beneficiary unfigured in the
time and place of the stage. Words intend . . . but who achieves? In
his struggle against Man, ORESTES' 'triumph' is wholly equivocal,
and it seems to be in these terms that Warner directs Ibbotson.

Materiality

Materiality is generally ob-scene in the Warner–Sophocles use of
myth. Hence the pomegranate-offerings are the more striking in
their materiality, and in the processual staging of this symbolically
rich materiality:

ELECTRA: Where must you go? What offerings are those?
CHRYSOTHEMIS: Our mother's, sent for our father's grave.
ELECTRA: Offerings – from her? . . .
E: to make him offerings?
C: And gave me these offerings for A.'s grave . . .
E: sister – these offerings:
Make none of them. The gods will not allow / Gifts from that
witch-wife . . .
. . . scatter them on the breeze
Or bury them deep. They must not . . .
she'll find them waiting,
Momentoes of what she did
. . . to send garlands of hate to the man she killed!
thanks . . . gratitude
. . . these grave-gifts . . .
Thow them away. Instead, offer him
A lock of your hair. And give him these gifts

> From me: poor gifts, but they are all I have . . . we'll garland
> the grave
> With richer gifts than any we give him now.
> (McLeish, lines 380–460)

The 'body' of CLYTEMNESTRA drawn in down the runnel in the
concrete from between the rear doors, and exposed, within the
frame of O.'s sustained trickery is similarly striking. In Mnouchkine's *Les Choréophores* Aegisthus too is slaughtered, and the
mother's body is drawn in, her thighs spread, and her lover lying
face down between those thighs, across her body, so that the image
is mordant and morbid in its enacting fatal sexuality on the bed
become tomb.

We can term all allusions (and elided allusions) to the pomegranates, a **lexical chain**, but that does not permit us to approach
the bases for its working as major force-field of immense power,
binding together the kinship scene with the spectators' different
sorts of knowledges and pleasures. We need instead to tie this
chain in again to the Processes and Participants which 'stage' it.
This rare materiality of the stage functions as a focus-point and a
point chaud (intensity) – or as a 'contingency in the flow' of performance energies, constituted in and by the kinship complex which is
Clytemnestra–Agamemnon–daughters–Aegisthus–(Orestes). This
kinship complex and the 'flow' of its interrelational energies (by
which I mean the elements and characteristics which are exchange-
able between the named 'peaks' or characters) takes the offerings
sent, borne, rejected, and in the production thrown and torn, not
'as themselves', nor even as 'indice pointing to something else' in
any simple sense, but as a dynamic orchestration combining the
symbolic, iconicity and indexicality. These are the means to the
complex production of 'attitude', attributed by us not just to
characters, but also to stagers. In this quality it might be said to
articulate (in a literal sense) the shifting conflicts of the kinship
scene, standing for different characters in different ways; and to
articulate the enunciators' esthetics and performance meta- praxis.
Its symbolic 'blood-letting' in the production acknowledges this
dramatic force in performance mode, and extends it.

Theatrical thematic systems

What we see operating here, through the action of the stage, is a

theatrical thematic system, which sets up a chain of echoes working along the lines established by this complex: fertility and infertility, the sewing of seeds, the letting of blood, Jungian as well as Freudian models of knowledge. But as **theatre thematics** it goes further, resonating with British social conditions of the late 1980s, which invite us to 'stage' Shaw's skinny, ceaselessly moving body again, in these terms: as icon of contemporary 1990s feminity, trapped between the excesses of worked energies, and the desire to love, to mother.

Thematic systems and 'orchestrations'

Inasmuch as characters are interrelated and complementary, the prioritisation of one actor–character complex will rebound upon all others, affecting casting, as well as those components coming from an actor's working contribution. In the given instance the network of complementarities does tend to mark an **actorly** gender-divide between Shaw/CLYTEMNESTRA–Parry and the Chorus, on the one hand, and SERVANT/ORESTES/PYLADES, on the other. But the divide is not hard and fast, and this is part of the production's strength. CHRYSOTHEMIS–Colverd is in relative terms plump, richly coloured, spatially-constrained by comparison with Shaw's range of movement; functional (same-gender comparison; kinship go-between); and characterised by the play between willingness and refusal. And AEGISTHUS–Case, the black actor, walks with head high, back straight, and powerfully-muscled, and responds with wit to ORESTES in the face of threat, despite the actor's inevitable place, in this performance, as stereotype of the male other. Both thereby break with the associated oppositions this type of gender-divide seems conventionally to activate, shifting us away from any suggestion of feminist politics of the 1970s.

4 Ideational function

Fourthly, the 86 lines are marked out, and can be blocked, in terms of the **Ideational Function,** involved with representations (or constructions) of 'world(s)' of the theatre fiction. Note, first, the difference between those elements on the basis of which we constitute the here-and-now of the fictional scene and its participant relations and events – the clustering of deictics ('I'/'he'; 'here'/ 'there'; 'this'/'that'; 'now'/'later', etc.) provides a forceful discursively-derived (and hence context relative) **diagram** for stage organisation of the present event (cf. Serpieri *et al.*, 1981) – and those elements constituting 'other times and other places': the mythological past; the recent past; the oracle-function; the kinship scene and its roles, relations and processes.

Note, second, the actional frames derived, *in minimal–logical terms*, from **inferred speech act function**, which will organise the complexes of stage activity: examples here are 'telling someone a tale'; 'introducing someone to an unknown place'; 'reminding someone of a shared past'. These *processed* or dynamised synoptic indices, concise and heavily 'loaded' through details available within any consensual semiotic (i.e. they become available as soon as we agree on the relation between *complex experience in 'our' world*, on the one hand, and on the other the validity of discursive cues which permit us to access that *experience of the world*), are elaborated, in the time and space of performance, in both strategic terms and tactically, revealing the minimal–logical/commonsensical, as well as the actorly specificity of habitus and ludicity. What we need to add to the 'discourse analysis' (symptomatic) processing is this final element of ludicity: the conditions of theatricality, dissect and then frame certain elements of the synoptic and certain sorts of processing of indices. For example, the 'speech-initiating function', in SERVANT, is doubled by the STAGE ENUNCIATION. Our knowledge of the double interlocuteur – both ORESTES *and* anticipated spectators – means that we do not simply attribute to SERVANT the social power commonly accruing to the 'right to initiate verbal interaction', locating the actor in a precise relation to ORESTES, but we also mentally and then actually locate the actor in an 'appropriate spatial relationship' with the spectators. In theatre uses, in short, the Ideational Function is always doubled, or contextualised (fiction) and then recontextualised (theatricality), to produce two sets of inferred asssumptions about 'experience in the world'. Acting- and staging-probabilities are derived from the intersection of these. Thus SERVANT:

- is **first speaker**, and thereby **draws gaze** and attention of spectators;

- addresses and names the other (thus, in minimal-logical terms, faces, looks at and thereby *points us to* the interlocuteur, who becomes spectator attention focus);

- establishes relation (solidarity + differentiation) through inter-personal deixis: 'We . . . you . . . we . . . your . . . I . . . you . . . I . . . you . . . We';

- establishes the other in kinship terms: 'son of; your father; your sister';

- names complex place, qualifies place ('rich in death'; 'where they butchered your father');

- specifies actional focus and possible actional frames anticipating fictional past and future/s: 'to avenge . . .'; 'We must make our plans'.

SERVANT here is consistently focused on the group, whereas ORESTES is focused on self:

S.: **We must make our plans:**	plural subject + modalised Material Process
O.: **My faithful friend . . . :**	conversational uptake: approval; strategic function: persuasion
This is my plan:	Shift from 'We/our' to 'This *is* my plan' – unmodalised Relational Process + proxal deictic 'this' – spectator attention focused on ORESTES
Listen carefully . . . guide my aim:	ambivalence of relationship: imperative + demand for help.

In minimal–logical everyday terms, which we overlay with minimal–logical theatre-staging terms, this observed difference will be 'felt-shown' by the actors, and will differently orient them in space, with regard to the audience, and with regard to each other. It will possibly influence (but not determine) focusing options like lighting.

ELECTRA

As peak in a complex network of interrelations, defined by that interrelationality, what does 'ELECTRA' enact? One of these net-works is provided through the Ideational Function, as the kinship unit (as social microcosm in-the-world). Because of the force of this network, almost ceaselessly activated through dense lexical chains which traverse the text, ELECTRA enacts the dynamic interface between (what are literally given as) Mother(-function) and Father(-function): as Infant-function she equates with ORESTES and CHRYSOTHEMIS. But this Mother–Father–Infant structure is overlaid with the system of gender, in terms of which ELECTRA lines up with CLYTEMNESTRA and CHRYSOTHEMIS against the male other – AGA-MEMNON/ORESTES – sharpening the conflictual potential, in terms of late-twentieth-century knowledges, because of the ques-tion of gender role-models within the family. If like-CLYTEMNESTRA in anatomy and expectation of social roles ('I have no husband, no children' (line 167) negatively reinforces the norm), ELECTRA is however established as negative field of force against CLYTEM-NESTRA ('the husband killed/The marriage-bed defiled' (lines 114–15); 'shall I call her/My unhappy mother, or Aegisthus' whore?' (lines 172–3); 'So the bitch-mother yaps' (line 298)). Further, ELECTRA is like-AGAMEMNON/ORESTES in aspiration. What emerges from this set of conflicts is the observation that ELECTRA is activated as dynamic site of shifting conflicts, between what we still tend to accept as the *nature–nurture problematic*.

What are the implications of this problematic for enactment? What happens when this complex is restaged within a changed dynamic context of volatile gender roles and relations, by an enunciatory team whose director and main actor are women? Add to this the restraints on uses of energy in Morand and Ibbotson, the soft body and voice-work of the latter, the smallness of the gesticular range, and Case who irresistibly, given the traditions of British theatre, enacts a psychosexual stereotype of otherness of male sexuality. ELECTRA is already the site of conflictual discourses and practices, in any late-twentieth-century activation of that symbolic network which is the writing. In the given staging, that conflictual potential is multiplied, but equally redirected, so that the stage enunciation marks its distance from, while enacting and dynamising, the dramatic writerly enunciation. And into the space which opens between the two springs the active subject–spectator, as negotiator, as 'traveller' between orders, and as practitioner of a complex specular-somatography, a voyage of the eye.

The implications for the actor (as ELECTRA) are these: s/he must be simultaneously strong in action, and blocked in action; strong in enactment (because, for example, a forceful woman actor, in the dynamised gender situation of 1989) of the terrible weakness of masculine-aspiration imprisoned within a female body and expectations, within a patriarchal culture. The strength comes largely from the fields of force we can locate in a voicing of this particular writing by McLeish, which places stress on the kinship unit and on ELECTRA's verbalisation of her place in it:

ELECTRA.:
Feeble
A child who will not grieve
For her father dead
(McLeish)

ELECTRA.:
A dull fool might forget
A father's miserable death
(Watling)

In McLeish the child–father relation coupled with a qualifier takes up first and last places in the three-line complex – both places functioning in English as **information focus**. McLeish chooses simpler clausal units, which in our terms function as **energy fluctuations within waves**, and he chooses lexical simplicity and avoids stereotypical 'poeticising' effects. These 'synoptic' options are dynamised and intersect with other networks and models of knowledge, in this case brought through the work-relation of the Warner–Shaw team, and through the psycho-soma specific to Shaw – who in 1991–2, in her work in Dublin in the Warner–Ibsen *Hedda Gabler* and now *Electra*, is back in the centre of critical acclaim. As Hedda, she offers another finely energised and wrought *somatic* work, widely read by critics as interiorisation, i.e. in psychologising terms.

It is the field of force, and not any unitary element of text, which intervenes to determine where in the clause 'He is here' – and indeed whether – the actor will mark one syllable with vocal stress. Unmarked by stress (through italics or punctuation) in the writing, and, in transitivity terms a Relational Process, which we commonly semiotise as static (it uses the verb to relate or equate two different elements), the voiced option can place stress on none or on any one of the three components. The choice to place stress will be determined by fields of force set up from the use in context of other textual elements; they are *carried over*, then, to the given text element, acting through it, but unavailable (because not able to be isolated) 'within it'. To stress any of the three options activates the field of 'contradiction', voiced against an assertion given elsewhere relating to one of '*He*' (and not an other), '*is*' (as distinct from 'is not'), or '*here*' (and not there); whereas in the unstressed option, the clause functions as simple declaration, and the peaking within the field disappears. The field of force of contradiction is not thus 'in the clause', but in its point-energised voicing, and it derives in textual terms from a spread of components across the text. In the case of the enactment of ELECTRA, such a field of force – of 'negativity', combined with 'interrogation' – comes from the tissue formed between these sorts of elements (lines 166–233):

Perceived force-fields of interrogation and negativity

Does he know?	Bitter
I have no husband,	Bitter
no children	. . . feast unspeakable
uncomforted	. . . his own death
burden	. . . fingers gripped me
. . . useless tears	Twisted and broke my life
Does he know . . . crimes	Punish them with pain bright
The wrongs . . . ? Does he care?	Deal dreadful death
Why does he say so, and never come?	Turn triumph to dust
flower . . . withered	I have no choice
hope is gone, my strength destroyed	I am on the rack
I have no children	. . . stubbornness born of pain
No loving husband	. . . my dying breath
I am no better than a slave	. . . feed on this hate
A drudge in my father's halls	What words can comfort me?
. . . in rags	Leave me, leave me
. . . the other slaves	I am sick, past cure
. . . feed on the scraps	. . . a long road /
	Of endless misery

The force-field of negativity, and energy-use

The observation of a force-field of negativity + interrogation of this sort – and particularly one in which, in interpersonal terms, no questions are answered by an interlocuter thereby negating a social convention – gives us an effective guide toward the 'bite and taste of the words in the mouth' for the actor, in any situation in which we are able to suppose a reasonable consensus as to language-use and affects. Once again, that 'reasonable consensus' relates only to strategic or institutionalised take-up, and cannot foresee the tactical skills of the actor, cannot foresee what is specific to Shaw's bodily range and to her vocal and muscular-contractual range, and to her sense of spirited play. What we can add to this chain of negativity + interrogation is the effect of contemporary context on the powerful Material Processes addressed largely in Imperative mood to the gods. Context, today, in the British community, probably largely inverts the effect these Processes would hypothetically obtain in a polytheistic or in a fatalistic monotheistic context. In the latter, invoking the gods empowers the just; in the former, invoking the gods and attributing to such an intervention effectivity within the world, by the same stroke must disempower ELECTRA/ORESTES, in the felt-judgement of many spectators. (The only means to counter this are through the theatrical figuring of such an intervention, through light, sound, music or immense amplification of the actorly play. But this would work against the human-centric 'Electra' of Warner.)

What we can foresee, on the basis of such a chain, is the potential for the formation, and fluctuation, of a wave of energy, which will transcend text-breaks, peak at the sorts of points noted, and – inasmuch as it is so strongly marked here – will flow through into other situations in which ELECTRA appears (e.g. lines 662–788, where SERVANT tells of ORESTES' death), but has no vocal participation. In this way it becomes a properly somatic 'character-trait'. In such a scene it will animate the same range of muscular flickerings, such that we shall continue to semiotise these as 'negative', as part of the force-field of negativity, even though they are not 'innately' so. In the sequence quoted ELECTRA–Shaw as muscular flickerings was readily semiotised, by me, as 'in agonised response to Servant's words' – i.e. I semiotise 'the same' muscular options differently, because the situation acts upon my interpretation of them.

'Situation' acts upon, to determine, semiosis of 'the same' muscular options – giving the lie to any proposed generalised and decontextualised 'semantics of body-language'. Inasmuch as ELECTRA is a force-field of negativity + interrogation caught within the kinship and gender networks, as we have seen, what shifts can we note which mark the character out along the sequence of performance-time and plot, providing the actor with that modulated range of attitudinal and actional potential we seem to require from characterisation? There seem to be at least three logics which come to organise 'what happens' (in Shaw's work) in the given instance:

(i) the 'organisational grid' or *dispositif*, observed in and derived from earliest narratological analysis or analysis of the **fabula** (Pavis, 1987) in dramatic writing, seems to posit that the outlining of a problematic situation 'leads to' attempts at intervention, followed by a 'consequential' return to one kind of 'order'; this teleological structure, determined by a pre-existing ideal template, set awry, and leading to the aspired goal of a return to order, is punctuated to coincide with

(ii) the 'performance structure', which we can approach from three perspectives:

(a) spectator expectations, energy-uses and restrictions, 'liberation' from these, suppressed/retained electromagnetic radiation which will be converted to applause;

(b) choices made by the theatre team with regard to production sequence and energy-uses.

(c) the shift and change within Shaw's uses of energy, such that there is enough changing interest to sustain attention, plus some kind of peaking coinciding with the progressive wearying of the spectators.

(iii) The logic of the third 'organisational grid' seems to be ideational, inasmuch as it relates to the ways in which different socio-cultural contexts would ask, and would frame 'possible responses' to, this question: *can* ELECTRA*–(Shaw) get what she wants?* Shaw gets what she wants, we have to suppose, through the rush of adrenalin, through its fragile mastery in the sustained bodywork and its elations; through her 'conquering' her own human frailties, and through the continuous and final spectator responses and critical acclaim. Through, indeed, her professionalism. These are the 'rewards' available to a certain sort of woman's work in the late twentieth century. But ELECTRA poses more problems, in that the penultimate situation of the character is displacement, from the centre-point of the kinship crisis, to a space now become that of outsider to (and not even onlooker on) the 'deeds done' by ORESTES:

ELECTRA:

> Lord Apollo, hear them; grant their prayers.
> I'm your servant; I've given you
> What gifts I had. Apollo, hear me now.
> On my knees I beg you
> Beseech you to help us.
> Smile on us. Make our plans come true.
>   . . . Hush, women; hush friends. Listen: The men are at work. It is now. . . . I must stand guard . . . We must wait for Aegisthus now. . . . The . . . woman . . . is dead? . . . The gods helped you before – pray
> That they are near to help you now.

The actional mode next adopted is that of verbal trickery of AEGISTHUS: this is 'progress' in ELECTRA, in the move from visceral truth-telling and moaning, to performance which convinces; but it is not a Material Process of intervention in and on the world. What follows is ELECTRA's decentring, after the ambiguous lines:

AEGISTHUS:

> . . . Learn from this corpse
> To bow to my yoke, to accept . . .
> Disobey, and you will suffer. Learn that now!

ELECTRA:

> My lesson is learned. I have understood,
> At last, to accept what I cannot change.
>
> (lines 1480–1)

There is a falling-away of ELECTRA energy here, and the spectators' attention is largely redirected to the ORESTES–AEGISTHUS debate which now returns to the words–deeds thematic system. This recurs frequently in the preceding scenes where ELECTRA wishes to speak (Verbal Process) and is silenced by ORESTES or SERVANT, in favour of deeds (Material Processes). Here it is dramatised between ORESTES and AEGISTHUS:

AEGISTHUS:
    Before you kill me, let me say this – . . .
ORESTES:
    Go inside, you, quickly. The answer now
    Is not more words: it is your death.

In this debate ELECTRA is decentred, becoming the word-goad to ORESTES' hesitation. In the Warner production this goading of the soft-bodied small-gestured Ibbotson is almost grotesque, as was the intensity of the ELECTRA–Shaw impassioned and lover-like reconciliation with ORESTES–Ibbotson. (This changes significantly at The Riverside, where ORESTES is taller, stronger in body and facial traits, moves faster, dynamically energised.)

Actional frames: between writing and spectating

The term 'reconciliation', as I have used it here, serves as label – product of dynamisation – to an *actional frame*, observed through the application of the Ideational Function to the writing, whereby it mediates between that writing used, and the user's conceptual world. In turn, this frame entails and organises, in any somatic approach, a prescribed number of constitutive somatic actions – including voicing – which emerge initially through actor-*habitus*. There are many such examples to be found in any writing for the stage. But this frame is at the same time overlaid by a number of other frames: the theatre relation provides the first. The actional frame 'reconciliation with lost brother' is thereby overdetermined by its orientation in space and time to the spectators, determining positions, direction of gaze, gestuality as visibility, spectator access to faces, and so on.

A second framing, which operates throughout any staging, comes from the overlay of an acting stylistics and the mise en scène – of which one function is to assure stylistic consistency. This overlay will act on, to constrain, the nature of the actorly interrelation, the amplification of gestuality, uses of lighting, sound, music: we can see this very clearly in the Mnouchkine staging where J-J. Lemètre's music serves as 'pulse' to the actions, and largely re-places, in Mnouchkine's recent work, that mode of actorly somatic work which spectators conventionally semiotise as character interiorities. The co-ordination here between music, individual actor differences of judgement and taste, and an overall actorly consistency I attribute to Mnouchkine as 'auteur', indicate a highly worked integration of overlays. So we are dealing not just with a reproduction of the 'everyday life actional and attitudinal complexes' which *habitus* entails, but with the various *dispositifs* or conceptual, organisational grids, which come to act on different instances of *habitus,* to co-ordinate and regulate these. It is through this piling up of strata, and the 'internal' organisation which comes from the intersection between strata, that we can see the specular–somatic economy of dramatic theatre at work. In the given instance, of 'reconciliation', what we need to be aware of is the way in which a further, highly deterministic transparency – derived from the dissemination of expert discourses of neo-Freudianism – comes to order the somatic work in the actional frame.

Models of knowledge and actional frames

Let me explain what I mean here: it is largely on the basis of the kinship reconciliation in the Barbican version (1988) that I suddenly – and with considerable reluctance – predicate the lover-like impassioned ELECTRA–Shaw as *hysteric*. My reluctance is threefold: in part it springs from the terms of the fiction, and my desire (working in spite of my knowledge of 'destiny', of tragedy) to see ELECTRA as strong enough to escape the conditioning imposed since AGAMEMNON's death; in part it springs from my contemporary, highly contradictory feminism, which prefers not to see a strong woman bound up in the chains of distorted energies, whatever their justly condemned cause; but in part the 'excess' here suddenly renders the work opaque, and through the two reactions produced above, I begin to wonder whether this particular excess works in the performance terms already established.

The to-and-fro play of semiosis is momentarily disrupted, and in the midst of spectating I begin to reassess what has already happened throughout the performance: there is a slipping and a splitting of attention from the immediate to the recent past, precisely at that instant which might be expected, otherwise, to mark a peak in involvement with the stage. Contemporary late 1980s' feminism, and the different 'expert discourses' entailed, suddenly 'shows through' the web of performance in its subtle combination of the fiction with contemporary life and its needs and desires.

The global and the immediate dramatic bases for ELECTRA as hysteric are all too clear, not the least inasmuch as Freud's reading of the Greeks plays so strong a role in the formulation of his theories of the psyche. And the McLeish translation plays into this 'commonsensical Freudianism' which indeed it might find difficult, now, to escape:

ELECTRA:
> O my dear . . . my darling . . .
> Your dear voice . . . you have come home . . .
> . . . Let me hold you . . . kiss you . . . forever . . .
> . . . O Orestes, never leave me,
> Never leave me again.
>
> (lines 1229–85)

The suspension points, breaking into speech, breathing, and energy-as-action in general – although energy here is maintained, and vibrates the more in the breaks – also serve to invite somatic intervention, and Shaw holds, touches, cuddles, embraces, weeps and beams, in a crescendo of physical intimacy which it is difficult not to see as a pathological displacement of genital sexuality in ELECTRA, produced, in terms of current conventions of theory, by the loss of the father, combined with the treacherous sexuality of the mother; and the consequential problematised sexual and kinship identity (as actional modes) of the daughter (see Rose, 1986, pp. 34–9). ORESTES then, potentially, acts out for ELECTRA all masculine roles, but because of the taboo on incest this merely leads to the setting of a more powerful trap to Woman.

In this staging, the Shaw–Ibbotson intimacy does not work in sexual terms: if Shaw can baby Ibbotson, there are scant somatic bases, precisely *because of* the choices of this staging, for the inescapable suggestion (promoted absolutely by Shaw's body work as this locks into scenarios characteristic of Freud's work), that he might be her mate. By way of contrast, Mnouchkine's *Les Choréophores* uses the tiny Nirupama Nityanandan as ELECTRA, and the much larger Simon Abkarian as ORESTES. Here, furthermore, the play begins with sibling reconciliation, so the ceaselessly worked but imploded energies in ELECTRA are not the prime focus, and the feminist critique of hysteria is not available. Nityanandan 'attempts to dance' (i.e. she performs a dancing and a stumbling) as the male dances, after ORESTES stumbles and falls; and the Chorus, under Catherine Schaub's leadership, makes a nonsense of the dramatic indication for 'choral work by Chorus', by literally hanging (off the surrounding walls) 'on ELECTRA's words' and shifts, swinging into the stage space in highly staged, group dance I predicate as 'passionate', as specific tonal and speed shifts in the continuous musical accompaniment command it. In Mnouchkine's choices we see the gender-stereotype complementarity, according to which Nityanandan's relative physical *inferiority* (sister smaller than brother) strains to be 'larger' (by adopting and failing at the brother's modes of action). On the contrary, in Shaw her physiognomy contrasted with that of Ibbotson produces the problematic disjunction, sister-dominant physically + dominated actionally.

A willed disjunction? Impossible for anyone to say, since we have seen that the will is complex, and can be wilful. What must be admitted is that this disjunction tears the fabric of the fiction, *for me*, tearing at the same time the commonsensical Freudianism it simultaneously enacts, so that everything is suddenly in question. In now 'classic' Lacanian terms, ORESTES at this point becomes ELECTRA's *little man*, the phallus with which she arms herself in order to intervene in the problematic situation. Is it the internalisation of everyday versions of expert discourses, lived out as 'intuitive' judgements of taste, that causes Warner to cast Ibbotson, and to restrain his muscular range, to make of him so soft a little member in Shaw's rangy and forceful game, who finally refuses to satisfy her in these terms? In choosing Case to activate in us irresistible – although wholly dubious – stereotypes of male vitality, she somatically compounds the reduction of ORESTES–Ibbotson, compounding what is given in the synoptic text as a deed yet to do, offstage: the killing of the substitute father.

Constraining ELECTRA

The woman-trap is quickly enacted in that ELECTRA is denied a *passionate* voice in the name of the deed of vengeance to be performed by men:

ORESTES:
    Electra, hush –
    . . . Electra, soon -
    . . . Soon will be the time: not now

... Electra, hush! ...
Say no more now. Tell me later ... Tell me later:
There is too much to hear, and time is short.
SERVANT: No more now ... Electra

(lines 1244-375)

The problem posed by this crescendo, and by this new predication, lies in the premonition that for this woman (combining, in newly problematic disjunction, ELECTRA and Shaw), there can now only be further loss, a new imprisonment. And it is the power of Shaw *as performer of immense energies* that makes this grotesque. Productively grotesque, without doubt, since, in the terms outlined by Pavis (1985), this sets up the conditions for our perception of a metatext. In my own terms, what it reveals as well is meta-performance (critiquing other traditions of performance) and metapraxis.

Femininity at work: performance as metapraxis

Part of the final effect of shifted force-fields comes from the finely tempered energetic bodywork of Case – the head remains high, the body does not slump or shake, the voice contests and reasons; and the inevitable comparison with Ibbotson/Case is telling. But the full effect comes from the thwarting of the maximal-wastage energetic input of Shaw, in the immense tamping down which emerges through the passive voice/Mental Process/Mental Process/Behavioural Process/negativised Material Process cluster of lines 1480–1. ELECTRA is not freed into action, into Material Processes, but only into (highly constrained) Verbal Processes, whereas, as we have seen, Shaw's lucid and forceful body-work acts in and on the theatre relation.

The conflation of the two produces an almost intolerable disjunction, at the end of the performance. I would be hard-pressed not to call it bitter, and not to claim that that bitterness is currently fashionable. By way of contrast, Mnouchkine systematically balances the ELECTRA–ORESTES relation with the dance-work of the Chorus, given – through the continuous music performed – a particular importance in the staging; and it is with the *élan* and passion with which this dancework is led by Catherine Schaub that the performance ends, with no bitter aftertaste. Here the team or collective is triumphant, and the audience responds in kind. There is no single starred work, and consequently there are no implications for me of a 'failure' or even a containment of ELECTRA. For Schlocker:

> [t]he main theme of the [staging] seems to be the act of watching, looking. . . . Rarely does one witness in theatre such an orgiastic dance that aims to ease the weight of tragedy by setting it on a flying carpet that never actually takes off. . . . [A] ritual code of a Far Eastern origin tames through body expression the Dyonisian excess of conflicting mythical powers. . . . Théâtre du Soleil has so far been a collective undertaking, acting individuality appearing only as a marginal feature, together with inner qualities. Something else . . . is more important and accomplished . . . [T]he main thing . . . lies in the coalescence of various styles, artistic expressions in the context of a total stage event, in the beauty of the set, in the expression of the tragic experience of the world, a desire for the magic of an ineradicable artistic imprint.
>
> (Schlocker, 1991)

Decentrings

This imprint, and the methods adopted by this company to achieve it, are together quite different from the *signature-event* which seems to typify both the apparent 'postmodernism' of Robert Wilson's work and the 'personal nostalgia' (a preferred focus of postmodernism) of Kantor's *Wielopole Wielopole*. Equally, the methods typified by Mnouchkine's stagings are far from those adopted by Warner, but in these two instances what we find are practices of decentring I want to call 'feminine' (but not 'female').

Warner has herself used decentring techniques earlier in the production, but in those instances what we can note is a staging option (and not a dramatic option) which can be seen to be in accordance with feminist theory of the 1980s, preoccupied with an ideological decentring away from the hero of the fiction or star of the stage, in favour of the team at work. I have already indicated that when SERVANT recounts-performs the trick tale for CLYTEM-NESTRA/ELECTRA/WOMEN, Morand as vocal focus loses out to the kinship conflict, which is what draws our shifting gaze. But Warner intervenes to add to this, 'with no textual basis' – other than what we might semiotise as 'concern' and 'interest about/ passion for ORESTES', from the words attributed to the Women.

What she does is to broaden the tissue of 'women's modes of involvement', to include not just an active Chorus – which is what we find, in the Mnouchkine–Schaub intervention, as a forceful and exhilarating substitute to pyschological interiorisation centred in the oneness of the actor – but a Chorus whose members are potentially singularised, and semiotised as 'bound-in emotionally' to the elements of the conflict.

This decentring by Warner is far from the effect noted by Pontbriand in Richard Foreman's work, although Warner's technique of decentring, which forges a vibrating network symbolic of kinship and sub-social groupings and clusters, drew to mind the Benjamin quotation, used by Pontbriand as title ('"The Eye Finds No Fixed Point On Which To Rest . . ."'). She notes that the 'experimental' 1968-and-after theatre of Foreman was one in which:

> The spectator . . . is bombarded by a multiplicity of visual and auditory events . . . there are continual changes of the geometrical stage set, even within an act . . . The lighting also changes continually; . . . The script is fragmented, made up of short, aphoristic, unconnected sentences . . . The text is almost shouted . . . Foreman himself is integrated into the actions of the actors. Usually seated in front of the stage in full view, with his back to the audience, he gives directions, regulates sound and light. (Pontbriand, 1982, p. 159)

Although "Foreman wants the spectator . . . to look between and among things . . . hence the ultimate fragmentation of elements", and although for Pontbriand this "purpose justifies his mania for manipulating effects" (p. 160), what is recounted is an instance of modernist confrontations with the still-prevailing 'telos of unity and harmony'. This is not the effect I find in Warner's work with her performers. She is dealing with decentring, the fanning-out of energies, precisely where they have always functioned unnoticed, and not with a re-centring on the metteur en scène as 'manic manipulator' – i.e. as *auteur*, in this instance. Warner's decentring leaves no anguishing void, into which the persona of the *metteur en scène* pops, because its interweaving of elements in any scene is such that the spectator is drawn in but not fixed; freed from obsessive focalisation, but neither bombarded nor liable to the sensation of loss which follows in the wake of manic fragmentation (and which Pavis has strongly criticised). Most importantly, Warner shows a network of working women, whom we semiotise within the fiction as affected and alienated and torn from within by masculine ideal and absences, intrusions, trickery and passionate interventions – and she does this by this somatic interactivity alone.

The terms recently set out by Bernard Dort in his *La Représentation émancipée* (*The Liberated Performance*) (Dort, 1988) for a theatre emerging from the various tyrannies of the recent past, seem better suited to the work of Warner as I have described it in its relation to the actor, to writing and to contemporary society. What Dort finally observes, here, seems to provide a fitting place for us to leave the scene:

> Perhaps it is time to return [to the historical nature of the goal of unification in staging], not to deny the importance of the metteur en scène and the latter's role in the show, but to signal the place of other components in it. . . . [T]he actor appears as much to destroy as to construct signs. On stage we certainly have a character or a rhetorical figure, but this incarnation or fabrication is never total. Behind the character the actor remains . . . At the very moment of dissolving into the stage fiction, the actor's body and voice remain to remind us that he or she is irreducible to whatever metamophosis is achieved. [. . . T]he metteur en scène loses sovereign power but this doesn't mean a return to a theatre of actors or a theatre of the text . . . Today through the progressive freeing of the different components of performance, it is opened onto an activation of the spectator. In this way it renews its links with what is possibly theatre's vocation: not to present a text or to organise a performance but to be a critique in action of signification itself. In this, acting comes back into its own. (pp. 173–84: my translation)

To be a critique in action of signification itself: theatre as theorter, in Ulmer's terms. Is this metasemiotic practice, as we conceive of it in the 1990s, very far from what Shakespeare played with in *Hamlet*?

Bibliography

Adorno, T., *Aesthetic Theory*, trans. C. Lenhardt (Routledge Kegan Paul, London, 1984).

Allen, R. (ed.), *Channels of Discourse* (Routledge, London, 1987).

Arac, J. (ed.), *Postmodernism and Politics, Theory and History of Literature*, vol. 28 (University of Minnesota Press, 1986).

Arens, K., 'Robert Wilson: Is Postmodern Performance Possible?', *Theatre Journal*, vol. 43 (1991).

Aston, E. and Savona, N., *Theatre as Sign System* (Routledge, London, 1991).

Austin, J. L., *How to Do Things with Words* (Penguin, Oxford, 1962).

Austin-Broos, D. (ed.), *Creating Culture* (Allen and Unwin, Sydney, 1987).

Bablet, D. (ed.), *Les Voies de la création théâtrale* (CNRS, Paris, 1970–92).

Banu, G., *L'Acteur qui ne revient pas* (Aubier, Paris, 1986).

——, *Mémoires du théâtre* (Actes Sud, Paris, 1987).

——, (ed.), *Kantor, l'artiste a la fin du XXe siècle* (Actes Sud, Paris, 1990).

Barba, E., 'Le Théâtre Kathakali', *Théâtres d'Orient: le Kathakali; l'Odissi* (Bouffonneries contrastes, no. 9, 1983).

——, 'Four Spectators', *The Drama Review*, no. 1 (1990).

Barba, E. and Savarese, N., *L'Anatomie de l'Acteur: Dictionnaire d'anthropologie théâtrale*, trans. P. Deschamps (Bouffoneries Contrastes, 1985).

——, trans. R. Fowler, *A Dictionary of Theatre Anthropology: The Secret Art of the Performer* (Routledge, London, 1991).

Barthes, R., *Image–Music–Text*, trans. S. Heath (Fontana, London, 1977).

——, *Camera Lucida*, trans. R. Howard, (Hill and Wang, New York, 1981).

——, *Selected Writings*, intro. S. Sontag (Fontana, London, 1982a).

——, *L'Obvie et L'Obtus* (Senil, Paris, 1982b).

——, *On Racine*, trans. R. Howard (Performing Arts Journal Publications, New York, 1983).

——, *The Responsibility of Forms*, trans. R. Howard (Blackwell, London, 1986).

Bateson, G., *Steps to an Ecology of Mind* (Penguin, London, 1978).

Baudrillard, J., *Simulations*, trans. P. Foss, P. Patton and P. Benchman (Semiotext(e), New York, 1983).

——, *The Ecstacy of Communication*, trans. B. Schutze and C. Schutze (Semiotext(e), New York, 1987).

——, *Revenge of the Crystal*, trans. P. Foss and J. Pefanis (Pluto Press, London, 1990).

Benamou, M. and Caramello, C. (eds), *Performance in Postmodern Culture* (Center for Twentieth Century Studies, University of Wisconsin-Milwaukee, Milwaukee, 1977).

Bennett, S., *Theatre Audiences* (Routledge, London, 1990).

Berriedale, K., *The Sanskrit Drama* (Oxford University Press, London, 1970).

Berger, J., *Ways of Seeing* (Penguin, London, 1972).

Billington, M., 'Writing for the Resistance', *Guardian* , 16 August 1990.

Birringer, J., *Theatre, Theory, Postmodernism* (Indiana University Press, Bloomington, 1991).

Blau, H., *The Audience* (Johns Hopkins University Press, London, 1990).

Blonsky, M. (ed.), *On Signs: A Semiotic Reader* (Blackwell, Oxford, 1985).

Bourdieu, P., *Outline of a Theory of Practice*, trans. R. Nice (Cambridge University Press, Cambridge, 1977).

——, *Distinction: A Social Critique of the Judgement of Taste*, trans. R. Nice (Routledge Kegan Paul, London, 1984).

Bradby, D., *Modern French Drama* (Cambridge University Press, Cambridge, 1991).

Bradby, D. and Schumacher C. (eds), *New French Plays* (Methuen, London, 1989).

Carroll, D., *Paraesthetics: Foucault, Lyotard, Derrida* (Methuen, London, 1987).

Champagne, L. (ed.), *Out From Under: Texts from Women Performance Artists* (Theatre Communications Group, New York, 1990).

Chtiguel, O., 'Without Theatre, the Czechoslovak Revolution Could Not Have Been Won', *The Drama Review*, no. 127, Fall (1990).

Clancy, P. , 'Artaud and the Balinese Theatre', *Modern Drama*, vol. XXVIII, no. 3 (1985).

Clifford, J. and Marcus, G., *Writing Culture* (University of California Press, Berkeley, 1986).

de Certeau, M., *Arts de faire* (Union Générale d'Editions, Paris, 1980a).

——, *La Culture au pluriel* (Christian Bourgeois, Paris, 1980b).

——, trans. S. Rendall, *The Practice of Everyday Life* (University of California Press, London, 1984).

——, trans. Brian Massumi, *Heterologies: The Discourse of the Other* (Manchester University Press, Manchester, 1986).

de Lauretis, T., *Alice Doesn't* (Macmillan, London, 1984).

——, *Technologies of Gender* (Macmillan, London, 1987).

Deleuze, G., *Nietzsche and Philosophy*, trans. H. Tomlinson (The Athlone Press, London, 1983).

Deleuze, G. and Guattari F., *A Thousand Plateaus*, trans. B. Massumi (University of Minnesota Press, Minneapolis, 1987).

Derrida, J., 'Limited inc, a b c . . .', trans. S. Weber S., *Glyph*, no. 2 (Johns Hopkins University Press, Baltimore, 1977).

——, *Writing and Difference*, trans. A. Bass (University of Chicago Press, Chicago, 1978).

——, *Positions*, trans. A. Bass (University of Chicago Press, Chicago, 1981).

——, 'To Speculate – On "Freud"', in M. Blonsky (ed.), *On Signs* (Blackwell, Oxford, 1985).

Dews, P., *Logics of Disintegration* (Verso, London, 1987).

Dolan, J., *The Feminist Spectator as Critic* (University of Michigan Press, Ann Arbor, 1988).

——, 'In Defense of the Discourse', *The Drama Review*, no. 123, Fall (1989).

Dollimore, J., *Radical Tragedy* (The Harvester Press, London, 1984).

Dollimore, J. and Sinfield A. (eds), *Political Shakespeare* (Manchester University Press, Manchester, 1985).

Dort, B., *La Représentation émancipée* (Actes Sud, Paris, 1988).

Durand, R., 'The Disposition of the Voice', in M. Benamou and C. Caramello (eds), *Performance in Postmodern Culture* (Coda Press, Center for Twentieth Century Studies, University of Wisconsin–Milwaukee, Milwaukee, 1977).

Eco, U., *A Theory of Semiotics* (Indiana University Press, Bloomington, 1976).

——, *The Role of the Reader: Explorations in the Semiotics of Texts* (Hutchinson, London, 1979).

——, *La Guerre du faux*, trans. Myriam Tenant (B. Grasset, Paris, 1985).

——, *Travels in Hyperreality* (Picador, London, 1986).

Elam, K., *The Semiotics of Theatre and Drama* (Methuen, London, 1980).

——, *Shakespeare's Universe of Discourse* (Cambridge University Press, 1984).

——, 'Text Appeal and the Analysis Paralysis', in T. Fitzpatrick (ed.), *Altro Polo – Performance: From Product to Process* (Theatre Studies Unit, University of Sydney, 1989).

Esslin, M., 'The Stage: Reality, Symbol, Metaphor', in J. Redmond (ed.), *The Theatrical Space* (Themes in Drama, Cambridge University Press, 1987).

Fawcett, R., Halliday, M., Lamb, S. and Makkai, A. (eds) *The Semiotics of Culture and Language, Language and Other Semiotic Systems of Culture* (2 vols, Frances Pinter, London, 1984).

Feral, J., 'Building up the Muscle: Interview with Ariane Mnouchkine', *The Drama Review*, no. 124, Winter (1989).

Feyerabend, P., *Against Method* (New Left Books, London, 1975).

Filipowicz, H., 'Expeditions into Culture: The Gardzienice (Poland)', *The Drama Review*, vol. 27, no. 1 (1983).

——, 'Gardzienice – A Polish Expedition to Baltimore', *The Drama Review*, no. 1, Spring (1987).

Foucault, M., *Les Mots et les choses* (Gallimard, Paris, 1966).

——, *The Order of Things* (Random House, New York, 1973).

Frow, J., 'Spectacle Binding – On Character', *Poetics Today*, vol. 7: 2 (1986).

Garnham, N. and Williams, R., *Media, Culture & Society: A Critical Reader* (Sage Publications, London, 1986).

George, D., *India: Three Ritual Dance-Dramas (Raslila, Kathakali, Nagamandala)* (Theatre in Focus, Chadwick-Healey, Cambridge, 1986).

——, 'Quantum Theatre – Potential Theatre: A New Paradigm?, *New Theatre Quarterly*, no. 181, (May 1989).

Goffman, E., *Presentation of Self in Everyday Life* (Penguin, London, 1956).

——, *Strategic Interaction* (Pelican, London, 1970).

——, *Frame Analysis* (Penguin, London, 1974).

Gregory, R., *The Oxford Companion to the Mind* (Oxford University Press, London, 1987).

Greimas, A., *Sémantique structurale* (Larousse, Paris, 1966).

——, 'The Love-Life of the Hippopotamus', ed. M. Blonsky, *On Signs* (Blackwell, Oxford, 1985).

——, *On Meaning: Selected Writings in Semiotic Theory*, trans. Paul J. Perron and Frank H. Collins (Frances Pinter, London, 1987).

Greimas, A. and Courtes, J., *Semiotique. Dictionnaire raisonne de la theorie du langage* (Hachette, Paris, 1979).

Habermas, J., 'Modernity – An Incomplete Project', trans. S. Ben-Habib, ed. H. Foster, *The Anti-Aesthetic* (Bay Press, Port Townsend, 1983).

Halliday, M., *Language as Social Semiotic* (Routledge Kegan Paul, London, 1978).

——, *An Introduction to Functional Grammar* (Arnold, London, 1985).

——,'Language and the Order of Nature', in N. Fabb, D. Attridge, A. Durant, C. MacCabe (eds), *The Linguistics of Writing: Arguments Between Language and Literature* (Manchester University Press, Manchester, 1987).

Hasan, R., 'Directions from Structuralism' in Fabb *et al.* (eds), *The Linguistics of Writing: Arguments Between Language and Literature* (Manchester University Press, Manchester, 1987).

Hjelmslev, L., *Prolegomena to a Theory of Language* (University of Wisconsin, Madison, 1961).

Hunter, I., 'Reading Character', *Southern Review*, vol. 16, no. 2 (1983).

Innes, C., *Holy Theatre* (Cambridge University Press, Cambridge, 1981).

Jakobson, R., *Questions de poétique* (Seuil, Paris, 1973).

Jameson, F., *Marxism and Form* (Princeton University Press, Princeton, 1971).

——, *The Political Unconscious – Narrative as a Socially Symbolic Act* (Methuen, London, 1981)

——, 'Pleasure: A Political Issue', *Formations of Pleasure* (Routledge Kegan Paul, London, 1983).

Kiernander, A., 'The Role of Ariane Mnouchkine at the *Théâtre du Soleil'*, *Modern Drama*, vol. XXXIII, no. 3 (1990).

Klossowicz, J., 'Tadeusz Kantor's Journey', *The Drama Review*, vol. 30, Fall (1986).

Kristeva, J., *Desire in Language: A Semiotic Approach to Literature and Art* (Blackwell, Oxford, 1980).

Kroker, A. and Cook, D., *The Postmodern Scene* (St Martin's Press, New York, 1986).

Kruger, L., 'The Dis-play's the Thing', *Theatre Journal*, October (1990).

Krysinski, W., 'Semiotic Modalities of the Body in Modern Theater', *Poetics Today*, vol. 2, no. 3 (1981).

Lacan, J., *The Function of Speech and Language in Psychoanalysis*, trans. and ed. A. Wilden (Johns Hopkins University Press, Baltimore, 1968).

——, *Ecrits: A Selection*, trans. A. Sheridan (Tavistock Publications, London, 1977).

——, 'Sign, Symbol, Imaginary', in M. Blonsky (ed.), *On Signs* (Blackwell, Oxford, 1985).

Lacoue-Labarthe, P. , 'Theatrum Analyticum', *Glyph* 2 (Johns Hopkins University Press, Baltimore, 1977).

Langer, S., *Philosophy in a New Key* (Harvard University Press, 1942).

Lemke, J., *Semiotics and Education* (Toronto Semiotic Circle: Monographs, Working Papers and Prepublications, 1984).

Levi-Strauss, C., *Structural Anthropology* (Basic Books, New York, 1963).

Lyotard, J.-F., 'The Unconscious as Mise en Scène', in M. Benamou and C. Caramello (eds), *Performance in Postmodern Culture* (Coda Press Inc., Center for Twentieth Century Studies, University of Wisconsin–Milwaukee, Milwaukee, 1977).

——, 'La Dent, la paume', *Des Dispositifs pulsionnels* (Christian Bourgeois, Paris, 1980).

——, 'The Tooth, The Palm', *Sub-Stance* 15 (1976).

——, *The Postmodern Condition: A Report on Knowledge*, trans. G. Bennington and B. Massumi (University of Minnesota Press, Minneapolis, 1984).

Macdonell, D., *Theories of Discourse*, Blackwell, Oxford, 1986).

Matejka, L. and Titunik, I. (eds), *Semiotics of Art: Prague School Contributions* (MIT Press, Cambridge, 1976).

McDougall, J., *Theatres of the Mind* (Free Association Books, London, 1986).

McLeish, K. (trans.), *Electra* (Cambridge University Press, Cambridge, 1979).

Melrose, R. and Melrose, S., 'Drama, "Style", Stage', in D. Birch and M. O'Toole (eds), *The Functions of Style* (Frances Pinter, London, 1988).

Melrose, S., 'Prospects for the Analysis of Performance', in G. McAuley (ed.), *From Page to Stage* (Theatre Studies Service Unit, University of Sydney, 1987).

——, 'Making Do: Strategies and Tactics in "New Performance" Pedagogy', *Contemporary Theatre Review* (1993).

——, '"Please please me": Sympathy and Empathy in Critical Metapraxis', *Contemporary Theatre Review* (1993).

——, 'The Kitchen as Eggshell: Documenting Bobby Baker's Live Art', *Hybrid*, June–July (1993).

Metz, C., trans. C. Britton, A. Williams, B. Brewster and A. Guzzetti, *Psychoanalysis and Cinema* (Macmillan, London, 1982).

Miller, B.S. (ed.), *Theater of Memory*, trans. Edwin Gerow, David Gitomer, Barbara Stoler Miller (Columbia University Press, New York, Guildford, 1984).

Miller, D. and Branson, J., 'Pierre Bourdieu: Culture and Praxis', in D. Austin-Broos (ed.), *Creating Culture* (Allen and Unwin, Sydney, 1987).

Mishima, Y., *Five Modern Noh Plays* (Vintage Books, New York, 1973).

Mnouchkine, A., *Théâtre du Soleil – Les Shakespeare – Richard II* (*Théâtre du Soleil et les Éditions Solin*, Paris, 1982).

——, 'en plein soleil', *Fruits*, no. 2/3 (1984).

Mulvey, L., 'Visual Pleasure and Narrative Cinema', in K. Kay and C. Peary (eds), *Women and the Cinema* (Dutton, New York, 1977).

Ohnuki-Tierney, E., *Illness and Culture in Contemporary Japan* (Cambridge University Press, Cambridge, 1984).

Oslzly, P., 'On Stage with the Velvet Revolution', *The Drama Review*, no. 127, Fall (1990).

Palmer, R., 'Toward a Postmodern Hermeneutics of Performance', in M. Benamou and C. Caramello (eds), *Performance in Postmodern Culture* (Coda Press Inc., Center for Twentieth Century Studies, University of Wisconsin-Milwaukee, Milwaukee, 1977).

Pavis, P., *Languages of the Stage* (Performing Arts Journal Publications, New York, 1982).
——, 'The Classical Heritage of Modern Drama', *Modern Drama*, vol. XXIX, no. 1 (1985).
——, *Dictionnaire du théâtre* (Editions Sociales, 1987).
——, *Theatre at the Crossroads of Culture* (Routledge, London, 1992).
Pêcheux, M., *Language, Semantics and Ideology*, trans. H. Nagpal (Macmillan, London, 1982).
——, Sur les Contexts épistémologiques de l'analyse de discours', *Mots*, no. 9, octobre (1984).
Peirce, C., in C. Hartshorne and P. Weiss (eds), *Collected Papers* (Harvard University Press, Harvard, 1931–58).
Pontbriand, C., '"The Eye Finds No Fixed Point . . ."', *Modern Drama*, vol. XXV, no.1 (1982).
Pradier, J.-M., 'Towards a Biological Theory of Performance', *New Theatre Quarterly*, vol. VI, no. 21, February (1990).
Pratt, M.-L., 'Ideology and Speech-Act Theory', *Poetics Today*, vol. 7, no. 1 (1986).
Propp, V., 'Fairy Tale Transformations', in L. Matejka and K. Pomorska (eds), ... (MIT Press, Cambridge, Mass., 1971).
Rose, J., *Sexuality in the Field of Vision* (Verso, London, 1986).
Ruby, C., *Les Archipels de la Différence* (Editions du Félin, Paris, 1989).
Said, E., *Orientalism* (Pantheon, New York, 1978).
de Saussure, F., *Course in General Linguistics*, trans. W. Baskin (McGraw-Hill, London, 1959).
Schechner, R., *Performance Theory* (Routledge, London, 1988).
——, *Between Theater and Anthropology* (University of Pennsylvania Press, 1985).
Schlocker, G., 'The Myth Dances', *Euromaske*, no. 3 (1991).
Schmitt, N., 'Theorising About Performance: Why Now?, *New Theatre Quarterly*, no. 23, August (1990).
Schumacher, C., *Artaud on Theatre* (Methuen, London, 1989).
Serpieri, A., Elam, K., Publiatti, P., Kemeny, T. and Rutelli, R., 'Toward a Segmentation of the Dramatic Text', *Poetics Today*, vol. 2, no. 3 (1981).
Silverman, K., *The Subject of Semiotics* (Oxford University Press, New York, 1984).
Stallybrass, P. and White, A., *The Politics and Poetics of Transgression* (Methuen, London, 1984).
Threadgold, T., Grosz, E., Kress, G. and Halliday, M. (eds), *Semiotics – Ideology – Language*, Sydney Studies in Society and Culture, no. 3. (1986).
Touraine, M. '*l'Individualisme: Le Grand retour*', *Magazine littéraire*, April/May (1989).
Ubersfeld, A., *Lire le théâtre* (Editions Sociales, Paris, 1978).
——, 'The Pleasure of the Spectator', *Modern Drama*, vol. XXV, no. 1 (1982a).
——, *L'Ecole du Spectateur* (Editions Sociales, Paris, 1982b).
Ulmer, G., *Applied Grammatology* (Johns Hopkins University Press, Baltimore, 1985).

——, *Teletheory: Grammatology in the Age of Video* (Routledge, London, 1989).

van Erven, E., *Radical People's Theatre* (Indiana University Press, Bloomington, 1988).

Weber, C. 'Brecht in Eclipse?', *The Drama Review*, vol. 24, no. 1 (1980).

Williams, R. and Garnham (eds), *Media, Culture and Society: A Critical Reader* (Sage, 1986).

Wilden, A., *System and Structure: Essays in Communication and Exchange*, 2nd edn (Tavistock, 1980).

Wright, E., *Postmodern Brecht* (Routledge, London, 1989).

Young, R. (ed.), *Untying the Text* (Routledge Kegan Paul, London, 1981).

Zarrilli, P., 'For Whom Is the "Invisible" Not Visible?', *The Drama Review*, T. 117 (1988).

Zeami, *La Tradition secrète du no*, trans. R. Sieffert (Gallimard, Paris, 1960).

——, *20 Plays of The Noh Theatre* (Columbia University Press, New York, Guildford, 1970).

Index

absences 9, 314
abstraction 246
accidental 21–2, 85–8, 201–2
actantial, actants 17ff
action
  actional frame 84, 130, 277,
    284, 307, 308
  actor as active agent 59, 133,
    147, 218, 227
  actor–character complex 155,
    229, 271, 295, 298
  and language 169
  dramatic, actorly 25, 214
  everyday, extra-daily 152, 213,
    240, 241, 242
  human 76
  in-the-world, on-the-world
    236, 289
  knowledge as 76, 225
  skills, work, of actor(s) 27, 90,
    104, 106, 111, 117ff, 126, 137,
    151, 160, 164, 205ff, 211,
    215, 221ff, 232ff, 237, 240ff,
    260–1, 267, 272, 295, 301
  somatic action 81, 89, 91, 141,
    227, 232, 235, 275, 285
  spontaneous and schooled 276
adequacy 24, 39, 45, 48, 49, 109,
  123
aesthetic, aesthetic pleasure,
  aesthetics 59
agency, of action 69, 80, 86–7, 99,
  129
alchemy 32, 145
analog, analogue 9, 38, 105,
  146–7, 169, 183, 191, 193
analysis
  actantial 17, 18, 21
  analogical 38
  discourse 45, 97, 125, 131, 209,
    243, 275, 299
  feminist 162
  Greimasian 18

models for, modes of 15
mood 294
of theatre, dramaturgical 6, 12,
  15, 20, 24, 57, 59, 63, 71, 154
of writing, text, narratological
  38, 57, 82, 169, 192, 204, 305
psychoanalysis, Freudian 14,
  120, 123, 128, 136, 151, 162,
  187, 209
psychoanalysis, Jungian 247
semiotic 3, 23, 61, 64, 248
social, cultural 8, 41, 45–6, 100,
  219, 256
systems 21
traditions of 37
transactional 109
analyst
  implicated in observation 33
  of performance, theatre 47, 57,
    214
  specificity of 195
anecdote 43, 51, 83, 84, 126
anthropology, anthropological 46,
  80, 126, 128, 180
appreciation 6, 60, 169–70, 188,
  229, 257
Aristotle 20, 188, 197
artefact 38
articulation 16, 37, 60, 134, 153,
  216, 232, 248
artifice 75
Asian theatre 150
assemblage 22, 73
association 15, 155, 226, 230
attic 264, 273ff
  see also doric
attitude, attitudes, attitudinal 26,
  30, 33–4, 37, 56, 72, 83, 86,
  88ff, 106, 116, 140, 179ff, 206,
  208, 228, 242, 249, 259, 290,
  297, 305, 308
audience 40, 41, 58, 69, 84, 124,

141, 152, 157, 170, 173, 203–4,
  209, 246, 280, 300, 311
aura 61, 246
auteur, auteurs 23, 24, 198, 308,
  313
  see author, authorial
authenticity 103, 174
author, authorial, authority,
  authorship 4–5, 14, 18, 20,
  23ff, 29, 40, 49, 56, 63–4, 73,
  77, 93, 97–8, 112–13, 128,
  142–3, 155, 169, 182, 186, 197,
  202, 208, 246, 284
avant-garde 38, 78
axis 6, 19, 20, 73, 105, 187, 189,
  191

Barthes, R. 7, 44, 59ff, 100, 117ff,
  140, 150, 151, 161, 163ff,
  176–7, 194, 196, 209, 215, 218,
  221, 225, 230, 261
Baudrillard, J. 42, 173
behaviour 18, 78, 80, 138, 179, 203
belief 3, 7, 34, 40, 42, 59, 63, 75,
  191
Benveniste 29, 47, 49, 157
binding-in, bound-in 36, 54, 100,
  103, 166, 205, 252, 253, 281,
  284, 313
biological determinism 180, 210
bipolar 57, 58
bite
  or nip (cf. Bateson) 213ff, 221,
    225, 230, 232, 234, 238, 270
  or nip, of words in the mouth,
    (cf. Bateson) 212, 218, 232,
    272, 304
Blau, H. 20, 214
blur 16, 27–8, 70, 98, 105, 137,
  145, 147, 179, 183, 292
'body language' 82–5, 106, 110,
  193
body-reasoning 104
bodywork 104–5, 118, 127, 159,
  204, 211, 215, 278, 305, 311
borrowings 17, 137
boundary 9, 36, 45, 85, 145, 239
Bourdieu, P. 6, 33, 37, 44, 60, 65,
  69–70, 73, 74, 85ff, 110, 122–3,

129, 132, 134, 139, 159, 161,
  169, 187, 196, 201, 208, 209,
  212, 225, 249, 256, 259
bricolage 17, 21, 22, 23, 166, 176
bunraku 116ff, 151, 177, 203, 205,
  247

castration 138, 180, 182, 186
catachresis 202, 209
catalysis 3, 7, 278, 292
categorisation 11, 27, 30, 210
catharsis, cathartic 67, 197, 233
causality 18, 84
centre, centring, decentring 4, 17,
  19, 25, 39, 61, 164, 194, 221,
  285, 293, 302, 306, 312, 313
character, characterisation
  actor–character(–spectator)
    complex 14, 37, 46, 62, 68,
      130, 165, 229, 253, 260, 271,
      283, 284, 295, 298
  binding-in of spectator 217
  character-types 264
  dramatic, constitution of 16,
      90, 93, 117–18, 156, 170, 187,
      220, 236, 258, 276, 285, 307
  enunciation of, by actor(s) 186,
      208, 220, 250, 290, 296
  epistemology of 18, 143, 153,
      164, 236, 245, 254, 264, 266,
      268, 274, 281, 284, 285
  examples of 184
  fictional, in fiction 229, 235, 267
  rel. to naturalism,
      'in-the-world' 122, 147, 271
  rel. to writing, author 5, 49,
      169, 267
  somatic, character-trait 262, 304
Chomsky, N. 17, 62
choreography, choreographic 274,
  275
cityscape 35, 75
clarity 16, 36, 42, 67, 104, 131,
  148, 180, 228
closure 30, 74, 152, 155, 195, 253,
  261
cobbling together
  see bricolage
codification 59, 61, 244, 257

codify, codified 40, 41, 53, 55, 79, 88, 106, 130, 243, 258, 264, 272, 284
collective, collective practice 20, 24–5, 29, 33, 39, 51, 52, 63, 64, 67, 70, 78, 123ff, 151, 164, 203, 214, 221, 224, 247, 248, 311
combination, combinatory 5, 7, 11, 19ff, 24, 49, 75, 80, 83, 92, 132, 144, 148, 151, 154, 170, 172, 190, 205, 215, 228, 260, 267, 275, 308
combinatory, combinatoire see Ubersfeld, A.
commonsense, commonsensical 7, 31, 42, 56, 77, 81, 98, 173, 181, 232, 237, 248, 269, 271, 274–5, 299, 309, 310
community theatre 70
competence 17, 55, 243
complementary, complementarity, complementarities 9, 10, 14, 28–9, 38, 55, 68, 71, 76, 80, 85, 98, 105–6, 146ff, 160, 162, 175, 183, 188–9, 245, 248, 259–60, 264, 270, 274, 282, 284–6, 291, 292–3, 298, 310
complex 14, 18, 20, 30, 42, 76, 81, 90, 100, 104, 127, 130, 138, 143, 145, 156, 159, 160, 176, 181, 188–9, 208, 211, 224–5, 229, 239–40, 253, 260, 271, 276, 283, 285, 295ff, 301–2
composition 21, 67, 207
condensation 18, 176, 183, 186, 194
conflict, conflicts, conflictual 18, 36, 86–7, 99, 102, 115, 117, 129, 140, 151, 179, 297, 301, 312, 313
confrontation 115, 137, 151
conjuring 92, 159, 281
connotation 49ff, 56
consciousness-raising 72
contestation 3, 9, 115, 127
context
    definition of 208
    discursive 112, 128
    of 'theatre analysis' 20

of theatre 11
    relativity of 299
    social, of theatre 42
    socio-historical 269
    specification of 250
    specificity of 50, 58, 129, 213, 236
contingencies 208, 236–7, 262, 266
continuum 9, 191, 193–4
contradiction 19, 44, 117, 169, 187, 224, 303
control
    authorial 197
    categorisation and 3
    globalising 42
    lucidity and 130, 249
    masterly 22
    muscular, somatic 100, 119, 151, 155, 159, 172, 233, 277
    passionate, effective 186
    representation and 115
    social 271
    theory of 22
    writerly 260
core 23, 97, 164, 165, 194
creativity 22, 33, 97
critic, critical 3–5, 30, 45–7, 59–60, 71, 73–4, 81, 92, 113, 117, 124–5, 142, 214, 222, 245, 267, 302, 305
cryptogrammar 259, 261
cunning 17, 22, 30, 79, 82, 85, 91–2, 104, 152, 162, 184, 195, 249, 277, 281
cybernetics 216
cynicism 40, 67, 233

de Certeau, M. 30, 33, 63, 71, 77, 90, 101, 115, 122, 141, 147, 185, 194, 209, 246, 255, 271
decision 3, 4, 68–9, 74, 81, 89, 91, 105, 136, 140, 152, 158, 160–1, 164, 204, 217, 222, 230, 248, 294
deep 18, 21, 22, 89
déhiscence 57, 58, 157, 278
deixis, deictics 43, 59, 147, 171, 260, 284–5, 298, 300
depoliticisation 44

Derrida, J., Derridean 5, 21, 24, 30, 45, 46, 57–8, 62, 97, 108, 114–16, 120, 150, 152, 155ff, 177, 202, 209, 211, 218–19
description 12, 48, 49, 59
desire, desire-trap, desires 12–13, 18ff, 27, 30–2, 34, 36, 39, 42, 73, 84, 91, 100, 102, 111, 117, 122, 128, 135, 141, 150–2, 155, 157–8, 163, 165, 168, 170, 172–3, 175, 182–3, 187, 188, 191, 195, 197, 208, 220, 226, 233, 251–2, 281, 298, 308
destinataire, destinator 18, 29
determinism 139, 140, 180, 210
didascalies 25, 130, 249
différance, deferral 24, 30, 57
difference
  as basis of articulation 16
  as basis of indentification 16
  as complementarity 38
  as distinction 62
  as otherness, in Derrida, in Artaud 116
  as principle of organisation 34
  between agendas (and perspectives) 5, 11, 49
  between semiotics and semiology 15
  binary 34
  biological, material 98
  class and socio-economic 86
  continuum of 191
  cultural 151
  difference-in-sameness 116, 153, 160
  difference-within-oneness 222
  exclusive 188
  gender 136, 139, 179, 182
  gender as cultural 102, 123, 178
  in material and mental process(es) 266
  in understanding 30
  mythologised 150
  observation of 179, 300
  observed by child 138
  of spectators 235
  radical 134, 145, 151
  rel. to character 264
  rel. to writerly practice 169
sight of 99
signs of 99
small-scale 222
digital, digitalisation 9, 16, 27, 38, 45, 60, 82–4, 101, 104–5, 119, 145ff, 159, 167, 183, 191, 193, 251
discours, discourse, discourse analysis
  "everyday commonsense discourse" 274
  analytical discourse 17
  critical discourse 4–5, 47, 73, 124
  discourse analysis 45, 97, 125, 209, 243, 275, 299
  discourse as site of meaning 247
  discourse of staging, *mise en scène* 22
  discourse of the Other 126, 131
  discourse of theatre semiotics 62
  external discourse 11
  fields of discourse, discursive systems, units 53, 65, 170, 236, 255
  fragmented, single-source 84
  master or "expert" discourse 24, 30–2, 42, 81, 84, 126, 141, 143, 152, 155, 248
  production of discourse 58, 110
  psychoanalytic discourse 188, 195
  rel. of discourse to esthetic phenomena 60
  rel. of discourse to experience 252
  scientific discourse 103
  semiological discourse 31, 43
  theatre discourse 45
  theoretical discourse 123, 211, 214
discrete 16, 37, 46, 68, 80, 92, 105–6, 133, 147–8, 156, 168, 183, 232
disenchantment 40, 59, 220, 233
disjunction 37, 44, 310, 311

disorder 77, 165, 224, 257
displacement 18, 105, 176, 183, 186, 194, 197, 203, 306, 309
dispositifs 91, 157, 197, 247, 283, 308
dissemination 30, 31, 45, 58, 90, 113, 126, 139, 142, 308
distinction 36, 62, 75, 167, 190–1, 273, 276, 289
diversity 17, 68, 89
doric 264, 273, 275–6
  see also attic
dramatisation 144, 165, 247
drives 17–18, 81, 122, 161, 167, 171, 218
dualism 104, 168
dynamic 61, 77, 106, 119, 194, 224, 233, 236, 256ff, 279–80, 283, 297, 301

ecosystem 257
effects, affects, affective 4, 27, 41, 83, 100, 114, 116–18, 120, 129, 133, 161, 202–3, 205–6, 224, 226, 231, 233, 245, 291, 302, 304, 313
Elam, K. 3, 7, 13, 14ff, 21, 24, 169, 191
Electra
  the character 138, 144, 155–6, 158–9, 163–5, 186–7, 198, 219, 232, 234, 237–9, 245, 253, 257, 262, 268, 286–7, 292ff, 301ff
  the play 59, 124, 151–2, 157–9, 163, 165, 184, 186–7, 195–6, 206, 235, 253, 263, 268, 284, 287, 300–1
enabling structure 86, 242, 275, 283
enchantment 40
energy, energetic
  energetic action-in-the-world 289
  energetic build-up 216
  energetic enthusiasm, belief 34, 222
  energy of audience,

energy-relations 63, 157, 160, 173, 197, 203, 207, 231, 233
energy-field, energy-focus 22, 148, 163, 186, 192, 213, 286, 295
energy-potential 184
energy-production, in performance, of actor(s) 42, 123, 140, 148, 155, 159, 173–4, 206, 223, 227, 231–3, 239–1, 277, 311
injection, input, of energy 80, 82, 147, 311
theories of energy, energy-use, energy-production 120, 216, 232, 240
theory of 'maximum wastage' of energy 82, 85, 151, 266, 290
use of, investment of, energy 4, 14, 63, 67, 93, 146, 176, 185–6, 189, 219–21, 232, 235, 238, 266, 271, 276–8, 305
Enlightenment 36, 37
entre les deux 23
enunciation, enunciator 30, 56, 138, 140, 150–1, 153, 156–7, 163, 164, 194, 207–8, 222, 229, 235, 247, 253, 260, 267, 270, 276, 278, 280–1, 289–90, 299, 301
episteme, epistemes, epistemological, epistemology 5, 8, 9, 13–14, 16–17, 30, 36, 45, 49, 56–7, 60, 74, 85, 90, 102ff, 115, 125, 136, 139, 141, 161, 165, 183, 209, 215, 218, 232, 248
ethnicity, ethnography, ethnological 45–6, 106, 128
event 4, 6, 8, 20–2, 27, 29, 30, 41ff, 52–3, 57, 62–3, 71, 75, 81, 83, 92, 97, 100, 109, 112, 120, 125–6, 154, 158, 164, 197–8, 219, 221, 225, 235, 242, 265, 283–4, 293–4, 299, 312
everyday life 33, 72, 86, 106, 122, 180, 212, 227, 229, 259–60, 308

evocation 132, 155, 157–8, 160, 202
exclusion 3, 49, 135, 136, 152
experience
  and feeling, emotion 27
  critical 60
  emotional 119
  esthetic 59, 60, 255
  human, everyday-lived 9, 13,
    16, 37, 40, 106, 110, 127, 249
  modes of 28
  of group work 23, 216
  of subject, spectator(s),
    audience 88, 123, 127, 145,
    152, 156–7, 160, 166, 173,
    176, 195, 197, 202, 220, 233,
    235, 255, 281
  re-experienced 280
  rel. to 'truth' 59
  rel. to discourse 44, 155, 252,
    263, 299
  rel. to dramatic text 125, 143
  rel. to language 45, 49, 97, 130
  social, cultural, psychological
    5, 29, 246
  socially symbolic 69
  somatic, of actor(s) 155, 215, 282
expert 30–1, 83–4, 126, 129, 136,
  143–4, 152, 155, 248, 266, 308, 310
expression 12, 61, 89, 155, 156, 194
exteriority 48, 89, 110, 117, 212,
  225, 229, 234
eyework, facework 21, 54, 83,
  164, 204, 228, 232, 284, 295

faith 39
Father-function 20, 172, 175, 189
teel
  of words in the mouth 202,
    204–5, 211–12, 216, 218, 230,
    232, 238, 249–51, 262, 272,
    287, 304
felt-experience 7, 8, 28, 105, 113,
  153, 155, 245, 260, 263, 267
feminine
  see gender
feminism 126, 263, 284, 308
fiction, fictionalisation 50, 55, 59,
  75, 89, 111, 117, 126, 128, 133,
  144, 151–2, 160, 164, 170, 172,
  175, 182, 186, 195, 198, 203,
  205, 208, 219, 232, 235, 252,
  267, 277, 283, 287, 291–2, 298,
  308, 314
field
  discursive 7, 8, 15, 46, 53, 65,
    115, 170, 210, 255
  divided, gendered 136
  energetic 158
  logically-stabilised 31
  of associative values 183
  of critical epistemology 74
  of cultural practice 214
  of energy, force 19, 148, 163, 176,
    204, 214, 277, 286, 297, 301–2
  of experience 235
  of intensity, in performance 53
  of relationships and values 246
  of theatre criticism and
    analysis 59
  of vision 216
  theatrical 226
figure 13, 23, 36, 67
focus 3–5, 12–13, 15, 17ff, 22, 24,
  43, 80, 98, 108–10, 121–2, 124,
  149, 156, 160, 186–7, 197, 213,
  222, 261, 263, 266, 275–6,
  284–5, 291, 295, 297, 299, 300,
  302, 309, 312
force, force-field, forces 7, 17, 19,
  24, 53, 56, 62, 74, 85, 92, 105,
  112, 117, 122, 128, 131, 137,
  141, 148, 160, 163, 175, 187,
  196, 202, 204, 207, 211, 213,
  218, 222ff, 229, 232, 234, 239,
  250, 253, 262, 277, 290, 296,
  301, 303, 311
Foucault, M. 11, 112, 271
foundations 33
founding scene, originary 21, 52,
  129, 139, 141, 158
'French' 47, 62
Freud, S., Freudian, Freudianisms 14, 20, 31, 45, 56, 77, 88,
  98, 100, 120, 123, 127, 131,
  133, 136ff, 143–4, 155, 160,
  164, 176, 178, 185, 188, 195,
  202, 240, 247, 251, 263, 298,
  309

Frow, J. 54, 188
functions 17–18, 30, 50, 51, 61,
    67–8, 74, 100, 105, 151, 163,
    165, 170, 181, 184, 186, 188,
    203ff, 211, 213, 214, 224, 226,
    228–9, 230, 236, 242, 243, 247,
    256, 260–1, 264–5, 282, 289,
    293, 295, 297, 303
gaze 25–6, 36, 40, 42, 48, 82–3,
    159, 161ff, 172, 174–5, 178,
    184–5, 203, 207, 217, 226, 229,
    231–2, 237, 266, 269, 271, 277,
    286, 294–5, 299, 307, 312
gender, gendered 18, 33, 77, 82,
    86, 100ff, 106–7, 123, 134,
    136ff, 154, 168, 172ff, 178–9,
    181ff, 187, 189, 195–6, 210,
    229, 231, 253, 287, 298, 301–2,
    305, 310
generative, genetic 17–18, 21–2,
    24, 45, 58, 81, 86, 89, 111–12,
    176
genre 6, 15, 102, 236–7, 260, 284,
    289, 294
gerund 159
gesture, gestuality 21, 48, 54, 82,
    83, 88, 117, 146, 165, 232, 252,
    261, 284, 290, 294, 307
goals 9, 39, 56
grammatologist 120
Greimas, A. 11, 17, 24
grids 29, 56, 91, 105, 157, 175,
    197, 254, 261, 283, 308
grounds 8, 14, 48, 67

Habermas, J. 37, 38, 73, 124
habitus 60, 85ff, 91, 93, 122, 128,
    134, 139, 160, 167, 173, 181,
    206, 208, 212, 225, 236, 242,
    245, 249, 259, 267, 273, 280,
    286–7, 299, 307, 308
Halliday, M. A. K. 14, 45, 54, 59,
    61, 77, 127, 143, 153, 194, 204,
    224, 235–6, 238, 249, 255ff,
    263, 265, 267, 269, 272ff, 278ff,
    283, 291
hallucination 151, 166, 175
halo, halo effect 165

Haptic function
    see Barthes, R.
hegemony 70
helper
    see actant
hermeneutic, hermeneutics 19,
    29, 44, 142, 170, 195, 201, 205,
    222, 283
hero 18, 164, 312
hesitation 3, 307
heterogeneity, heteroglossia,
    heteropraxia 22, 47, 64, 222
heuristic tools 43
hierarchisations 17, 114
history 4, 9, 33, 36, 42, 45–6, 72,
    79, 86, 88–9, 99, 129, 132, 134,
    141, 160–1, 169, 187, 195, 204,
    211, 242, 246, 256–7, 293
humanism 5, 41, 220
Hunter, I. 40, 144, 266
hypostasis 9
hypothesis, hypothetical 6, 8, 15,
    18, 30, 38, 49, 50, 52, 65, 74,
    83, 129, 150, 169, 191, 229,
    235, 278
hysteria 123, 186, 309

iconicity, indice, index, indexical,
    indexicality, *see* Peirce, C.
idealisation 46, 54, 62, 97, 172
identity, identification 14, 20,
    33, 34, 53, 77–8, 88, 101,
    103, 106, 123, 139, 164,
    170–1, 174, 180, 183, 188,
    196, 264, 265, 309
ideology 20, 23, 88, 108, 113, 142,
    169
Imaginary 55–6, 57–8, 125, 136,
    147, 149–50, 154, 156, 158,
    166–7, 169–71, 174–5, 178,
    181–3, 185, 187, 190, 196,
    205–6, 208, 210, 213, 216, 224,
    234, 240
immanence 139, 189
impulses 17
incest 33, 168, 180, 186, 309
indeterminacy 45, 87, 114, 235
inferential 160, 164, 208

institutions, institutions of theory
4, 33, 49, 76–8, 83, 86, 92, 99,
101, 107, 114–15, 185, 187, 189,
190, 194, 254–5, 262, 276, 284
intensity, intensities 40, 51, 53, 61,
186, 196, 230, 243, 281, 297,
307
intent 6, 25, 112, 117–18, 132–3,
165, 267
interaction, interactive 6, 8, 19,
42, 61, 71, 76, 82–4, 88–9,
91–2, 100, 106, 109, 124, 145,
153, 155–7, 161–3, 170, 186,
195, 204, 206–7, 216, 223, 229,
236, 239, 248–9, 256–7, 277,
282, 299
interdiscursive, interdiscursivity
15, 47, 73, 126, 127–30, 152,
161, 254
interpraxia, interpraxis 47,
129–30, 152, 254, 294
INTERPRETANT
see Peirce, C.
interrelationality 285, 295, 300
intersubjective 131, 157, 162, 236,
249
intertextual, intertextuality 15,
33, 127
intervention 20, 22, 24–5, 29, 31,
36, 38, 41, 43, 48–9, 52, 64,
72–4, 78–9, 81, 86, 103, 126,
130, 138, 150, 153–4, 160,
180–1, 186–7, 194, 209, 213–14,
245, 250, 261, 270, 284, 286,
293–4, 304–6, 309, 313
intuition, intuitive 43, 82, 104,
110, 127–8, 258, 266–7, 310
isomorphicity, isomorphism 194

kabuki 138, 151, 153, 156–7, 204
kinetic, kinetics 234
kinship 33, 129, 140, 159, 170,
181, 187–8, 207, 286–7, 293–4,
297ff, 305–6, 308–9, 312–13

l'insaisissable, unseizable
see Ubersfeld, A.
Lacan, J., Lacanian 28, 45, 57, 98,
101, 106–7, 131ff, 141, 147,

157, 161, 165ff, 170ff, 178ff,
185–6, 188–9, 195, 214, 216,
277, 310
Lacoue-Labarthe, P. 20, 187
language, *langue* 6, 7, 17, 20, 26,
43, 45, 53, 55, 59, 70, 80, 92,
97, 100, 110, 125, 131, 167,
188, 196, 209, 231, 235, 251,
254–5, 258, 260, 273
see also Saussure, F. de
libido, libidinal 32
lie, truth, truth-regime 15, 34–5,
59, 90, 103, 111, 113, 141,
168–9, 174, 195, 203, 210, 254,
292, 294, 304, 306
linguistics 5–7, 15–17, 45–6,
61, 97, 105, 148, 209, 235,
238, 255
logic, logically-stabilised,
logically-unstabilised 7, 31,
34, 37, 45, 74, 81, 103, 105,
108, 136, 142, 180, 234, 257–8,
260, 279–80, 295, 305
logocentric, logocentricity,
logocentricist 11, 15, 103, 110,
131, 256, 260
ludicity 299

mainstream, marginalisation 27,
33, 52, 59, 68, 70, 83, 92, 99,
103, 131, 137, 182, 185, 190,
209, 243, 245, 273
masculine
see gender
master discourse 24, 31–2, 43, 141
Material Process
see Halliday, M. A. K.
materiality 21, 25, 54, 101, 143,
144, 162, 168–70, 174, 179,
198, 207, 226, 230, 247, 263,
296–7
meaning
'goal' of 28
deferred 58
felt-meaning 27
in systemic-functional
linguistics 258
location, site of 4, 239, 247
meaning-field 53

meaning – *continued*
  meaning-potential 148, 206,
    214, 224, 228, 236
  meaning-production 6, 24, 34,
    53, 57, 61–2, 161, 201, 203,
    225, 232
  minimally-coded 82
  rel. to feeling 61
Mental Process
  see Halliday, M. A. K.
metaphor, metaphors,
  metaphoric 8, 12–13, 18, 20,
    22, 29, 32, 58, 61–2, 76, 83, 91,
    97, 104–5, 109–10, 114, 115,
    127, 132, 142, 145, 157–8, 160,
    166–7, 186, 189, 194, 204, 210,
    216, 221, 223, 236, 239, 243,
    259, 277, 279, 280
metaphysics 174
metapraxis 75, 159, 267, 270, 272,
  276, 279, 280, 282, 297, 311
metasemiotics 258, 267
metatext 12, 140, 146, 222, 284,
  294, 295, 311
methodologies 3, 17, 31
metonymic 18, 20, 54
metteur en scène, mise en scène 11,
  14, 18, 20, 22, 24–5, 46–7, 51,
  63, 69, 76, 80, 86, 92, 98, 105,
  112, 119, 122, 124, 126, 128,
  130, 132, 140, 146, 152–3, 156,
  172, 184, 194, 202, 206–7, 212,
  216, 221, 224, 229, 231, 239,
  245, 249, 257, 261, 270, 284,
  294–5, 307, 313
Metz, C. 6
microcosm 33, 69, 301
mimesis 157
minimal 16, 21, 29, 52, 82, 90,
  130, 132, 143, 156, 215, 228,
  232, 237, 242, 269, 271, 275,
  282, 291, 299–300
misrecognition 151, 169, 182, 185,
  195, 277, 291
Mnouchkine, Ariane 39–40, 69,
  82, 106, 111, 137, 150, 151,
  153–4, 156–7, 172–3, 185, 196,
  204, 220, 225, 233, 272, 284,
  307, 308, 309–13

models 3, 9, 11, 24, 45, 54, 58, 90,
  143, 150, 222, 247–8, 251, 257,
  263, 268, 283, 298, 301, 302
modernism
  see postmodernism
modes
  fictional 143
  of action, actional 27, 46, 76,
    90, 98, 122, 138, 181, 189,
    193, 195, 208, 249, 261–2,
    277, 287, 293, 309
  of analysis 97
  of intervention 31, 36, 41, 49,
    64, 187, 245
  of knowing, of knowledge 115,
    123, 284
  of practice 4, 28, 78, 126, 144,
    193, 201, 207, 243, 260
  of representation 44
  of signification 103
  of writing 33
  psychoanalytic 17
  symbolic 18, 127, 170, 175, 221
morality 38
morpheme 15
Mother-function 137, 175, 189
moves 40, 54, 76, 77, 109, 265, 307
Mukarovsky 6
multiplicity, multivariate 16, 21,
  23, 41, 70, 88, 154ff, 168, 184
muscular, muscularity, muscular
  memory, reticular 40, 61, 93,
  100, 118–20, 151, 158–9, 163,
  172, 176, 204–6, 210, 212, 215,
  221, 226–7, 230, 233, 235, 241,
  249, 251–2, 271, 295, 304, 310

narrative, narratological,
  narratology 6, 17, 29, 102,
  179, 195, 305
natural, naturalism 12, 18, 26, 34,
  36–7, 76, 98–9, 116ff, 122, 140,
  181–3, 229, 233, 242, 256, 258,
  260, 262, 271, 273, 290
negativity 33, 34, 37, 74, 99, 103,
  138, 145, 147, 166, 168, 207,
  209, 240, 270, 303, 304
neo-Freudian
  see Lacan, J.

network 24–5, 49, 138, 159, 181,
    183, 186, 195, 205, 208, 263,
    295, 298, 300–1, 313–14
nominalisation
    see Halliday, M. A. K.
nostalgia 4, 40, 71–2, 158, 312
nucleus 22

opaque, opacity 73, 151–2, 245,
    251, 253, 256, 291, 295, 308
    see also Pêcheux, M.
opposer
    see actants
oppositionality 115–16, 135, 179
options
    performance 16, 170
    writerly 234
Other, otherness 83, 110, 114,
    123–4, 126ff, 135, 137, 141–3,
    150, 165, 169, 175, 183,
    189–90, 194, 213, 301

paradigm, paradigmatic 5, 6, 18,
    84
paralinguistic 97
parataxis, paratactic 83, 264, 275,
    291
    see also Halliday, M. A. K.
parole
    see Saussure, F. de
particle, particularity 45, 60, 78,
    193
passion 32, 43, 81, 112, 155, 159,
    163, 186, 198, 311–12
patriarchy 49, 100, 103, 178
Pavis, P. 3, 7, 11ff, 17, 19–20,
    22–4, 38ff, 47, 58, 67, 71, 75,
    88, 90, 140, 146, 202, 221, 225,
    250, 258, 284, 305, 311, 314
peak 14, 17, 160, 186–7, 222, 236,
    264, 275, 300, 304, 308
Pêcheux, M. 31, 73, 74, 125–7,
    129–31, 142, 145, 147, 151,
    161, 205, 234, 245–6, 250–1,
    257, 291
pedestrian, pedestrian-as-artist
    see de Certeau, M.
Peirce, C. 11, 24–6, 28–9, 109
performance, performativity

'curtain calls' 41
'standing for' 'the author' 112
Ancient Greek 184
and enunciation 157
bodies, somatic practice in 106,
    145, 183, 252, 276
conditions of 32, 89
constitution and use of 134
creative impetus of 51
metapraxis of 297
rel. to dramatic text, writing
    129, 131, 243, 263, 280
rel. to everyday practice 155
rel. to gender 173, 179
rel. to theatricality 271
response(s) of spectator(s) 44,
    63, 230
semiotics of 9, 121, 217, 221
specular-somatic economy of
    203
structure of 305
use of language in 214
why it 'works', or not 235
perspectival 64, 152, 157, 173,
    192, 283–4
phallus, phallocentric, phallo-
    cratic 100, 185–6, 189, 310
phenomenon, phenomenological
    7, 8, 59, 92, 105, 182, 183, 186,
    229, 232, 265, 269, 284
phenotypes
    see Halliday, M. A. K.
philosophemes 209
Platonism, Platonic 209
pleasure 12, 16, 23, 26, 44, 52, 65,
    66ff, 73, 91, 107, 123–4, 131,
    144, 151, 155, 161, 165, 175,
    187–9, 206, 219–20, 224, 226,
    239–40, 242, 245, 251
poaching
    see de Certeau, M.
polyphony 64, 121, 122
popular culture 44–5, 70, 121
post-Thatcherite 70
postmodern, postmodernist,
    postmodernity 4, 22, 32, 38ff,
    49, 58, 67, 72, 77, 86, 88, 110,
    114–15, 120–1, 137, 154, 183,
    195, 203, 233, 237, 283, 312

poststructuralism, post-structural-
ist 57, 91, 120, 180
power 6, 7, 9, 24, 25, 33, 38, 67,
70, 77, 83, 89, 112, 117, 120,
127, 155, 158, 185, 196, 226,
246, 260, 268, 284, 297, 299, 311
practice
'down-breaking' 64
collective 20, 39, 70, 164
communicative 110
critical 30, 81, 142
cultural 59, 65, 73, 91, 99, 107,
117, 138, 141, 180, 194, 212,
234, 243
cultural, modes of 28
discursive 5
ethnographic 265
everyday 49, 259
fields of 31
human 152
interactive 84
logic of 105
metasemiotic 314
modes of 78, 126, 193
of actor(s) 205
of pleasure 44
of the gaze 42
performance 69, 129, 272
postmodern 67
semiotic 16, 85, 255
signifying 119
somatic, muscular 46, 48, 93,
104, 279
somatic-discursive 196
stage 156, 188
symbolic 106, 207, 258
theatre 4, 6, 15, 21, 43, 51,
114–15, 123, 127–8, 137, 156,
166, 202, 204, 209, 222, 278,
284
writerly 169
practitioner(s)
enunciation of 280
of body intelligence 83
of semiotics, semiology 3, 41
of specular-somatography 301
of stage 226
of theatre 23, 32, 60, 69, 76, 91,
110, 121, 128–30, 151, 160,

170, 174, 176, 186, 193, 201,
210, 215, 220, 224, 225, 269
rel., 'contract', with
spectator(s) 13, 19, 133, 157
relations within group of
208–9, 214, 221, 223, 237,
247, 284
Prague School 8
praxis 53, 67, 276
procedures 4, 5, 7, 9, 14–15, 17,
43, 62, 129, 131, 201, 213, 245,
246–7, 271
process, processes, processual
decision-making 3, 68, 105, 136
dramatic writing as 246
esthetic 23
human relations 207
in Halliday 249, 264
institutionalised 78
intersubjective 162
intertextual 33
logical 29
Material (in Halliday) 235, 290,
295
Mental (in Halliday) 236, 311
multi-modal 64
nominalisation 273
of seduction 278
of stage 283
of the psyche 205
performance 204
primary 190
production 233
reading 50, 127
rel. to nominalisation 43
rel. to system 255
Relational (in Halliday) 236,
302
relations of 159
secondary 149
somatic 261, 263
stage figuring 148
up-building 7
verbal 145
Verbal (in Halliday) 306
projection 18, 67, 90, 143–4, 149,
182, 236, 266, 291, 295
Propp, V.
see narrative

protomorphic 133–4
proxemic, proxemics 21, 37, 54, 83, 232, 261, 284, 290
psyche 104, 125, 144, 154, 181, 196, 202–3, 205, 227, 229, 251, 309
psycho-soma 201–3, 205–7, 209–10, 212, 215, 226ff, 232, 234, 238, 267, 290, 302
psycho-somatic 7, 76, 164, 203, 285
psychology, psychologisation 170

quantum physics, quantum theory 45, 165, 254, 255
quoting, quotation
see postmodern

rationalism 72, 104
reality effects 116–18
recognition 16, 23, 49, 63, 98, 114, 149, 156, 172, 245, 251, 266
reduction, reductive 20, 45, 185, 310
referent 29
register
see Halliday, M. A. K.
Relational Process
see Halliday, M. A. K.
relative, relativity 15, 25, 29, 45, 64, 68, 70, 114, 136, 181–2, 195, 208, 227, 236, 262, 290, 298, 299, 310
REPRESENTAMEN
see Peirce, C.
representation, representationality 5, 6, 28, 42, 44, 55, 60, 63–4, 68, 72, 110, 114ff, 121–2, 137–8, 150–1, 155ff, 164, 178, 181, 184–5, 187, 207, 223, 253, 270, 283, 298
repression 148, 164, 203
residue 14, 66, 212, 241, 283
resolution 20, 103, 140, 150, 197
responsibility 5
Rheme
see Halliday, M. A. K.
rhizome 62, 157, 244

risk-taking 211–13
role 24, 26, 40–1, 45, 55, 68, 75, 93, 118–19, 122, 132, 153, 169, 170–1, 173, 186–7, 210, 212, 235, 253, 267, 283, 287, 294–5, 301, 309
Rose, J. 171–2, 174–5, 189, 196, 309
rupture 5, 135, 151
Russian Formalism 82

sado-masochism 20, 137
de Saussure, F., saussurean, saussureanism 5, 6, 11–12, 14–15, 17, 21, 24–5, 29, 30, 34, 46, 50, 105
scenarios 8, 14, 17, 20–1, 31, 59, 112, 115, 127, 132, 163, 179, 181–2, 184, 188, 207, 251, 309
schema 19, 22, 24–5, 50, 92, 131, 161, 229, 238
scriptural economy
see de Certeau, M.
secretions 42, 67, 173
seduction, seductive 92, 121, 185, 207, 277, 278, 281
seed, seme, semiotic, semiotics
'new semiotics' 80
'pre-symbolic' 100
'semiotic reach' 238
'whole human semiotic' 90, 236, 254, 268, 275
body-semiotic 102, 176
everyday practice 85
of performance 217
of theatre which 'works' 243
open systems 256
Peircian 191
radical semiotic subjectivity (Lacan) 139
rel. with real 189
resonance 159
seed pod, metaphor of 58, 62
semiotic myths (Lacan) 106
semiotic play 57
semiotic potential 201
semiotic system, language as 47
semiotics of writing for the stage 3
social semiotic 212, 299

seed, seme, semiotic, semiotics –
  continued
  structural semiotics 33
  the semiotic project 21, 26, 39,
    41, 60
semiology, semiological,
    semiologist
  'spontaneous' 87
  critique of 44
  established discourses and
    procedures 43
  model of knowledge 30
  modernist 7
  position concealed 73
  structural 115
  traditional 211
  Eco, Umberto 34
semiotise, semiotisation, semiosis
  'beyond' 63
  'connoted' 50
  complementarity 286
  complex subject-functions 30
  connotational 54
  gender relations 314
  humanism 173, 220
  interrelational norms 293
  minimal-logical 271
  notions of 46
  play of, spectating 308
  rel. to emotion 119, 203
  rel. to enunciation, writing 163,
    235
  rel. to group 70
  rel. to process 302
  rel. to psychoanalysis 135
  textual complementarities 264
sense, sensorium 7, 34, 41, 47, 56,
  63, 92, 112, 132, 142, 181, 184,
  187, 202, 208, 216–18, 226,
  230, 232, 242, 245, 258, 260,
  262, 264, 270, 280–1, 290, 297,
  304
separatism 180
seriousness 32, 77, 275
sex 42, 67, 173
sh'te 53
Shakespeare 5, 40, 51, 57, 59, 113,
  151, 156–7, 252, 314
Shaw, F. 124, 137, 140, 151, 158,

  184, 195, 204, 219, 234–5, 238,
  245, 257, 262, 284, 294, 302
sign
  see seed, seme, semiotic,
    semiotics
signifiance, *signifiant*, signification 6, 102–3, 132, 161, 164,
  194, 314
signifiant
  see Saussure, F. de
signifié, signified, signifier 6,
  24–6, 34, 50, 230
  see also Saussure, F. de
signifying practice 99, 119, 222
simulacra, simulacrum,
    simulation 41–2, 67, 74–5,
    121, 173
simultaneity 6, 105
singular, singularities, singularity
  7, 20, 24, 30, 33, 40, 43, 52, 58,
  73, 98, 120, 122, 126, 149, 154,
  161, 165, 176, 181, 197, 201,
  208, 213, 225, 229, 242, 245,
  248, 251, 254, 260, 266
site 4, 9, 20, 27, 52, 81, 99, 114,
  118, 132, 136, 140, 170, 171,
  173, 183, 208, 221, 225, 226,
  229, 230, 245, 247, 250, 295,
  301
sleight of hand, cunning, artifice
  17, 22, 30, 75, 79, 82, 85, 91–2,
  104, 142, 152, 162, 184, 195,
  249, 277, 281
social, social subject 7, 24, 33–4,
  37, 41–3, 45, 52, 54, 61, 68, 70,
  72, 74, 84, 86–7, 89–91, 97–8,
  100, 103–4, 112, 114, 116,
  121–2, 130, 138, 144, 166, 172,
  180, 186, 189, 196, 209, 211,
  213, 217, 220, 229, 231, 235,
  243, 245–6, 249, 251, 254, 256,
  258, 264, 265, 277
socio-historical 141, 202, 269
socio-pragmatic 7
somatic, somatic practices 40, 46,
  48, 56, 63, 76, 80, 85, 90, 100,
  129, 141, 149, 153, 162, 177,
  183, 186, 190, 193, 195, 201,
  204, 210, 219, 222, 226, 229,

232, 239, 241, 243, 246, 249,
252, 258, 261, 262, 266, 272,
275, 277, 282, 285, 290, 295,
302, 307, 309, 314
somatography 196–8, 204, 301
space 14, 23, 26, 27, 31, 40, 43,
48–9, 55, 57, 68, 72, 74, 77, 78,
81–2, 90, 99, 106, 117, 122,
130, 147, 152–3, 155, 157,
162–3, 165, 173, 176, 182,
185–6, 215, 225, 230, 234, 237,
239, 246, 253–4, 257, 260–2,
276, 283, 293, 295, 299–301,
306, 307, 310
specificity 7, 8, 15, 50, 58, 72, 90,
155, 166, 178, 180, 183, 192,
195, 242, 263, 299
spectacle, spectator, spectators,
specular 7, 12–13, 19, 22, 27,
29, 37, 40, 46, 52, 56, 61, 63,
67, 72, 76, 79, 84, 86, 88, 92,
106, 117, 119, 121, 127, 132,
137, 140, 147, 149, 152, 157,
160, 163, 170, 172, 175, 176,
181, 186, 194, 196, 201, 206,
212, 214, 219, 225, 228, 233,
239, 242, 245, 254, 261, 266,
271, 276, 281, 284, 290, 294,
299, 304, 313
specular–somatic 52, 56, 106, 175,
191, 202–3, 206, 208, 213–14,
225, 247–8, 281, 295, 308
speech acts
see Austin, J., Pratt, M.-L.
stage, staging, stagings 14, 18,
20–2, 27, 31–2, 36, 38, 40–2,
46–7, 49–50, 52, 54ff, 64–5, 67,
73, 75, 88, 106, 121, 124,
127–8, 130, 133, 143, 145,
147–8, 151, 156, 163, 165, 183,
185, 191, 193, 195, 198, 202–3,
205, 211, 222, 229, 231, 237,
245–6, 248, 252, 264, 270, 284,
290ff, 299–301, 307, 309,
311–12
standing-for
see Peirce, C.
Stanislavski, Stanislavskian 48,
100, 113, 204, 229

strategy, strategic, in Bourdieu
85, 89, 91, 92, 159, 201
strategy, strategic, in de Certeau
76, 78–9, 85, 92, 147, 185, 201
structure, structural analysis 18,
33, 59, 60–1, 86, 91, 128, 140,
159, 179, 228, 242, 275, 283,
284, 301, 305
subject, subjectivity 7, 17–19, 23,
27, 30–3, 51, 59, 65, 68–9,
71–3, 76, 86, 87ff, 98ff, 112–13,
115–16, 121–2, 126–8, 131,
133ff, 139, 151, 156, 161, 166ff,
174, 180, 182, 187–9, 195,
204–5, 207, 235, 238–9, 245,
249, 251, 253–5, 257–8, 260,
267, 269, 295, 300, 301
sublime 219
substance 8, 99, 121, 234
substitute 9, 36, 48, 117, 157, 184,
189, 191, 233, 310, 313
subtext
see discourse, logocentricity
superordinate 45, 73
surface 18, 22, 23, 49, 61, 97
suture, sutures 197
symbol
see Peirce, C.
symptom, symptomatic
see Peirce, C.
syncretic 12
synergy 32, 78, 148, 175, 248
synesthesia 48, 214, 218, 261
synoptic, "in place", dynamic, "in
flux", see Halliday, M. A. K.
syntagm, syntagmatic 5, 6, 15
synthesis 38, 83
system 4, 12, 26–8, 31, 34, 37,
46–8, 50–1, 60–2, 77, 79, 82,
91, 121, 136, 158, 191, 203,
205–6, 214, 221, 224, 226–8,
230, 233, 236, 245–6, 252ff,
260, 263ff, 278, 284, 286,
294–5, 298, 301, 306
Systemic Functional
see Halliday, M. A. K.

taboo 33, 168, 176, 180, 182, 183,
309

tactics
  see de Certeau, M.
tactile 227
taste 5, 7, 30, 37, 59, 65, 69, 70,
    81, 86, 90, 114, 119, 124, 174,
    212ff, 218, 225, 230, 232, 234,
    249, 266, 270, 275, 304, 307,
    310
teleology, teleological 22, 28, 51,
    109, 305
television 48, 54, 68, 71, 72, 75,
    84, 148, 197
text
  'traces' within 130
  analysis of 192, 204
  analyst of 225
  body as, in performance 210
  dramatic 4, 65, 129, 269
  element(s) of 18, 127, 303
  functions 105
  materiality of 143
  modalities of 73
  opacity of 245
  options 140
  politics of 57, 103, 131
  practice(s) of 15
  producer of 143
  production and use of 33
  rel. to 'unconscious' 132
  rel. to author 24
  rel. to dramatic character 267
  rel. to mainstream 185
  rel. to theatricality 58, 97, 121,
      218
  rel. to user 236
  signature 112
  Sophoclean 221
  synoptic ("in place": Halliday)
      54, 91, 106, 127, 247, 263,
      275, 291, 310
  theatre performance as 6
  which 'works on several
      levels' 142
Textual Function
  see Halliday, M. A. K.
textualise, textualisation 4, 5, 145,
    291
theatre collective 151
Théâtre du Soleil 39–41, 68, 111,

150, 156, 173, 185, 204, 220,
    233
theatricality 13, 27, 47, 50–3, 56,
    58, 151, 170, 173–4, 193, 198,
    202, 219, 221–2, 226, 228,
    232–4, 237–8, 242–3, 249, 266,
    271, 276, 278, 280–1, 290–1, 299
thematic, thematisation
  see Halliday, M. A. K.
Theme
  see Halliday, M. A. K.
theoretical
  'French' 11
  abstraction 246
  discourse 30, 47, 123, 141, 211,
      214
  discourses, genre-specific 6
  fields 151
  legitimacy, of authorial theory
      24
  position 68
  writers, French 275
theory
  actantial 24
  authorial 20
  chaos 247
  cultural 73
  dramas of 101
  feminist 312
  Freudian 195, 240, 263
  game of 114
  gendered 168, 210
  gendered, scene of (1970s &
      1980s) 184
  generative 22
  history of, recent 9
  history of, rel. to theatre 4
  institutions of 101
  linguistic 12
  literary 6, 103
  of agency 80
  of blocked Imaginary 170
  of complementarities 28
  of différance (Derrida) 30, 57
  of energy 120, 219, 232
  of enunciation (Benveniste) 29
  of forgotten history (Bourdieu)
      187
  of habitus (Bourdieu) 60, 249

of human subjectivity 136, 182
of intertextuality 15
of mimesis 157
of multiplicity 156
of negativity 145
of otherness 123, 131
of representation 55, 110
of speech act(s) 169
of synergy 32, 78
of tactics (de Certeau) 122
of theatre practice 204
pedagogic practice of 14
political 189
postmodern 22, 43
psychoanalytic 129
quantum 46
rel. to practice 5
semiotic (Lacan) 106
social (Habermas) 124
social, 19th century 151
socio-political 44
somatic 207, 216
stage of 32
staging, dialogue of 65
theatre as metaphor for 115
totalising, of society and
    culture 180
wave 193
therapy, therapeutic 77, 191, 227
thrust 23, 213, 223, 227, 240, 241,
    277, 282
tools
    see heuristic
traces 8, 37, 40, 64, 99, 119,
    126-7, 129-30, 151, 205,
    240, 245, 250
trait 33, 234, 262, 304
transformation 47, 67, 72, 130,
    152-3, 183, 236
Transitivity
    see Halliday, M. A. K.
translation 26-7, 33, 40, 45, 81,
    86, 89, 109, 128, 275, 291, 309
transparent, transparency 28, 151,
    250, 276, 295, 308
triad
    see Peirce, C.
truth, truth-regime
    see lie

turnabouts 9
typical, typicality 18, 41, 76,
    78, 80, 181, 190, 208, 266,
    273, 276

Ubersfeld, A. 7, 11ff, 26, 30, 34,
    35, 50, 62-3, 143, 166, 189,
    206, 217, 254, 267
Ulmer, G. 20, 30, 32, 43, 75, 83,
    84, 88, 115, 120-1, 123, 126,
    129, 144, 195, 201-2, 209, 210,
    214, 216-17, 314
un-speakable, unspoken 63, 126,
    129, 166, 205, 231
uncertainty 31, 224, 235
unconscious, concept of 88, 126,
    132-4, 145, 161, 167, 191, 194,
    196, 198, 208, 259
unit 16, 19, 22, 29, 33, 51, 72, 82,
    92, 100, 140, 159, 170, 183,
    191, 228, 236, 247, 294, 301,
    302
universal 15, 30, 49, 53, 68, 69,
    71, 75, 113, 121, 129, 136, 141,
    158, 246
univocal 41
unseizable, *l'insaisissable*
    see Ubersfeld, A.
unthinkable 21, 52, 251
up-down 9, 191, 194
utterance 108, 193

value 5, 7, 65, 101, 105, 110, 113,
    114, 136, 147, 178, 180, 202,
    216, 228, 265
variables 23
vision, visual 18, 20, 23, 30-1, 36,
    61, 91, 133, 137, 148, 164, 216,
    222, 227
Vitez, A. 41
voice, voicework, voicing 49, 54,
    72, 81, 84, 93, 97, 117, 118,
    125, 173, 196, 201, 204, 207,
    211, 221, 230, 236, 261, 271,
    279, 286, 290, 293, 301, 307
void 13, 14, 26, 313
voyeurism 123, 162

Warner, D. 59, 69, 124, 137–8, 140,
    148, 151–2, 154–6, 159, 164–5,
    172, 184, 187, 196–8, 204, 206,
    219, 235, 245, 262–3, 284, 293ff,
    302, 304, 307, 310, 312–14
wastage
    see Barba, E.
waves, wave theory 53, 162, 193,
    302
web 23, 92, 242, 295, 308
whole, wholeness 22, 24, 48, 67,
    90, 143ff, 155, 158, 169, 191,
    205, 207, 213, 228, 236, 237,
    254, 268, 275, 291
Wilden, A. 9, 25, 105, 135, 136,
    141, 145, 170, 178, 183, 185,
    190–2, 212, 240, 251, 257
Woman, women
    see Rose, J.
work, virkje ('struggle against a
    burden') 58, 70, 131, 148, 183,
    195, 203, 221, 234, 242, 283
    'the work' 6, 119, 258
    body-work, somatic, muscular,
        voice 100, 106, 118–20, 153,
        159, 163–4, 186, 189, 196,
        202, 205, 219, 247, 252, 278,
        285, 295, 301, 307–9, 311
    energetic 140, 231
    of the actor(s) 16, 23, 63, 78,
        84–5, 89, 113, 122, 126, 133,
        151, 156, 166, 172, 206–7,
        213, 215, 222–3, 227, 229,
        239, 272, 295
    of the spectator(s) 27, 148, 157,
        167
    symbolic, intellectual 61, 83,
        92, 181, 211, 214, 225, 232,
        253, 277
    theatre, collective 23, 62, 64, 69,
        86, 104, 116, 146, 221, 243, 302
    woman's 137, 138, 305
world-out-there 112
writerly
    components 83
    constitution of character 19
    constructs 204
    control 260
    dramatic enunciation 301

options 234
practice of division and
    difference 169
practices, in dramatic theatre 7
rel. to other production
    elements 283
rel. to speaking 113
speech 276
writing
    'in depth' 195
    'male' 159
    'paternalistic' 103
    about performance 124
    analysis of 169
    as collective intertextual
        process 33
    as-voice 230
    by an other 133
    dramatic 63
    dramatic, 'under-written' 142
    dramatic, analysis of 224
    dramatic, as interpretation of
        theatricality 52
    dramatic, canon of 137
    dramatic, character-complex 90
    dramatic, deictics in 147
    dramatic, rel. to 'natural
        language' 259
    dramatic, rel. to human
        discourse 242
    dramatic, rel. to performance 131
    dramatic, rel. to somatic trait 262
    dramatic, socio-functional
        conception of 251
    eruption of body into 102
    group, collective 121
    in-use 201
    mode of 279
    play of, in work of actor(s) 211
    rel. to field of experience 235
    rel. to performance 215
    rel. to theatre 47
    Shakespearean 157
    Sophoclean 186
    speaking and writing subjects
        74
    stress in, typographic 302
    symbolic network of 301
    use of 248